seats, votes, and the spatial organisation of elections

G. Gudgin and P. J. Taylor

with a new introduction by R. J. Johnston

ecpr PRESS

© G. Gudgin and P. J. Taylor

© R. J. Johnston (Introduction)

First published in 1979
by Pion Limited

First published by the ECPR Press in 2012

The ECPR Press is the publishing imprint of the European Consortium for Political Research (ECPR), a scholarly association, which supports and encourages the training, research and cross-national cooperation of political scientists in institutions throughout Europe and beyond. The ECPR's Central Services are located at the University of Essex, Wivenhoe Park, Colchester, CO4 3SQ, UK

All rights reserved. No part of this book may be reprinted or reproduced or utilised in any form or by any electronic, mechanical, or other means, now known or hereafter invented, including photocopying and recording, or in any information storage or retrieval system, without permission in writing from the publishers.

Typeset by Anvi Composers
Printed and bound by Lightning Source

British Library Cataloguing in Publication Data
A catalogue record for this book is available from the British Library

ISBN: 978-1-907301-35-3

www.ecprnet.eu/ecprpress

ECPR – Monographs

Series Editors:
Dario Castiglione (University of Exeter)
Peter Kennealy (European University Institute)
Alexandra Segerberg (Stockholm University)
Peter Triantafillou (Roskilde University)

Other books available in this series

ECPR Classics:
Beyond the Nation State: (ISBN: 9780955248870) Ernst Haas

Citizens, Elections, Parties: Approaches to the Comparative Study of the Processes of Development (ISBN: 9780955248887) Stein Rokkan

Democracy: Political Finance and State Funding for Parties (ISBN: 9780955248801) Jack Lively

Electoral Change: Responses to Evolving Social and Attitudinal Structures in Western Countries (ISBN: 9780955820311) Mark Franklin, Thomas Mackie, and Henry Valen

Elite and Specialized Interviewing (ISBN: 9780954796679) Lewis Anthony Dexter

Identity, Competition and Electoral Availability: The Stabilisation of European Electorates 1885-1985 (ISBN: 9780955248832) Peter Mair & Stefano Bartolini

Individualism (ISBN: 9780954796662) Steven Lukes

Modern Social Policies in Britain and Sweden: From Relief to Income Maintenance (ISBN: 9781907301001) Hugh Heclo

Parties and Party Systems: A Framework for Analysis (ISBN: 9780954796617) Giovanni Sartori

Party Identification and Beyond: Representations of Voting and Party Competition (ISBN: 9780955820342) Ian Budge, Ivor Crewe, Dennis Farlie

People, States and Fear: An Agenda for International Security Studies in the Post-Cold War Era (ISBN: 9780955248818) Barry Buzan

Political Elites: (ISBN: 9780954796600) Geraint Parry

State Formation, Parties and Democracy (ISBN: 9781907301179) Hans Daalder

System and Process in International Politics (ISBN: 9780954796624) Morton Kaplan

Territory and Power in the UK: Territory and Power in the UK (ISBN: 9780955248863) James Bulpitt

The State Tradition in Western Europe: A Study of an Idea and Institution (ISBN: 9780955820359) Kenneth Dyson

contents

New Introduction: Seats, Votes and the Spatial Organisation of Elections Revisited by *Ron Johnston*	ix
Preface	xli

1 Translating votes into seats

1.1 Seats and votes	1
1.1.1 Electoral reform	2
1.2 The spatial organisation of plurality elections	4
1.2.1 The distribution of party voters	5
1.2.2 Drawing constituency boundaries	8
1.2.3 The interaction of voters and boundaries	11

2 A modelling framework for the seats-votes relationship

2.1 The frequency-distribution approach	13
2.1.1 The constituency proportion distribution	14
2.1.2 Basic types of seats-votes relationships	17
2.2 The normal distribution and the cube law	20
2.2.1 Normal predictions of seat proportions	22
2.2.2 The cube law as a normal model	26

3 Explaining the cube law

3.1 The binomial method	32
3.1.1 Variants on the binomial distribution	33
3.1.2 The distribution of constituency proportions and spatial clustering	35
3.2 The Markov method	39
3.2.1 A model of individual voters	40
3.2.2 A model of clusters of voters	42
3.3 An empirical investigation of the Markov explanation	47
3.3.1 The sample survey	48
3.3.2 The political mosaic of Newcastle upon Tyne	49
3.4 The normal distribution as an electoral norm	52

4 Malapportionment, nonuniform swing, and nonnormality

4.1 Malapportionment	55
4.1.1 The effective party vote proportion	56
4.2 Nonuniform swings	59
4.2.1 Variations in patterns of swing	59
4.2.2 Simple random or linear swing-votes relationships	61
4.2.3 Other swing-votes relationships	64
4.3 Nonnormality in constituency proportion distributions	65
4.3.1 Nonnormality 1: skewness	68
4.3.2 Nonnormality 2: kurtosis and bimodality	71
4.3.3 Empirical studies of constituency proportion distributions	73
4.4 The components of electoral bias	86

5 Three-party elections

5.1	The three-party seats-votes relationship and the election triangle	93
	5.1.1 Election triangles	94
5.2	The case of nationally uniform third-party vote	96
	5.2.1 Equal attraction rates	97
	5.2.2 Unequal attraction rates	99
5.3	Nonuniform levels of third-party support	102
	5.3.1 Independent variable support for the third party	102
	5.3.2 Third-party support related to major-party strength	106
	5.3.3 Regional variation in third-party support	107
5.4	Empirical applications	109
	5.4.1 Three-party elections in Britain	109
	5.4.2 A permanent minority: Social Credit in New Zealand	116
5.5	Conclusion: three-party elections, the Achilles heel of the plurality system	119

6 Decisionmaking in electoral districting

6.1	Types of districting agencies	122
	6.1.1 Partisan decisionmaking	122
	6.1.2 Nonpartisan decisionmaking	125
	6.1.3 Bipartisan districting	127
	6.1.4 Beyond the USA	131
	6.1.5 The question of South African elections	133
6.2	A statistical framework	140
	6.2.1 Constituencies as combinatorial structures	140
	6.2.2 Algorithms for finding feasible solutions	143
6.3	The two-constituency case	146
	6.3.1 Alternative solutions	146
	6.3.2 Constituencies for Sunderland	149
	6.3.3 Districting decisions of alternative agencies	151
	6.3.4 A formal derivation of majority-party bias	152
6.4	Extensions to more than two constituencies	154
	6.4.1 Variance and party fortunes	155
	6.4.2 Constituencies for Newcastle upon Tyne	156
	6.4.3 Congressional districts for Iowa	158
6.5	Is there a satisfactory districting procedure?	160

7 Beyond pluralities

7.1	Systems of voting	162
7.2	Majority systems of voting	165
	7.2.1 The alternative vote in Australia	165
	7.2.2 The double ballot in France	169
	7.2.3 A majority-vote system for Britain	172

7.3	The single-transferable-vote system	176
	7.3.1 STV in Ireland	176
	7.3.2 STV for British elections	179
7.4	A mixture of pluralities and PR	188
	7.4.1 The 'mixed system' in the Federal Republic of Germany	190
	7.4.2 Additional members for the British parliament	192
7.5	Conclusions: electoral engineering	195

8 Concluding comments and summary   200

Appendix 1

Alternative approaches to explaining the cube law	205
March's behavioural rationalisation	205
Taagepera's communication theory	208
A game-theoretic approach	211

Appendix 2

Functional relationships between seats and votes in multiparty elections	213
Qualter's multiparty equation	213
A general seats-votes equation	215
Casstevens and Morris's decomposed system	218
Spafford's regression approach	219

Appendix 3

Derivation of the seats-votes relationship: uniform support and even attraction	222

Appendix 4

Derivation of the seats-votes relationship: uneven attraction from major parties	223

Appendix 5

Construction of figure 5.10	225

Appendix 6

Derivation of equations for linear relations between third-party support and the strength of other parties	226

Appendix 7

Alternative explanations of bimodal CPDs	228

References   231

Index   237

new introduction | seats, votes and the spatial organisation of elections revisited[1]

Ron Johnston

Political science was only a small discipline in the United Kingdom before the 1970s (Grant 2010). Within it the study of elections was dominated by David Butler, his students and collaborators. He was by then well-known for his *The British General Election of...* series of books and, through his collaboration with Donald Stokes on the first British Election Studies, for importing the survey-based approach to studying voting behaviour from the United States (Butler and Stokes 1969, 1974). Although rigorous in its procedures, this work was not heavily quantitative, as the term would now be understood. At that time, British students of elections were lagging behind their American counterparts in the sophistication of their quantitative methodologies.

British geography in the 1970s was in the throes of what many termed a 'theoretical and quantitative revolution'. Its roots were American – being launched there in the late 1950s and having achieved a considerable presence within a decade (Taylor 1976; Johnston and Sidaway 2004). Quantitative spatial science was the discipline's new paradigm, an approach rapidly taken up by a few British pioneers, initially focused on Cambridge (Haggett 1965; Chorley and Haggett 1964, 1967) and Liverpool (Gregory 1962). Peter Taylor was one of the first generation of British postgraduates to adopt that paradigm, with a PhD at Liverpool (1966–1970) on 'Interaction and distance: an investigation into distance decay and a study of migration at a microscale', which used nineteenth-century census data and from which he published two pioneering papers on spatial interaction models (Taylor 1971a, 1971b). In 1968 he was appointed to a Demonstratorship in the Department of Geography at the University of Newcastle upon Tyne: he spent the 1970–1 academic year on leave at the University of Iowa, one of the early cores of the quantitative revolution where some of the staff and graduate students were interested in matters electoral (Johnston and Pattie 2012a).

One of Pete's early interests in the application of quantitative methods within geography was classification and regionalisation (Taylor 1969; Spence and Taylor 1970) – the division of a territory into coherent 'regions' on pre-defined criteria. Bunge (1966) had already made the connection between this and the definition of electoral districts. Iowa was being redistricted – the 1970 census figures required its number of Representatives to be reduced from seven to six – and researchers

---

[1] I am grateful to Graham Gudgin and Peter Taylor for their support of this project to reprint the book and for their valuable comments on this introductory essay. I am also grateful for comments from Adrian Blau, Kelvyn Jones, Charles Pattie, Colin Rallings, Michael Steed, Michael Thrasher and Paul Wilder.

there were exploring the use of computer algorithms to create new configurations of districts. Pete compiled an annotated biography of materials on districting (Taylor 1972), undertook a review of districting algorithms (Taylor 1974), and proposed a new measure of shape to be used in defining compact electoral districts (Taylor 1973a).[2]

On his return to the UK and a lectureship at Newcastle, an early paper on 'Some implications of the spatial organisation of elections' (Taylor 1973b) set out the core of the argument developed fully in *Seats, Votes and the Spatial Organisation of Elections* (hereafter *SV*). Pete's return to Newcastle coincided with Graham Gudgin's arrival there as a Demonstrator. He too was an early convert to geography's quantitative revolution – his first degree was in geography and he then obtained a mathematics degree in order to get on top of the revolution. His PhD was on regional economic growth and he built on this to pursue his later career in economics (Gudgin 1978; Fothergill and Gudgin 1982). At Newcastle, he and Pete began to collaborate on electoral research, and a stream of papers emerged in the following years – though not without difficulties, as they described in the Preface to *SV*. One of them (Gudgin and Taylor 1974) extended and formalised the case made in Taylor's 1973 paper for the centrality of geography to the operation of single-member plurality electoral systems.[3]

The focus of their attention was the translation of votes into seats. This had already attracted David Butler's attention. His appendix on 'The relation of seats to votes' in *The British General Election of 1945* (McCallum and Readman 1947) addressed the issue that if the Conservative and Labour parties had won equal shares of the votes cast then, Labour would have won 54 more seats than its opponent (Butler 1947: 282). He suggested that this 'potential injustice' logically could be the consequence of three main causes (1947: 284):

1. Geographical chance, i.e. boundaries working as if 'gerrymandered' slightly in one side's favour.
2. Extra-fickle areas. (By extra-fickle areas he meant marginal constituencies where the swing to the winning party was much larger than elsewhere.)
3. Unequal populations in constituencies.

Of these, the third was the most likely cause, reflecting the major shifts in population distribution since the last redistribution of constituencies in 1918 (including those generated by World War II); Butler's conclusion was that the redistribution then being undertaken should remove the 'potential injustice'.[4]

---

2   This work, and the subsequent exploration with Graham Gudgin of the combinatorial issues involved in the amalgamation of smaller units into constituencies, also fed in to Pete's path-breaking work with Stan Openshaw on the modifiable areal unit problem, one of the most intractable and important problems in spatial analysis (Openshaw and Taylor 1980).
3   Amazingly, Web of Knowledge[(C)] indicates no citations for either of these papers – even though the second cites the first!
4   He noted that at the 1945 election Labour was advantaged by the size differentials (the average constituency that it won had 50,785 voters compared to 56,713 in those won by the Conservatives) but disadvantaged by the latter (Labour won 42 seats with majorities of 20,000 or more

After two more elections, Butler returned to the issue in the first edition of *The Electoral System in Britain, 1918–1951* (Butler 1953). By then Kendall and Stuart (1950) had identified a 'law of cubic proportions' operating in the translation of votes into seats in Great Britain whereby:

$$S_1/S_2 = (V_1/V_2)^3$$

with V_1 and V_2 being the percentage share of the votes won by parties 1 and 2, and S_1 and S_2 their percentage shares of the seats. Thus if party 1 won 52 per cent of the votes and party 2 got 48 per cent, the 'law' would produce

$$S_1/S_2 = (52/48)^3 = 1.38$$

so that party 1 would get 58 per cent of the seats and party 2 would have 42 per cent. This regularity informed Butler's analysis of the 1950 and 1951 results, at both of which he noted that the 'Conservatives would have won more seats than Labour for any given percentage of the total vote' (Butler 1953: 193).

More generally, Butler identified two regularities in British election results. The first was that the winning party tended to get a larger percentage share of the seats than of the votes. Secondly, the translation process did not operate equally for the two main parties: writing about the 1950 and 1951 elections, for example, he noted that to secure a majority of seats Labour needed to gain about two percentage points more (some 500,000) votes than the Conservatives – who could gain a majority of the seats with two percentage points less of the votes than Labour (Butler 1953: his table showing this – p.193 – provided a template replicated in more recent analyses of how the system operates: Curtice 2010). Butler estimated that in 1945 there was a bias favouring Labour (an 'error' in the prediction of its share of the seats relative to that of the votes) of six seats, but this changed to one against it of 18 and 21 seats respectively at the next two elections.[5] He saw these as relatively unimportant when set against a 'clear and steady relationship between seats and votes' (Butler 1953: 194). What biases there were tended to be self-cancelling, with some of the generating processes favouring the Conservatives and others Labour.

Butler identified four factors that were necessary to produce the 'winner's bonus' that characterised most British general election results:[6] a two-party system; political homogeneity across the country (i.e. uniform swings in support from one party to the other between elections); 'fair and equal constituencies', with little variation in constituency electorates favouring one party; and similar geographical distributions of support for each. The biases – the potential injustices of his earlier analyses – would emerge because 'If the supporters of one party tend to be more concentrated than those of the other, the former may squander many more votes than the latter in building up huge majorities in safe seats' (1953: 196).

---

compared with only 8 by the Conservatives).

5   A brief overview of the use of 'bias' in this context – in contrast with the concept of 'disproportionality' – is in McDonald (2009).
6   In 1951 Labour won more votes but fewer seats than the Conservatives; the situation was reversed in February 1974.

He also suggested that the absence of bias would occur when 'there is no especial concentration of vote-splitting third-party candidates in marginal seats' (1953: 199). He summarised his findings as (Butler 1953: 198–199):

The major parties seem likely to receive roughly equal and predictable treatment at the hands of the electoral system:

(a) when two parties are predominant in all constituencies,

(b) when any variations in the swing between them are distributed at random in relation to the majorities,

(c) when there is no party bias in the size of constituencies,

(d) when there is no especial concentration of vote-splitting third-party candidates in marginal seats, and

(e) when neither party's support is more concentrated in safe constituencies than the other's.

In the book's second edition, he stated that nothing in the results of the 1955 and 1959 elections 'invalidates the general argument' (Butler 1963: 203). His list of the factors that might result in bias however excludes one – differential turnout – that was of only very minor relevance in the 1950s and 1960s but became one of the major causes from the 1990s on as turnout fell rapidly, especially in areas where Labour tended to be the strongest party (Johnston *et al.* 2001, 2006).[7]

Butler's intuitive appreciation of the situation was continued in subsequent analyses of the results for *The British General Election of...* series, undertaken by Michael Steed after 1964. He continued Butler's practice of providing a histogram of the swing across all constituencies between elections (to test the homogeneity assumption) and assessing whether the cube law continued to fit well given that the graphs were clear on the relative uniformity. In 1966, for example, he noted that the observed regularities in the recent past continued to operate: between 1959 and 1966, for example, a uniform swing model predicted a Labour gain of 100 seats from the Conservatives – the actual figure was 103. By 1970, however, although the swing histogram still indicated considerable uniformity, nevertheless variations across regions and constituency types were increasingly apparent within this overall pattern, which – along with greater malapportionment (a redistribution due to be introduced in 1969 had been voted down by the Labour government because it would probably have damaged their chances at the next election: Rossiter *et al.* 1999a) – may have been the reason why the anti-Labour bias, so apparent in 1955, had largely disappeared by 1970; the Conservative benefit then was only 10 seats (Steed 1971: 414). By the time of the next election, when much of the malapportionment had been removed by introduction of the new constituencies, the usual relationship had broken down because of significant inter-regional and urban-rural variations in swing (Steed 1974: 325). Tactical

---

7   Interestingly, differential turnout was cited by Quandt (1974) as one of the factors that might generate biased election results away from those predicted by the cube law.

voting was becoming more common as well. Eight months later, Steed (1975: 353) noted that 'there was a considerably lower turnover of seats than would have been produced by uniform movement of votes' – presaging his classic paper with John Curtice (Curtice and Steed 1982) that focused on the various geographical variations in swing that by then characterised British elections and were the reason why the cube law's obsolescence was being declared.

Despite this conclusion, however, by the time Taylor and Gudgin started their work the cube law had been incorporated into what Upton (1985: 388) called 'the general folklore of political science', even though Tufte (1973: 523) had wondered whether 'there actually *is* a theory behind' it. So was the general belief that operation of the electoral system included a 'built-in' bias against Labour – indeed against parties of the left more generally, as evidence from Australia, Canada and New Zealand indicated (Taylor and Gudgin 1977; see also Rodden 2006, 2010; Chen and Rodden 2010). These observations, together with US work on gerrymandering and redistricting, underpinned the programme of work that resulted in *SV* (with Gudgin and Taylor 1974, providing an early and clear overview of its arguments[8]).

*****

Gudgin and Taylor's papers and *SV* were elements of their general critique of the plurality electoral system produced through a sustained, scientific analysis of how the system works – a system with an 'important weakness that the relationship between total votes gained and number of seats won is uncontrolled, arbitrary, sometimes unpredictable, and in some circumstances open to abuse' (*SV*, "preface" on page xli). They stress in the Preface to *SV* that the book is '*a technical statement about how a particular system works,* and no more' ("depends upon how the seats are won at the particular election. There are no electoral rules, perhaps there can be no rules, to cover such an eventuality—it just 'happens' occasionally with plurality voting systems. To any student of politics such events represent a challenge that requires some explanation, and the two examples quoted above have been so treated (Butler, 1952; Steed, 1974). We follow this second, more 'academic' approach to the iniquities of plurality voting systems in this book. Our purpose is to increase understanding of how votes are translated into seats in such systems. Although we realise that many readers will find ammunition in the pages that follow to justify their reformist arguments, this monograph is intended to be a technical statement about how a particular system works, and no more." on page xlii; their emphasis). Its underpinning argument is that how votes are translated into seats reflects the interaction of two maps – the spatial distribution of the pattern of support for each political party across the country and the grid of constituency (electoral district) boundaries superimposed upon that map, within which votes are cast and counted as the basis for the allocation of legislative seats.

---

8   That paper had, as an epigram, a quote from a general secretary of the British Labour party that 'There is no greater gamble on earth than a British general election'; their goal was to formalise that gamble – indeed to show that, given certain pre-conditions, it was not a gamble at all as the outcome is very predictable.

After an introductory chapter that briefly describes the electoral system in each of the six countries on which most of the book focuses – Australia, Canada, New Zealand, South Africa, the United States, and the United Kingdom (with most attention paid to the last of these; almost all other studies at the time were of a single country only) – the first part examines how votes are translated into seats, beginning with an evaluation of the cube law. Kendall and Stuart's (1950) classic paper showed that the 'law of cubic proportions', as they termed it, only applied when a party's percentage of the votes cast across all constituencies (its CPD) was normally distributed, with a standard deviation of 13.679. The distributions for the 1935, 1945 and 1950 elections had standard deviations which approximated that figure (as they did at the subsequent four elections: Curtice and Steed 1986: Table 2). Nevertheless, as they also noted, those distributions were not normal – which in 1950 produced an 'error' of 40 seats in the predicted difference between the two main parties (hence the 'built-in' anti-Labour bias that Butler observed).

These observations raised three questions addressed in detail in *SV*:

1. Why did the British parties' CPDs (constituency proportion distributions) have standard deviations close to 13.679, so that the leading party benefited in the translation of votes into seats?;

2. What was the outcome of the translation process when the standard deviation was either substantially larger or substantially smaller than 13.679?; and

3. What caused the non-normality in those CPDs which meant that one party benefited more from the exaggerative element of the cube law's operation than the other?

A modelling framework was established, whose key feature was the spatial clustering of voters of different political persuasions. This operates at a much smaller scale – of socially relatively homogeneous public and private sector housing estates, for example – than that of Parliamentary constituencies (which averaged some 60,000 voters each in the UK at the time). Three aspects of the geography of support for the parties are then crucial: the size of the clusters; their relative homogeneity (this assumption was later explored by Upton 1985, applying a theory of crowd behaviour developed by Penrose 1953); and their clustering within constituencies. Formal modelling of their geography under certain conditions – which held in the UK in the period Gudgin and Taylor were studying, as shown by a small empirical example of Newcastle upon Tyne – indicated that the interaction of these three produced a CPD that resulted in a cube law-type outcome. Where those conditions did not apply – as in New Zealand at the time – then the CPDs did not underpin a cube-law outcome. The law's relevance to the UK was thus serendipitous: it was not the system's design that produced the winning party's bonus of seats relative to votes but rather the interaction of three geographies that could not be pre-determined (local cluster size, their relative homogeneity, and clustering within constituencies); different geographies would result in different translation outcomes, different seats:votes relationships.[9]

This theoretical discourse is buttressed by intensive empirical explorations. The strict operation of the cube law in real world situations depends on five basic assumptions being met, the first four of which are inherently geographical – that:

1. constituencies have equal sizes;
2. change over time in a party's support is either uniform across all constituencies or unsystematic (e.g. not concentrated in certain regions);
3. the CPDs are normal with a standard deviation of approximately 13.679;
4. the constituency boundary mesh is laid across the clusters in an arbitrary or random way; and
5. elections are fought by two parties only.

None of these is entirely valid, and the less representative they are of the empirical situation the more complex the translation process. Much of the remainder of *SV* examines each assumption in turn, both theoretically and through empirical examples.[10] Malapportionment, non-uniform swing, and non-normal CPDs are treated first, with the last of the three getting extended treatment which shows how different types and degrees of skewness and kurtosis impact on the seats:votes relationship. This leads to the development of a measure of bias for and against parties – the difference between its share of the votes and of the seats – and its decomposition into malapportionment and distribution effects, with the latter further decomposed into that based on the operation of the cube law (which is non-partisan, because it operates equally for both parties) and a residual element (which is partisan, because it has a negative impact on one of the parties and a positive one on the other). Three-party elections are treated separately, with an innovative use of electoral triangles to predict the third party's performance and illustrate why, in most situations, it suffers from a 'savage bias' against it.

Having identified the major sources of bias, *SV* presents a method of decomposing the aggregate measure to establish the relative importance of the contributing components. That method was criticised by Chisholm *et al.* (1981), with a follow-up clarification by Gudgin and Taylor (1982) – who had published full details of an extended approach (with an analysis of the 1979 British general election) to incorporate turnout and minor party, as well as the malapportionment and distribution components, in Gudgin and Taylor (1980; their first 'success' in getting a paper accepted in a leading political science journal: the extension was also undertaken by Grofman *et al.* 1997, without reference to Gudgin and Taylor's 1980 paper[11]). Chisholm *et al.* (1981: 218) concluded that 'the problem

---

9   Gudgin and Taylor discuss other attempts to provide a theoretical basis for the cube law – such as March (1957) and Theil (1970) – noting that the latter provided a modelling approach rather than an explanation.

10 The text and appendices provide full proofs for all of the arguments developed – as the Preface indicates – with inputs from statisticians at the University of Newcastle.

11 Blau's (2002, 2004) later work incorporated the Edgeworth curve that allowed both the standard deviation and the kurtosis of the CPD to be varied (see Edgeworth 1897).

of unintentional bias in British elections is small, so small as to be regarded as trivial': later research (Johnston *et al.* 2001) showed that this was the case for the 1970s elections that Chisholm *et al.* studied – not because there was no bias but because the various components were self-cancelling, some favouring the Conservatives and others advantaging Labour because of the way the various maps interacted then. In the 1980s, however, Johnston *et al.* (2001) showed that there was a considerable non-trivial bias favouring the Conservatives and from 1997 on, a very substantial one favouring Labour.

The next part of the book moves on to policy implications; it removes the assumption that the mesh of constituency boundaries is not created in such a way that biased election outcomes are produced. Traditionally, it was believed that redistricting (the US term)/redistribution (the UK term) is either a partisan activity undertaken to produce a biased outcome that favours the party(ies) undertaking the task (the gerrymanderers) or a non-partisan activity undertaken by neutral bodies which results in a non-biased outcome. *SV* destroys that myth of 'nonpartisan cartography', showing that nonpartisan districting – by bodies such as the UK's Boundary Commissions – can, indeed, is very likely to, produce biased outcomes. The only difference between it and partisan districting (gerrymandering) is that – as they quote Nagel (1965) – it is 'only non-partisan in the sense that it is unpredictable as to which party it will favour' (*SV*, p. 127); the result is what they term an 'unintentional gerrymander'. This conclusion is again reached through a formal modelling process, with convincing (if small) examples. Districting is a combinatorial problem – and hence an important example of the modifiable areal unit problem. It involves taking a large number of small areas (electoral wards in the UK case) and grouping them together into constituencies that meet pre-defined criteria, such as size. There is thus a number of possible outcomes for the redistricting of any area, which may vary in their electoral outcomes according to the way the partisan characteristics of the small areas are grouped together. Some of the configurations may favour one party, others may favour its opponent; if more are of the first type than the second, then – *ceteris paribus* – it is likely that the neutral Commission will select from that majority group. This is unlikely to be as biased towards the party concerned as would be the case if it was gerrymandering a solution to promote its own electoral interests – although *SV*'s theory of decision-making in electoral districting does not rule this out: it all depends on the between-district variances in the parties' share of the votes cast across all possible outcomes.

Most of *SV* deals with plurality elections held in single-member constituencies but when the book was written there was considerable debate in the UK over electoral reform (Finer 1975) – in part responding to the apparent perversity of the result of the February 1974 general election, when Labour came second in votes cast, but won more seats than the Conservatives. So *SV*'s final chapter applies its analytical approach to other systems – the alternative vote (Australia); the double ballot (France); STV (Ireland); and MMP (Germany). It concludes that the last of these – since adopted in New Zealand (among other countries: Shugart and Wattenberg 2001) and for elections within the UK to the Scottish Parliament, the

National Assembly of Wales, and the London Assembly – is the best because,

> all arbitrary unintentional effects may be abolished and the debate can become directly concerned with theories of representation and not with their partial reflections in voting systems. The additional member system is simply the most reliable tool available for the respectable electoral engineer; it takes the geography out of elections (*SV*, p.199).[12]

*****

SV was a highly innovative book – indeed a classic. It was innovative not only in tackling a large problem – the translation of votes into seats, mainly in single-member plurality elections – comprehensively but also for doing that in a rigorous mathematical/statistical framework. It not only demonstrated conclusively why there is normally a 'winner's bias' at such elections but also, as was stressed in the conclusion, why there is also usually a 'savage bias against minor parties' – and all because of geographies. Because of the rigorous approach, and the associated detailed proofs provided in the appendices, the book explains electoral outcomes rather than just providing some empirical understanding based on limiting assumptions, which is what the cube-law does.

SV is a classic not just because of its innovativeness and coherence but also because it has never been bettered. Others – such as Taagepera and Shugart (1989) – have followed its lead but *SV* remains the foundation on which any future work should be based. But has it been as influential as it might/should have been? Clearly there have been followers, as discussed below, but the rigorous theory has often been bypassed for the empiricism that remains a characteristic of much work on electoral systems, particularly in the UK.[13] *SV* was occasionally cited as providing an argument for why the cube law was no longer a valid benchmark for analysing the seats:votes relationship in British election results, but without addressing its detailed arguments setting out why the cube law was a special case dependent on particular interacting geographies (as in Norris and Crewe 1994).[14]

Why? In part this is because of some of the features of inter-disciplinary research. *SV* was written by two geographers, and published by a company with no record (past or future) of books in political science, but a very successful small stable of journals in geography/social science, perception, and physics. Further – as they report in their Preface to *SV* – Gudgin and Taylor were almost completely unsuccessful in getting papers accepted by political science journals, in part, it seems, because those journals' editors, and so presumably the discipline they served, were not attracted to their rigorous mathematical arguments and statistical testing. (The only paper accepted by such a journal before *SV* appeared – Taylor and Gudgin 1975 – discussed British non-partisan cartography without any theoretical

---

12 Elsewhere, Taylor (1985; Taylor and Lijphart 1986) wrote of proportional tenure over time as an alternative perspective on proportional representation.
13 According to Google Scholar the book has been cited 152 times (I am responsible for about one-sixth of those!), almost none of those citations being by UK political scientists (though, as indicated here, there were some).
14 In that sense, the book was probably 'more sighted than cited'!

foundations; it met the then current disciplinary preference for empiricism.) Thus political scientists were not exposed to their work in the mid-1970s, and although the theory was published elsewhere in a journal of quantitative social science (Taylor and Gudgin 1976), the amount of extra-disciplinary literature-searching and -referencing by political scientists was small (geographers were – are? – much more active outwith the 'closed' realms of their own discipline: Laponce 1980; Johnston 2003). In reviewing the under-developed state of research into electoral systems and their impacts a few years after *SV* was published, Lijphart (1985: 4) noted that 'political scientists have not paid sufficient attention to the highly sophisticated and highly relevant work being done by political geographers' (citing *SV* as a prime example).[15] In part that conclusion remains valid.[16] There is now much more interaction among political scientists and the small number of geographers who have continued along the path set out by Gudgin and Taylor – notably through the EPOP (Elections, Public Opinion and Parties) specialist group of the UK Political Studies Association. Nevertheless, whereas the papers that those geographers publish in political science journals tend to get cited, those that appear in geography journals do not.

The book was reviewed in almost all of the major geographical journals of the time, and those reviews were overwhelmingly positive if not laudatory:[17] the most critical (Chisholm *The Geographical Journal*, 1982) concludes that it has a 'somewhat mechanistic, statistical framework' but also that it is a 'fine piece of work', both 'elegant and logical'. Reviews by political scientists were few, and there were none (as far as can be ascertained) in political science journals. In one of the four (in *Political Geography Quarterly*, 1982), Ian Budge (from the University of Essex, which by then had established its reputation for world-leading analytical political science) congratulated the authors on their 'formal rigor' and precise testing – noting that this probably 'put off the politics journals' – and concluded that its 'rigour and intellectual quality [...] make its reading an exciting and satisfying experience'. Patrick Dunleavy was less congratulatory (in *Regional Studies*, 1981) claiming that the book was difficult for a political scientist to review because it was not located within the discipline's broader concepts and too much of it was empiricist and technical: nevertheless he concluded that although

---

15 Unfortunately, he had previously misquoted them by stating that 'The cube law is based on the assumption of equal districts and a random delineation of district boundaries' (Lijphart 1985: 429). *SV* is also misquoted in Campbell's (1997: 267) book on bias in US House elections, to the effect that 'electoral system bias [...]. occurs when "one party tends to win smaller constituencies than its rival"'. (This book, published in 1997, includes no reference to any British work on bias other than *SV*, plus Taylor and Johnston's (1979) textbook.)

16 Although *SV* is in the bibliography of Taagepera and Shugart's (1989) analysis of the seats:votes relationship, for example, neither author appears in the index and the chapter (16) which, it is claimed, 'will give a rational basis for the seat-vote equations' (1989:172) makes no reference to Gudgin and Taylor's theoretical structure (or indeed any other).

17 Those 'discovered' include: Chisholm, *The Geographical Journal*, 1982; O'Loughlin, *The Geographical Review*, 1982; Archer, *Economic Geography*, 1982; Mercer, *Progress in Human Geography*, 1982; Massam, *Annals of the Association of American Geographers*, 1982; Paddison, *Environment and Planning A*, 1982.

the authors were 'time-bound in their methodology', and somewhat paradoxically given his earlier comments, that 'the book successfully pushes beyond some of the naive early political science accounts still given credence in the discipline' – which was Gudgin and Taylor's goal! Jeffrey Stanyer (in *International Journal of Urban and Regional Research*, 1982[18]) claimed that although the book was a 'very detailed and careful examination of the working of one type of electoral system' it was 'less substantial, less original and less interdisciplinary than [the authors] [...] obviously believe'. It was less substantial because 'it defines the democratic process too narrowly' and omits topics such as competition, turnout and legislative behaviour – the first is considered; the second could well have been included, and undoubtedly would have been two decades later when it became more important; and the link between the third and the seats:votes relationship is very hard to discern. It was less original because others – not mentioned – have considered the issue: Gudgin and Taylor do not 'break fresh ground' but rather bring together 'diverse lines of investigation by others [...] integrating them in a single framework' (a major and important research task of itself, but Stanyer's claim of no 'fresh ground' is readily countered by much that is clearly original in *SV*). This links to the third criticism: the book was not very interdisciplinary because 'there is very little geography and the political theory is old fashioned': the heart of the book **is** geography (Fotheringham's review in *Urban Studies*, 1981, argues that 'Gudgin and Taylor's contribution lies in the attention devoted to the spatial or territorial aspects of election results'!) and the book is built around the cube law because that dominated discussion of the seats:votes ratio at the time. Fotheringham wondered whether Gudgin and Taylor were giving disproportionate attention to the seats:votes relationship, however, claiming that 'Procedures for selecting parliamentary candidates and access to the decision-makers could be considered closer to the heart of representative democracy.'

A review in a statistical journal was also less than laudatory, asserting that although 'interesting and provocative' *SV* contained 'numerous errors and frequent fuzziness' (Potthoff in *Journal of the American Statistical Association*, 1983) – although it later qualifies that claim by stating that Chapter 5 and the associated appendices only 'appear to contain frequent errors or, at best, results based on inappropriate models' and he implies that some of the 'errors' are no more than typographical. He suggests that the issue of tactical voting should have been given more attention, particularly with regard to support for the Liberal party, which could have been based on other work on voting behaviour and the translation of votes into representation (such as Condorcet's theory) which is very marginal to Gudgin and Taylor's core concerns. It is far from a crushing critique, however, and avoids any mention of the book's core arguments that for the cube law to apply, certain geographical criteria have to be met and various techniques for redistricting can influence how those geographies interact and generate biased election outcomes; instead much of Potthoff's discussion suggests that he was treating the book as a text rather than a research monograph.

---

18 I have been unable to find any reviews by political scientists in political science journals.

A further reason why *SV* did not get the attention it deserves is that it was one of the authors' last pieces of writing on elections. Long before *SV* was published, Graham Gudgin had moved from Newcastle to jobs in Norwich, London, Cambridge and then Belfast and Oxford Economics Ltd., as an economist. Apart from a few essays, Peter Taylor did no further work on electoral systems after 1979, moving into the field of world systems analysis and the role of cities in globalisation. Thus they were not actively promoting their arguments.[19] These were published and available for others to follow-up – which a few did – but perhaps the lack of a personal presence (although EPOP was not formed for another decade so the opportunities were few) and a continuing stream of work (some of which might well have been more acceptable to political science journals than was the case in the 1970s) meant that the arguments, to the extent that they were encountered in the first case, disappeared from sight.

*****

In the three decades since it was published, parts of *SV* have attracted more attention, and been the foundation of further work, than others. Initially, redistricting/redistribution was the focus. Ron Johnston had been working with Pete Taylor on a number of topics in the late-1970s (a collaboration that climaxed in the 1979 publication of their *Geography of Elections*), and on learning that he didn't intend to take the work further, Ron – with Pete's support – sought a research grant to extend the studies of the Boundary Commissions (Pete and Graham having previously failed to get such support – as described in the Preface to *SV*). In 1978 he got a one-year grant from the Social Science Research Council to build a computer program that would identify all the possible configurations of constituencies within local government areas that met two major constraints (contiguity and a maximum deviation around the average electorate). He was fortunate in attracting David Rossiter as the researcher who wrote the program (Rossiter and Johnston 1981), which was applied to a number of areas, confirming and extending *SV*'s conclusions (based on two exemplar cases only) that the largest party in each area was likely to win a disproportionate share of the seats there relative to its share of the votes (Johnston and Rossiter 1983). Non-partisan cartography by a neutral Boundary Commission more likely than not, produced a biased outcome favouring the strongest party in each local area (the UK constituency-building exercise then involved treating each of the major local government areas separately, with very few constituencies combining wards in more than one of those areas). They also used the computer program to generate an alternative configuration for new constituencies for Sheffield from that provisionally recommended by the Boundary Commission for England in its Third Periodic Review. This was considered at the Public Inquiry, after which the Assistant Commissioner recommended, and the Commission accepted, that

---

19   One exception was a joint session that Peter Taylor, Ron Johnston and Michael Steed addressed at the Royal Geographical Society in 1984 (Johnston 1985b; Taylor 1985 and subsequent discussion on pp.344–346 following Taylor's paper).

it replace the provisionally-recommended configuration. Representatives of the Labour Party present at the hearing, were attracted by the existence of the program and cited it in evidence in their (failed) legal case in 1982–1983 which sought to get the Commission's full set of recommendations set aside because it was possible, using computers, to produce greater equality across constituencies than was present in the set to be presented to Parliament (Rossiter *et al.* 1999a; Johnston *et al* 1984). They lost their case because the judges who heard it interpreted the legislation as indicating that British redistributions were to be exercises in the exercise of neutral judgement balancing a range of factors, not just in accountancy.

For most of the 1980s little else was done that stemmed directly from *SV*, however; later work by Cirincione *et al.* (2000) extended the computer algorithm developed by Rossiter but difficulties in getting it published in American journals, saw their work come to a premature end.[20] Instead, the geographical study of elections focused on the map whose contours *SV* took as axiomatic – the clustering of party supporters which generated the CPDs that underpinned the bias produced when the mesh of constituencies was laid across it. In the UK, for example, Gudgin and Taylor assumed (quite reasonably; most other analysts then did the same) that voting behaviour was dominated by a class cleavage, and that there was considerable class segregation as a result of housing market operations. This was challenged by more sophisticated analytical research (e.g. Crewe and Payne 1976; Curtice and Steed 1982; Johnston 1985a; Johnston *et al.* 1988), which identified complex patterns of voting with clear spatial components – some of it at the micro-scale focused on the hypothesised neighbourhood effect (Johnston and Pattie 2006) and multi-level analyses indentified the amount of variation at a variety of spatial scales (Jones *et al.* 2007); little was done, however, to link these to the formal models of clustering developed in *SV*.

Non-partisan cartography and unintentional gerrymanders returned to the academic agenda in the early 1990s. The biases these could generate were largely ignored during the 1980s, mainly because little evidence of their severity was adduced – indeed, later research suggested that the various bias components balanced each other out so that neither Labour nor the Conservatives enjoyed an advantage over the other in the 1970s-1980s (Johnston *et al.* 2001). Labour lost the 1983 and 1987 general elections by wide margins in the distribution of votes, however, but won a substantially larger share of the seats, whereas the 'savage bias' against the minor parties (particularly the Liberal/Social Democrat Alliance) continued; it was the status quo. After the 1992 election, however, interest in the bias reappeared. Taylor and Gudgin (1977; see also Rodden 2006, 2010; Chen and Rodden 2010) had argued that the electoral prospects of left-wing parties in Australian and New Zealand were poor because of their positively-skewed CPDs,

---

20 For a critique of that and similar approaches see Altman and McDonald (2007). One interesting American citation of *SV* was in a court case challenging a Texan redistricting that would generate a more biased outcome than a previous redistricting plan – implying a gerrymander: *amici curiae* brief of Heslop *et al.* in the case of *Jackson et al.* v *Perry* in the United States Supreme Court. For the decision in that case, see http://www.supremecourt.gov/opinions/05pdf/05–204.pdf.

and the 1992 UK general election result appeared to sustain that conclusion. Johnston *et al.* (1994, 2002) explored whether that was so. Instead of adopting the method of measuring and decomposing bias developed in *SV* (and in earlier Australian and later US analyses: Rydon 1957; Soper and Rydon 1958; Grofman *et al.* 1997), they turned to an alternative methodology developed by a New Zealand political scientist (Brookes 1959a, 1960) which had been applied by Johnston (1976a, 1976b): its metric was more easily interpreted and did not use the cube law as the benchmark against which to measure bias.

This renewed interest in the translation of votes into seats and the biases that might ensue was treated in detail and depth in Roger Mortimore's (1992) D.Phil thesis at the University of Oxford – which was unfortunately not published either as a monograph or a series of papers.[21] It was a wide-ranging analysis of the structure and operations of the Boundary Commissions in the period 1950–1987 and of the various constraints within which they operated, notably the 'Rules for redistribution', and included a discussion of partisan bias and its measurement. Having criticised Gudgin and Taylor for their use of the cube law as the benchmark he advanced the case for using Brookes' algebra, although using a different measure of swing to that deployed by Johnston; he also extended the number of components into which the bias measure was subdivided to make it more relevant to the UK case – introducing, for example, a 'third party win' component alongside those of malapportionment, differential turnout, third party vote share and geographical distribution. Those adaptations to Brookes' method were extended by Rossiter *et al.* (1999b).

Analyses of biases in the 1979–1992 sequence of elections showed that growing regional differentiation in support for the two main parties (see also Curtice and Steed 1982, 1986) and an increase in the number of seats where the Conservatives and the Liberal/SDP Alliance occupied first and second places shifted the CPD standard deviations well away from that required for the cube law to operate. In seats where the Conservatives and Labour occupied the first two places, there was a strong distribution bias component working against Labour, partly countered by a smaller malapportionment component, which in 1983 and 1992 cancelled out the pro-Conservative distribution effect. Meanwhile, in the seats contested by the Conservatives and Liberals the bias favoured the former at each election from 1964–1992, predominantly because they benefited from the distribution component (Johnston *et al.* 1994).

Bias – as against disproportionality (what Gudgin and Taylor referred to as non-partisan bias in *SV*, resulting from operation of the cube law; partisan bias was the residual) – was firmly brought back onto the agenda after the 1997 UK general election. This was fought in a new set of constituencies defined by the Boundary Commissions earlier in the decade. As part of their evaluation of the election outcome and the impact of the political parties on the Commissions' work, Rossiter *et al.* (1999a) calculated the extent of bias. They argued – following

---

21 He did not enter academia but instead joined the polling firm MORI where he is now a head of political research and has published widely on voting behaviour in the UK.

Butler and Mortimore by adapting Brookes' approach – that if there were no bias then if the two main parties had obtained the same share of the votes cast, they should have been allocated the same share of the seats. Using a uniform swing across constituencies (also assumed in *SV*), they constructed a notional election where Labour and the Conservatives had the same vote percentage (with the shares obtained by other parties and the percentage turnout in each constituency being held constant), and found that Labour would have won 82 more seats (out of a total of 659) than the Conservatives (Rossiter *et al.* 1997a, 1997b). This bias estimate was a major surprise, not only because of its size but also because the operation of the UK electoral system was widely believed always to favour the Conservatives.[22] The bias was even larger at the next two elections: with equal vote shares Labour would have obtained 142 more seats than the Conservatives in 2001 and 112 in 2005 (Johnston *et al.* 2002, 2006). Even in 2010, when Labour lost by a substantial margin to the Conservatives, with equal vote shares Labour would have won 54 more seats than their main opponent (Johnston and Pattie 2010, 2011a).

The size and changed nature of this bias stimulated new research into its causes which built on the foundations provided by *SV* but extended it into areas not considered by Gudgin and Taylor, except in their 1980 paper. One was the impact of the geography of abstentions. Turnout at UK elections has fallen substantially since the 1970s, much more so in Labour-supporting areas than in those where the Conservatives are strong; by 2005 this provided a larger component of the anti-Conservative bias than malapportionment – Labour also tends to be stronger in the smaller constituencies, for a variety of reasons (Johnston *et al.* 2006; Borisyuk *et al.* 2010a). But much more important was the changing geography of support for Labour, away from the positive skewness of its CPD as recorded in *SV*. Part of this reflected the country's changing economic and social geographies: the decline of the large-scale heavy industries and coal-mining meant that Labour no longer had clusters of northern constituencies with very large majorities, a trend exacerbated by the reduction in the power and size of the trades unions that had mobilised much support there, as well as in the public housing estates where many of the 'better quality' dwellings were sold to the sitting tenants. It also reflected a change in Labour's support base. The absolute and relative decline of the 'working class' meant that the probability of it being the largest party after any election was declining (Crewe 1986). It needed to broaden its base, a situation recognised by New Labour under Tony Blair after 1994, and its success in attracting middle-class support, especially in 'the south', contributed to its 1997 and 2001 landslide victories. The party's CPD changed during this period from one characterised by positive skewness as described in *SV* to negative skewness (as was also the case for left-wing parties in Australia and New Zealand). The extensive biases that New Labour enjoyed from 1997 reflected that; in 2001, for example, of its bias of 142 seats, 78 resulted from its vote distribution being much more efficient than the

---

22 This finding was cited as one of the reasons why the UK's electoral system should be reformed in the 1998 report of the Jenkins Commission.

Conservatives' (Johnston et al. 2002).

Alongside this body of research based on Brookes' algebra, John Curtice expanded on his analyses with Michael Steed of the cube law's failure (Curtice and Steed 1982) with a simple measure of bias that did not decompose it into the various factors that they accepted generated such bias (as in Curtice 2001[23]) and tables such as those pioneered by Butler (1953) which showed the difference between the two main parties in the size of their lead in vote shares needed to obtain a majority of seats (see also Curtice 2009, 2010). Curtice and Steed (1986) extended their argument in a later paper which incorporated the results of the 1983 election. In 1982 they had argued that the changing geography of voting in the UK had undermined the electoral system's 'exaggerative quality', but the 1983 election result – a Conservative landslide in terms of seats won – suggested otherwise; they argued that the 'exaggerative quality' reflected the operation of certain contingent circumstances (1986: 210) and that trends in voting behaviour – the growth of a third party and widening inter-regional and urban-rural differentials – made these less likely to occur (although there was still a pro-Conservative bias to recent results). They concluded (1986: 218) that:

> We have demonstrated [...] that the single member plurality electoral system has now almost lost its ability to exaggerate the relative electoral strength of the Conservative and Labour parties in terms of the seats that they win.

In this they were prescient but premature. The 1987 election was very largely a re-run of 1983; 1992 was a transitional contest in terms of the seat:votes ratio; and then 1997 heralded a three-election sequence at which the exaggeration properties were re-established (notably in 2005 when a narrow Labour victory in votes nevertheless delivered a substantial Parliamentary majority). Only in 2010 were the contingent conditions – the relative vote shares of the three main parties plus their geographies – again in place to illustrate the veracity of Curtice and Steed's conclusion. It still remains moot, however, whether the system's 'tendency to exaggerate the lead of the Conservatives over Labour or vice versa at Westminster elections has all but disappeared' (1986: 220). What if Labour again won just over 40 per cent of the votes, perhaps 7 percentage points more than the Conservatives and twice the Liberal Democrats' share? Of course, that question may never be answered, not necessarily because such a result may not recur but rather because in 2011 the Conservatives changed the rules for constituency definition, requiring them all to be within +/-5 percentage points of the UK-wide quota (they also reduced the number of MPs: Johnston and Pattie 2011c, 2012b; Johnston, Pattie and Rossiter 2012); Curtice and Steed suggest that the exaggerative effect may remain in place with larger constituencies, but the increase resulting from the new rules – an average English constituency with some 5,000 more voters in 2015 compared to 2010 – may be insufficient for that to become apparent.

Adrian Blau's (2002) Oxford D.Phil thesis took an alternative approach to

---

23 In that paper, Curtice refers to *SV* in a footnote pointing to other analyses of the bias, but – like many others who note the book – does not address the main issues raised there.

the analysis of election results, seeking to measure and then decompose bias in the actual result rather than by first constructing a notional result whose validity rested on certain key assumptions – such as the applicability of a uniform swing across constituencies – which characterises Brookes' algebra. His work – initially stimulated by 'discovering' *SV* in a library when he was doing work for a geography undergraduate degree project – produced results, for both the size and direction of the bias and the relative importance of its major components, that largely parallel those generated using the Brookes' algebra (compare his Table 1 – Blau 2004 – with Table 4.1 in Johnston *et al.* 2001), but with some notable disagreements: the biggest relate to the 1983 general election which the Conservatives won by a landslide over Labour (which in turn only just beat the SDP-Liberal Alliance into third place), circumstances in which the assumption of a uniform swing was least appropriate. Where the two leading parties were close in their vote totals – as in 1992 – the differences in the two sets of estimates are small, because of the absence of a heroic assumption regarding the use of a uniform swing when generating the 'notional election result' that is central to Brookes' algebra.

Clearly, the cube law no longer has much traction, leading commentators (e.g. Blau 2010; Curtice 2009, 2010) to conclude that the plurality electoral system is no longer fit for purpose as many conceived it – to deliver majority government by the largest party. Some politicians, notably in the Liberal Democrat party, agree – but not the Conservatives. They believed that the main source of their underperformance in the translation of votes into seats at recent elections has been a function of malapportionment, despite academics' arguments to the contrary (McLean *et al.* 2009; Thrasher *et al.* 2011; Borisyuk *et al.* 2012). Hence their legislation in 2011 for a new set of rules to be applied by the Boundary Commissions whereby all UK constituencies – with few exceptions – will have electorates within +/-5 percentage points of the electoral quota (Johnston and Pattie 2012b). These new constituencies are to be in place in time for the 2015 general election (when the number of MPs is also to be cut from 650 to 600); will the bias have gone – or will interacting geographies still matter?

The declining relevance of the cube law to understanding the translation of votes into seats at UK general elections over the three decades since Gudgin and Taylor did their research, means that their method of estimating the various bias components is also obsolete. They computed the amount of partisan bias, for example, as that remaining when the cube law effect has been taken into account – both Mortimore (1992) and Blau (2002) arguing that this is a weak foundation on which to build a methodological procedure.[24] Their approach could have been modified by estimating the amount of non-partisan bias using whatever power relationship best-fitted the seats:votes relationship at the election being analysed,

---

24 Mortimore (1992: 5) was particularly scathing, arguing that to predict a party's 'unbiased seat share' using the cube law was 'crude' and 'obviously mistaken' because it was based on a 'dangerous circularity' which amounts to calculating 'nothing more than a measure of the extent to which the electoral system fails to behave in accordance with their own predictions; this is surely futile'!

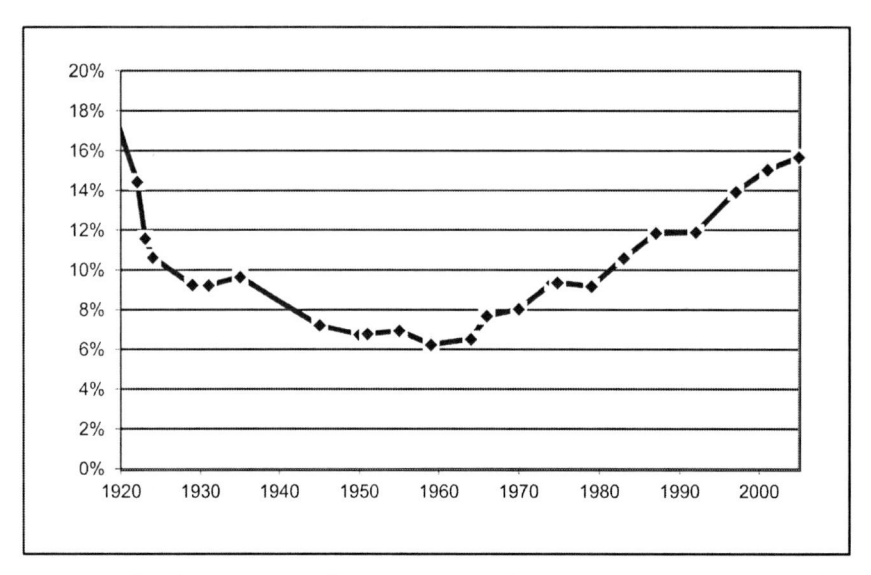

Figure 1: The changing spatial concentration of Conservative voters at British general elections, 1918–2005 (reproduced from Dorling 2010: 175, with the author's permission)

but such ad hoc arrangements are themselves unsatisfactory – and out of line with the rigorous approach adopted in *SV*. The alternative approaches using different algebras – although themselves problematic because of the assumptions they make – offer measurements that are better suited to situations where no one empirical relationship holds across time and space. But recognition of that situation in no way gainsays Gudgin and Taylor's major contribution in showing that the CPDs underpinning a particular seats:votes relationship reflect the interaction of three geographies; as the nature of those geographies and their interactions changes, so do the relationships – which is the fundamental lesson to be learned from their pioneering work.

Much of the analysis of bias since 1992 has accepted *SV*'s reasoning but not revisited it (analysts have largely sustained the intuitive empirical tradition of British psephology rather than the theoretical approach of *SV* – as in Johnston *et al*. 2001). A revisit could be extremely profitable, however, since some of Gudgin and Taylor's assumptions – particularly those regarding the size and homogeneity of the clusters of party support, and the macro-scale clustering of those clusters – are now harder to sustain. (This is exemplified in one brief study that did address the core of the argument in *SV*, that the weakening of the cube law relationship probably indicates a change in the nature of residential clustering in the UK, but not then exploring whether this has been the case: Maloney *et al*. 2003. A study which focused directly on the degree of clustering, in Taiwan, is Lin and Lee 2009). Given the decline of the class cleavage and the growth of 'valence politics' (Clarke *et al*. 2009), the models underpinning the CPDs that generate the cube law and its variants are obsolescent; how different might the model predictions be with different assumptions. In some ways the geography of support has not changed, but in others it has. Figure 1 (taken from Dorling 2010: 175) shows the spatial concentration of the Conservative vote since the 1920s: the larger the value on the vertical axis the greater the degree of concentration, so Conservative support was least clustered spatially in the post-war decades but is now as concentrated again as it was in the 1920s. And part of the reason for the changing geography has been the activities of the parties themselves. *SV* takes no account of the interactions between the two maps. The UK's redistribution procedure is not as non-partisan as Gudgin and Taylor imply – although it was much more so in the 1970s than it has been since. In the 1980s the Labour party realised that it could influence the definition of constituency boundaries during the public consultation stage, particularly through the presentation, at the public inquiries, of alternative configurations of constituencies within individual local authority areas that served its electoral interests – alongside criticism of options offered by its adversaries. Labour clearly outflanked the Conservatives in doing this during the redistribution that preceded the 1997 general election, with an impact on the resulting biases (Rossiter *et al.* 1999a), and both parties put substantial effort into similar attempts to influence the map's boundaries at the next redistribution a decade later.

With the map in place, the parties then seek to influence their support within each constituency – but in some much more than others. The conventional wisdom in British political science until the 1980s was that local campaigning had little impact on election outcomes; the national campaign – increasingly focused on the mass media – was what mattered (hence the observed uniform swing) and, to pirate another piece of political accepted wisdom, all else was embellishment and detail. Since then, however, a substantial body of research has shown that how much a party's candidates spend on the local campaign – mainly on canvassing voters to identify supporters and then mobilise them to turn out on election day – has a significant impact on how well they perform there (Johnston 1987; Johnston and Pattie 2006) as do other aspects of local electioneering such as the number of active party workers (Denver and Hands 1997; Fisher *et al.* 2011a, 2011b). Increasingly, the central party organisations have recognised the importance of these campaigns and have provided strong direction – plus, in some cases, resources – with which to make them more effective. But those campaigns are geographically very variable. Candidates and local parties don't devote much effort raising and spending money and putting activists on the streets in constituencies where defeat is almost certain. Nor do many of them focus substantial resources on the seats where victory is ensured – just enough to guarantee that turnout of supporters is sufficient to make that happen. Most effort is spent – and encouraged by the national party organisations – in the marginal constituencies, where failure to mobilise sufficient of the latent support may make the difference between success and failure (Johnston *et al.* 2012a).

This geography of campaigning is reflected in the CPDs; if a party pays little attention to the hopeless seats where all of its votes would be wasted, then its CPD could well be negatively skewed and its vote distribution (assuming that it is not a minor party) would be more efficient than if it turned out supporters where their votes were not going to count; the more resources a party has to commit to such local campaigns, therefore, and the more effective they are the better the outcome for it from the votes-into-seats translation. The changing skewness of Labour's CPDs for the elections from 1992 on was enhanced by the growth of anti-Conservative tactical voting.[25] In seats where Labour candidates occupied a poor third place its supporters were more likely to vote Liberal Democrat to try and prevent a Conservative victory locally, thus reducing the number of Labour wasted votes there and extending the negative skewness of the party's CPD. In seats where the Liberal Democrats were in third place, on the other hand, substantial numbers of their supporters switched to Labour for the same reason, thus generating more Labour victories, by relatively small margins, than might otherwise have been the case – again making for a more efficient CPD.

This changing situation, since the period when Gudgin and Taylor did their research, has had one major impact. *SV* includes analyses of the results of the 1974 general elections in the UK, which marked the start of the third and fourth party surges in support. The analyses of their impact in *SV* largely focused on them remaining as minor parties, but this has not been the case. The Alliance did not make a major breakthrough in the 1980s, nor did the Liberal Democrats in the 2000s; in addition Plaid Cymru remains a minor party in most of Wales for elections to the UK Parliament and the SNP has not successfully challenged Labour's Scottish hegemony in general elections (and its success at the 2011 election to the Scottish Parliament may not translate into a similar outcome at the next general election – scheduled for 2015). The Liberal Democrats have remained a strong third force across the UK, however, although not reaching the threshold that *SV*'s modelling indicated would lead to their seats share being commensurate with their percentage of the votes.

Two issues follow from this. The first is the geography of the Liberal Democrat post-1970s, and especially post-1990s, surge. Like most minor parties, the savage bias against them in the votes-to-seats translation reflected the inefficiency of their CPD – too many of their votes were obtained in relatively small percentages in constituencies where they came third; furthermore, where they won more than one-third of the votes they were more likely to come second rather than first, than was the case with the other two parties (Borisyuk *et al.* 2012). The party faced a difficult strategic choice: should it campaign widely across the country, aiming to win as much support as possible but probably winning few seats; or should it focus its limited resources on a few areas where it had a reasonable

---

25 March's (1957) analysis of the cube law provoked a brief response from Brookes (1959b) who used his algebra to assess the amount of bias in New Zealand's recent election results. He concluded that 'the logic of March's analysis is that any party handicapped by the gerrymander effect will reshuffle its coalition, i.e. will increase its bid for voters in marginal seats until its support is more strategically balanced. The New Zealand Labour party has given every appearance in recent elections of attempting to do this' (1959b: 291). It apparently had little success, but that was not the case several decades later when the British Labour party adopted a similar strategy (Johnston and Pattie 2006: 296–298).

chance of winning (Denver 2001). At most elections it selected the latter option, on the grounds that by winning representation in Parliament it could gain visibility and credibility on which to base future campaigns during which it could spread its appeal outwards from its cores of support (Dorling et al. 1998). This strategy was allied with one aiming to build its presence in local governments. Winning seats there – and in some cases either sharing or gaining outright power on local authorities – also helped in building visibility and credibility; voters who observed Liberal Democrats as successful local councillors might be more prepared to support them in Parliamentary contests. Through this strategy (on which see the example in Ashdown 2008) the Liberal Democrats increased their number of MPs considerably between 1992 and 2005 while their vote share remained relatively stable. Most of their initial successes were in seats that the Conservatives might otherwise have won, especially in the south of England, but increasingly there were Liberal Democrat successes in Labour's northern heartlands; they won control of several city councils (Sheffield, for example) and then gained Parliamentary seats in those cities, notably in 2005 when they campaigned strongly against Labour's invasion of Iraq and introduction of top-up University fees (Fieldhouse, Cutts and Russell 2006).

Geography was thus key to the post-1970 Liberal Democrat advance. With over one-fifth of the votes at a sequence of elections – at the last two of which the winning party got no more than 36 per cent – some argued that Britain now had a three-party system, although on the ground that appeared as three two-party systems (Johnston et al. 1994; Johnston and Pattie 2011a). Some 54 per cent of seats at the 2005 election had the Conservative and Labour candidates in the first two places; in another 20 per cent Conservatives and Liberal Democrats occupied the first two places with Labour often a poor third; and in a further 19 per cent, the first two places were occupied by Labour and Liberal Democrat candidates: some 7 per cent of the seats were in a fourth 'other' category – most of them in either Scotland or Wales where a nationalist party occupied one of the first two places. There was a clear geography to that division: most of the seats where Labour and the Liberal Democrats occupied the first two places were in either northern England or London, for example, whereas most of those where the Conservatives and Liberal Democrats were the main contenders were in southern England outside the country's main urban areas (Johnston and Pattie 2011a).

Given the emergence of this three-party system, the measurement of disproportionality and bias – whether using the procedure applied in *SV* or that based on Brookes' algebra – appeared incongruous, treating the Liberal Democrats as a 'minor party' rather than a major player the geography of whose support had a crucial influence, not only on its own performance in winning seats, but also its opponents'. Work was undertaken to take this into account by extending Brookes' formulation to a three-party situation. After an initial exploration (Borisyuk et al. 2008) a full procedure was outlined (Borisyuk et al. 2010b) and applied to recent elections (Thrasher et al. 2011; Borisyuk et al. 2012). This showed that in 2010 both the Conservatives and Labour benefited from having relatively efficient CPDs (bringing them 36 and 31 more seats respectively than might have been expected from the average situation given the observed share of the votes) whereas the Liberal Democrats' CPD was extremely inefficient (a bias against it for that component of 74 seats).[26] Labour benefited from higher levels of abstention in its seats than in those held by the Conservatives as well as, slightly, from malapportionment, so that overall the bias towards it was 63 seats compared to a positive bias of just 13 for the Conservatives and a negative bias of 76 seats for the Liberal Democrats (Thrasher et al. 2011).

That small component of the pro-Labour and anti-Conservative bias in 2010 rather undermined the Conservatives' case that they were discriminated against by malapportionment – but it didn't prevent them rewriting the rules to ensure that all constituencies in future have electorates within 5 percentage points of the national average. The 2010 figures for the malapportionment bias component were the smallest for all elections since 1983, reflecting the equality across the new constituencies introduced for that election (other than in Scotland, where the most recent redistribution was in 2004). But the three-party calculations show that malapportionment has never been a major contributor to the bias: it was at its largest in 1992, when it contributed 18 of the 55-seat positive bias enjoyed by Labour. Since 1983 abstentions have provided a larger source of positive bias for Labour than malapportionment and since 1997 they have been a larger source of negative bias for the Conservatives. But the main source of bias overall – and especially for the Liberal Democrats – has been the efficiency of each vote party's distribution: this was positive for the Conservatives at all elections since 1983 bar two (2001 and 2005) and also positive for Labour, except in 1997 when it won a landslide victory and its share of the seats was more commensurate to its share of the votes in a three-party contest than at any of the other three elections. It was always negative for the Liberal Democrats – by as many as 79 seats.

A major reason for this situation is well-known, and was dealt with in *SV*: the Liberal Democrats' CPD has been very positively-skewed, with a relatively low mean. Another reason adds a further complexity. In a three-party situation (with minor parties also fielding candidates in some constituencies, including some who perform well – such as the Greens in 2010 in a small number of seats) a seat could be won with as little as one-third of the votes cast and any candidate with more than 40 per cent should anticipate victory. In 2010, only one seat was won with less than 30 per cent of the votes cast (Norwich South, by the Liberal Democrat candidate with 29.4 per cent of the votes; the Labour candidate got 28.7 per cent, the Conservative 22.9 and the Green 14.9). All candidates who got more than 45 per cent of the votes won the seat, but there was a considerable difference among those who got 40–45 per cent:[27] 67 of the 71 Labour candidates with that share

---

26 The procedure operates by estimating the average outcome from all six possible distributions of a particular share of the votes. Thus if at an election party A got 41 per cent of the votes, party B 33 per cent and party C 26 per cent the procedure allocates those shares (41–33–26) to each ordering of the parties in turn (i.e. ABC, ACB, BAC, BCA, CAB, CBA), estimates the number of seats each would win at each of those 'notional elections' and takes the mean over all six as the norm against which the actual outcome is compared.

27 There is a small number of cases of candidates getting more than 45 per cent of the votes but

won, as did 66 of the 77 Conservatives, but only 11 of the 22 Liberal Democrats. With a substantial share of the votes, Labour and Conservative candidates were much more likely to win than Liberal Democrats (the same difference applied for those candidates with 30–40 per cent: Borisyuk *et al.* 2012). The reason for this was that in many cases where the Liberal Democrats were relatively strong (with more than 30 per cent of the votes) one of the other two parties was relatively weak, making the seat in effect a two-party race so that the Liberal Democrats' main opponent was very likely to get an even larger share; where either Labour or the Conservatives got over 30 per cent of the votes, on the other hand, all three of the main parties performed relatively well, so that a vote share of 35 per cent was more likely to deliver them victory than it was for the Liberal Democrats. The nature of the local competitive situation was an important determinant of conversion rates – of votes into seats – and the Liberal Democrats suffered from that in 2010 (and in several of the preceding elections too) as well as from having an inefficient (positively-skewed) CPD.[28]

*****

The core argument in *SV* is that in the operation of single-member plurality electoral systems geography matters because of the interaction of two maps – of parties' voting strength and of constituency boundaries – with the detailed contours of the first map reflecting the interaction of three other maps (the clustering of voters of different political persuasions, the homogeneity of those clusters, and their size relative to that of the constituencies). Others have followed Gudgin and Taylor's lead by stressing that conclusion (Johnston *et al.* 2001: 226). But Gudgin and Taylor took the argument further than any other UK scholars, through their evaluation of bias in other types of electoral system, concluding that it – and thus geography – mattered in most (see also Johnston and Pattie 2011b).

The exception, they claimed, is the additional member system – MMP/AMP. This is not necessarily so. Under MMP/AMP a proportion of the seats is allocated to single-member constituencies, where biases will probably be produced (as has been the case in both Germany and New Zealand, where minor parties have generally experienced 'savage bias' against them). The remainder are allocated to the parties according to their performance in a PR election, once the results of the constituency contests are taken into account. Thus, for example, in a 100-seat legislature where 50 seats are allocated according to the list contest a party with 30 per cent of the votes would be allocated 30 seats; if it won 25 of the constituency contests it would get five additional seats from its list, to ensure proportional representation. Any biases at the constituency contests (if the party won only 30 per cent of the votes there then it would be over-represented if it won 25 – half – of

---

failing to win the seat: at Chelmsford in 1983, for example, the Liberal candidate – Stuart Mole – won 47 per cent but lost to the Conservative – Norman St John-Stevas – who got 47.6 per cent.

28 Labour also benefited in this 'conversion' process because of its strengths in Scotland and Wales where the Conservatives and Liberal Democrats have been particularly weak (at least in major parts of each country) for much of the last two decades.

the single-member seats) should be erased by the list contest.

But that may not always be the case depending on details of the system. For example, the size of the list component of the legislature may be insufficient to ensure strict proportional representation if a party wins more seats in the constituency contests than its share of the list contest votes entitles it to. If the total size of the legislature is fixed, this could result in a party being over-represented: if, say, it won 30 per cent of the list votes in the above example but 33 of the constituency seats, then three of the seats that should have been allocated to other parties cannot be, and as a consequence they are underrepresented. This has been the outcome in some of the MMP/AMP elections to the Scottish Parliament and the National Assembly of Wales, for example, where the list elections are fought not as a single national contest but rather as a series of regional contests. In Wales, for example, there are 40 constituency seats and 20 list seats, with the latter contested in five regions each returning four AMs. In one region in 2007 (South Wales West) Labour won 35.8 per cent of the list votes with the Conservatives getting 21.7 per cent, Plaid Cymru 17.7 per cent and the Liberal Democrats 12.4 per cent. With eleven seats in total allocated to the region, the Liberal Democrats could have expected to be allocated one seat and Labour 4; but Labour had won all seven of the constituency seats, and as a consequence the Liberal Democrats' vote share was insufficient to gain them any representation (Hix *et al.* 2010). Again, geography militated against the smaller party winning representation. In some systems – New Zealand and Germany but not Scotland and Wales – this problem is circumvented by allowing any such 'additional seats' to be retained, with the size of the legislature being enlarged accordingly until the next election.[29] Thus if a party won 30 per cent of the votes in the list contest for a 100-member legislature, with half of the seats being allocated according to the list result, and won 33 of the constituency seats, the outcome would be it getting 33 seats in a 103-seat legislature, which is a slight bias in its favour (32 per cent of the seats for 30 per cent of the votes).

Some systems have threshold requirements for the allocation of list seats, to reduce the chances of minor parties winning representation: in New Zealand, for example, to qualify for list seats a party has to win either 5 per cent of the list votes or at least one of the constituency seats. The first of these criteria means that the larger parties will be slightly over-represented. The latter, however, can mean that if a small party has sufficient support in one area so that it wins a single constituency, then even if it has less than 5 per cent of the list votes it gets an allocation of seats. A party with 3.5 per cent of the votes which wins one constituency would be entitled to four seats in a 120-member legislature, for example; the geography of its support would be crucial to its winning representation and parties' there develop their campaigning strategies accordingly.[30]

---

29 This is commonly known by the German term *überhangmandat*.
30 At the 2011 general election in New Zealand, for example, it was claimed that the National (centre-right) party leader had done a deal with the leader of a small right-wing party (ACT) not to compete hard in the seat where he was standing so that he could win it and thus possibly gain

In other words, unless you go to the extreme and totally remove geography – by having a single PR election for a national constituency, as in Israel and the Netherlands – it is almost certain to play some part, and to be used by the parties, in the translation of votes into seats. Taking geography out of elections, which Gudgin and Taylor see as the action of a 'respectable electoral engineer', is almost impossible – and if you do, then the members of your legislature have no links to particular areas (communities); it is a placeless democracy (as proposed in Rehfeld 2005).

*****

Seats, Votes and the Spatial Organisation of Elections not only drew attention to what was already known in an informal way – that geography is key to the outcome of single-member plurality elections, as well as to contests held under a number of different electoral systems – but also, and most importantly, established why this is the case in a rigorous, formal set of arguments. It conceptualised the problem of disproportionality and bias in the translation of votes into seats in a systematic modelling framework underpinned by clear theoretical arguments. Those arguments and models continue to frame research questions – *Seats, Votes and the Spatial Organisation of Elections* established a paradigm that still has much energy; party competition has changed but the framework remains as valid now as it was 40 years ago.

---

a further 2–3 seats for his party even though it was going to fall short of the 5 per cent threshold; at the time the National party candidate was ahead in the constituency according to the opinion polls. The National leader presumably calculated that 3–4 seats for a minority party that would almost certainly support his government was a better option than winning the seat alone for National. Against that, the Labour and Green parties wondered whether to canvass their supporters to vote for the National party in that constituency, thereby forestalling the tactic. The ACT candidate won the seat with 45 per cent of the votes to National's 37 per cent (their shares at the 2008 contest were 56 and 22 per cent respectively); the combined Labour and Green share of the vote fell from 21 to 15 per cent. Because the ACT party did virtually no campaigning elsewhere in the country, however, it obtained only just over 1 per cent of the list votes and qualified for no further seats!

References

Altman, M. and McDonald, M. (2007) The limitations of quantitative methods for analyzing gerrymanders: indicia, algorithms, statistics and revealed preferences. Available at http://papers.ssrn.com/sol3/papers.cfm?abstract_id=998728.

Ashdown, P. (2008) *A Fortunate Life: The autobiography of Paddy Ashdown*, London: Aurum Press.

Blau, A. (2001) 'Partisan bias in British general elections', in J. Tonge, L. Bennie, D. Denver and L. Harrison (eds) *British Elections and Parties Review, Volume 11*, London: Frank Cass, pp. 46–65.

— (2002) *Seats-Votes Relationships in British General Elections, 1955–1997*, Oxford: University of Oxford: D.Phil Thesis.

— (2004) 'A quadruple whammy for first-past-the-post', *Electoral Studies* 23: 431–453.

— (2010) 'Majoritarianism under pressure: the electoral and party systems', in R. Hazell (ed.) *Constitutional Futures Revisited: Britain's Constitution to 2010*, Basingstoke: Palgrave Macmillan, pp. 233–248.

Borisyuk, G., Johnston, R. J., Rallings, C. and Thrasher, M. (2010a) 'Parliamentary constituency boundary reviews and electoral bias: how important are variations in constituency size?', *Parliamentary Affairs* 63: 4–21.

— (2008) 'Measuring bias: moving from two-party to three-party elections', *Electoral Studies* 27: 245–256.

— (2010b) 'A method for measuring and decomposing electoral bias for the three-party case, illustrated by the British case', *Electoral Studies* 29: 733–745.

Borisyuk, G., Johnston, R. J., Thrasher, M. and Rallings, C. (2012) 'Unequal and unequally distributed votes: the sources of electoral bias at recent British general elections', *Political Studies* (forthcoming).

Brookes, R. H. (1959a) 'Electoral distortion in New Zealand', *Australian Journal of Politics and History* 5: 218–233.

— (1959b) 'Legislative representation and party vote in New Zealand', *Public Opinion Quarterly* 23: 288–291.

— (1960) 'The analysis of distorted representation in two party, single member elections', *Political Science* 12: 158–167.

Bunge, W. (1966) 'Gerrymandering, geography and grouping', *The Geographical Review* 55: 256–263.

Butler, D. (1947) 'The relation of seats to votes', in R. B. McCallum and A. Readman (eds) *The British General Election of 1945*, London: Oxford University Press, pp. 277–292.

— (1953) *The Electoral System in Britain, 1918–1951*, Oxford: Clarendon Press.

— (1963) *The Electoral System in Britain since 1918*, Oxford: Clarendon Press.

Butler, D. and Stokes, D. (1969) *Political Change in Britain: Forces shaping electoral choice*, London: Macmillan.

— (1974) *Political Change in Britain: The evolution of electoral choice*, London: Macmillan.

Campbell, J. E. (1997) *Cheap Seats: The Democratic Party's advantage in U.S. House Elections*, Columbus: Ohio State University Press.

Chen, J. and Rodden, J. (2010) 'Tobler's law, urbanization, and electoral bias: why compact, contiguous districts are bad for the Democrats', Available at http://polmeth.wustl.edu/media/Paper/florida.pdf.

Chisholm, M., Devereux, B. and Versey, R. (1981) 'The myth of non-partisan cartography: the tale continued', *Urban Studies* 18: 213–218.
Chorley, R. J. and Haggett, P. (eds) (1964) *Frontiers in Geographical Teaching*, London: Methuen.
— (1967) *Models in Geography*, London: Methuen.
Cirincione, C., Darling, T. and O'Rourke, T. G. (2000) 'Assessing South Carolina's 1990s Congressional redistricting', *Political Geography* 19: 189–211.
Clarke, H. D., Sanders, D., Stewart, M. C. and Whiteley, P. F. (2009) *Performance Politics and the British Voter*, Cambridge: Cambridge University Press.
Crewe, I. (1986) On the death and resurrection of class voting: some comments on *How Britain Votes*. *Political Studies* 35: 620–638.
Crewe, I. and Payne, C. (1976) 'Another game with nature: an ecological regression model of the British two-party vote ratio in 1970', *British Journal of Political Science* 6: 43–81.
Curtice, J. (2001) 'The electoral system: biased to Blair?', *Parliamentary Affairs*, 54: 803–811.
— (2009) 'Neither representative nor accountable: first-past-the-post in Britain', in B. Grofman, A. Blais and S. Bowler (eds) *Duverger's Law of Plurality Voting: the Logic of Party Competition in Canada, India, the United Kingdom and the United States*, New York: Springer, pp. 27–46.
— (2010) 'So what went wrong with the electoral system? The 2010 election result and the debate about electoral reform', *Parliamentary Affairs* 63: 623–638.
Curtice, J. and Steed, M. (1982) 'Electoral choice and the production of government: the changing operation of the electoral system in the United Kingdom since 1955', *British Journal of Political Science* 12: 249–298.
— (1986) 'Proportionality and exaggeration in the British electoral system', *Electoral Studies*, 5: 209–228.
Denver, D. (2001) 'The Liberal Democrat campaign', *Parliamentary Affairs* 54: 638–649.
Denver, D. and Hands, G. (1997) *Modern Constituency Electioneering: Local campaigning at the 1992 general election*, London: Frank Cass.
Dorling, D. (2010) *Injustice*, Bristol: Policy Studies Press.
Dorling, D., Rallings, C. and Thrasher, M. (1998) 'The epidemiology of the Liberal Democrat vote', *Political Geography* 17: 45–70.
Edgeworth, F. Y. (1897) 'Miscellaneous applications of the calculus of probabilities', *Journal of the Royal Statistical Society* 61: 534–544.
Fieldhouse, E., Cutts, D. and Russell, A. (2006) 'Neither north nor south: the Liberal Democrat performance in the 2005 general election', *Journals of Elections, Public Opinion and Parties* 16: 77–92.
Finer, S. E. (ed.) (1975) *Adversary Politics and Electoral Reform*, London: Anthony Wigram.
Fisher, J., Cutts, D. and Fieldhouse, E. (2011a) 'Constituency campaigning in 2010', in D. Wring, R. Mortimore and S. Atkinson (eds) *Political Communication in Britain: The leader debates, the campaign and the media in the 2010 general election*, Basingstoke: Palgrave Macmillan, pp. 198–217.
— (2011b) 'The electoral effectiveness of constituency campaigning in the 2010 British general election: the triumph of labour?', *Electoral Studies* 30: 816–828.
Fothergill, S. and Gudgin, G. (1982) *Unequal Growth: Urban and regional employment change in the UK*, London: Heinemann.
Grant, W. (2010) *The Development of a Discipline: The history of the Political Studies Association*, Chichester: Wiley-Blackwell.

Gregory, S. (1962) *Statistical Methods and the Geographer,* London: Longman.
Grofman, B., Koetzle, W. and Brunell, T. (1997) 'An integrated perspective on the three potential sources of partisan bias: malapportionment, turnout differences, and the geographic distribution of party vote shares', *Electoral Studies* 16: 457–470.
Gudgin, G. (1978) *Industrial Location Processes and Regional Employment Growth,* Westmead Hants: Saxon House.
Gudgin, G. and Taylor, P. J. (1974) 'Electoral bias and the distribution of party voters', *Transactions, Institute of British Geographers* 63: 53–73.
— (1980) 'The decomposition of electoral bias in plurality elections', *British Journal of Political Science* 10: 515–522.
— (1982) 'The myth of non-partisan cartography: clarifications', *Urban Studies* 19: 405–407.
Haggett, P. (1965) *Locational Analysis in Human Geography,* London: Edward Arnold.
Hix, S., Johnston, R. J. and McLean, I. (2010) *Choosing an Electoral System,* London: The British Academy.
Jenkins, R. (1998) *Report of the Independent Commission on the Electoral System,* London: HMSO, Cm 4090-I.
Johnston, R. J. (1976a) 'Spatial structure, plurality systems and electoral bias', *The Canadian Geographer* 20: 310–328.
— (1976b) 'Parliamentary seat redistribution: more opinions on the theme', *Area* 8: 30–34.
— (1985a) *The Geography of English Politics: The 1983 general election,* London: Croom Helm.
— (1985b) 'People, places, parties and Parliaments: a geographical perspective on electoral reform in Great Britain', *The Geographical Journal* 151: 327–338.
— (1987) *Money and Votes: Constituency campaigns spending and election results,* London: Croom Helm.
— (2003) 'Geography: a different sort of discipline?', *Transactions of the Institute of British Geographers* NS28: 133–141.
Johnston, R. J., Cutts, D. J., Pattie, C. J. and Fisher, J. (2012a) 'Spending, contacting and voting: the 2010 British general election in the constituencies', *Environment and Planning A.*(forthcoming).
Johnston, R. J., Openshaw, S., Rhind, D. W. and Rossiter, D. J. (1984) 'Spatial scientists and representational democracy: the role of information-processing technology in the design of parliamentary and other constituencies', *Environment and Planning C, Government and Policy* 2: 57–66.
Johnston, R. J. and Pattie, C. J. (2006) *Putting Voters in Their Place: Geography and elections in Great Britain,* Oxford: Oxford University Press.
— (2010) 'The local campaigns and the outcome', in N. Allen and J. Bartle (eds) *Britain at the Polls 2010,* London: Sage Publications, pp. 203–239.
— (2011a) 'The British general election of 2010: A three-party contest or three two-party contests?', *The Geographical Journal* 177: 17–26.
— (2011b) 'Electoral systems, geography, and political behaviour: United Kingdom examples', in B. Warf and J. Lieb (eds) *Revitalizing Electoral Geography,* Farnham: Ashgate Publishing, pp. 31–58.
— (2011c) 'Parties and crossbenchers voting in the post-2010 House of Lords: The example of the Parliamentary Voting System and Constituencies Bill, *British Politics* 6: 430–452.
— (2012a) 'Kevin Cox and electoral geography', in A. E. Jonas and A. Wood (eds)

Territory, Space and Urban Politics, Aldershot: Ashgate Publishing.
— (2012b) 'From the organic to the arithmetic: new redistricting/redistribution rules for the UK', *Election Law Journal* (forthcoming).
Johnston, R. J., Pattie, C. J. and Allsopp, J. G. (1988) *A Nation Dividing? The electoral map of Britain 1979–1987*, London: Longman.
Johnston, R. J., Pattie, C. J., Dorling, D. and Rossiter, D. J. (2001) *From Votes to Seats: The operation of the British electoralsSystem since 1945*, Manchester: Manchester University Press.
Johnston, R. J., Pattie, C. J. and Fieldhouse, E. A. (1994) 'The geography of voting and representation: regions and the declining importance of the cube law' in A. Heath, R. Jowell and J. Curtice (eds) *Labour's Last Chance? The 1992 election and beyond*, Dartmouth: Aldershot, pp. 255–274.
Johnston, R. J., Pattie, C. J. and Rossiter, D. J. (2012b) '…somewhat more disruptive than we had in mind': the Boundary Commission for England's 2011 proposed redistribution of Parliamentary constituencies', *The Political Quarterly*, (forthcoming).
Johnston, R. J. and Rossiter, D. J. (1983) 'Constituency building, political representation and electoral bias in urban England', in D. T. Herbert and R. J. Johnston (eds) *Geography and the Urban Environment, Volume 3* ,Chichester: John Wiley, pp. 113–156.
Johnston, R. J., Rossiter, D. J., Pattie, C. J. and Dorling, D. (2002) 'Labour electoral landslides and the changing efficiency of voting distributions', *Transactions of the Institute of British Geographers* NS27: 337–361.
Johnston, R. J., Rossiter, D. J., and Pattie, C. J. (2006) 'Disproportionality and bias in the results of the 2005 general election in Great Britain: evaluating the electoral system's impact', *Journal of Elections, Public Opinion and Parties* 16: 37–54.
Johnston, R. J. and Sidaway, J. D. (2004) *Geography and Geographers: Anglo-American human geography since 1945*, 6th edn, London: Edward Arnold.
Jones, K., Johnston, R. J., Burgess, S. M. and Propper, C. (2007) 'Region, local context, and voting at the 1997 general election in England', *American Journal of Political Science* 51: 640–654.
Kendall, M. G. and Stuart, A. (1950) 'The law of cubic proportion in election results', *British Journal of Sociology* 1: 183–197.
Laponce, J. A. (1980) 'Political science: an import-export analysis of journals and footnotes', *Political Studies* 28: 401–419.
Lin, T.-M. and Lee, F.-Y. (2009) 'The spatial organization of elections and the cube law', *Issues & Studies* 45: 61–98.
Lijphart, A. (1984) 'Advances in the comparative study of electoral systems', *World Politics* 36: 424–436.
— (1985) 'The field of electoral systems research: a survey', *Electoral Studies* 4: 3–14.
McCallum, R. B. and Readman, A. (1947) *The British General Election of 1945*, London: Oxford University Press.
McDonald, M. (2009) 'The arithmetic of electoral bias: with applications to U. S. House elections', Available at http://papers.ssrn.com/sol3/papers.cfm?abstract_id=1451302
McLean, I., Johnston, R. J., Pattie, C. J. and Rossiter, D. J. (2009) 'Can the Boundary Commissions help the Conservative party? Constituency size and electoral bias in the United Kingdom', *Political Quarterly* 80: 479–494.

Maloney, J., Pearson, B. and Pickering, A. (2003) 'Behind the cube rule: implications of, and evidence against, a fractal electoral geography', *Environment and Planning A*, 35: 1405–1414.

March, J. G. (1957) 'Party legislative representation as a function of election results', *Public Opinion Quarterly* 21: 521–542.

Mortimore, R. (1992) *The Constituency Structure and the Boundary Commissions: the rules for the redistribution of seats and their effect on the British electoral system, 1950–1987,* Oxford: University of Oxford, D.Phil Thesis.

Nagel, S. S. (1965) 'Simplified bi-partisan computer districting', *Stanford Law Review* 17: 863–899.

Norris, P. and Crewe, I. (1994) 'Did the British marginals vanish? Proportionality and exaggeration in the British electoral system revisited', *Electoral Studies* 13: 201–221.

Openshaw, S. and Taylor, P. J. (1980) 'The modifiable areal unit problem', in N. Wrigley and R. J. Bennett (eds) *Quantitative Geography: a British view,* London: Routledge and Kegan Paul, pp. 80–90.

Penrose, L. S. (1953) *On the Objective Study of Crowd Behaviour,* London: Lewis.

Quandt, R. E. (1974) 'A stochastic model of elections in two-party systems', *Journal of the American Statistical Association* 69: 315–324.

Rehfeld, A. (2005) *The Concept of Constituency: Political representation, democratic legitimacy, and institutional design,* New York and Cambridge: Cambridge University Press.

Rodden, J. (2006) 'Red states, blue states and the welfare state: political geography, representation, and government policy around the world', Available at http://www.wcfia.harvard.edu/sites/default/files/Rodden2006.pdf.

— (2010) 'The geographic distribution of political preferences', *Annual Review of Political Science* 13: 321–340.

Rossiter, D. J. and Johnston, R. J. (1981) 'Program GROUP: the identification of all possible solutions to a constituency-delimitation problem', *Environment and Planning A* 13: 231–238.

Rossiter, D. J., Johnston, R. J. and Pattie, C. J. (1997a) 'Estimating the partisan impact of redistricting in Britain', *British Journal of Political Science* 27: 319–331.

— (1997b) 'Redistricting and electoral bias in Great Britain', *British Journal of Political Science* 27: 466–472.

— (1999a) *The Boundary Commissions: Redrawing the UK's map of parliamentary constituencies,* Manchester: Manchester University Press.

— (1999b) 'Integrating and decomposing the sources of partisan bias: Brookes' method and the impact of redistricting in Great Britian', *Electoral Studies* 18: 367–378 (and 19: 649–650).

Rydon, J. (1957) 'The relation of seats to votes in elections for the Australian House of Representatives, 1949–1954', *Political Science* 9: 49–61.

Shugart, M. S. and Wattenberg, M. (eds) (2001) *Mixed-Member Electoral Systems: The best of both worlds?,* New York: Oxford University Press.

Soper, C. S. and Rydon, J. (1958) 'Under-representation and electoral prediction', *Australian Journal of Politics and History* 4: 94–106.

Spence, N. A. and Taylor, P. J. (1970) 'Quantitative methods in regional taxonomy', *Progress in Geography* 1: 1–64.

Steed, M. (1971) 'The results analysed', in D. Butler and M. Pinto-Duschinsky, *The British General Election of 1970,* London: Macmillan, pp. 386–415.

— (1974) 'The results analysed', in D. Butler and D. Kavanagh, *The British General Election of February 1974*, London: Macmillan, pp. 275–312.
— (1975) 'The results analysed', in D. Butler and D. Kavanagh, *The British General Election of October 1974*, London: Macmillan, pp. 293–339.
Taagepera, R. and Shugart, M. S. (1989) *Seats and Votes: The effects and determinants of electoral systems*, New Haven CT: Yale University Press.
Taylor, P. J. (1969) 'The locational variable in taxonomy', *Geographical Analysis* 1: 181–195.
— (1971a) 'Distance decay curves and distance transformations', *Geographical Analysis*, 3: 221–238.
— (1971b) 'Distances within shapes: an introduction to a family of finite frequency distributions', *Geografiska Annaler B*, 53: 40–53.
— (1972) 'An annotated bibliography on topics related to political districting', in J. Liittschwager, *Redistricting Report* (for the State of Iowa Legislature's Committee on Reapportionment).
— (1973a) 'A new shape measure for evaluating electoral district patterns', *American Political Science Review* 67: 947–950
— (1973b) 'Some implications of the spatial organisation of elections', *Transactions, Institute of British Geographers* 60: 121–136.
— (1974) 'Electoral districting algorithms and their applications', *Working Paper No 2*, Quantitative Methods Study Group, Institute of British Geographers.
— (1976) 'An interpretation of the quantitative debate in British geography', *Transactions, Institute of British Geographers* NS1: 129–142.
— (1985) 'All organisation is bias: a political geography of electoral reform', *The Geographical Journal* 151: 339–343.
Taylor, P. J. and Gudgin, G. (1975) 'A fresh look at the Parliamentary Boundary Commission', *Parliamentary Affairs* 28: 405–415.
— (1976) 'The statistical basis of decision making in electoral districting', *Environment and Planning A* 8: 43–58.
— (1977) 'Antipodean demises of Labour', in R. J. Johnston, (ed.) *People, Places and Votes: Essays on the electoral geography of Australia and New Zealand*, Armidale: University of New England, pp. 111–120.
Taylor, P. J. and Johnston, R. J. (1979) *The Geography of Elections*, London: Penguin.
Taylor, P. J. and Lijphart, A. (1986) 'Proportional tenure versus proportional representation: introducing a new debate', *European Journal of Political Research* 13: 387–399.
Theil, H. (1970) 'The cube law revisited', *Journal of the American Statistical Association* 65: 1213–1219.
Thrasher, M., Borisyuk, G., Rallings, C. and Johnston, R. J. (2011) 'Electoral bias at the 2010 general election: evaluating its extent in a three-party system', *Journal of Elections, Public Opinion and Parties* 21: 279–294.
Tufte, E. R. (1973) 'The relation between seats and votes in two-party systems', *American Political Science Review* 67: 540–554.
Upton, G. J. G. (1985) 'Blocks of voters and the cube law', *British Journal of Political Science* 15: 388–398.

| preface

Unlike the majority of democratic countries most English-speaking nations retain the plurality system of elections in which the winner takes all within each individual constituency. This 'first-past-the-post' system leads to the important weakness that the relationship between total votes gained and number of seats won is uncontrolled, arbitrary, sometimes unpredictable, and in some circumstances open to abuse. Exaggerated majorities for winning parties are a common feature of the system, but it is also capable of awarding victory in seats to a party with a minority of votes. The latter negation of democracy is particularly likely to disadvantage left-wing parties, and has done so on several occasions in a number of countries. Minor parties are treated in especially arbitrary ways by the system. Often their significant voting strength is nullified by the award of a derisory number of seats. Sometimes a minor party achieves a rough proportionality in seats and votes, but it is very rare for such a party to gain positively from the system. The final important area in which the system exhibits severe structural weakness concerns gerrymandering. The territorial nature of the system provides an invitation to adjust boundaries for political gain. In Britain the neutrality of the Boundary Commissions makes gerrymandering appear to be a nonissue. However, neutrality merely ensures that no bias is intended. In practice neutral Boundary Commissions can unintentionally favour one party over others since strict fairness requires more than not intending to exhibit bias.

The above list of iniquities of the so-called 'Anglo-Saxon' democratic systems has provided the stimulus for carrying out the research upon which this book is based. It is important, however, to recognise that criticism of such voting systems may take on two separate guises. One quite natural reaction is to turn to the democratic countries which mostly practise some form of proportional representation and to advocate the spread of such 'equitable' voting systems to the remainder of the democratic world. In Britain, for instance, this reaction has been represented by a growing literature which proposes electoral reform of this type (Finer, 1975; Rogaly, 1976; Hansard Society, 1976; Mayhew, 1976). A second reaction has been to dwell upon the problems of plurality-type systems of voting and to try to explain why it is they operate in the way they do. In this case it is the arbitrary nature of the first-past-the-post system which is emphasised (Taylor and Gudgin, 1975). By this we mean that plurality voting systems have evolved in an almost unplanned way so that they produce electoral effects which have never been explicitly advocated, voted upon in parliament, and then set into operation. Take, for instance, the following question: under what circumstances should a party with the highest total of votes be given the second largest number of seats in parliament? Such a situation has occurred twice in recent British elections—to Labour in 1951 and to the Conservatives in February 1974—but the topic has never been explicitly discussed in parliament. Rather it is simply an arbitrary result that depends upon how the seats are won at the particular election. There are no electoral rules, perhaps there can be no rules, to cover such an eventuality—it just 'happens' occasionally with plurality voting systems. To any student of politics such events represent a challenge that requires some explanation, and the two examples quoted above have been so treated (Butler, 1952; Steed, 1974). We follow this second, more 'academic' approach to the iniquities of plurality voting systems in this book. Our purpose is to increase understanding of how votes are translated into seats in such systems. Although we realise that many readers will find ammunition in the pages that follow to justify their reformist arguments, this monograph is intended to be *a technical statement about how a particular system works,* and no more.

The central thesis of this book is that the relationship between seats and votes depends on two things. The first is the spatial distribution of party support across a country. The second is the way in which the grid of constituency boundaries is placed on top of the geographical pattern of support. The interplay between these two aspects is responsible for the weaknesses of the system. Occasionally these prove to be extreme but the factors translating votes into seats in a nonproportional way play a part in all plurality elections. The importance of the seats-votes relationship makes it surprising that relatively little academic attention has been attracted to the subject. A truly vast literature analyses the determinants of the number of votes gained by individual parties, but the step from votes to seats has been underresearched.

One reason for the lack of research is the complexity of the subject. The simple nature of the election system conceals surprisingly complicated mechanisms relating seats and votes. The purpose of this book is to describe these mechanisms. *Chapter 1* describes the electoral rules in the five countries from which most of the empirical material is drawn. This is followed by the core of the argument in *chapter 2,* which describes a model of the seats-votes relationship. This leads from first principles to a position in which the relationship can be described by one of a series of simple mathematical functions of which the famous 'cube law of elections' is one.

Chapter 3 provides an explanation of why the model and its mathematical forms, including the 'cube law', occur in practice. The argument is developed in statistical terms, and its crux concerns the way in which party voters are distributed between constituencies. The end result is an equation which relates seats to:

(1) the overall vote gained by a party,
(2) the number of constituencies,
(3) the form of clustering of voters on the ground.

This is illustrated and tested empirically for Newcastle upon Tyne by using a polling-day survey of three thousand voters. The accordance between the theory and the reality are sufficiently close to indicate that this chapter develops the first satisfactory explanation of the cube law and allied seats-votes relationships. *Appendix 1* reviews the work of others on explaining the cube law.

Chapters 2 and 3 are confined to two-party elections and are based on somewhat simplified electoral assumptions, although the degree of reality is quite sufficient to account for the major elements in the relationship between seats and votes. In *chapter 4* the simplified assumptions are dropped in order to discuss a range of situations which occur in actual electoral systems. These include varying constituency size (malapportionment), swings which are nonuniform between constituencies, and finally the overconcentration of support for a party in its strongholds. Each of these is a variant on the simple model of chapter 2, and each is an aspect of actual elections, which influences the relationship between seats and votes. The chapter ends with an equation which demonstrates how differences between seats and votes (that is, bias) can be accounted for by these various components.

The development towards more realistic and more complex electoral conditions is continued in *chapter 5,* in which an analysis is conducted of the seats-votes relationship for three-party contests. The extra ingredient created by the presence of an additional party proves to be the increased likelihood of instability of election results when certain thresholds are attained by the third party. Below these votes thresholds third parties are often considerably disadvantaged in seats, but when the third party has a quarter to a third of the total votes the situation can change violently. With three relatively evenly balanced parties, small shifts in votes can produce landslides in seats. Again the critical factor is the spatial distribution of support, and in this chapter a method is developed of translating votes into seats for specified types of spatial distribution.

Each of the preceding chapters is concerned with how seats and votes are related under 'natural' conditions. In most countries there is, however, some degree of political involvement in the process of drawing constituency boundaries (electoral districting), which results in a seats-votes relationship that differs from what might be expected given a more random arrangement of boundaries. In the USA and South Africa the seats-votes relationship has changed radically in the postwar period and in both cases the process of electoral districting is one likely cause. In the USA the result has been to diminish greatly the number of marginal constituencies and to make elections less responsive to shifts in public opinion. In South Africa the result has been a very large bias operating in favour of the National Party, to the extent that South Africa can be viewed as being effectively a one-party state. In *chapter 6* the American system is described along with an account of the recent 'reapportionment revolution'. This is followed by an account of computer districting, and an application of one districting algorithm to the problem of calculating the entire range of feasible districting solutions in three case studies. The results from the case studies lead to a theory of districting agencies which predicts the type of solution associated with particular types of districting agency. Surprisingly, the consequences of a neutral agency like the British Boundary Commission are likely to be the same as those of an agency aiming to gerrymander in favour of the majority party. The case of South Africa is considered in a separate section.

The problems engendered by the plurality system are in the rare category of human problems which can be effectively banished 'at a stroke'. As we have already noted, most democracies other than the English-speaking ones use some form of proportional representation (PR), and this could also easily be adopted by the remaining non-PR countries. In chapter 7 the alternative-vote, single-transferable-vote, and additional-member systems are analysed. The discussion is somewhat less formal than in previous chapters but the methods developed in those chapters are used to bring out the likely consequences of a switch from the plurality system.

We hope that this book will prove of interest to a range of people interested in elections. In particular we anticipate that three audiences will be most directly concerned. For political scientists this volume represents the first comprehensive analysis of the seats-votes relationship and contains much that will be completely new to most readers. In the USA, we hope that the book will help place the massive recent interest in reapportionment into a framework within which it can be viewed more rationally.

For geographers the interest should be two-fold. First, the work serves as an example of the spatial organisation of a particular and important type of human activity. Second, specialist political geographers will find material, some of which they will already be familiar with, brought together in a single volume for use in teaching and research. The content of the book has already served as part of a final-year option course for geography students at The University of Newcastle upon Tyne.

Finally, the book will be of relevance to those concerned with the legal aspects of elections. Electoral law requires to be built upon a foundation of understanding, since, as argued in chapter 6, fairness and predictability of consequences depend on much more than mere legislative intent. In the USA political interest in reapportionment has been strongly paralleled by legal interest, and in Britain also lawyers are likely to become increasingly involved in electoral matters as devolution and European integration proceed, and to throw open fundamental questions of parliamentary representation. In past debates on electoral laws, Butler (1963, page 144) has argued that "When electoral matters have been discussed in Parliament during the past thirty years there has very seldom been any illusion to the hard facts about the working of the system". Steed (1975b) illustrates this further with the particular example of the debate surrounding the 1885 electoral reforms upon which modern British elections are based. He shows that the single-member plurality system was chosen in part on the expectation that it would tend to produce proportional representation! We trust that this monograph will serve to ensure that such misunderstandings remain historical curiosities.

For each of these audiences and for other readers we have tried to develop the technical aspects of the argument as gently and clearly as possible. The technicality forms an integral part of the book, and we have felt it essential to be explicit as to how each conclusion was reached. It is hoped that occasional outbreaks of algebra do not put off those who have an otherwise strong interest in the subject matter.

The work on which this volume is based has a relatively long history stretching back to 1972. One author had previously been interested in electoral districting while working in the USA, but the main thrust came from a common interest in elections while at the University of Newcastle upon Tyne. For both of us the work has been a rewarding experience, and has demonstrated to us both the considerable advantages of cooperative research. In this case each phase of the work has been jointly and equally developed step-by-step.

Even joint authors would be in a poor state without very considerable assistance from many other people. Generous help with data sources has been gratefully received from many quarters. Ron Johnston made available his data bank of New Zealand elections, and Don Parkes, Stu Daltrey, and Tony Hellen each helped to provide results from the countries with which they were associated. When gaps appeared in our set of election results embassies proved a reliable and efficient source, and we have the embassies of Australia, South Africa, and Canada to thank for their assistance. The survey data used in chapter 3 was collected by over fifty students on a cold winter day in 1974. We wish to thank the University of Newcastle Research Fund and the Department of Geography for jointly covering the cost of this data collection exercise.

Mathematics and computing have been two areas in which help was continually needed. Dave Tarn took charge of all computing and we have him to thank for virtually all the tabulations and many computer diagrams. All of the finished diagrams were produced by Olive Teasdale and we are grateful for her quick and efficient work upon them. Members of the Statistics Department at the University of Newcastle were generous with their time. Graham Upton and Victor Barnett helped to clarify several matters and we are particularly indebted to Peter Diggle for some important proofs which we could not have produced ourselves.

One disappointment for us has been the fact that several areas of empirical work have been less fully developed that we would have wanted. The causes of this shortcoming lie, we feel, in the subtle but strong institutional barriers which militate against interdisciplinary research, regardless of the esteem which the latter enjoys in public debate on research matters. Since this type of experience is unlikely to be unique to ourselves, or even to the two disciplines involved, we hope that by publicising difficulties that are usually politely ignored they may be diminished in the future.

Our experiences in this area have been both serious and comic. When we were approximately halfway through this research we attempted to obtain SSRC support so that one of us could work full-time on the project to speed the work along and specifically to develop the empirical side of the work. Unfortunately support was not forthcoming, despite SSRC's public advocacy of 'interdisciplinary' and 'applied' research, for reasons that were never made formally clear to us. We were left with the strong impression that rejection was related to opposition to research on elections being done by other than political scientists. This view has been bolstered by the treatment of our research papers by journals concerned with politics. Whereas we have found no difficulty in publishing our results in geography and related journals we have had no luck in the politics field and this is where the comedy has often crept in. As well as the predictable editor's comment that our papers are too mathematical for a politics readership, we have actually had one article accepted for publication on condition we missed out the middle section – the argument on how we reach our conclusions; only the conclusions were required! In another case a politics journal turned down an article for being too statistical and referred us to a statistics journal whose editor promptly referred us back to the original politics journal. Yet another paper has the distinction of being turned down by politics journals on three continents. In each case the paper was rejected with no criticism of its content except that the topic was not considered to be of interest to the readership. In 1975 we decided to stop submitting papers to politics journals and to concentrate instead in putting together our work into a single volume. The result is before you.

Graham Gudgin
Department of Economics
University of Cambridge

September, 1978

Peter J Taylor
Department of Geography
University of Newcastle upon Tyne

To
Enid and Lynette

chapter one | translating votes into seats

The word democracy means, literally, 'government by the people'. Up until the eighteenth century the term was restricted to describing political systems in which the population governed directly through large meetings without recourse to elections and representative institutions (Holden, 1974). Such 'pure' democracy is difficult to imagine in complex societies. Hence an 'indirect' or representative form of democracy has evolved whereby government is by the *elected representatives* of the people. Such systems of government raise a whole host of problems in terms of the relationship between representatives and the people being represented. This book treats one of these problems in some detail: we investigate how the votes cast for a political party are translated into seats for the party's candidates in the legislature, parliament, or assembly. This is a key relationship which lies at the very heart of modern representative democracy.

1.1 Seats and votes

If it is accepted that the relationship between seats and votes is a fundamental and critical characteristic of modern democracies then it follows that electoral laws should spell out precisely what this relationship will be. It may be argued, for instance, that a party should receive the same proportion of seats as its proportion of votes. Such exact proportional representation defines an ideal deterministic relationship

$$S = V, \qquad (1.1)$$

where S is the percentage of seats and V is the percentage of votes for a party. This is just one of innumerable deterministic relationships which could be laid down in an electoral law to govern the seats-votes relationship. Unfortunately electoral laws are not always so directly concerned with this relationship. This is illustrated by figure 1.1 where 664 election results for parties in twenty countries for 115 elections between 1945 and 1965 are shown (Rae, 1971). Although a clear trend emerges so that a higher percentage of votes usually leads to a higher percentage of seats, there is a wide variety of seats-votes relationships. This simply means that a certain percentage of the vote may mean a different electoral outcome for different parties at different times in different countries. There is no universal seats-votes relationship in representative democracy.

It is, of course, naive to expect otherwise. Representative democracy was not invented by one group of people in one country at one particular time to be diffused unaltered to the rest of the world. Rather it has evolved piecemeal in different ways in different European and European-settled countries over two centuries. In some cases new representative institutions have been devised whereas elsewhere existing institutions have been gradually 'reformed'. This obviously relates to the different contexts within which modern political institutions have developed. In Britain a reform movement had to contend with a parliament that could boast of a tradition going back to the thirteenth century. In the United States the Constitution was framed upon the experience of colonial assemblies. In France and most other European states there was little or no direct tradition of responsible legislatures, so change was often more revolutionary. In all of these cases there is one single theme running through the changes. This is the trend towards more explicitly democratic forms of government. Notions of what is meant by 'more democratic' have varied but generally we can see that most changes have led to more and more people having more and more say in the composition of the legislatures. This trend has produced a variety of forms of representative democracy, which is reflected in figure 1.1.

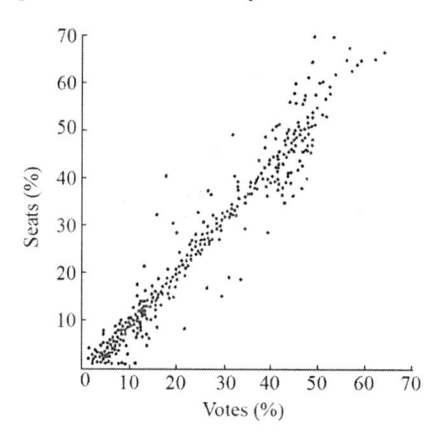

Figure 1.1:   Seats and votes for 664 parties in 115 elections

1.1.1 Electoral reform

This democratic trend can be described in terms of four major types of electoral reform.

The first and most basic democratic change is clearly *reform of the suffrage*. Restrictions on who should vote have been based on numerous criteria, the most common of which are property qualifications, age, and sex. Early franchise reform involved bringing the male middle-class citizens into the system. The nineteenth century saw most European and North American restrictions on the male franchise abolished, and female suffrage became generally available in the first quarter of the twentieth century.

Reform of the suffrage is not effective if the people entitled to vote are not free to vote as they wish. To ensure this requires *reform of electioneering*. This involves ensuring fair practices in terms of voter registration, and preventing intimidation by employers and landlords and corrupt buying of votes by candidates. Extension of the franchise with the resulting larger numbers of voters makes corruption more difficult but these problems were only brought fully under control with the institution of secret voting and adequate policing of anticorruption laws.

Even if every adult is able to vote as he or she wishes this still does not ensure that each elector is equally provided for. If one voter is part of a large constituency while another is part of a very small constituency we would consider the first voter to have less influence on an election than the second voter. This of course involves the problem of the 'rotten boroughs' in Britain, and early reformers realised that reform of the suffrage and electioneering must be complemented by *reform of the distribution* of constituencies. Thus there has been a trend towards constituencies of more equal size right through into the twentieth century in Britain, North America, and Europe. In the former two cases this has been as far as the reform movement has progressed. However, in Europe a fourth set of reforms can be identified, which have not got beyond the debating stage in Britain and North America.

Even if every adult is able to vote as he wishes in equal-size constituencies, this still does not ensure that every voter influences the composition of his legislature. For instance in Britain, Lakeman (1974) has pointed out that the borough constituency of South Shields, which was created in 1832, has *never* returned a Conservative Member of Parliament. This does not mean that South Shields voters have not voted Conservative but simply that such voters have always been in a minority. In fact representation for South Shields would not have been affected if every one of the Conservative voters over nearly 150 years had never bothered to vote. All of these votes have been literally wasted. Similarly most Labour votes in many southern county constituencies have been wasted throughout most of the twentieth century. Of course most Liberal votes are now wasted everywhere. This can be viewed as a type of disenfranchisement of the voter despite his going through the motion of depositing his vote in the ballot box. In Europe this situation has been viewed as unsatisfactory and has led to a *reform of representation.* This has involved a change in the system of voting to one which takes into account everybody's vote in allocating seats in the legislature. Such voting systems are usually based on proportional representation. Starting in Denmark in 1855, the proportional-representation reform movement swept all before it in Europe so that by the 1920s all countries had adopted this type of voting system. This even included France for a short time (1917-1927), the Irish Republic despite its British links, and the British Parliament itself for the university seats. Fundamental reform of representation, however, has not come to Britain and the United States, and the 'Anglo-Saxon democracies' (also including Canada, Australia, South Africa, and New Zealand) have stopped short of the total electoral reform experienced by most European democracies. Five of these countries (Australia is the odd man out—see chapter 7) have retained the plurality system of voting, under which a candidate wins a seat by gaining a plurality of the votes (more votes than any other candidate) in spatially defined constituencies. The contrast between these countries and those with reformed voting systems is clearly illustrated in figure 1.2 where the data displayed in figure 1.1 are separated into two graphs. The first [figure 1.2(a)] shows seats-votes relationships in these 'Anglo-Saxon democracies' where a wide scatter of results is very evident. The European democracies (with the exception of France), on the other hand, employ proportional representation systems which produce, with only a few minor discrepancies, a close approximation to the deterministic relationship of equation (1.1) [figure 1.2(b)]. The major variations observed in figure 1.1 can now be seen to be due to a relatively small number of election results produced by the residual group of countries which have not experienced a reform of their system of representation.

It is not the purpose of this discussion to investigate the political and historical reasons for this anomaly but rather to consider the operation of such 'unreformed' representative democracies. Figure 1.2 shows that the proportion of the vote that a party receives in elections in these countries only *partly* determines the number of seats that are won. In this monograph the additional factors which produce the election outcome above and beyond the actual level of a party's vote are investigated. We largely restrict this investigation to consideration of representation in plurality-type elections with single-member constituencies where the candidate with most votes wins the seat. In such situations the major additional influences upon election results are associated with the spatial organisation of the election.

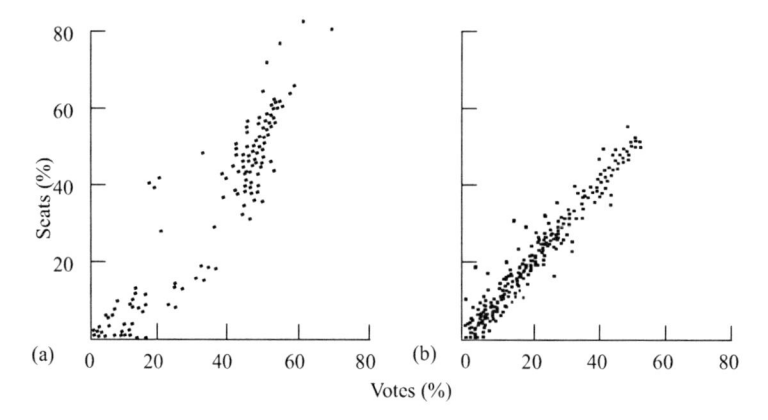

Figure 1.2: Seats and votes for different systems of voting: (a) plurality; (b) proportional representation

1.2 The spatial organisation of plurality elections

Plurality elections are used to elect representatives in the lower houses of five countires—United Kingdom, United States, Canada, New Zealand, and South Africa (France and Australia use related 'majority type' elections which are considered in chapter 7). This monograph concentrates on analysis of elections from all five countries but places particular emphasis on British-American contrasts[1].

In all cases there are two basic elements underlying the final electoral outcome—the spatial distribution of voters and the spatial distribution of constituency boundaries. It is the interaction between these two spatial distributions which produces the allocation of seats by parties in the national legislature. Both types of distribution vary among the five countries to produce different relationships between votes and seats. Each distribution element is considered in turn.

1.2.1 The distribution of party voters

The support for political parties varies from place to place. The reason for this is simply that different parties attract the support of different societal groups, which are themselves unevenly distributed across the country. Hence the electoral geography of a country will typically reflect certain elements of the social geography of that country; which particular elements will depend on the nature of the party system that operates within the country.

Party systems are based upon fundamental social cleavages within a country, both past and present (Rokkan, 1970). Four major social cleavages have been identified on the basis of territorial, religious, urban-rural, and social-class differences. Rokkan (1970) treats these cleavages in an evolutionary sequence which produces modern party systems. The importance of each cleavage varies from country to country and this is reflected in the variations in party systems. Rokkan is largely concerned with European party systems but his ideas have been extended to North American (Cox, undated). In this context a fifth social cleavage needs to be added to our list—ethnic differences (Taylor and Johnston, 1978). For present purposes it need only be noted that each social cleavage has specific implications for the spatial pattern of party voters. This requires consideration in some detail.

Patterns of party voters can be viewed as lying on a continuum in terms of spatial segregation. At one extreme a party's voters are totally separated from all other voters. Total separation can only occur in theory, but it was almost produced in practice in the case of the Irish Nationalists before the creation of the Irish state in 1921. In contrast, party voters could be totally intermingled spatially. This would be approximately the case if a social cleavage based upon sex became the dominant basis of party politics. If all women voted for a 'Women's Party' such support would be evenly

---

[1] Plurality electoral laws have been employed in several non-European former British colonies since their independence (for example, India). Economic and cultural differences are so large, however, that these examples are not used. However, the general methodology developed below should be applicable to analysis of such elections.

spread across the country and intermixed with opposing voters (men) at the scale of individual households.

The five social cleavages produce levels of spatial segregation lying between these two extremes. Obviously territorial cleavages produce most separation, especially when the party is dominant in its 'home territory' as in the Irish Nationalist example. The religious cleavage may interact with the territorial cleavage, as in Ireland, to produce segregation at both a large and a small scale: in Belfast, for instance, religious segregation and the resulting electoral geography is at an intraurban scale. Rural-urban cleavages produce segregation between regional and intraurban scales. Finally social class and ethnic differences are usually most finely separated at the intraurban scale. Hence all the major cleavages underlying party systems produce some form of spatial segregation of party voters although there are major variations in the scale at which the geographical separation occurs.

How do the five countries with plurality elections fit into this scheme of things? They can be ordered in terms of the degree of a social-class basis to voting as follows.

United Kingdom
The main cleavage is along social-class lines, producing the Labour Party and the Conservative Party (Alford, 1963). This dominates voting behaviour although other cleavages are represented—territorial cleavages by the nationalist parties in Wales and Scotland, a religious cleavage represented by Republican and Unionist parties in Northern Ireland, and a lingering urban-rural cleavage reflected in Labour's continuing relative weakness in rural areas (Crewe and Payne, 1976). Despite these various elements of the party system, the electoral geography of Britain (the UK, excluding Northern Ireland) is largely reflected in the pattern of social classes across the country.

New Zealand
The main cleavage is again one of social class, producing the Labour Party and the National Party (Robinson, 1967). This cleavage dominates voting behaviour although ethnic and rural-urban cleavages are weakly represented. Labour always wins four Maori constituencies and the minor Social Credit Party draws support from rural areas. Neither element severely distorts the main social cleavage underlying New Zealand's electoral geography, which once again reflects the pattern of social classes.

United States
Since the renaissance of the Democratic Party in 1932, the American party system has included a social-class cleavage (Chambers, 1967). The social-class cleavage does not dominate the voting as in Britain and New Zealand, however. Ethnic differences are important and often reinforce class differences, as with the solid Black support for the Democrats. At a local level, religious differences may be important but they in turn closely

relate to ethnic differences. Urban-rural contrasts underlie voting in some areas although the pattern varies—Republicans being urban-based in the South, Democrats being urban-based in the Midwest, for instance. In addition to these variations, the US has a major territorial cleavage reflected today in the South with its traditionally strong support for the Democrats. Hence America's electoral geography reflects a rather heterogeneous pattern of party support.

Canada
According to Alford (1963), Canada has little or no class voting. The two main parties are the Liberals and Progressive Conservatives, whose support is based upon provincial-level ethnic alliances (Blake, 1972). In fact regional differences dominate Canadian voting patterns (Simeon and Elkins, 1974; Schwartz, 1974). A major territorial cleavage is reflected in Quebec with its strong support for the Liberals and now increasing support for the French wing of the minor party Social Credit. The other minor party, the New Democrats, is explicitly working class and represents the social-class cleavage in a minor way. Even this party, however, has an essentially regional base to its support pattern. Canada's electoral geography is thus very 'regional' in nature (Campbell and Knight, 1976).

South Africa
This is a special case because of severe franchise restrictions. Only the white minority have the vote and within this racial group an ethnic cleavage dominates the voting (Heard, 1974; Peele and Morse, 1974). The Afrikaaner population has the National Party and the English-speaking whites have the United Party and more recently the Progressive Party. This ethnic cleavage reflects territorial, religious, and urban-rural differences in producing the electoral geography of the state (Farquharson, 1959). The country did originally have a Labour Party but it was not able to survive in a society where racial and ethnic cleavages dominate, so by the 1950s it had virtually disappeared as an electoral force.

The five countries have now been ordered in terms of the degree to which a social-class cleavage underlies their voting patterns. Rokkan identifies social class as the most recent cleavage to affect party systems and argues that it has tended to make party systems more alike. This is only partially reflected in our set of five countries although it should be noted that the ethnic basis of much voting in North America and South Africa does incorporate a class element since ethnic groups are themselves class-related. Furthermore, in terms of spatial segregation, ethnic differences will often operate at the same scale as class differences, especially in urban areas. Hence, within urban regions at least, the degree of spatial separation of party voting will not necessarily show major differences among our five countries despite alternative bases of voting. This feature is particularly emphasised by the rapidly increasing levels of urbanisation in North America and South Africa.

The argument in this section can be summarised as follows. In Britain and New Zealand the electoral geography largely reflects the pattern of social classes, in the USA this pattern is also found but is distorted by ethnic patterns and a distinctive territorial element in the South. In Canada and South Africa ethnic and territorial patterns underlie the electoral geography to the general exclusion of direct effects of social class. In all cases the party systems exhibit marked patterns of spatial segregation among party supporters.

1.2.2 Drawing constituency boundaries

Unlike the spatial distribution of voters, the organisation of constituency boundaries is explicitly part of a country's electoral law. The laws concerning boundary drawing consist of two parts. First there are rules to be adopted in drawing boundaries. These may relate to such things as population limits for constituencies or adherence to local-government boundaries. Second, and much more important, there is the question of who shall draw the boundary lines. This is a politically sensitive issue for several reasons. At the scale of the individual representative a new boundary around a constituency may either end a political career or else make a seat much safer in a subsequent election. At a wider scale, boundaries may completely change an overall seats-votes relationship. Quite simply, boundaries may be manipulated to favour one party over another. Such 'gerrymandering' seems to operate independently of the particular rules adopted. There are usually so many different feasible ways of dividing up an area into constituencies under any set of rules that choosing a particular solution to favour one party is an easy task when the boundary drawing is in political hands. Hence the question of 'who draws the boundaries' is clearly the most important aspect of a country's electoral law. Each of the five countries which have a plurality system of election will now be considered in terms of political control of the drawing of constituency boundaries.

United Kingdom

The electoral law controlling constituencies in the UK is largely to be found in the 1949 Redistribution of Seats Act. This act specifies that constituencies are to be revised periodically to take into account the population changes since the previous redistribution. Three main rules are specified: the 'population rule' requires constituencies to be of roughly equal population; the 'boundary rule' requires constituencies largely to follow local-government boundaries, and the 'geography rule' enables allowances to be made for particular problems of areas with poor accessibility (Taylor and Gudgin, 1976a). The boundary and geography rules may override the population rule so that a wide range of population sizes among constituencies typically results (MacKay and Patterson, 1971, Rowley, 1970; 1975a). These rules are applied by four Boundary Commissions, one for each of the four 'home countries'. These commissions are explicitly neutral in a party political sense. Not only do the rules involve no political considerations, but the membership of the commissions is itself nonpolitical. It is a semijudicial body which reports its findings to Parliament via the Home Secretary. The only political involvement comes when their proposals have to be agreed in Parliament. This has sometimes led to controversy (Butler, 1955a; Steed, 1969) but at no time does anybody except the commissioners actually draw constituency boundaries. Hence this case will be identified as involving minimum political involvement in boundary drawing.

New Zealand
New Zealand constituencies are delimited largely on the basis of the Electoral Act of 1956. The basic thinking behind the act is similar to that of the British case (Jackson, 1962). Under this Act New Zealand has to be divided into seventy-six European constituencies of approximately equal population but other criteria, such as accessibility, have to be taken into account. The boundary drawing is left to the Representation Commission, who are required to change the boundaries after each census. There is one major difference between this agency and British boundary commissioners. The New Zealand body includes similar official members as does the British body but also includes two political members, one representing the Government and the other the Opposition. Although, unlike Britain, the decisions of the Representation Commission are final in law and do not require parliamentary approval, a political input does occur at the crucial boundary-drawing stage. Hence New Zealand may be said to have more political involvement in drawing constituency boundaries than Britain.

United States
In the USA party political involvement is even further developed (Hacker, 1964). The US Constitution prescribes that "each house shall be the judge of the elections, returns, and qualifications of its own members". This has been interpreted as meaning that delimiting constituencies is a political decision. Although there have been a variety of rules relating to population equality, compactness, and contiguity in American electoral history (Hacker, 1964), the overwhelming feature of all of this has been the political involvement. This has taken two forms. First there has been the refusal of state legislatures to redraw their district boundaries as the population distribution has changed. This enabled rural interests to maintain control despite widespread urbanisation of the population. All this changed with the reapportionment revolution of the 1960s whereby the Supreme Court enforced a policy of equipopulous districts (Baker, 1966). The courts have not curtailed the second type of political involvement, however. State legislatures still have power to draw their own district boundaries and those for the US Congress (Jewell, 1962). In effect this involves setting up districting agencies which are overtly political in nature. Where one party controls the legislature it is able to

carry out direct gerrymandering despite Supreme Court population controls; where no single party is able to control the state legislature a political compromise is usually produced by members of both parties. Either way the USA represents the opposite of the British case, with explicit party political involvement instead of political neutrality.

Canada
Canada has had a revolution in its districting procedures even greater than that of the USA since this has involved both the rules adopted and the question of who draws the boundaries. Up until 1964 the electoral law was derived from the 1867 North America Act, which was interpreted as allowing government control of districting with absolutely no rules to curtail their activity. In practice rural constituencies were made smaller than urban constituencies but otherwise there were no clear bases for the districting. The actual boundary drawing was carried out by a committee of the House of Commons on which the government party's majority was the key feature. Hence political involvement was total and accusations of gerrymandering common (Ward, 1967). All this changed in 1964 with a new electoral law which laid down rules for districting to be carried out by neutral boundary commissions for each province separately. These commissions have nonpolitical members under the direction of the Representation Commissioner. They have to work within population guidelines and take into account such features as accessibility before submitting their plans to Parliament. Here members have the opportunity to refer parts of the maps back to the commissions but after these objections have been considered by the commission, their final map is subject to no further changes (Ward, 1967). In theory this procedure seems to be as nonpolitical as the British case. In practice, things are slightly different. The century of detailed parliamentary involvement in boundary drawing is difficult to overturn with one change of law. In fact after the first redistricting by the commissions (1966) there were numerous parliamentary objections to particular parts of the submitted maps. Political involvement now depends upon how responsive the commissioners are to parliamentary criticism. In the event they made twenty-four amendments to their original plan for Ontario, amended eight seats in Quebec, six in British Columbia, and two in Manitoba. Clearly there remains some political influence on the boundary drawing but the power now lies squarely in nonparty hands (Lyons, 1969).

South Africa
The situation with regard to drawing constituency boundaries is somewhat contradictory. On the one hand, the rules and procedures are very much like the British case (Heard, 1974). Constituency boundaries are drawn by a delimitation commission, which since 1965 has acted over the whole country. The commission's rules involve obtaining approximately equal numbers of white voters per constituency, subject to other criteria such as

accessibility, existing boundaries, and sparsity of population. This latter criterion has been traditionally used to give more seats to rural areas and hence has favoured the National Party. This practice dates back to before the rise to power of this party in the 1948 election (Lakeman, 1974). Since 1948, however, there have been accusations of gerrymandering. Although the commissioners are not party nominees, they are appointed by the government (by the state president since 1961) and it has been suggested that they favour the National Party. Farquharson (1959) notes that the urban concentration of United Party voters may lead to some boundary discrimination against that party but he feels that "the Commission has not gone out of its way to remove anomalies, and has indeed introduced some new ones". He then goes on to give examples. Political involvement in boundary drawing in South Africa may be left as problematical at this stage.

Further details of the electoral laws of the five plurality countries can be obtained from the references given in the discussion. This section has just given a basic comparative outline of the districting procedures, which can be summarised as follows: The degree of political involvement in the drawing of lines is a crucial feature of districting practice and it varies from the largely neutral British case through the slight party involvement in New Zealand to the total party involvement in the USA. Canada has changed from the American end of the spectrum to the British end and there is dispute on South Africa's position along this spectrum.

1.2.3 The interaction of voters and boundaries

The five countries with plurality elections have now been designated in terms of patterns of party support and types of districting procedures. The actual outcome of an election in one of these countries will depend on the interaction between these two types of spatial distribution. Constituency boundaries are placed upon the mosaic of party voters and every party returns a member to the parliament for every constituency where its supporters form a plurality. Hence the electoral outcome depends upon both the pattern of party votes and the location of constituency boundaries. These are the additional factors which affect election results, above and beyond the proportion of votes which a party receives. Figure 1.3 shows those factors operating in a variety of situations. One hundred and thirty-two elections in six two-party plurality election contests are shown (Tufte, 1973). The first two graphs in the top row show the effect of an interaction between neutral boundary lines and class-based party systems. The result is a reasonably linear seats-votes relationship. The other four graphs show situations where political involvement in the districting has tended to distort the seats-votes relationship so that the points are more scattered. These graphs are an initial indication of how, within the single plurality voting system, there is great variety in outcome relating to the spatial organisation discussed above. The major purpose of this monograph is to develop an understanding of this variety of outcomes. The following chapter begins to develop such an understanding by tracing the links between seats and votes in countries with neutral boundary delimiters and party allegiance based upon social class.

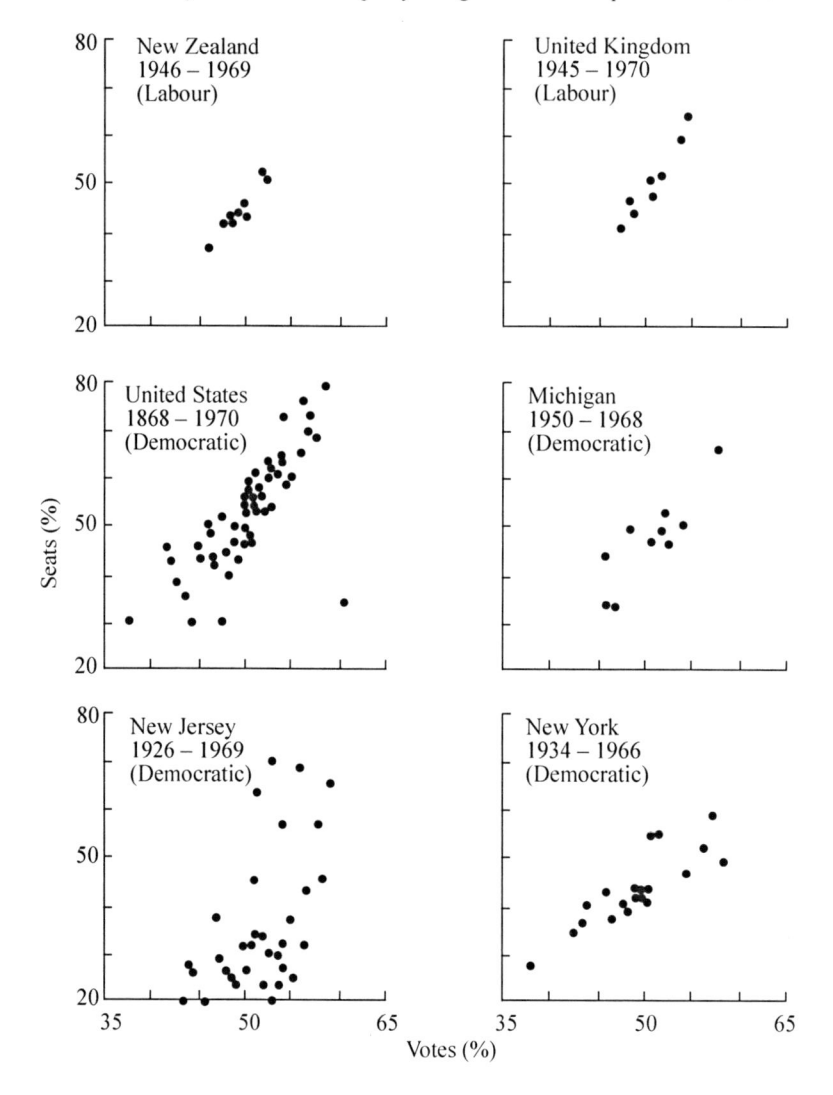

Figure 1.3: Seats and votes for six sets of plurality elections

chapter two | a modelling framework for the seats-votes relationship

The purpose of this chapter is to present a framework for studying the way in which the plurality election system translates votes into seats. In this chapter the concern is with modelling rather than with explaining the relationship. The model will show more or less precisely how aggregate numbers of seats are related to aggregate numbers of votes, and will allow predictions from votes to seats. Although a model partly constitutes an understanding, it by-passes more basic questions related to why a particular seats-votes relationship should occur whereas others do not. The question of accounting for the occurrence of the particular relationship which typifies two-party, class-based elections concerns the interrelation of distributions of voters and constituencies which was discussed in the last chapter. Before proceeding to this topic it is necessary to lay the basic groundwork in this chapter.

In order to simplify the analysis, it is assumed in what follows that elections are two-party contests fought on equal-size constituencies that have not been gerrymandered. This precludes full discussion of elections in the USA, Canada, and South Africa, so the main empirical examples will be from Britain and New Zealand. This chapter is, however, largely theoretical in content and empirical analyses are largely left to subsequent chapters where the assumptions used in this chapter are progressively relaxed.

2.1 The frequency-distribution approach

The precise connection between votes gained and seats won by a party at a particular election can be easily computed as long as results are available for each constituency. All that is required is that the number of constituencies in which the party obtains more votes than its opponents is counted. This simplicity may be extended to the situation where prediction of the seats a party will win at a forthcoming election is required. When the existing votes per constituency are used, all that is required are estimates of change in party votes since these can be applied to the constituencies to provide predicted votes per constituency. This may be based upon an overall national swing applied to each constituency, or alternatively a more subtle treatment of groupings of constituencies may be used (Brown and Payne, 1975). Whatever method is used, however, the share of seats between parties is merely a matter of counting, once the votes split in each constituency has been estimated.

This empirical method is quite satisfactory for analysing the seats-votes relationship for several purposes. Moreover, with the use of computers it is not even necessarily long-winded. It is principally useful in two ways. In predicting results for any given election, it will produce results as accurate as the voting forecasts on which it is based. It can also produce generalisations of the seats-votes relationship by relating changes in votes to changes in seats between elections over a period of years. In postwar British elections, for example, a simple graph reveals that a 1% change in aggregate (national) votes produces a change in seats of approximately 3%. Figure 1.3 shows this relationship quite clearly, as the linear trend extends nearly 24% on the seats axis but only 8% along the votes axis. New Zealand elections show a similar but less distinct trend.

In this chapter interest will be focused upon models of the electoral system and will not be concerned with precise descriptions of the form discussed in the previous paragraphs. These models will be diagrammatic or algebraic descriptions of election results which capture the essential features, but not necessarily the exact details. Such models are meant to be simplifications of the real situations in the sense that they are brief and concise descriptions. Since some readers may find such simplifications more complicated than reality because of the mathematics involved, it is perhaps worth stating clearly why it is advantageous to adopt this approach. The principal advantage is in the clarity gained by generalised mathematical description. A relatively short mathematical expression can, in the case of elections, describe all the relevant details of an election, and this allows an overview which is not possible with a mass of individual constituency results. The gain in clarity of an overall view is a vital ingredient in permitting analyses to proceed beyond description. Since our aim is to understand the plurality election system, it is important that we concentrate on the features of general importance, despite the fact that our descriptions may not fit any one single election, nor be as accurate predictors of election outcomes as is the detailed empirical approach. This is, however, a relatively small price to pay, since through models, mechanisms underlying the system can be discovered which would otherwise remain hidden among the mass of detail.

2.1.1 *The constituency proportion distribution*

The essentials of the seats-votes relationship can be seen quite clearly by means of the frequency distribution of party results (by constituency) for a single election. This frequency distribution, which we will refer to as the *constituency proportion distribution*, or CPD for short, is constructed by counting the number of constituency results *for any one party* which lie in a sequence of vote categories; for example, 0%-10%, 10%-20%, etc, as illustrated in figure 2.1. Frequency distributions for actual British and New Zealand elections are displayed in chapter 4, Canadian elections in chapter 5, and United States and South African elections in chapter 6.

These frequency distributions contain almost as much information as we need to know about elections in order to analyse the plurality system. The number of constituencies to the right of the 50% point on the votes axis gives the aggregate number of seats won by the party in question. The proportion of the votes won can also be assessed from the frequency distribution if constituencies have equal electorates or, at least, if differences in sizes of electorates are randomly spread between parties. Otherwise the recorded total votes cast for the party over the whole country is of more use. Furthermore, in the two-party situation the distribution for one party is the mirror image of the other. Finally it should be noted that it is common for elections in which two parties dominate the voting, but in which minor parties also take part, for the frequency distributions to be concocted out of the two-party vote alone. If, in a given constituency, party A gains 45% of the vote, party B, 45%, and party C, 10%, then the revised figures, ignoring the third party, would be 50% for both party A and party B.

The accuracy and hence utility of CPDs depend on the size of the classes of voting proportions. Thus, 5% size bands (0%-5%, 5%-10%, etc) are more accurate than 10% size bands (0%-10%, 10%-20%, etc), and so on. As the category size gets smaller, the accuracy increases. In the limiting case, a frequency distribution is arrived at which does not consist of discrete categories at all, but instead is a continuous distribution as in figure 2.2(b). In the case of a continuous frequency distribution, the number of constituencies in any range of vote proportions (for example, 5%-10%) is given by the proportion of the area under the curve lying in that range. In practice, tables are usually available to calculate these areas. The subsequent modelling will be concerned with continuous frequency distributions, since these are analytically easier to handle although discrete distributions will be used for illustrative purposes.

Two further formalities remain before any practical insights may be gained. It is first useful to construct cumulative frequency distributions as in figure 2.3(a). The proportion of constituencies in which the party in question gains *less* than a given percentage of the votes can be read directly from such distributions (that is, the frequency distribution is

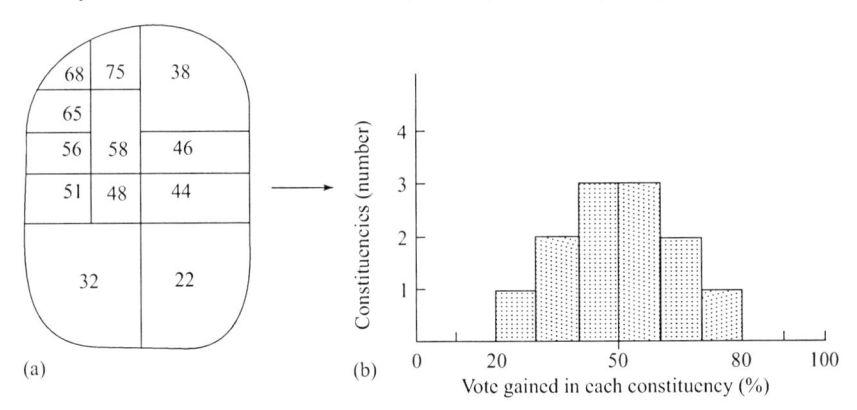

Figure 2.1: Construction of a constituency proportion distribution: (a) spatial distribution of support for party A (% of votes by constituency); (b) constituency proportion distribution for party A

cumulatively aggregated from the left). These cumulative CPDs are important because under certain conditions they specify exactly the proportion of seats that a party wins for a given level of (overall) vote. Hence, cumulative CPDs can also be seats-votes curves. The reason for this is shown in figure 2.3(b). In this diagram three aggregate vote levels are depicted ($x < 50\%$, $x = 50\%$, $x > 50\%$). The upper set of frequency distributions show how the size of the shaded area is related to the vote percentage x. This shaded area in fact represents the percentage of seats won (if symmetry is assumed), as is seen in the lower distributions. Each lower distribution can be viewed as the corresponding upper distribution which has been flipped about its central axis and then moved along the votes line until its central axis is aligned with x. The shaded area then comprises those seats which the party wins, that is, those in which it gains more than 50% of the votes.

Second, the approach based on frequency distributions gains in simplicity with an assumption of swings *between elections* which are nationally uniform across constituencies. That is to say, if there is a national swing to party A, between two elections, of $x\%$ then the swing in each individual constituency is of $x\%$ also. The empirical validity of this requirement also will be examined below in chapter 4 and it is sufficient for present purposes to note that the swings observed in modern elections in Britain and New Zealand are normally uniform enough to allow us to proceed. Later, this assumption will be dropped to reflect real elections more closely.

The simplification gained through this requirement can be appreciated by looking again at the constituency proportion distribution. If the swing is the same in each constituency, then the whole distribution moves to the right or left along the scale by the amount of the swing. The movement is a rigid translation in which the distribution preserves its shape. With this type of movement, it is a relatively simple matter to calculate what proportion of the distribution, and thus of the seats, cross the 50% line (and hence change hands) for any given swing in votes. Without this requirement, the distribution would change shape to some extent with any

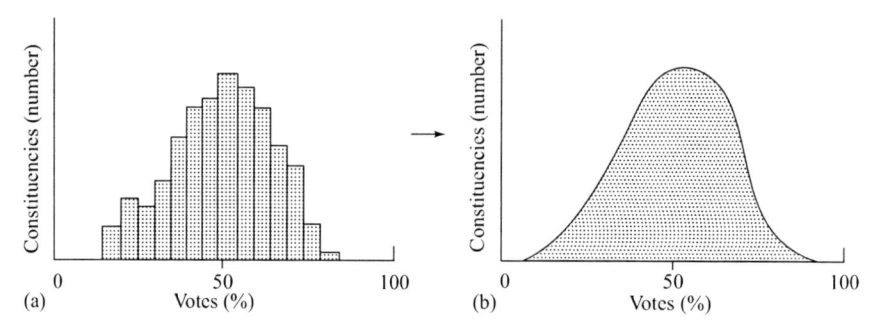

Figure 2.2:   Constituency proportion distributions: (a) discrete; (b) continuous

change in aggregate party support, and the relationship would lose some of its simplicity.

To summarise thus far, the aim is to model elections by using simplified frequency distributions incorporating several not fully realistic requirements. Besides the insistence on two-party contests, these are equal-size electorates (and turnout) and a uniform swing between constituencies. None of these requirements is so severe as to nullify the usefulness of the following analysis.

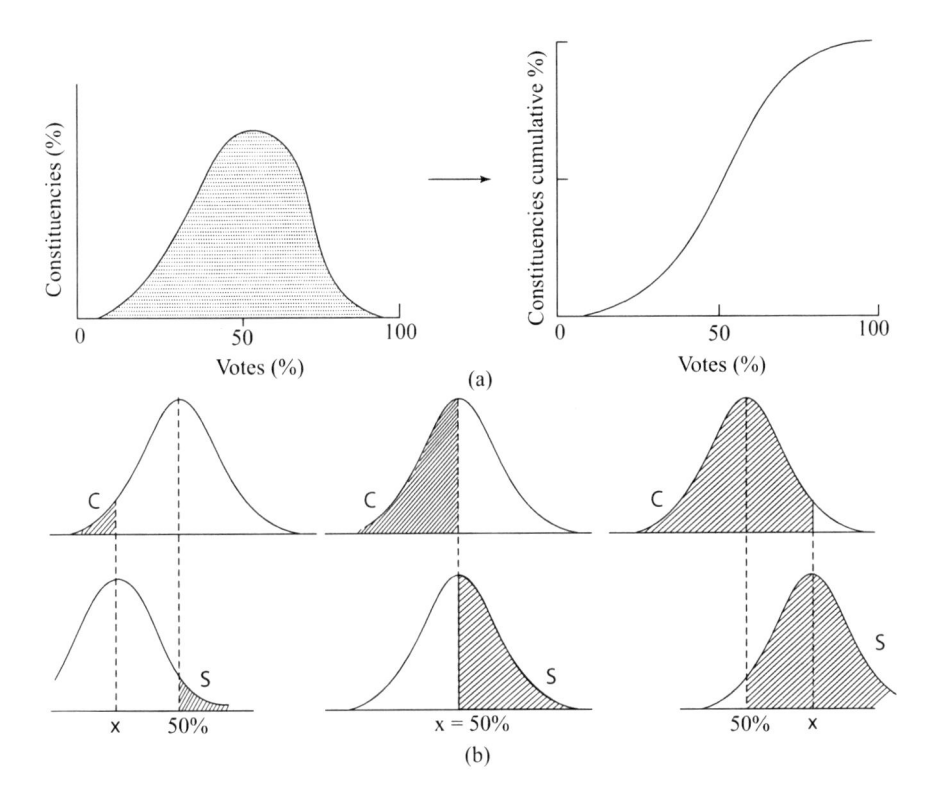

Figure 2.3: (a) Construction of a cumulative CPD; (b) the use of the cumulative CPD as a seats-votes curve

2.1.2 Basic types of seats-votes relationships

The position has now been reached where exploration of the seats-votes relationship can begin. First, observe that in order for the seats proportion to mirror the votes proportion, regardless of level of swing, a rectangular distribution is needed as in figure 2.4(a). Here a swing of $x\%$ in the aggregate votes shifts the whole distribution $x\%$ to the left or right. This moves the same proportion of the rectangle onto the other side of the

50% 'winning post' as is moved along the scale. The impossibility of an even swing when some constituencies are already close to 0% or 100% in their support for one party or the other can be safely ignored. In real elections extreme results are rare, and moreover, without correspondingly extreme swings, these play no part in changing the outcome of elections. The rectangular distribution produces a cumulative frequency-distribution function with a slope of one as in figure 2.5(a). In this case, $S = V$ where S is the percentage of seats gained by party A and V is the percentage of votes gained by party A. In both cases, S and V refer to the aggregate or 'national' situation and not to individual constituencies.

This type of frequency distribution produces proportional representation because the constituencies are spread equally along the range of possible vote percentages. There are as many constituencies with extreme results as there are 'marginals' (those with majorities close to 50%). In stable electoral conditions, swings of more than plus or minus 5% from equality between the parties are uncommon. As a result, all that is needed to produce proportional representation in the changes (but not necessarily in the election as a whole) is that the frequency distribution should be rectangular and contain 10% of the seats in the range 45%-55%. The rest of the distribution does not influence changes if these constituencies never change hands.

If the frequency distribution is more concentrated around 50% than the rectangular distribution, then the plurality election system will accentuate the advantage gained in vote proportion by the victorious party. Figures 2.4(b) and 2.4(c) both depict CPDs of this accentuated seat-proportion type.

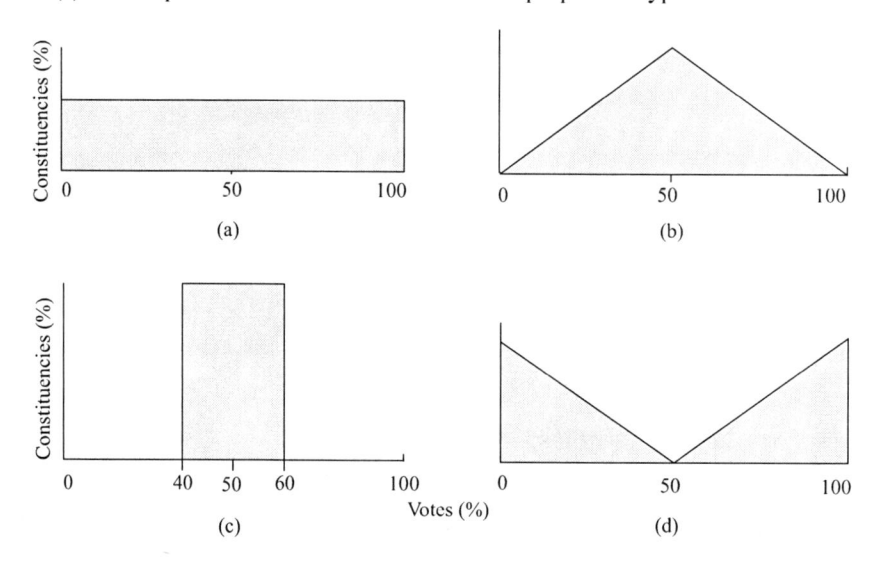

Figure 2.4: Hypothetical examples of CPDs: (a) rectangular (or uniform) distribution; (b) triangular distribution; (c) alternative rectangular distribution; (d) V-shaped distribution

In both cases, a movement (swing) of the distribution by x% in either direction will tend initially to move a proportion of the distribution (that is, constituencies) greater than x% across the 50% 'winning post'. As can be seen in figures 2.5(b) and 2.5(c), the two cumulative distribution functions both have slopes in excess of one (greater than 45°) for small swings. In the case of the truncated rectangular distribution in figure 2.4(c), the seats-votes relationship is given by: $S = aV$, where a is a constant greater than one. In the case of the triangular distribution, the relationship is nonlinear, but has a slope of greater than one close to 50%.

In contrast, a frequency distribution more dispersed from the 50% point than is the rectangular distribution, will tend to damp down the change in seats occasioned by any given swing in votes. As with the accentuating distributions, those parts of the distribution relevant to the small swings commonly met in practice are of most concern. In this case, as in figure 2.4(d), a swing of $x\%$ would cause a proportion of seats smaller than $x\%$ to change hands, as long as x was relatively small. Further swings in excess of $x\%$ would cause increasingly large transfers of seats between the parties. Figure 2.5(d) illustrates the situation quite clearly. For relatively low swings, the electoral system would be fairly insensitive. A declining major party, with its votes distributed in this way, would thus lose its proportion of seats more slowly than its votes.

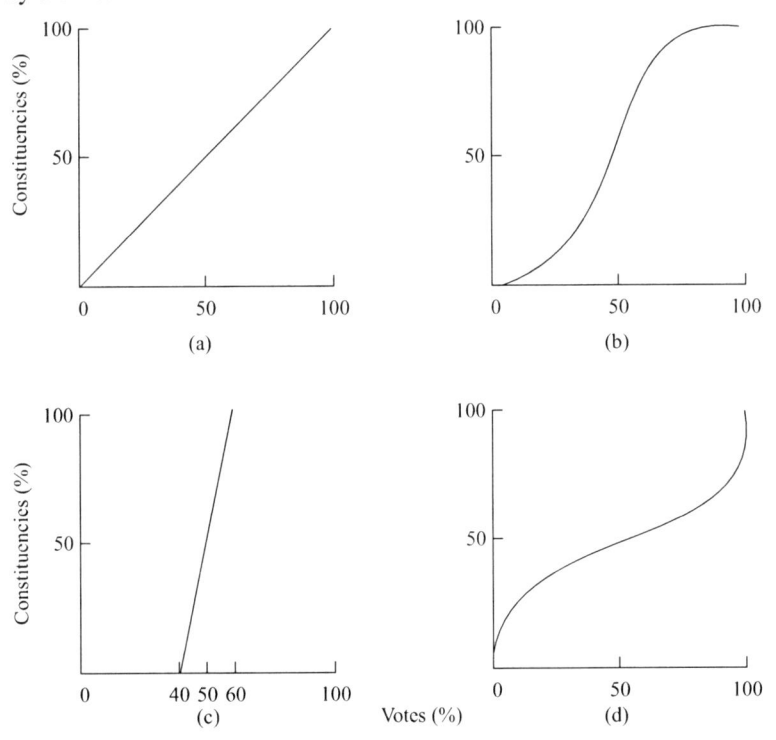

Figure 2.5: Hypothetical cumulative CPDs: (a) rectangular distribution; (b) triangular distribution; (c) alternative rectangular distribution; (d) V-shaped distribution

When the diagram in figure 2.1 above is reversed, it is obvious that each type of frequency distribution implies a certain geographical pattern of support. The rectangular distribution would mean the same number of constituencies at each level of support for a given party: the support for party A would be concentrated in some constituencies, relatively sparse in a similar number, and mixed in different proportions in, again, similar numbers. This, in fact, implies a relatively high degree of spatial clustering (either in one region or in large 'patches'), but in a highly artificial way. There is no obvious way that normal socioeconomic and cultural forces influencing the distribution of social classes or culture groups would produce this constrained pattern. However, for a small range close to the centre of the frequency distribution current American elections are approximately rectangular. This situation may have been produced by the artificial means of fixing the district boundaries to make it so and is discussed in chapter 6.

The V-shaped frequency distribution is easier to imagine. This implies a highly clustered support for each party with a relatively high degree of spatial segregation. Parties based on regional interests (for example, Irish Nationalists in UK elections before 1921), in which the party gains most of the votes in its 'home' area and few elsewhere, would be of approximately this type.

Among the frequency distributions under discussion here, the triangular type of distribution implies the greatest mixing of voters in constituencies. Each party has areas in which it is more dominant, but most constituencies contain supporters of both parties in approximately similar proportions. With modern social class-based parties, the geographical mixing of social classes at scales smaller than the typical constituency does result in many constituencies being relatively close contests. The clustering of working-class voters in city centres and in mining and industrial areas also produces areas of dominance, as does the clustering of right-wing voters in rural areas and in resort towns. In the USA the existence of some regionally based support in the Southern Democrats, over and above the class-based cleavage, has spread the frequency distribution to a greater extent than in the more 'nationalised' circumstances of Britain or New Zealand.

An approximately triangular type of distribution is, in fact, the most commonly observed, as will be seen in the next section. As a consequence, the plurality election system in most situations tends to accentuate in seats the advantage gained in votes by the winning party. In practice, the plurality system tends to favour winning parties disproportionately, thus forming its most distinctive feature. It is this feature that we model here.

2.2 The normal distribution and the cube law

In this section the plurality system will be modelled rather more rigorously. To do this, a remarkable statistical regularity known as the normal (frequency) distribution will be taken as a case study. This distribution is drawn in figure 2.6 and is described by the function

$$f(V) = \frac{1}{\sigma(2\pi)^{1/2}} \exp\left[\frac{(V_i - \overline{V})^2}{2\sigma^2}\right], \tag{2.1}$$

where
- V_i is the proportion of the vote in constituency i,
- $f(V)$ refers to the frequency of these vote proportions,
- $\overline{V}$ is the overall (national) proportion of the vote,
- σ is the standard deviation of the constituency proportions around the overall proportion. This 'parameter' controls the spread of the distribution around its mean: the larger σ, the 'wider' the distribution.

This frequency distribution results when a large number of independent forces, each individually small, are added together to produce an aggregate effect. In the case of elections, these forces are the influences on the number of supporters of party A (and hence of party B) in each constituency. In a class-based cleavage, these numbers are largely the result of a complex of socioeconomic forces, given that an individual's political allegiance has more to do with social background than with the stimuli of campaigns or current issues.

It is a matter of empirical observation that two-party frequency distributions from most British elections this century, in New Zealand elections, and in US elections (omitting the states of the 'Deep South') until the recent reapportionment revolution are all approximately 'normally distributed' (Kendall and Stuart, 1950). As a result it is realistic in these cases to use a normal distribution, with a specified standard deviation, as our 'model' frequency distribution. Also, since tables exist for the area under the normal curve, it is an easy matter to read off the proportion of seats won for any level of votes. All that needs to be specified, aside from the overall proportion of votes won, is the standard deviation. The relationship between seats and votes is then given by the cumulative normal distribution as in figure 2.7. As can be seen, this is an S-shaped relationship with a steeply sloped and almost linear central section.

The slope of this central section is always greater than one, and in detail is controlled by the standard deviation of the distribution. The lower

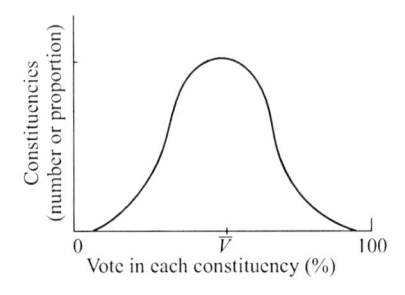

Figure 2.6: A normal constituency proportion distribution

limit on the standard deviation is zero, in which case all constituencies would be identical as microcosms of the national voting split. The upper limit is not strictly determinate, but given that there are limits of 0% and 100% on the range of constituency voter proportions, an arbitrary limit of 20% can be imposed. With larger standard deviations, the distribution steadily becomes nonnormal, although the theoretical upper limit for the standard deviation of *any* distribution in this range is 50% (Gudgin and Taylor, 1974, page 73). The slope of the cumulative normal distribution at $V = 50\%$ with a standard deviation of 20% is approximately two[1]. For small standard deviations, the slope of the cumulative distribution is large, eventually approaching infinity for minutely small standard deviations.

The importance of the slope of the cumulative distribution at (and near) 50% is that it forms the multiplier which accentuates the proportion of seats gained for a given increase in the percentage of votes won by a party. A slope of two implies that each 1% in votes gained over 50% produces a 2% gain in seats won. A very large slope gives a very large multiplier. This accords with intuition since a large slope is produced by a small standard deviation, which itself indicates that most constituency contests are marginal. Hence a small overall swing in votes will make a high proportion of seats change hands. The multiplier is somewhat smaller than the slope at 50% when national swings are large, in contrast to when swings are small enough to keep the overall vote proportions close to 50%. However, for most swings met in real elections, the multiplier as calculated above is good enough.

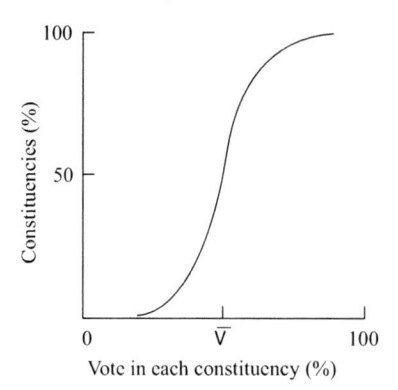

Figure 2.7: The cumulative normal distribution

2.2.1 Normal predictions of seat proportions

We now have a model, which is applicable to a number of elections in different countries, based on the normal distribution. In this model, the proportion of seats (S) won by the major party in an election is given by

$$S = \Phi(z) \tag{2.2}$$

---

[1] The slope of the cumulative normal distribution at its mean is given by $1/[\sigma(2\pi)^{1/2}]$, which in this case is $1/(0.2 \times 2.507) \approx 1.99$.

Table 2.1: The cumulative normal distribution for predicting seat proportions
$[z = (V - 0.5)/\sigma]$

z	S	z	S	z	S	z	S	z	S
0.00	0.5000	0.50	0.6915	1.00	0.8413	1.50	0.9332	2.00	0.97725
0.01	0.5040	0.51	0.6950	1.01	0.8438	1.51	0.9345	2.01	0.97778
0.02	0.5080	0.52	0.6985	1.02	0.8461	1.52	0.9357	2.02	0.97831
0.03	0.5120	0.53	0.7019	1.03	0.8485	1.53	0.9370	2.03	0.97882
0.04	0.5160	0.54	0.7054	1.04	0.8508	1.54	0.9382	2.04	0.97932
0.05	0.5199	0.55	0.7088	1.05	0.8531	1.55	0.9394	2.05	0.97982
0.06	0.5239	0.56	0.7123	1.06	0.8554	1.56	0.9406	2.06	0.98030
0.07	0.5279	0.57	0.7157	1.07	0.8577	1.57	0.9418	2.07	0.98077
0.08	0.5319	0.58	0.7190	1.08	0.8599	1.58	0.9429	2.08	0.98124
0.09	0.5359	0.59	0.7224	1.09	0.8621	1.59	0.9441	2.09	0.98169
0.10	0.5398	0.60	0.7257	1.10	0.8643	1.60	0.9452	2.10	0.98214
0.11	0.5438	0.61	0.7291	1.11	0.8665	1.61	0.9463	2.11	0.98257
0.12	0.5478	0.62	0.7324	1.12	0.8686	1.62	0.9474	2.12	0.98300
0.13	0.5517	0.63	0.7357	1.13	0.8708	1.63	0.9484	2.13	0.98341
0.14	0.5557	0.64	0.7389	1.14	0.8729	1.64	0.9495	2.14	0.98382
0.15	0.5596	0.65	0.7422	1.15	0.8749	1.65	0.9505	2.15	0.98422
0.16	0.5636	0.66	0.7454	1.16	0.8770	1.66	0.9515	2.16	0.98461
0.17	0.5675	0.67	0.7486	1.17	0.8790	1.67	0.9525	2.17	0.98500
0.18	0.5714	0.68	0.7517	1.18	0.8810	1.68	0.9535	2.18	0.98537
0.19	0.5753	0.69	0.7549	1.19	0.8830	1.69	0.9545	2.19	0.98574
0.20	0.5793	0.70	0.7580	1.20	0.8849	1.70	0.9554	2.20	0.98610
0.21	0.5832	0.71	0.7611	1.21	0.8869	1.71	0.9564	2.21	0.98645
0.22	0.5871	0.72	0.7642	1.22	0.8888	1.72	0.9573	2.22	0.98679
0.23	0.5910	0.73	0.7673	1.23	0.8907	1.73	0.9582	2.23	0.98713
0.24	0.5948	0.74	0.7704	1.24	0.8925	1.74	0.9591	2.24	0.98745
0.25	0.5987	0.75	0.7734	1.25	0.8944	1.75	0.9599	2.25	0.98778
0.26	0.6026	0.76	0.7764	1.26	0.8962	1.76	0.9608	2.26	0.98809
0.27	0.6064	0.77	0.7794	1.27	0.8980	1.77	0.9616	2.27	0.98840
0.28	0.6103	0.78	0.7823	1.28	0.8997	1.78	0.9625	2.28	0.98870
0.29	0.6141	0.79	0.7852	1.29	0.9015	1.79	0.9633	2.29	0.98899
0.30	0.6179	0.80	0.7881	1.30	0.9032	1.80	0.9641	2.30	0.98928
0.31	0.6217	0.81	0.7910	1.31	0.9049	1.81	0.9649	2.31	0.98956
0.32	0.6255	0.82	0.7939	1.32	0.9066	1.82	0.9656	2.32	0.98983
0.33	0.6293	0.83	0.7967	1.33	0.9082	1.83	0.9664	2.33	0.99010
0.34	0.6331	0.84	0.7995	1.34	0.9099	1.84	0.9671	2.34	0.99036
0.35	0.6368	0.85	0.8023	1.35	0.9115	1.85	0.9678	2.35	0.99061
0.36	0.6406	0.86	0.8051	1.36	0.9131	1.86	0.9686	2.36	0.99086
0.37	0.6443	0.87	0.8078	1.37	0.9147	1.87	0.9693	2.37	0.99111
0.38	0.6480	0.88	0.8106	1.38	0.9162	1.88	0.9699	2.38	0.99134
0.39	0.6517	0.89	0.8133	1.39	0.9177	1.89	0.9706	2.39	0.99158
0.40	0.6554	0.90	0.8159	1.40	0.9192	1.90	0.9713	2.40	0.99180
0.41	0.6591	0.91	0.8186	1.41	0.9207	1.91	0.9719	2.41	0.99202
0.42	0.6628	0.92	0.8212	1.42	0.9222	1.92	0.9726	2.42	0.99224
0.43	0.6664	0.93	0.8238	1.43	0.9236	1.93	0.9732	2.43	0.99245
0.44	0.6700	0.94	0.8264	1.44	0.9251	1.94	0.9738	2.44	0.99266
0.45	0.6736	0.95	0.8289	1.45	0.9265	1.95	0.9744	2.45	0.99286
0.46	0.6772	0.96	0.8315	1.46	0.9279	1.96	0.9750	2.46	0.99305
0.47	0.6808	0.97	0.8340	1.47	0.9292	1.97	0.9756	2.47	0.99324
0.48	0.6844	0.98	0.8365	1.48	0.9306	1.98	0.9761	2.48	0.99343
0.49	0.6879	0.99	0.8389	1.49	0.9319	1.99	0.9767	2.49	0.99361
0.50	0.6915	1.00	0.8413	1.50	0.9332	2.00	0.9772	2.50	0.99379

where $\Phi(z)$ is the (cumulative) normal distribution function specified by $1/(2\pi)^{1/2} \int_{-\infty}^{z} \exp(\frac{1}{2}u^2) du$ and $z = u = 1/\sigma(\bar{V} - 0.5)$ for $\bar{V}$ and σ as defined in equation (2.1). This equation may appear quite fearsome to the nonmathematician but in practice it is seldom directly used since tables exist for $\Phi(z)$. Just such a standard table is reproduced here (table 2.1) and will be used to illustrate the simplicity of the normal-distribution approach.

The proportion of seats won, as predicted by equation (2.2), is determined by $\bar{V}$, the mean constituency vote proportion (which under the assumptions of the model is equal to the aggregate national vote proportion), and also by σ, the standard deviation of the distribution. Seat predictions are found as follows. Assume that a party wins 55% of the overall vote and $\sigma = 10\%$. Hence $V = 0.55$, $\sigma = 0.10$, so $z = (0.55 - 0.50)/0.10 = 0.5$. In table 2.1 for $z = 0.5$, $\Phi(z) = 0.6915$, producing the prediction that a party with 55% of the vote will win nearly 70% of the seats under a normal CPD situation with $\sigma = 0.10$. This relatively large winner's 'bonus' is due to the relatively small standard deviation. Note that with $\sigma = 0.20$, $z = 0.25$ and $\Phi(z) = 0.5987$ in table 2.1. Here 55% of the vote wins only 60% of the seats. This is the first direct illustration of how effects other than the simple vote proportion for a party may be modelled to produce alternative seat proportions. The standard deviation of the CPD constitutes a link between the spatial organisation (electoral geography) and electoral outcome (seats won) through its implicit measurement of marginal seats in the normal-distribution model. It does this because, in measuring the spread of a CPD, the standard deviation indicates the degree to which party support varies between constituencies.

This model can now be applied to actual elections for which the standard deviation of the CPD is known. The standard deviations for selected British elections since 1923 are shown in table 2.2 and those for New Zealand elections since 1957 in table 2.3. The fact that the New Zealand values are consistently below the British standard deviations will be briefly discussed in the next chapter. At this point it should be noted

Table 2.2: *Standard deviations of selected British CPDs since 1923. Sources: data for elections of 1935, 1945, 1950 from Kendall and Stuart (1950); data for other elections calculated*

Election	Standard deviation for major party	Election	Standard deviation for major party
1923	14.6	1955	14.9
1924	14.0	1966	14.6
1929	18.0	1970	14.6
1935	13.3	1974 (February)	16.5
1945	13.5	1974 (October)	17.3
1950	13.8		

how similar the standard deviations are, both between the countries and over time within each country. There are many obvious differences over both time and place which may be reflected in the standard deviations in the two tables but nevertheless all values lie between the two hypothetical examples of 10% and 20% used above. In the subsequent discussion, those largely two-party elections in Britain from 1945 to 1970 will be used to illustrate this approach. Normal-distribution predictions are given for these elections in table 2.4, column (4). These predictions can be

Table 2.3: Standard deviations of New Zealand CPDs since 1957

Election	Standard deviation for major party	Election	Standard deviation for major party
1957	11.2	1969	11.9
1960	11.6	1972	11.4
1963	12.6	1975	10.8
1966	12.9		

Table 2.4: Actual and predicted seat proportions for some British elections, 1949–1970 for the Labour Party

Election	$\overline{V}$ (two-party)	Seats (%) all parties	two parties	Normal predictions σ varies[a]	$\sigma = 0.137$	Deviations (5)–(4)	(5)–(3)
	(1)	(2)	(3)	(4)	(5)	(6)	(7)
1945	54.8	61.4	64.9	63.9	63.6	−0.3	−1.3
1950	51.5	50.4	51.4	54.2	54.2	0.0	+2.8
1955	48.3	44.0	44.5	45.4	45.0	−0.4	+0.5
1966	53.5	57.6	58.9	59.4	60.0	+0.6	+1.1
1970	48.1	45.6	46.7	44.8	44.5	−0.3	−2.2

[a] From table 2.2.

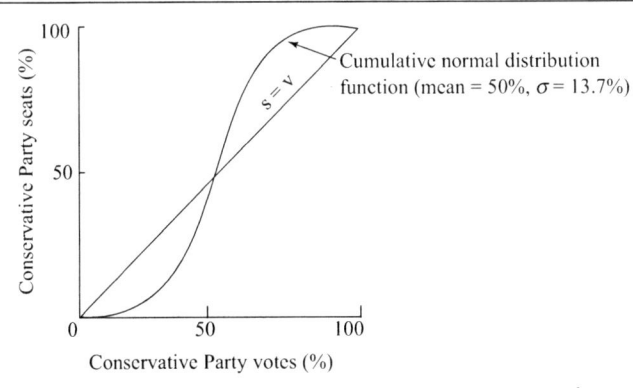

Figure 2.8: Actual and predicted results in two-party contests for UK elections, 1945–1970

compared with the actual two-party seat percentages in column (3). The model predicts the percentage seats to within an accuracy of about 1.5%, or nine seats on average. These errors are small and may be accounted for by violations in the assumptions of the model which we deal with in the next chapter. The actual and predicted values for 1945-1970 are graphed in figure 2.8.

2.2.2 The cube law as a normal model

For the purposes of this chapter, the next step is to attempt to simplify the relationship further than as expressed in equation (2.2). This can be achieved by noting that, although the standard deviation controls the form of the seats-votes relationship within the normal-distribution model, small differences in standard deviation have little effect on the seat predictions. For instance, when the percentages of seats won in five British elections since 1945 are predicted by using a constant standard deviation of 13.7%. in all elections, the predictions are little different [columns (5) and (6) table 2.4].

The advantage in using this particular standard deviation is that the slope of the cumulative normal distribution function at $V = 50\%$ is almost exactly three. This permits a simpler expression to be used without any important loss of accuracy. Since the direct relationship between percentage of seats and percentage of votes is given by the cumulative distribution function, any simple expression relating S and V should be of approximately the same form. One simple function which adopts the correct S-shaped form in the range zero to one is:

$$\left(\frac{S}{1-S}\right) = \left(\frac{V}{1-V}\right)^k, \quad 0 < S, V < 1 \tag{2.3}$$

(Note: S and V are the *proportion* of seats and votes respectively of party A.) Isolating S, we get the form

$$S = \frac{V^k}{V^k + (1-V)^k} \tag{2.4}$$

The function, equation (2.4), is graphed for various values of k in figure 2.9. When $k = 3$, the function is known as the law of cubic proportions or, more simply, as the cube law. It turns out that this function is extremely close to the (cumulative) normal distribution function for corresponding k and σ.

Kendall and Stuart (1950) demonstrate, for example, that for $k = 3$ (the cube law) equation (2.4) is almost exactly equal to the normal distribution function with a standard deviation of 0.137. (This section can be omitted by the nonmathematical reader without losing the continuity of the argument.)

They do this, firstly, by expressing equation (2.3) as follows:

$$\frac{S}{1-S} = \left(\frac{\frac{1}{2}+x}{\frac{1}{2}-x}\right)^3, \quad -\tfrac{1}{2} < x < \tfrac{1}{2} \tag{2.5}$$

where x is the proportion of votes expressed as a deviation from 0.5. Isolating S once again gives

$$S = \frac{(1+2x)^3}{2(1+12x^2)} \tag{2.6}$$

The (noncumulative) frequency distribution can be found by differentiating equation (2.6), that is

$$f(x) = \frac{dS}{dx} = \frac{3(1-4x)^2}{(1+12x^2)^2}, \quad -\tfrac{1}{2} < x < \tfrac{1}{2} \tag{2.7}$$

The mean of this distribution is zero, since the variable x was expressed as a deviation from 0.5. To find the standard deviation, we need the square root of the integral of $x^2 f(x)$ over the interval $-\tfrac{1}{2}$ to $+\tfrac{1}{2}$, that is

$$\sigma = \left[\int_{-\frac{1}{2}}^{\frac{1}{2}} x^2 f(x) dx\right]^{\frac{1}{2}},$$

which reduces to

$$\sigma = \frac{4\pi}{27/3^{\frac{1}{2}}} - \frac{1}{4}$$

$$\sigma = 0.137$$

Kendall and Stuart also derive the skewness and kurtosis, both of which are extremely close to the theoretical values for the normal distribution.

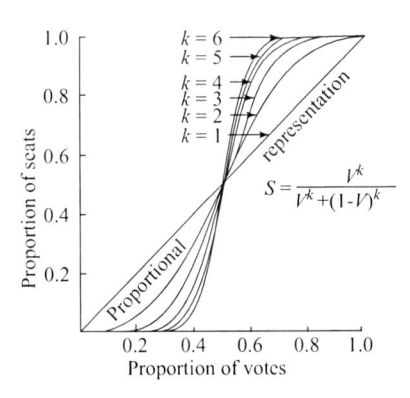

Figure 2.9: Alternative power laws, $k = 1–6$

The distribution function of a normal distribution with $\sigma = 0.137$ is compared with that of the cube law in column (4) of table 2.5[2]. The largest discrepancies occur in the critical region around $V = 0.5$ but are nevertheless small, amounting to the equivalent of two seats in British elections. A slightly more accurate approximation in the critical regions is given by a normal distribution with $a = 0.133$. This is derived by calculating a variance which is correct at $V = 0.5$ rather than being the best approximation over the whole distribution as in the Kendall and Stuart derivation.

Table 2.5: Distribution functions of normal and cube-law curves. Source: Kendall and Stuart (1950) and calculated by authors

V	Cube-law	Normal ($\sigma = 0.137$)	(2)–(3)	Normal ($\sigma = 0.133$)	(2)–(5)
(1)	(2)	(3)	(4)	(5)	(6)
0.00	0.0000	0.0001	−0.0001	0.0001	−0.0001
0.05	0.0001	0.0005	−0.0004	0.0004	−0.0003
0.10	0.0014	0.0017	−0.0003	0.0013	+0.0001
0.15	0.0055	0.0053	+0.0002	0.0042	+0.0013
0.20	0.0154	0.0141	+0.0013	0.0121	+0.0033
0.25	0.0357	0.0338	+0.0019	0.0301	+0.0056
0.30	0.0730	0.0719	+0.0011	0.0663	+0.0067
0.35	0.1350	0.1364	−0.0014	0.1297	+0.0053
0.40	0.2286	0.2324	−0.0038	0.2261	+0.0025
0.45	0.3539	0.3574	−0.0035	0.3535	+0.0004
0.50	0.5000	0.5000	0.0000	0.5000	0.0000
0.55	0.6461	0.6426	+0.0035	0.6465	−0.0004
0.60	0.7714	0.7676	+0.0038	0.7739	−0.0025
0.65	0.8650	0.8636	+0.0014	0.8703	−0.0053
0.70	0.9270	0.9281	−0.0011	0.9337	−0.0067
0.75	0.9643	0.9662	−0.0019	0.9699	−0.0056
0.80	0.9846	0.9859	−0.0013	0.9879	−0.0033
0.85	0.9945	0.9947	−0.0002	0.9958	−0.0013
0.90	0.9986	0.9983	+0.0003	0.9987	−0.0001
0.95	0.9999	0.9995	+0.0005	0.9996	+0.0003
1.00	1.0000	0.0001	+0.0001	0.9999	+0.0001

[2] It may be objected that the normal models give predictions of some small proportion of seats for 0% votes and that they do not give a total 100% seats to a party with 100% votes. This is because the normal distribution is a continuous distribution with no limits to its range whereas the vote proportions may only range from 0 to 1.00. This 'unrealistic' aspect of the normal model is of no practical importance but it may be noted that in contrast Thiel (1970) has shown that power laws of the cube-law type do not have this problem and may be preferred on these grounds. Mathematical niceties aside, the advantages of viewing power laws as approximations to normal models far outweigh this objection.

In this case we calculate the slope of the normal distribution function at $V = 0.5$, that is

$$\text{slope at } V = 0.5 = \frac{1}{(2\pi)^{\frac{1}{2}}\sigma} \approx \frac{0.4}{\sigma}.$$

However, it can be shown that the slope of a function (2.3) at $V = 0.5$ is equal to the value of the exponent k, which in the cube-law case is three[3]. Hence the normal distribution which most closely approximates the cube law close to $V = 0.5$ has a standard deviation which fits the expression

$$\frac{0.4}{\sigma} = 3,$$

or

$$\sigma = \frac{0.4}{3} = 0.133.$$

Column (5) of table 2.5 shows the improved accuracy near $V = 0.5$, and column (6) demonstrates that this is achieved at the expense of less accuracy elsewhere.

The cube law $\{S/(1 - S) = [V/(1 - V)]^3\}$ thus corresponds to a normal distribution with a standard deviation of 0.137 or 0.133 (depending on the type of approximation criteria). In most subsequent discussion Kendall and Stuart's original approximation (0.137) is used. Similar calculations reveal that a square law $\{S/(1 - S) = [V/(1 - V)]^2\}$ corresponds to a normal distribution with a standard deviation of approximately 0.20.

The basic material for constructing a realistic model of the seats-votes relationship is now complete, and it may be worthwhile to summarise the steps in the argument:

1. Many elections using the plurality system have frequency distributions of constituency vote proportions which are approximately normal in form.

---

[3] With the use of equation (2.4), in general for $0 \leq V \leq 1$ the first derivative (slope) is given by

$$\frac{dS}{dV} = \frac{[V^k + (1-V)^k]kV^{k-1} - V^k[kV^{k-1} - k(1-V)^{k-1}]}{[V^k + (1-V)^k]^2},$$

which reduces to

$$\frac{dS}{dV} = \frac{2kV^k(1-V)^{k-1}}{V^{2k} + 2V^k(1-V)^k + (1-V)^{2k}},$$

but when $V = 0.5$, $(1 - V) = 0.5$, so that

$$\frac{dS}{dV} = \frac{2kV^{2k-1}}{4V^{2k}}$$

$$= k$$

Hence the slope of the curve at $V = 0.5$ is given by the exponent in the original function.

2. This fact can be used in modelling such elections, since the proportion of votes won is the proportion of the normal distribution lying above $V = 50\%$. This proportion can be read from tables of the normal distribution (table 2.1).
3. This expression using the normal integral can be expressed in a simpler functional form by using power relationships of the form

$$S = \frac{V^k}{V^k + (1-V)^k}$$

However, this saves little time or effort compared with using tables of the normal distribution.

4 For modern British elections, square or cube laws ($k = 2$ or 3 respectively) will give the best predictions (on the assumption that k is restricted to integer values). This is because the square law corresponds to a standard deviation of 0.200 and the 'cube law' to a standard deviation of 0.137 or 0.133. Most modern British elections have frequency distributions with standard deviations which lie within this range. For British elections 1945 to 1970, the cube law (or the normal distribution function with a standard deviation of 13.7%) gives seat predictions which are accurate to within 1.5% on average (figure 2.9).

The 'cube law' [or other power 'laws' with the form of equation (2.4)] are particularly simple representations of the seats-votes relationship. The cube law, which is the commonly used power law, is usually plucked from nowhere. The advantage of emphasising the frequency distribution is that the process linking seats to votes is clearly in view. As a result it is easier to modify the model or to explain the relationship. In this situation, as in many others in the social sciences, a great deal of flexibility can be gained by modelling the process rather than the pattern resulting from it. This is attempted in the next chapter.

chapter three | explaining the cube law

At the beginning of chapter 2 it was suggested that the framework presented there would form the basis of analyses to uncover the mechanisms underlying the seats-votes relationship in plurality elections. It is the purpose of this chapter to attempt to justify this aim by presenting explanations of the cube law.

As indicated in chapter 2, the cube law is only one of many feasible relationships between seats and votes. It has attracted a good deal of attention because of its apparent applicability to a range of elections in several countries. However, the cube law serves as a description of the seats-votes relationship only because it adequately describes the relevant aspects of the normal constituency proportion distribution (CPD) which are characteristic in elections which the cube law fits. It is the existence of the normal CPD, and in particular the narrow range of observed values for the standard deviation, which are important and which this chapter seeks to account for. The argument in this chapter is thus more general than explanation solely of the cube law. The latter does, however, provide a particular, and salient, focus for the analysis.

In one sense the connection between the cube law (or related laws') and the normal CPD with the appropriate standard deviation is all that is required to explain this type of seats-votes relationship. The desire to understand why simple relationships such as the cube law hold in a variety of electoral circumstances could stop at this point. This would, however, leave unanswered questions as to why the normal distribution should occur in the first place, and why standard deviations of a particular magnitude should commonly occur. It is answers to these questions which are attempted in this chapter. This more fundamental explanation of the cube law can only be achieved through understanding the underlying mechanism of the seats-votes relationship based upon the interaction of voting patterns and constituency boundaries. It is this mechanism which is investigated in great detail in this chapter.

Authors from a variety of disciplines have attempted explanations of the cube law in a variety of ingenious ways, reflecting a diversity of methodology in the social sciences. These alternative explanations are briefly described and evaluated in appendix 1. The approach adopted here is closest to that of the mathematical statisticians who have investigated the problem. They treat frequency distributions as the end result of probability processes. It is thus no surprise to observe that statisticians faced with normal CPDs have immediately looked around for probability processes, having some real world plausibility, which could mathematically generate the frequency distributions. The earliest attempts in this direction appear to be those of Edgeworth in 1898, but the major effort was that of Kendall and Stuart in 1950. The latter outline two types of probability approach, which can be termed the 'binomial' and the 'Markov' methods. The first is based on the independent probabilities of voters supporting one or other party, while the second emphasises connections (dependence) between voters. Both of these approaches are discussed below.

3.1 The binomial method

The link between processes (of voting) and patterns (in this case, CPDs) in probability modelling can be illustrated initially by using a simple coin-tossing analogue. Assume that all voters are totally uninterested in political parties but that voting is compulsory. Each voter might then toss a coin before voting and decide his choice of party on the landing of the coin. On the assumption of 'fair' coins throughout the country, each person would have the same probability, 0.5, of voting for party A (say) and each constituency would also have this probability. However, although on average all constituencies would have half their voters supporting party A, in each election constituencies would differ among themselves owing to random variations inherent in the voting process. (It is important to notice the difference between the probability of an event and its subsequent realisation: constituencies may share the same probabilities, but have different realisations.)

This voting process may be generalised slightly to allow individual probabilities of supporting party A different from 0.5 as long as all voters throughout the country adhere to the same fixed probability, say 0.6. Although such modelling is patently unrealistic, it can be used as an initial step towards greater realism since it is interesting to see what CPDs such processes produce.

This process, described by statisticians as a set of independent Bernoulli trials, is one in which each act of voting is a trial and each set is a constituency. The resulting frequency distribution is the binomial distribution, which is a discrete analogue of the normal distribution and for large numbers of trials becomes indistinguishable from the normal. The unreality of the process is reflected in the resultant frequency distributions, which have very much smaller variance than those met in real elections. For example, if each constituency has 60000 voters and $p_i = p = 0.5$ (where p is the probability of supporting party A and i refers to individual constituencies), then the standard deviation is given by $[n(p-p^2)]^{1/2} = 122$ or 0.2% of the constituency electorate. With such a small standard deviation, the great majority of constituency results would be within ±0.5% of the overall (national) result. The frequency distribution would be virtually a single column based on 0.5. The standard deviation of 0.002 is very much smaller than the cube-law standard deviation of 0.14, and standard deviations of the elections illustrated in tables 2.2 and 2.3, that is, in the range 0.10 to 0.20.

3.1.1 Variants on the binomial distribution

When compared with reality, the assumptions of the binomial model are therefore too restrictive. A more realistic model can be introduced by relaxing the assumption that voters are acting entirely in a random fashion. This implies a relaxation of the assumption that the national propensity to support either party is faithfully reflected in each constituency. In fact, deviations away from these 'binomial' assumptions can occur in two ways. First a regular (at least more-regular-than-random) distribution of voters among constituencies can be assumed. This would be modelled by a binomial type of distribution, but one with a smaller variance than that of the binomial distribution itself. The probability distribution which is described by these assumptions is the Poisson variation of the binomial (sometimes called the 'subnormal' variation, and not to be confused with the Poisson distribution itself). In this case, the probability of voting for either party remains constant between constituencies but varies within them. A hypothetical example would be a 'women's party'. Since the proportion of women to men does not vary much from area to area, constituency election results would be similar, although within each constituency there would be a sharp voting cleavage dependent on sex. As the variance decreases, the situation approaches the deterministic case where all constituencies are identical and any party, with however a small majority in the country as a whole, would win all the seats.

Second, a more realistic variant on the binomial distribution is the so-called Lexis case. In this distribution, the probabilities p_i vary *between*, but not *within*, constituencies. The underlying process being hypothesised here is one in which voters with different propensities of support are segregated into distinct constituencies, but within each constituency the voters all have the same support probabilities, although they may not all actually vote the same way. As before, the actual votes (realisations) are random outcomes given some prior probability. The resulting frequency distribution naturally depends on the way in which the p_i vary among constituencies. Once again this depends on the spread of voters of various political complexion among constituencies, and this type of probability process does not suggest any particular way of dealing with these spatial distributions. To model reality, all that is required is that the distribution of p_i s should itself be approximately normal, with the desired variance[1]. It is possible to discuss circumstances under which realistic versions of the Lexian process might be applicable, but first it is important to summarise the models discussed so far, and to point out that in each case the process described above has a spatial equivalent. The different versions of the binomial model which have been outlined above are summarised in columns (1) and (2) of table 3.1.

---

[1] This is technically achieved by using a mixing distribution to specify the p_i, and the most common is the continuous beta distribution. This is a very flexible distribution capable of assuming a wide variety of forms (Gudgin and Taylor, 1974, page 58).

From a spatial viewpoint, it can be seen that a binomial frequency distribution can also result from a process of distributing voters between constituencies. If supporters of two parties are *randomly* spread among constituencies with the constraint that their combined numbers must equal the constituency electorate, then the simple binomial distribution results[2]. As before, the variance resulting from a random spread of votes is much smaller than that observed in real elections. If the process of

Table 3.1: Characteristics of binomial models

Probability model	Relevant characteristics	Spatial distribution	Voting process
Binomial 1	symmetrical, small variance	random (NB this involves a degree of clustering)	propensity to vote for either party is the same in each constituency
Binomial 2: Poisson's case	symmetrical, very small variance	dispersed (tending to regularity)	levels of support vary within but not between constituencies
Binomial 3: Lexis case (beta-binomial)	symmetrical or asymmetrical, larger variance	more clustered than random	varying levels of support between but not within constituencies

---

[2] Unconstrained random distributions in space produce Poisson distributions. However, in the case of two-party elections with a fixed size of constituency, and the voters of each party distributed randomly, we have two Poisson variables, X_1, X_2, subject to the condition that $X_1 + X_2 = n$ (that is, a constant). The resulting distribution is binomial: $p(X_1 = r | X_1 + X_2 = n) = $ binomial (r, n, λ) where λ is the mean of X.

Proof

$$p(X_1 = r | X_1 + X_2 = n) = p(X_1 = r | X_2 = n - r)$$

$$= \frac{p(X_1 = r) p(X_2 = n - r)}{p(X_1 + X_2 = n)}$$

$$= \frac{\lambda_1^r \exp(-\lambda_1)}{r!} \frac{\lambda_2^{n-r} \exp(-\lambda_2)}{(n-r)!} \bigg/ \exp(-\lambda_1 - \lambda_2) \frac{(\lambda_1 + \lambda_2)^n}{n!}$$

$$= \frac{n!}{r!(n-r)!} \frac{\lambda_1^r \lambda_2^{n-r}}{(\lambda_1 + \lambda_2)^n}$$

$$= \binom{n}{r} \lambda_1^r (1 - \lambda_1)^{n-r}$$

since $\lambda_1 + \lambda_2 = 1$.

spatially distributing voters results in a pattern more regular than random, or in other words is less clustered than a random distribution, then the resulting frequency distribution is that of Poisson's case with its very small variance. The more realistic Lexis case reflects a spatial process in which voters for any one party are more clustered than randomly spread voters would be.

In this slow progress towards a realistic model of a process underlying observed frequency distribution, the situation reached is that in which p_i must vary between constituencies, or from a different point of view, party supporters are more clustered than are randomly spread supporters. The Lexian model is unrealistic for its assumption of homogeneity (at least, in propensities) within constituencies, and in addition is of little use in considering the distribution of support between constituencies. On the first point, it can be noted at once that the internal homogeneity of constituencies is relatively unimportant as long as constituency sizes are large. Departures from the assumption of homogeneity have relatively little effect on the form or variance of the Lexian distribution. This can be seen by examining the equation for the variance of the distribution of constituency proportions:

$$\text{var}(x) = \frac{p(1-p)}{n} + \frac{n-1}{n}\text{var}(p_i). \tag{3.1}$$

The two elements on the right-hand side correspond first to the *within-constituency* variance, and second to *between-constituency* variance. The element $p(1-p)$ has a maximum value of 0.25, and in a situation approximating that in the UK is divided by $n = 60000$, giving an upper limit on $p(1-p)/n$ of 4×10^{-6}.

To achieve the 'cube-law variance' of 0.019, var(p_i) has itself to equal ~0.019 since the within-constituency element is too small to have any real influence. If the voters within any constituency are heterogeneous in their voting propensities, then the within-constituency variance, surprisingly, is smaller (Feller, 1968, page 231). In less technical terms, this means that the form of the resulting frequency distribution depends hardly at all on the composition of support within constituencies, and almost wholly on the distribution of constituency (average) support probabilities. To model a realistic process, it is necessary to concentrate solely on the distribution of (constituency support probabilities, ignoring all else in the knowledge that it is unimportant. For practical purposes, an assumption of internal homogeneity is as good as any, and has the advantage of simplicity.

3.1.2 The distribution of constituency proportions and spatial clustering

The major disadvantage of the binomial (Lexian) approach is its ultimate failure to throw much light on the reasons for the existence of normal distributions with relatively high variance. A review of this approach has had the merit of emphasising the need to account for the greater than random clustering of voters between constituencies. It is to this that attention must now be turned initially in a nonrigorous way and later in probability terms.

In accounting for realistic frequency distributions, it is also necessary to account for the similarities observed in different countries and for stability over time. In all of these respects, spatial processes appear the most plausible contenders to explain the distribution of the p_is. What is required in spatial terms is some explanation for the observed degree of clustering of party support. In very general terms, the clustering is easily explicable. Political support in Britain and New Zealand is class-based. Similarly, class forms the major criterion for residential segregation. In the towns (containing 80% of UK population) there are working-class districts and middle-class districts, and moreover towns vary considerably in their overall social composition, reflecting wide contrasts in dominant economic function as between industrial and resort towns, for example. In the numerically less important rural areas, spatial segregation by class (and hence party affiliation) is maintained first and foremost by the existence of mining areas, but also by commuter belts. In agricultural areas, with little industry or commuting, segregation of voters is much less marked. However, in advanced countries such areas form the minority, are declining in importance, and in the UK, as an extreme case form a very small element.

It should be noted at this point that we are assuming a population of electors with fixed *propensities* of support. Moreover, the discussion here depends on a relationship between propensity and social class. The argument employed in this section, being a general one, does not need a firmer basis than the existence of a broad relationship between social class and voting intention as described in chapter 1.

The connection between clustering of voters and form of frequency distribution can be explored further in the following examples. If voters are clustered and the clusters are evenly spread, then the frequency distribution depends on the relative sizes of the clusters and the constituencies. Clusters which are much larger than constituencies will result in U-shaped frequency distributions. Successively smaller cluster-constituency ratios will change the form of frequency distribution, firstly towards a rectangular distribution, and for a ratio of less than one towards a unimodal distribution resembling the normal. These points are illustrated in figure 3.1. Clusters of only one voter each, randomly spread over the space of constituencies, lead to the binomial distribution.

It is now possible to bridge the gap between what is known about the spatial clustering of voters and what is known about frequency distributions. As a general rule, clusters of voters are much smaller than constituencies in the economically developed countries under discussion. Within towns, socially homogeneous districts are much smaller than constituencies.

In Britain, working-class areas (for example, council estates and inner-city districts) are typically much smaller than the 60000 voters of an average constituency. In rural areas, coalfields and commuter belts are both areas in which clusters of supporters are more densely concentrated, but neither type of area is in practice homogeneous enough to be considered a single cluster. The nature of spatial economics is such that the different levels in the social hierarchies are functionally interrelated and have to live in proximity to one another to avoid long journeys to work. Coalfields have shopkeepers and professional and administrative workers as well as miners; while commuter belts have manual service workers. In addition commuter areas are typically interwoven with older, more mixed communities.

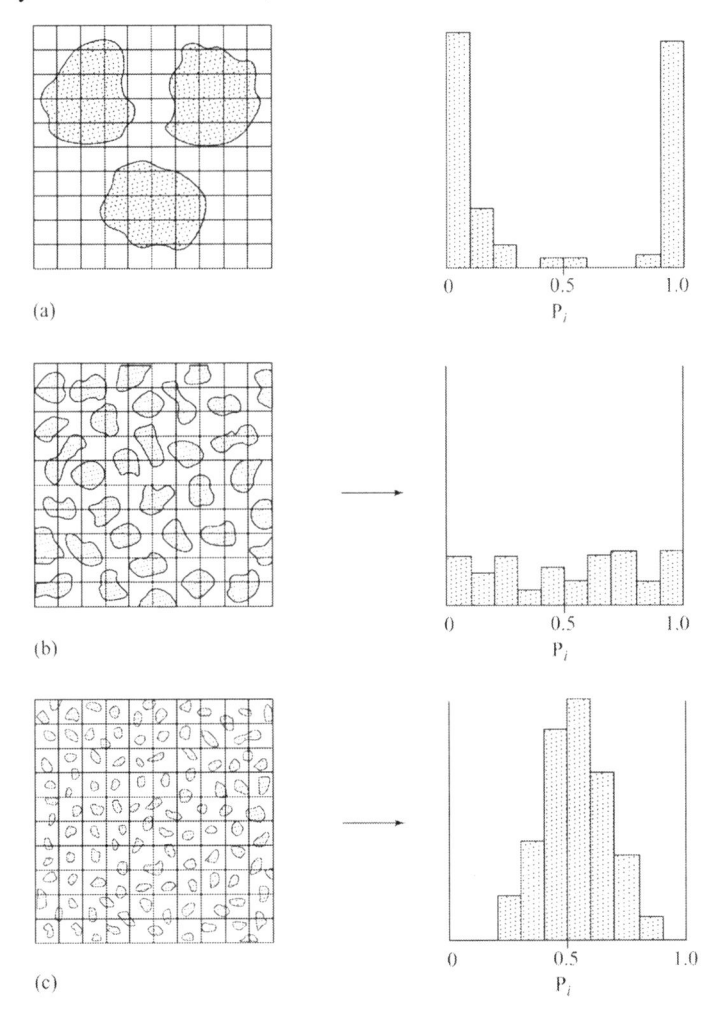

Figure 3.1: Relationships between clusters of voters (stippled areas) and size of constituency (a single square of the grid)

The consequence in both cases is that clusters of party support are spatially interwoven with one another within constituencies, and do not individually become as large as the 60000 of UK constituencies, or the quarter million of US Congressional Districts.

In practice, the spatial distribution of party support accords with that of figure 3.1(c), and hence a unimodal frequency distribution results. The existence of relatively large clusters, as in city centres, and of relatively dense concentrations of clusters, as in mining areas, means that constituency results are spread widely around 50% (on the assumption of two evenly matched parties). On the other hand, extreme results close to 0% or 100% are rare. Since the average size of cluster is well removed from the one-voter size underlying the binomial distribution, the standard deviation of real world distributions is larger than the 0.002 of the binomial, but at the same time is smaller than 0.20, which is approximately the upper limit for the bell-shaped type of distribution.

These sorts of consideration give a ready explanation for similarities between countries and stability over time. From the standpoint of time first, broad spatial patterns change only slowly with fundamental economic or social changes or dramatic alterations in the dominant means of transport. As long as the principal electoral cleavage and the nature of the major parties remains unchanged, the CPD is unlikely to change radically. Within the UK a century of change, political as well as economic and social, has had little impact except perhaps to effect some increase in the variance of the distribution (see Edgeworth, 1898, and chapter 4). Tables 2.2 and 2.3 have already shown that Britain and New Zealand display normal CPDs and it can now be further noted that similar bell-shaped distributions have been found in the USA and South Africa in the past and may even be derived from Canada's multiparty elections. These examples are discussed in later chapters. Here only the point made in chapter 1 need be considered, namely that ethnically based voting will often produce a type of voting mosaic very similar to that produced by class-based voting, to produce CPDs with far larger variances than those predicted by the simple binomial model.

One possible significant difference between these countries, however, is in population size. The five countries vary from two million people up to two hundred million. It is possible that sizes of coherent social areas also vary greatly, but if so, then as long as constituencies remain much larger, this variation is unimportant. The figures below show that the

	Population (million)	Voters per constituency
South Africa (whites)	2.3	13000
New Zealand	2.6	16000
Canada	19.0	49000
UK	55.6	63000
USA	203.2	240000

larger countries have larger constituencies, although less than in proportion to their size. [See Taagepera (1972) for an attempt to model the relationship.] Even in New Zealand and South Africa the average size of constituency is relatively large and likely to be considerably larger than the sizes of homogeneous social areas.

The argument thus far can now be summarised as a preface to a more rigorous approach. The binomial approach proves to be of limited use, in that after a little analysis the investigation rests solely on empirical considerations of the voting mosaic and constituency size. Two important results do emerge from this approach, however. First, random spatial distributions, which can be used as a basis for comparison, produce low-variance frequency distributions. The factors which lead to real world CPDs must therefore involve a higher degree of clustering of voters. Second, the average propensities of constituencies to support a party are important whereas variation within constituencies (that is, around the constituency average) is not important. These two facts provide a basis for an empirical investigation of the sorts of factors which could lead to a normal frequency distribution of the 'cube law' type. Empirically it is observable that homogeneous clusters of social groups (which we use as a proxy for party support) are smaller than constituencies in the UK, and probably in all of the countries considered here. A little more theory serves to show that a reasonably even spread of clusters forms a frequency distribution of approximately the correct type as long as the clusters are significantly smaller than constituencies, but considerably larger than a single voter. The weakest link in this chain of reasoning is the last, since the size of variance of the frequency distribution is a critical factor and yet there is no accurate or rigorous link between it and the processes outlined above.

3.2 The Markov method

The other principal approach based on probability stresses connections between voters rather than (independent) probabilities of supporting one party or the other. A Markov system is one in which the probability of a given event depends only on the outcome of the preceding event. In electoral terms, electors with fixed votes can be thought of as being allocated to constituencies. For any constituency the probability of a voter being a party A supporter depends only on whether the last voter allocated was a party A supporter. The higher the correlation between successive allocations, the higher the degree of clustering of supporters between constituencies. Hence, the Markov scheme like the Lexian is a way in which we can move away from the low-variance, random distributions to more realistic ones with greater degrees of clustering. Both schemes provide methods of generating frequency distributions, but the Markov scheme has advantages in allowing a more rigorous specification of the process needed to generate the cube-law variance.

3.2.1 A model of individual voters

Let there be fixed proportions p and $(1 - p)$ of supporters of parties A and B, respectively, in a given population of voters. To allocate voters to constituencies, firstly choose one voter at random. The next voter is then allocated also at random, but with a probability determined as follows: Let α be the probability that if a party A supporter has been allocated, then the next voter also supports party A, and let β be the probability of a party A supporter following a party B supporter, such that $\alpha > \beta$, and $\alpha - \beta = \varepsilon$ (say).

Then for a series of 'trials', each consisting of n allocations, the resulting frequency distribution of trial outcomes has the following characteristics.

(1) It tends to normality as n approaches infinity (Uspensky, 1937, page 301). In fact, the distribution tends to be quite close to normality for small values of n; for example, for $n = 25$, Uspensky (1937, page 229) shows that the frequency distribution closely approximates the normal distribution.

(2) If p_i is the observed proportion of party A supporters in the ith trial, then the mean value of the p_i s in samples of n is p; that is, the overall proportion of party A supporters in the population. The same of course holds of $(1 - p)$, party B supporters (Uspensky, 1937, page 223).

(3) The variance of the p_i s is given by

$$\text{var}(p_i) = \frac{p(1-p)}{n} \frac{(1+\varepsilon)}{(1-\varepsilon)}. \tag{3.2}$$

(Uspensky, 1937, page 225).

The Markov scheme supplies a process leading to the required normal distribution and if one includes an expression for variance, which can be tied to empirical cases, it will lead in particular to the 'cube law' variance. The process posited is one in which voters are allocated to constituencies. What is being modelled in this case is the complex of 'natural' socioeconomic factors which lead to the distribution of social classes (and hence political allegiance) among constituencies. The only really active element in the probability process is the dependence between one allocation and the next. How is this dependence to be interpreted? One obvious connection between voters which will fulfill the requirements of a dependence relationship is social class. If we proceed as before, with only two classes, once a working-class voter is allocated to a constituency then it is more likely that other working-class voters will also be allocated to it rather than middle-class voters being allocated there. The mechanisms underlying such dependence are those of occupation and of residential segregation. An industrial town means that more working-class than middle-class voters are 'allocated' to its constituencies. Similarly, a suburban or commuter-belt area will have more middle-class voters 'allocated' to it.

It is easier to imagine such a process occurring at a smaller spatial scale, that of coherent social areas. In this case the first voter allocated will set the general tone and there will be a high likelihood that subsequent voters have the same support propensities. Thus the process begins with an arbitrary voter and continues with a high probability of selecting similar voters. A change from one party to the other is analogous to skipping from a working-class district to a middle-class one (or vice versa) in selecting voters. The analogy between the spatial process and the probability model is not rigorously made, nor is the process entirely realistic (mainly because of considerations of internal voting homogeneity of social areas). Both aspects can be improved, but first the degree of dependence that is needed in this simple model to achieve the required 'cube law' variance will be derived.

The expression for the variance of the distribution [equation (3.2)], in fact, relates three properties of the model. These are: the proportions of supporters of the two parties in the population as a whole, p, $1-p$; the constituency size, n; the dependence between voters, which can be interpreted loosely as the degree of clustering $(1+\varepsilon)/(1-\varepsilon)$. Since the variance of the normal distribution underlying the cube law is 0.137^2, that is 0.019,

$$\frac{p(1-p)}{n}\frac{(1+\varepsilon)}{(1-\varepsilon)} = 0.019.$$

If the two parties are assumed to be evenly balanced in the nation at large,

$$\frac{0.5 \times 0.5}{n}\frac{(1+\varepsilon)}{(1-\varepsilon)} = 0.019,$$

that is,

$$\frac{1+\varepsilon}{1-\varepsilon} = \frac{0.019}{0.25}n = 0.076n \quad \text{or} \quad \varepsilon = \frac{0.076n-1}{1+0.076n}.$$

For a fixed constituency size, n, of 60000,

$$\varepsilon = \frac{4560-1}{4560+1} = 0.9996.$$

Since $\alpha + \beta = 1$[3], $\quad \alpha = \tfrac{1}{2}\varepsilon + \tfrac{1}{2} = 0.9998.$

---

[3] In accordance with Uspensky (1937, page 223)

$$p = \frac{\beta}{1-\varepsilon} = \frac{\beta}{1-\alpha+\beta}$$

since $\varepsilon = \alpha - \beta$. Thus

$$p(1-\alpha+\beta) = p - \alpha p + \beta p = \beta, \quad \text{or} \quad \beta(1-p) = p - \alpha p = p(1-\alpha).$$

Hence

$$\beta = \frac{p(1-\alpha)}{1-p}.$$

In our case, $p = 0.5$, so $p/(1-p) = 1$, and $\beta = 1 - \alpha$. In other words, $\alpha + \beta = 1$.

The degree of dependence between successive voters has thus to be extremely high in order to achieve the variance of cube-law dimensions. An initial selection of a party A voter leads to a probability of 0.9998 of the next voter having the same allegiance, and so on through the trials. This gives a probability of only one in five thousand of changing from one party to another, or, in terms of the clustering interpretation, implies an average cluster size of 5000 voters. Table 3.2 shows how the average cluster size varies with size of constituency. This table implies that the existence of the cube law as an accurate descriptor of the seats-votes relationship would require homogeneous clusters of about 16000 voters in the USA, 5000 in the UK, and 1100 in New Zealand or South Africa.

Table 3.2: Average size of cluster [1/(1 − α)] and size of constituency (n) to generate cube-law variance

n	α	1/(1 − α)
250000	0.99994	16667
60000	0.9998	5000
30000	0.9996	2500
15000	0.9991	1111
1000	0.9870	77
100	0.8837	9

3.2.2 A model of clusters of voters

A modification to this basic model permits a considerable improvement in the realism of the process. Since the process being described is based on clusters of voters, these clusters can be fed into the model right from the start. Assume a situation in which two types of clusters of voters exist. One is a working-class cluster with proportions of 0.7 supporting party A and 0.3 of supporting party B. The second is a cluster of middle-class voters in which the proportions are reversed. Now allocate to constituencies, not voters, but clusters of voters. In this case the variance of the resulting frequency distribution is given by[4]

$$\text{var}(p_i) = (2r-1)^2 \frac{p(1-p)}{n} \frac{(1+\varepsilon)}{(1-\varepsilon)}, \qquad (3.3)$$

where r is the proportion of 'working-class' voters supporting party A (or 'middle-class' voters supporting party B).

---

[4] We are indebted to P Diggle (University of Newcastle) for the following proof. Let (X_n) be a discrete time random process, and let (Y_n) be a derived process such that $Y_n = aX_n + b$, for arbitrary constants, a, b, ε, R.

Let $\overline{X} = \frac{1}{n}\sum_{i=1}^{n} X_i$ and $\overline{Y} = \frac{1}{n}\sum_{i=1}^{n} Y_i$

Theorem. Whatever the correlation structure of the process (X_n)

$$\text{var}(\overline{Y}) = a^2 \, \text{var}(\overline{X}).$$

To reach the 'cube law' variance of 0.019 with $r = 0.7$, as specified in the above example (and $p = 0.5$ as before),

$$[(2 \times 0.7) - 1]^2 \frac{0.25}{n} \frac{(1+\varepsilon)}{(1-\varepsilon)} = 0.019,$$

$$\frac{1+\varepsilon}{1-\varepsilon} = 0.475n, \quad \text{or} \quad \varepsilon = \frac{0.475n - 1}{0.475n + 1}.$$

For a constituency size of 60000 and a cluster size of, say, 1000 voters, $n = 60000/1000 = 60$.

For $n = 60$, $\varepsilon = 0.932$ or $\alpha = 0.966$, table 3.3 gives values of α for various cluster sizes (n) within three sizes of constituency, on the

Lemma. For arbitrary random variables, X, Y, if $Z = aX+b$ and $W = cY+d$, then
$\text{cov}(ZW) = ac\, \text{cov}(XY)$.
Proof: $E(Z) = aE(X) + b$, $\quad E(W) = cE(Y)+d$.
Hence
$E(ZW) = acE(XY) + adE(X) + bcE(Y) + bd$,
$E(Z)E(W) = acE(X)E(Y) + adE(X) + bcE(Y) + bd$,
and
$\text{cov}(ZW) = E(ZW) - E(Z)E(W) - ac\{E(XY) - E(X)E(Y)\} = ac\, \text{cov}(XY)$.
Proof: For the process (Y_n),

$$\text{var}\left(\sum_{i=1}^{n} Y_i\right) = \sum_{i=1}^{n} \text{var}(Y_i) + 2\sum_{i<j}^{n} \text{cov}(Y_i, Y_j)$$

$$= \sum_{i=1}^{n} a^2 \text{var}(X_i) + 2\sum_{i<j}^{n} a^2 \text{cov}(X_i, X_j)$$

$$= a^2 \text{var}\left(\sum_{i=1}^{n} X_i\right).$$

In particular, let (X_n) be a two-state Markov chain with states $(0, 1)$ and let

$$Y_n = (2r - 1)X_n + (1 - r).$$

Then (Y_n) is also a two-state Markov chain with states r and $(1 - r)$ respectively.

It follows from the theorem that $\text{var}(\overline{Y}) = (2r - 1)^2 \text{var}(\overline{X})$. However, the variance of (X_n) is given by Uspensky (1937, page 225) as

$$\text{var}(\overline{X}_n) = \frac{p(1-p)}{n} \frac{(1+\varepsilon)}{(1-\varepsilon)},$$

where p, ε, n are as defined previously.
It follows immediately that

$$\text{var}(\overline{Y}) = (2r - 1)^2 \frac{p(1-p)}{n} \frac{(1+\varepsilon)}{(1-\varepsilon)}.$$

assumption of a 0.7 proportion of support for the area's 'natural' party (for example, the working-class party in a working-class area). The α values in this case can be interpreted as the degree of concentration of clusters among constituencies. A value of $\alpha = 0.5$ indicates that the clusters are randomly allocated among constituencies, whereas higher values indicate greater degrees of concentration. For example, given a constituency size of 60000 voters (table 3.3), there are a variety of ways in which the variance of 0.019 can be achieved. In each case the clusters have support proportions of 0.7 and 0.3 for the two parties. Clusters of 20000 voters distributed almost randomly among constituencies will result in the correct variance. Smaller-sized clusters can achieve the same result, but only if they are themselves more concentrated. Clusters of twelve thousand voters have to be mildly concentrated ($\alpha = 0.7$). Smaller clusters need to be strongly concentrated in order to keep the variance large. Evenly spread clusters would tend towards the low-variance binomial distribution as the size of cluster became small. In order to counteract this effect, the clusters must themselves become concentrated in relatively few constituencies, to create the extreme election results which produce a large variance value.

As a model of the real world, this modified Markov scheme does not differentiate between contrasting types of 'concentration of clusters'. One type is regional segregation, in which party A clusters are concentrated in one or more regions of a country and absent or scarce elsewhere. At the other extreme, constituencies with concentrations of clusters may be scattered throughout the country (for example in city centres). Intermediate types are also possible, but all are equivalent *ceteris paribus* as far as the model is concerned.

As expected, a larger size of constituency (table 3.3) produces the same frequency distribution with larger clusters. For constituencies with 250000 voters (corresponding approximately to US congressional districts), mildly concentrated clusters of 50000 voters will produce the cube-law variance. With small constituencies, the clusters are correspondingly smaller. The cube-

Table 3.3: Dependence (α) between clusters of voters to generate cube-law variance

Cluster sizes (voters)	Constituency size (voters)		
	250000	60000	15000
500	0.996	0.983	0.935
1000	0.992	0.966	0.877
2000	0.983	0.935	0.781
3000	0.975	0.905	0.705
6000	0.952	0.825	0.543
12000	0.908	0.705	-
20000	0.856	0.575	-
50000	0.705	-	-
85000	0.570	-	-

law distribution could result from elections in New Zealand or South Africa, for example, if the 0.7 : 0.3 clusters were mildly concentrated ($\alpha = 0.7$) and contained about 3000 voters.

In each of the above examples, the internal form of the clusters was maintained at support levels of 0.7 and 0.3 for the two parties respectively. With fixed support levels (and fixed constituency sizes) the size and spatial concentration of the clusters can be varied while the resulting variance is kept constant. It is also possible to vary the internal composition of the clusters and this is done in table 3.4, in which the single constituency size of 60000 voters is used. The r value, as before, is the proportion of voters in a given cluster supporting that cluster's 'natural' party. The proportion supporting the other party is $(1 - r)$. The column $r = 0.7$ is repeated from table 3.3 to allow comparison between the tables.

If the clusters of voters were to be less homogeneous (for example, $r = 0.6$), then in order to produce a variance of 0.019 the clusters would either have to be larger (than for $r = 0.7$), or alternatively would have to be more concentrated among constituencies, or both. With greater internal homogeneity, the opposite is true. As the homogeneity increases, successively smaller, or alternatively less concentrated clusters will achieve the required effect. As an example, moderately concentrated ($\alpha = 0.7$) clusters of 6000 voters, which were relatively homogeneous in their party support ($r = 0.8$) would produce the cube-law distribution.

The Markov approach thus tells us that, for a given size of constituency, the variance of the CPD depends on three things, each of which can vary independently of the others:

The size of clusters, defined as the number of voters comprising the cluster.
The internal homogeneity of clusters, that is, the proportion of voters who support one party rather than another. The least homogeneous clusters occur when the proportion is 0.5 — half of the voters support one party, while half support the other. The other extreme is a proportion of 1.0, when all the voters vote the same way.

Table 3.4: *Dependence (α) between clusters of voters and homogeneity within clusters to generate a cube-law variance (for constituencies of 60000 voters)*

Cluster sizes (voters)	Cluster homogeneity (r)			
	0.6	0.7	0.8	0.9
500	0.996	0.983	0.962	0.934
1000	0.991	0.966	0.927	0.877
2000	0.983	0.935	0.864	0.781
3000	0.974	0.905	0.809	0.704
6000	0.950	0.825	0.679	0.543
12000	0.905	0.705	0.514	0.273
20000	0.851	0.575	0.276	0.263

The concentration of clusters between constituencies. Clusters can be spread among constituencies in a variety of ways, ranging from complete uniformity, through randomness, to high concentration in a few constituencies. In measuring the probability that if one cluster is allocated to a particular constituency, then the next one allocated has the same political complexion, the α value is also a measure of the concentration of clusters.

Any combination of size, concentration, and homogeneity of clusters will produce a normal distribution with some variance. In order to arrive at any specific variance, only certain combinations of the three variables will suffice. In general, if internal homogeneity is increased, then to retain a constant value of variance, cluster size and/or concentration must be decreased.

For anyone interested in spatial patterning, the simple link between a frequency distribution and the three components of spatial pattern outlined above suggests exciting possibilities. The frequency distribution, a one-dimensional quantity, holds some information about two-dimensional spatial patterns. The fact that frequency distributions are often more easily available or can be easily compiled, whereas spatial distributions are difficult to measure or are unknown in detail, means that the Markov method will allow information to be gleaned which would otherwise be inaccessible or difficult to gain.

In the specific case of elections the method has allowed the identification of the combinations of circumstances in which 'cube-law distributions' will be produced. The particular combination existing in any one country is a matter for empirical investigation, and this will be explored in the following section. For the present, the important thing is the finding that a range of plausible circumstances will produce the required result. For UK elections, with constituencies of approximately 60000 voters, it is plausible to think that mildly concentrated clusters of 6000 voters with 0.7:0.3 support levels do exist in reality. In addition, any one of the three figures may be changed if unrealistic, as long as compensating changes in the other figures are realistic. The other highly plausible aspect is the scale dependence of the relationships. Countries with large populations tend to have large constituencies, and are also likely to have more and larger cities and larger social areas within them—although this relationship is less obvious when agricultural areas are considered. As long as the size of social areas (clusters) and the size of constituency vary approximately proportionately with the size of electorate, the variance of the CPD will remain the same. Hence the curious fact, originally noted by Kendall and Stuart (1950), that CPDs are, or were, remarkably similar for countries at scales as radically contrasting as those of New Zealand, the UK, and the USA.

This is still the situation, to some degree, for Britain and New Zealand as shown by tables 2.2 and 2.3. There are, however, consistent differences between the standard deviations of CPDs in the two countries, as was noted in chapter 2 and these may now be considered in the light of the Markov model. The most obvious difference between Britain and New Zealand is of course constituency size. Note, however, that, all other things being equal, smaller constituencies will tend to produce larger variances. Hence on these grounds alone it would be expected that New Zealand should have *larger* CPD standard deviations than Britain whereas the converse is true. The modelling above suggests that the smaller constituencies must be more than compensated for by one of the following:

(1) lower homogeneity of areas (r), suggesting different types of social areas than Britain or else different levels of class voting;
(2) smaller clusters of voters than in Britain;
(3) less concentration of clusters among constituencies than in Britain.

Any one, or combination, of the above could override the constituency-size 'effect' to generate the lower New Zealand variances. Hence the Markov model suggests some interesting empirical investigations that would be in order to sort out this situation.

Although the Markov model may be used to suggest empirical investigations, it should also be noted here that several aspects of the model remain unrealistic. Perhaps the most obvious one is the equal-constituency-size assumption within countries when malapportionment is known to exist to varying degrees as described in chapter 1. This is not a major problem for the modelling, however, and is discussed as such in chapter 4. The nature of the clusters themselves, on the other hand, presents more serious difficulties. The model assumes fixed homogeneity and constant cluster size. Social areas, the clusters, are obviously graded to some extent in terms of social class and hence possibly also of voting. This situation is incorporated into the model as a simple dichotomy of types. Furthermore it is a simple matter of everyday observation to note that areas of relatively homogeneous social composition vary widely in size. A straightforward illustration might be council estates in the UK. These largely working-class areas vary in size from a street or two up to well over ten thousand voters. Other types of social area are less easily defined, but nevertheless vary considerably in size. Both the homogeneity and the size of the clusters will themselves form frequency distributions, and in principle the fixed homogeneity and constant cluster size could be replaced by such frequency distributions in an improved, albeit more complex, model. This modification is not attempted here and both the homogeneity and the size constants may be thought of as the averages of their respective distributions. It seems unlikely that replacing these means with the full range of possibilities from frequency distributions would materially alter the conclusions.

3.3 An empirical investigation of the Markov explanation

The Markov model used in the last section led to the conclusion that the cube law would be generated in a plurality voting system if voters were spatially arranged in clusters so that the size, the homogeneity, and the concentration of clusters were related within fixed ranges. The question is whether these relationships and ranges of values are realistic. If the size, homogeneity, and concentration of clusters are measured empirically in Britain, will the observed values generate the cube law, which is known to provide a good approximation in British elections?

3.3.1 The sample survey

To answer this question a survey of the residential pattern of voters was conducted in February 1974 in Newcastle upon Tyne. This is a city with a population of a quarter of a million, forming part of the Tyne and Wear conurbation. The majority of the work force are employed in service occupations despite the city's industrial image. Like most British cities the electorate contains a majority of Labour voters with a typical split in recent elections being 58% Labour and 42% Conservative. Since a more widely based survey was beyond the resources of this study, the Newcastle example stands as an illustration and a test case.

The survey method involved interviews with 2518 voters as they left polling stations in the General Election of February 1974. Interviewers were spread across all fifty-nine polling stations in two of the four Newcastle constituencies[5]. Each polling station was manned for six hours in total, spread between three different periods of the day. These covered working hours, periods of travel to (or from) work, and midday/ evening periods in an effort to counteract potential biases due to variations in political complexion of voters at different times of the day. In the event this was perhaps unnecessary, since the aggregate proportions supporting each party were virtually identical irrespective of whether or not this sampling design was utilised in calculations. The relevant questions asked concerned party support and street of residence.

The accuracy of the results can be assessed by comparing the sample results with the actual election results in the two constituencies. The comparative figures are given in table 3.5 and a clear tendency towards

---

[5] The survey was conducted in the Newcastle North and Newcastle West constituencies. Resources limited the survey to two constituencies, and these were chosen as covering a wide spectrum of social areas. Every polling station within these constituencies was surveyed for a balanced sample of six of the fourteen hours on polling day. A total of fifty-four undergraduate and postgraduate interviewers undertook the survey work, which consisted of approaching voters as they left the polling station after voting. Instructions were given that interviewers after completing an interview should approach the next voter to leave the polling station, and continue in this way for an hour. In some areas this procedure resulted in all voters being approached, in others, especially at busy times, only a minority sample were approached. Each voter was asked six questions on current and previous voting behaviour, address and occupation, but only the address and stated current voting preference were analysed for this study. Despite previous doubts, the great majority of voters cooperated willingly in the survey. Interviewers were asked to record the refusal rate, and the overall estimate was 15% of those approached.

underestimation of Conservative support can be observed. This is not due to sample error, since the samples are large and the standard errors are close to 1%. The inaccuracy is very probably caused by a systematic tendency for those refusing to assist in the survey to be Conservative voters. The overall proportion of those approached who refused to cooperate was estimated by interviewers to be about 15% although much higher proportions were reported from strongly middle-class areas. One group which showed some reluctance to take part was old people, and once again these were more likely to be Conservative supporters than Labour supporters. This explanation is supported by the arithmetic since if 10% of those approached in West refused to cooperate, and 15% in North, with all of these being Conservatives, then the correct proportions are achieved. In the work reported below all of the figures have been multiplied by the ratio of the actual to the estimated proportions.

Table 3.5: Survey and actual results of the February 1974 General Election in Newcastle upon Tyne, West and North

	Labour		Conservative		Liberal	
	survey	actual	survey	actual	survey	actual
Newcastle West	66.7	60.1	33.3	39.9	-	-
Newcastle North	38.2	33.4	34.8	43.6	27.0	23.0

3.3.2 The political mosaic of Newcastle upon Tyne

Although the location of voters was ascertained down to the scale of the individual street, sample sizes were too small to assess the political complexion of each street. The smallest scale at which we could *directly* describe the spatial distribution of voters was that of the polling district. These contain an average of two thousand voters and it was of interest to test whether this scale would be fine enough to identify coherent clusters of voters.

In fact the polling-district scale is too large. This can be seen in figure 3.2 in which frequency distributions of polling districts are constructed for Conservative support. In both cases the distributions appear to be trimodal, indicating the existence of distinct Conservative and Labour areas, but also of a mixed category of polling district containing both types of area. The form of the distribution suggests that the polling-district boundaries do not coincide with those of distinct clusters, but also that the clusters are smaller than polling districts. If the clusters were a size similar to that of polling districts then the distributions would be more uniform; if they were larger, there would be a stronger tendency than that observed towards bimodality. On the other hand, the distributions do suggest the existence of a substantial degree of clustering (as opposed to a random distribution of party supporters).

Since sample sizes prevent a direct mapping of clusters at much below the polling-district scale an indirect method was adopted, based on a classification of housing types by rateable value and other characteristics, together with the results of the election survey. Because the housing information was available for the whole of Newcastle, clusters of voters were identified for the whole city and not just for the two constituencies in the election survey.

Rateable values are available for every house in Newcastle and modal values for each street were made available for us from another research project. (We are grateful to Dr A Kirby of Reading University for these data.) This was supplemented by information on types of housing in terms of whether the street consisted largely of flats, of houses, or of houses with garages. Finally, lists were available of all streets in Newcastle with houses which were wholly or predominantly council-owned. From these data Newcastle was divided into two types of area—type A, pro-Conservative, and type B, pro-Labour. The following rules of allocation of streets were adopted:

1. All streets designated council-owned were allocated to type B.

2. All remaining streets with houses with garages were allocated to type A.

3. Of the remaining streets (noncouncil flats and houses without garages), the lowest-rated streets were cumulatively added to type B until it comprised 58% of the total streets.

4. All remaining streets were added to type A. The break point came at a rateable value (1973) of £151.

The result of this exercise is that 58% of streets are designated type B and 42% type A. The ratio 58 : 42 was chosen because this is the 'normal' balance between Labour and Conservatives in recent elections.

When two types of street are mapped, large clusters of similar types are found, particularly in the area near the river, on council estates, and in middle-class districts to the north and east. From this map, clusters of streets were defined to represent type A and type B neighbourhoods. Since our model treats all clusters equally we need empirically to derive

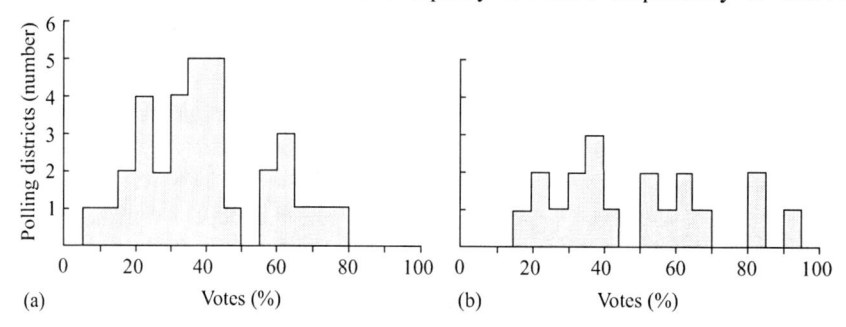

Figure 3.2: Conservative votes in Newcastle polling districts: (a) Newcastle West; (b) Newcastle North

approximately equal-size clusters. This has two effects on our definitions of clusters. First all 'outliers' of streets—that is, one type of street or streets surrounded by the other type—were eliminated as clusters if they consisted of one or two streets only. In fact, in every case these streets were found not to be dissimilar from their neighbours in terms of rateable value, they just happened to fall the other side of the £ 151 arbitrary threshold from neighbouring streets. In no case therefore were genuinely distinctive and separate neighbourhoods eliminated by this procedure.

Second, the large homogeneous areas of like streets had to be broken down into zones of approximately equal size. This was achieved by employing 'natural' barriers such as main roads as boundaries. The resulting definitions of neighbourhoods are to some degree arbitrary and are certainly subjective but they do give a mosaic of residential areas which captures more of the real pattern than use of 'official zones', such as enumeration districts or wards, can possibly do.

The final result is the pattern of 180 neighbourhoods shown in figure 3.3. This is the political mosaic of Newcastle upon Tyne. It is the pattern of voting behaviour upon which the constituency boundaries have to be placed. These boundaries are also shown in figure 3.3. From this map it is possible to estimate the spatial dependency from the contiguity relations of the neighbourhoods. This is done simply by identifying those neighbourhoods which are surrounded to a greater extent by unlike areas than by like areas. There are eleven such areas, so the degree of dependency is estimated as $\alpha = 169/180 = 0.94$.

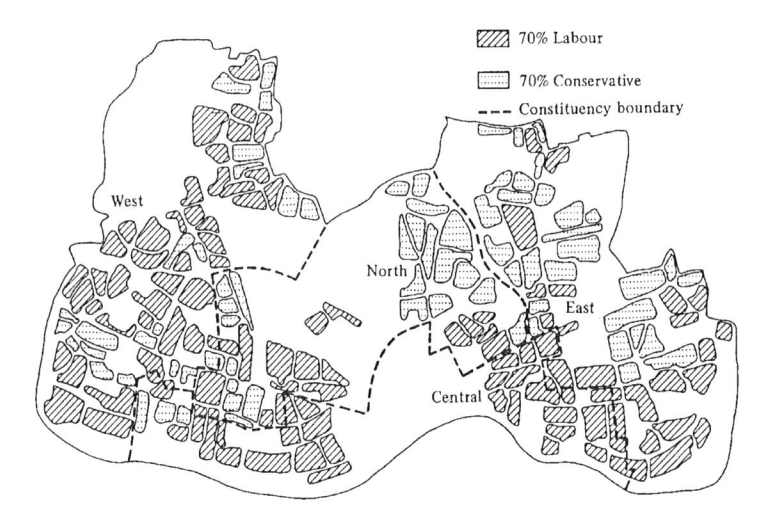

Figure 3.3:   The electoral mosaic of Newcastle upon Tyne

The second necessity is that of estimating the degree of political homogeneity within each type of area. From the election survey, it is possible to assign voters directly to either type A areas or type B areas. The proportion of Conservative voters in type A areas was estimated at 75% (having corrected for the bias due to undercounting of Tory voters), whereas in type B areas the proportion voting Labour was 66%. Since the Markov model requires an equal degree of homogeneity in both types of areas, to maintain its simplicity, it seems reasonable in this case to use a common proportion of 70%.

It is now possible to use this information in the Markov formula to estimate the variance of a CPD which would result from the size, the homogeneity, and the concentration of clusters of voters as observed in Newcastle. Since

$\alpha = 0.94$, $\quad \beta = 0.06 \quad$ and $\quad \varepsilon = (\alpha - \beta) = 0.88$.

Also,

$r = 0.7$, $\quad p = 0.58$, $\quad$ and $\quad q = 0.42$.

(In fact it makes negligible difference whether or not p and q are set at Newcastle levels or are alternatively retained at $p = q = 0.5$ as before.)

Finally, the number of clusters per constituency is $180/4 = 45$. Thus

$$\mathrm{var}(x) = \frac{1}{n}(2r-1)^2 \, pq \, \frac{(1+\varepsilon)}{(1-\varepsilon)} = 0.014.$$

This compares with the variance of 0.019 for the normal distribution underlying the cube law. This slightly lower variance would by itself result in a power-law relationship between seats and votes which had an exponent of 3.3 rather than 3.0 as in the case of the cube law. The correspondence is obviously very close and the results give strong encouragement for the Markov model as an explanation of the cube-law phenomenon. Not all of the British (or any other) electorate is city-based and it seems likely that the stronger clustering in suburban areas and coalfields will tend to increase the variance of the national CPD, that is, will move it in the direction of the observed variance of the national distribution. It is plainly possible to conduct a great deal more research into this question but the results from Newcastle are highly satisfactory.

3.4 The normal distribution as an electoral norm

This empirical illustration of the Markov model is the final element in the argument of this chapter. It is now appropriate to summarise this argument.

1. The basic mechanism behind a normal CPD can be investigated by viewing such distributions as the outcome of probability processes.
2. The binomial method can generate such distributions but gives little insight into the existence of observed levels of variance.

3. The Markov method can generate CPDs with the required variance on the basis of plausible processes.
4. The final model specifies the relationship between size of constituency, size of clusters of voters, homogeneity of clusters, concentration (or spatial autocorrelation) of the clusters, and variance of the CPD.
5. Finally the implications of this modelling need to be reemphasised. The combination of factors which produce the cube-law-like seats–votes relationship depends upon the voting cleavage and the spatial form that it takes, With elections fought as national contests along class lines it is the spatial pattern of social classes which determines the particular seats–votes relationship modelled above. All that is required to produce normal CPDs, however, is that the clusters of voters are significantly smaller than the constituencies, as illustrated for Newcastle upon Tyne. Such clustering of voters is to be expected even where ethnically based voting is the basic cleavage, although the particular form of clusters will obviously vary. Hence the normal distribution can be viewed literally as the norm, or standard, form of CPD for modern plurality elections. The seats–votes relationship which results from this type of CPD is not an arbitrary matter, but is instead a direct reflection of the spatial distribution of voters among constituencies. In conclusion the modelling presented above can be viewed as both an explanation of the cube law and as setting up a standard form against which actual CPDs may be compared. It is this second role which is developed in the subsequent chapters.

chapter four | malapportionment, nonuniform swing, and nonnormality

Although it has been argued that the normal distribution and its associated power laws can be considered standard situations against which actual elections may be compared, this does not imply that normal CPDs are the inevitable result of plurality elections. In fact the cube law has never achieved universal acceptance even for British elections (Butler, 1951; 1952; 1955b). In the context of plurality elections in general, the law has recently come under quite severe criticism from Tufte (1973), on the basis of the seats-votes relationships presented above as figure 1.3. After showing that the cube law only fits one of the six examples he goes on to assert that

"The real theoretical defect of the model, however, is that it hides important political issues. The law implies that the translation of votes into seats is:

(1) unvarying over place and time, and

(2) always 'fair', in the sense that the curve traced out by the law passes through the point (50% votes, 50% seats), and the bias is zero" (Tufte, 1973, page 546).

The truth, of course, is that the cube law, like any other model or theory which attempts to generalise beyond the particular, will only accurately describe reality when its assumptions are satisfied in the particular situation being modelled. It would simply seem to be the case that the cube law's assumptions are badly violated in five of the particular election series which Tufte has chosen to study.

If assumptions are violated then naturally the predictions of the model will be that much less accurate. This is, of course, a matter of degree. No model's assumptions will fit perfectly in any application although if a model is to be useful it is to be expected that its assumptions are approximately met on numerous occasions. Hence an empirical evaluation can be made of a general model by asking two questions about its assumptions: (1) How well do they tend to fit reality? and (2) What effect do observed violations have on the actual predictions of the model? In this chapter a beginning is made towards answering these two questions.

The cube law depends on five major assumptions:

(1) Equal-size-constituency assumption: all constituencies are weighted equally in the model although it is known that there are variations in numbers of voters per constituency in real elections.

(2) Uniform-swing assumption: equal swings are specified for all constituencies irrespective of the level of voting for either party (that is, an increase of $x\%$ in a party's share of the national vote is reflected as an $x\%$ increase in every constituency).

malapportionment, nonuniform swing, and nonnormality | 55

(3) Constituency-proportion-distribution assumption. The cube law relates to the particular frequency distribution specified in chapter 2.
(4) Two-party assumption: the cube law makes no reference to other parties which may distort the relationship between the two main parties.
(5) Constituency-boundary assumption: the probability modelling of the last chapter is based upon arbitrary placement of boundaries around voters with no manipulation of the districting to produce a particular electoral outcome. This latter assumption is clearly related to the CPD assumption since manipulation of districting involves producing a favoured CPD which, as will be shown, typically differs from the CPD underlying the cube law. In the context of the present discussion, however, it is convenient to keep these two assumptions separate and to treat them in different parts of the subsequent argument.

Each of these five assumptions is dealt with in turn and the first three are the subject matter of this chapter. Strangely, given Tufte's criticism above, these topics are dealt with in conjunction with the notion of electoral bias. This is defined simply as the difference between the percentage of votes a party receives and the percentage of seats it wins. It is highly unlikely that a party winning 50% of the vote will win exactly 50% of the seats, as the cube law predicts. However, rather than dismissing the model on these grounds, one can relate this 'error' to the violated assumptions so as to produce an explanation for the bias. Hence this chapter concludes by returning to the law (or rather the CPD upon which it is based) as a standard so as to both measure and understand electoral bias. The view taken here is quite straightforward: the model's idealistic assumptions are inevitably violated in real elections and the effects of such divergences between model and reality are used constructively to further understanding of plurality elections.

4.1 Malapportionment

There will never be an election in which each constituency has exactly the same number of voters. Even if a perfect apportionment were carried out, by the time an election was held the figures upon which the constituencies were based would be out of date. Hence there will also always be malapportionment to some degree.

Malapportionment is an easily understood electoral abuse. If one voter resides in a constituency twice as large as a neighbouring constituency, he may claim that his vote is worth only half that of a voter in the other constituency. For this reason reform of distribution has been a relatively successful activity, especially in the USA after the reapportionment revolution. In chapter 1 this reform of distribution was distinguished from the central concern of this monograph, the reform of representation. This is because reform of distribution deals with the issue of representation at the level of the individual voter whereas representation of aggregates of voters supporting political parties is the prime interest in this research.

Although malapportionment discriminates against individual voters in terms of where they happen to live, it may not necessarily discriminate against one political party or the other. For instance, if both parties win equal proportions of large and small constituencies then malapportionment will not affect the party representation. On the other hand, the distribution problem will be related to party representation where one party tends to win smaller constituencies than its rival. In this situation the party winning smaller constituencies requires fewer votes to gain seats and hence the malapportionment will be reflected in the seats-votes relationship. Therefore malapportionment may affect the balance of parties in parliament and this possibility has not been incorporated in the cube law and related modelling of the last chapter.

4.1.1 The effective party vote proportion

Comparisons between the proportion of seats a party wins and the proportion of votes it receives are based upon overall national aggregates of seats and votes. For any party the proportion of the vote may be obtained by simply adding up its vote in every constituency and dividing by the total vote or, as we deal with here, the total vote cast for the two main parties. As was pointed out in chapter 3, this overall proportion of the vote may not be the same as the mean of the CPD. Where every constituency is the same size the overall vote proportion will equal the average constituency proportion. Furthermore where both parties win equal proportions of seats in constituencies of various sizes the overall vote proportion will again equal the average constituency proportion. Otherwise these two estimates of a party's voting strength will differ. The cube law and other modelling based on CPDs is derived from the latter measure, whereas most seats-votes comparisons will be based upon the overall vote proportion for a party.

Which is the 'correct' measure of a party's voting support? In a sense both measures are correct, depending upon the scale of analysis adopted. Obviously if the national strength of a party is of interest then the figure to use is the overall vote proportion for the party. Plurality elections, however, are not organised as national events but are actually numerous local contests at the constituency scale. The cube law and any other model linking seats to votes in a plurality election is forced to treat the constituency as its basic unit of analysis. Hence within the realms of plurality elections the 'correct', or rather the effective, measure of a party's voting strength is the average constituency proportion of the vote. It is this 'effective' vote for a party which swings along the vote axis with the CPD in the modelling developed in the last chapter.

A simple example will help clarify the argument. Assume a country of ten constituencies with a total of one thousand voters. A perfect apportionment would produce constituencies of one hundred voters each.

If party A received all the votes in six of these constituencies and only these votes, the overall proportion would be 600/1000 = 0.6 and the average constituency proportion would be

$$(1.0 + 1.0 + 1.0 + 1.0 + 1.0 + 1.0 + 0.0 + 0.0 + 0.0 + 0.0)/10 = 0.6 \, .$$

Overall vote proportion equals average constituency proportion as expected. Now assume a redistribution so that party A's territory is apportioned into eight constituencies of seventy-five voters each and the remaining territory has just two constituencies of 200 voters each. This malapportioned situation produces the same overall vote proportion but the average constituency proportion now rises to

$$(1.0 + 1.0 + 1.0 + 1.0 + 1.0 + 1.0 + 1.0 + 1.0 + 0.0 + 0.0)/10 = 0.8 \, .$$

It is this figure of 0.8 which is the *effective* vote for party A, helping them to win eight seats despite an overall vote proportion of only 0.6.

In one study of electoral biases, Soper and Rydon (1958) prefer to use the median rather than the mean of a party's distribution as their measure of 'effective vote'. It is easy to see why this should give so much better prediction results. The median is closer to the mode than the mean and is *not* influenced by the many excess votes in the tail of the distribution. The median may be an adequate solution for simple election-prediction purposes but by ignoring the skewness of the distribution it is of little or no interest in trying to understand electoral bias. The correct measure of central tendency for assessing a party's voting strength among constituencies must be its mean value since it reflects all votes cast and not just the rank order of constituencies.

From the discussion so far it can be concluded that malapportionment may be easily incorporated into the modelling framework developed in chapter 2. All that is required is that the effective vote for a party, the average constituency proportion, is used rather than the overall vote proportion. The discussion need not terminate here, however. What about the difference between the actual proportion and the effective proportion? This must be of interest to reformers of representation since it reflects a bias against one party or the other. In fact the difference between the actual and the effective vote proportions has been used by researchers as a measure of the malapportionment effect on a party (Soper and Rydon, 1958; Brookes, 1959; 1960; Sickels, 1966; Johnston, 1976a; 1976b). In the simple hypothetical example above, for example, the malapportionment effect is a massive +20% for party A since their actual 60% of the vote was worth 80% in winning seats. Another way of interpreting this malapportionment effect is to say that in order to maintain its seat total under a new 'fair' redistribution, party A would need a swing of 20% in their favour.

The use of this measure of malapportionment effect can be illustrated with a very interesting study of US congressional elections by Sickels

(1966). He analysed all congressional elections from 1946 to 1964 for individual states returning ten or more congressmen to Washington. His purpose was to evaluate the importance of the reformers' victories in the reapportionment revolution. By 1966 it was clear that malapportionment was to be largely eliminated in congressional districts. However, Sickels recognised that this victory would be a rather hollow one if, in fact, malapportionment had not been a major cause of party disadvantage in the House of Representatives. He tested this possibility by computing the malapportionment effect for the party which controlled the state legislature when the congressional districts were drawn. The results are shown in table 4.1. In the vast majority of cases malapportionment had a minimal effect on party advantage. He is therefore able to conclude that the malapportionment that existed in congressional districts was not a cause of bias towards one party or the other in the electoral system. If state legislatives were carrying out discriminatory districting during this period they were not using malapportionment as a method for penalising their opponents. Thus with this very simple analysis Sickels is able to show the irrelevance of the reapportionment revolution, at least at the congressional scale, for issues of party representation.

The work of Sickels shows clearly how malapportionment can be evaluated as an electoral abuse in party terms. Although in US congressional elections malapportionment does not seem to have been important in terms of party advantage, the rural-urban differences in constituency sizes in other countries reported in chapter 1 may well result in party advantage in these cases. This is the situation in South Africa (Heard, 1974), for instance, and in Canada (Spafford, 1970). This question will not be pursued further here, however, but will be taken up again in section 4.4, when the importance of malapportionment will be assessed alongside the other elements which contribute to electoral bias.

Table 4.1: Malapportionment effects by states, US House of Representatives: 1946-1964 (after Sickels, 1966)

Malapportionment effect for a party with power to gerrymander	Number of states
− 0.04	0
− 0.03	6
− 0.02	8
− 0.01	30
0.00	90
+ 0.01	43
+ 0.02	22
+ 0.03	12
+ 0.04	5
+ 0.05	0

In the meantime the analysis of CPDs will be based upon the effective vote, the distribution mean, hence avoiding the malapportionment problem.

4.2 Nonuniform swings

The discussion on the seats-votes relationship in chapter 2 was based on the assumption that uniform swings prevailed in all constituencies. Since this assumption, like the equal-size assumption, is not reflected in any real elections, it is important to discover what effect nonuniform swings will have on the working of the power-law model.

The uniform-swing assumption was a valuable aid in the initial investigation of seats and votes since it allowed a change in votes to be treated as a rigid movement of the CPD along the votes axis. As the CPD moved along the axis, successively more of its area, representing numbers of seats, passed the 50% winning post and became transferred from one party to another. If the form of the CPD could be specified reasonably simply, then it was possible to derive a straightforward expression linking change in seats to change in votes. However, if the swing varies from one constituency to another then the *shape* of the distribution will change as well as its position on the axis, and matters are no longer so simple.

4.2.1 Variations in patterns of swing

The 'swing of the pendulum' has long been a popular way of viewing changes from election to election, with television pundits operating a 'swingometer' on election night. However, the concept of the swing has come in for some criticism in recent years. Simple gross measures of changes in votes between parties will typically hide a multitude of different types of change. With survey data these more subtle flows of opinion can be found and Butler and Stokes (1974) describe and illustrate several examples. However, for aggregate analyses such as ours, simple gross measures of change are all that is necessary. Nonetheless one aspect of the debate concerning swing is relevant and needs to be commented upon briefly.

There are several ways in which the gross change in party support at an election can be measured. The Nuffield studies of British elections compute the average of the change in the two major parties' vote as their measure of swing. Such parties' vote is calculated as a proportion of the total votes cast. However, the modelling reported above has been concerned with change in the proportions of the two-party vote only. In this case a gain for one party must be exactly matched by a corresponding loss by the other party so no averaging of the two changes is necessary. Since the change is based on a smaller total vote, two-party swing will inevitably be slightly larger than the overall average swing. For instance between the February and October 1974 British elections, the overall average swing to Labour was 2.2% and the two-party swing was 3.3% (Steed, 1975a). Despite this systematic discrepancy, findings relating to the overall average swing will be used and considered in the light of the two-party modelling. Although the magnitude of the two measures will differ slightly, the *pattern* of the two swings should be almost identical, specifically in terms of variations which are of concern here.

Perfect uniformity of swing in an election would be represented by equal proportionate change in party votes over all constituencies. In this situation every constituency would record the same swing. Deviations from this theoretical ideal will be represented by constituency variations about the overall national swing. This can be measured by the standard deviation of the constituency swing values. When this has been carried out for pairs of modern British elections the standard deviation has been found to be very small, between 1% and 3%. Hence variations in party votes over time are much smaller than variations over space, which, as we have seen, are sometimes up to ten times larger. This national uniformity in terms of electoral change has elucidated much comment concerning the 'nationalisation' of electoral forces in Britain (Stokes, 1967) and the most complete discussion of its causes can be found in Butler and Stokes (1974).

If uniformity of swing is a fact of British elections, what of other countries? Stokes (1967) specifically notes the higher standard deviation of swings for pairs of recent American congressional elections. His British-American comparisons are shown in table 4.2, where we see US standard deviations of just over 5%. We have added further examples to table 4.2. New Zealand elections show a pattern very much like the British examples, while Canada has an extremely high standard deviation even in comparison with the USA. Hence once again we find Britain and New Zealand elections most closely approximating a cube-law assumption and the USA, and Canada in particular, severely violating the assumption.

The importance of these varying levels of violation of the uniform-swing assumption will depend on the relationship between the variations in swing and the party voting. For instance, a situation of no change in

Table 4.2: Swing figures from four countries. Sources: USA and Britain—Stokes (1967), Butler and Stokes (1974); New Zealand and Canada—calculated by authors

Elections	Swing	σ	Elections	Swing	σ
Britain			*USA*		
1945-1950	4.5	3.7	1952–1954	4.3	5.2
1950-1951	0.7	1.4	1954–1956	2.2	5.1
1951-1955	1.8	1.4	1956–1958	6.9	5.5
1955-1959	1.2	2.2	1958–1960	2.7	5.6
1959-1964	3.5	2.4	*New Zealand*		
1964-1966	3.2	1.7	1957–1960	5.0	2.0
1966-1970	4.4	2.1	1963–1966	4.1	2.3
1970-1974	0.9	2.9	1972–1975	8.1	2.9
			Canada		
			1972–1974	8.4	12.3

overall party support could result from a significant loss of votes in critical marginal seats being balanced by a gain in votes in that party's strongholds. A party in this situation would find itself losing seats without any overall loss of votes. On the other hand if swings tended to be of below-average size in marginal seats then a party with an overall positive swing would find its rate of seat capture disappointing in comparison to what could have been achieved by uniform swing of the same aggregate magnitude.

4.2.2 Simple random or linear swing-votes relationships

The modification of the model to include nonuniform swing in fact turns on the relationship between strength of swing and level of support. For relationships which are random or linear, a simple adjustment to the model is possible because the general nature of the CPD does not change for realistic magnitudes of swing. A normal distribution remains normal, for instance, in the face of swings which are either unrelated to party support or else are linearly related to it. What does change is the spread, or variance, of the distribution (as well as its mean of course). Since the relationship between seats and votes based on the normal distribution depends on the variance, the nature of this relationship alters when the variance changes.

The exact effect of random or linearly related swings upon the variance can be obtained by using the 'trick' of viewing the distribution of swings across constituencies as a frequency distribution. In this case the swing is measured as the absolute change in the proportion of the (two-party) vote won by one of the parties (that is, a change from 40% to 50% in one constituency represents a swing of 10%). The CPD for one election can now be seen to be the sum of two distributions, one being the CPD from the preceding election while the other is the swing distribution.

The variance of the sum of two distributions is easily obtained by using the standard statistical expression (the sum of two frequency distributions is obtained by adding term by term, that is, constituency by constituency):

$$\text{var}(a + b) = \text{var}(a) + \text{var}(b) + 2\,\text{cov}(a, b). \qquad (4.1)$$

In the present context a is the CPD from the preceding election, b is the swing distribution, and cov(a, b) is a measure of association between strength of swing and level of support[1].

With the use of this expression to calculate the variance of the new CPD, the latter can now be manipulated exactly as before, that is, as if we were sliding a rigid distribution along the scale of votes. The calculation

---

[1] Cov(a, b) is the covariance of a and b, and is a statistical measure akin to the correlation coefficient; indeed it is an unstandardised correlation coefficient. The expression can be reformulated in terms of the more familiar correlation coefficient denoted here as corr(a, b), that is

$$\text{var}(a + b) = \text{var}(a) + \text{var}(b) + 2[\text{var}(a)]^{1/2}[\text{var}(b)]^{1/2}\text{corr}(a, b) \,.$$

of the seats won can be undertaken by using tables, or by computing the appropriate power law and working directly. As argued in chapter 2, the power exponent is computed most simply (and most accurately in the context of realistically small swings) with the formula

$$k = \frac{1}{(2\pi\sigma^2)^{1/2}} = \frac{1}{2.5071\sigma} = \frac{0.3989}{\sigma} \approx \frac{0.4}{\sigma},$$

where k is the exponent in the power relation

$$\frac{S}{1-S} = \left(\frac{V}{1-V}\right)^k$$

For example if a cube-law distribution ($\sigma^2 = 0.0187$) is altered by nonuniform swings in the form of a swing distribution with a variance of 0.0025[2], with swing unrelated to party strength, then the new CPD has a variance equal to:

$$0.0187 + 0.0025 + (2 \times 0) = 0.0212.$$

The appropriate power exponent is then equal to

$$\frac{0.3989}{0.0212^{1/2}} = \frac{0.3989}{0.1456} = 2.74,$$

that is,

$$\frac{S}{1-S} = \left(\frac{V}{1-V}\right)^{2.74}$$

For random swings, or swings which are linearly related to party strength, the argument is now complete. Given the variance of the CPD of one election, the variance of the swing distribution, and a measure of the relation between strength of swing and level of party support, it is possible to specify the power law appropriate to the following election. This power law will then describe the relationship between the overall (national) swing and the change in seats.

Since the swings are unknown before the event this method does not help much with election prediction (unless realistic assumptions can be made), but then this is not the aim of the exercise. What is gained is a further insight into the mechanics of the process by which votes are translated into seats. Some immediate conclusions can be drawn from equation (4.1). First, if the swings are variable over constituencies, but in a way which is unrelated to the level of party support (that is, swings are random with respect to support), then

$$\text{cov}(a, b) = 0.$$

---

[2] This value is the variance of a distribution of proportion swings, unlike the standard deviations of percentage swings given in table 3.1. This variance is the equivalent of a percentage standard deviation of 5%.

Since variances are always positive (being squares of numbers) and because var(b), the variance of the distribution of swings is not zero[3] by assumption, then in this case the variance of each successive CPD will increase. This in turn means a more spreadout distribution and thus fewer marginal seats. The ratio of seats change to votes change (which is 3.0 under the cube law) will decline, and hence over a period of time the accentuating 'winners' bias of plurality elections will diminish. This is a result which is far from immediately obvious although a little clear thought suffices to show that it is in fact correct.

In Britain (at least until 1974) there has been no consistent tendency for the CPD variance to increase for either major party nor has this been the case in postwar elections in New Zealand. In the USA, however, the variance of the CPD for US congressional elections has shown a long-run tendency to increase (Tufte, 1973), but whether this is due to the process discussed above, or to other effects such as gerrymandering is not currently apparent. It can be noted, though, that with a swing variance typical of US congressional elections (0.0025), it would take only eight elections for a cube law to be transformed into a square law, if there was no relationship between size of swing and prior level of votes. To investigate whether or not this process was occurring we would need to measure the correlations between swing and prior strength for successive elections, and also to have some measure of the effects of gerrymandering. We consider this latter possibility in chapter 5.

In Britain and New Zealand, if there is no tendency for CPD variances to increase, then there must be some counteracting tendency which leads to a *negative* association between swing and prior voting strength. This could be either the effect of a weak process of social mixing or the effect of a growing dominance of national over local communications on electoral matters. In the former case the decline of mining employment in coalfield areas in Britain and the increasing affluence of the working class would lead to the erosion of support in Labour's strongholds. In the latter case if the local pressures which reinforce the locally dominant party allegiance are relatively weakened then once again party strongholds will be eroded.

If the CPD variance remains stable through successive elections, then

$$\text{var}(a + b) = \text{var}(a),$$

which implies

$$\text{var}(b) + 2\,\text{cov}(a, b) = 0 \quad \text{or} \quad \frac{\text{var}(b)}{2} = -\,\text{cov}(a, b).$$

---

[3] A variance of zero would indicate no variation, a uniform swing, whereas we are assuming non-uniform swing.

In Britain the variances of the swing distributions are low (0.0004), and hence a very slight association between swing and voting strength would suffice to maintain a stable CPD variance. The necessary covariance would be −0.0002, giving a correlation coefficient of only −0.07. With the range of swing distribution variances observed in Britain between 1945 and 1970 the required correlation coefficients would range from −0.05 to an exceptional −0.27. If no association were assumed then it would take almost fifty elections for a cube-law situation to be converted to a square-law situation. Because the variance of the swing distribution is so low in Britain, indicating highly nationalised elections, a strong *positive* association would be needed to bring a rapid reduction in the exponent of the seats-votes relationship.

The relationship between swings, seats, and votes, and the questions of social integration and nationalisation of contests are fascinating ones, which it is unfortunately not possible to develop in this study.

4.2.3 Other swing-votes relationships

There may be relationships between swing and level of support which are neither random nor linear. In these cases the shape of the CPD will tend to diverge from normality and it is no longer a simple matter to specify the resulting seats-votes relationship. Some of the most obvious alternative relationships are the following:

(1) Swing increases (or decreases) with level of support at an increasing (or decreasing) rate. Such a nonlinear relationship should be relatively easy to model since there are several well-used functions to describe this situation. However, since the authors are not aware of any actual cases of such swing patterns it is not proposed to develop this type of swing here beyond noting, informally, that such a violation of the uniform-swing assumption will have an effect similar to that on the linear case in increasing the variance of the CPD, though accentuated.

(2) Swings may be lower in marginal constituencies than in other constituencies. This will have a profound effect on the seats-votes relationship, in that fewer seats will change hands. There is evidence that such swings occurred in Britain between the two 1974 elections (Steed, 1975a), resulting in a smaller than expected Labour victory. If this type of swing became a consistent feature of British elections it would obviously negate cube-law predictions and lead to distortions of the normal CPD. However, it is again not proposed to develop an *ad hoc* approach to modelling the seats-votes relationship in this situation without further empirical knowledge of its importance.

(3) The association between swing and level of support may differ between those seats which are held by the party and those which are not. This seems to be the situation to some degree in American congressional elections since 1964 with the increase in so-called 'incumbency voting'. In this situation a party with a swing in its

direction will achieve a higher swing in the seats it already holds but a lower swing in seats held by the other party. Since it is among these latter constituencies that the party expects to win additional seats, it follows that this type of swing will have rather obvious and profound effects on the seats-votes relationship. Quite simply fewer seats will change hands and the CPD will tend towards bimodality. This evidence for such a change in American elections is discussed along with an alternative and possibly complementary explanation in chapter 7.

(4) Finally one type of swing which is common is the regionally differentiated type. If regional differences affect large parts of a country, with high swings in say a quarter of the country and low or intermediate swings in other large sections, then the likelihood is that both parties will be affected. The result is likely to do little to affect an underlying random or linear relationship between swing and support levels.

High or low swings in a relatively small area may have some effect if they are confined to one dominant type of constituency. The 'Enoch Powell effect' in the English West Midlands in 1970 and 1974 affected several marginal constituencies which changed hands and distorted the general relationship. Such cases are relatively rare, however, and can be dealt with as special minor cases (see Taylor and Johnston, 1978).

The arguments of this section can be summarised as follows:

(1) The effect of nonuniform swings on the power-law models depends upon the swing-votes relationship.
(2) Where this relationship is random or linear a simple expression can be derived for a revised variance of the new CPD.
(3) This expression can be used to evaluate the effect of nonuniform swings: in Britain and New Zealand the swings will have no noticeable effect on the CPD whereas larger swing variances in the USA and Canada will have more definite influences but these will be compounded with violations of other assumptions dealt with in the next two chapters.
(4) Other swing-votes relationships are more difficult to model although they may sometimes be treated as special cases.

In all cases nonuniform swing distorts the initial CPD and hence effects the seats-votes relationship. The time has come to consider violations of this basic assumption of the modelling, the normal CPD.

4.3 Nonnormality in constituency proportion distributions

Since the cube law and similar power 'laws' directly reflect normality in the underlying CPDs, it is important to examine the effects of nonnormality in the form of the seats-votes relationship. The general position can be summarised briefly. In the UK and to a lesser extent in New Zealand, and in the USA and South Africa before 1960, the CPDs were all approximately normal in form. None was exactly normal, so deviations from normality will have had some affect on the rate at which vote gains were multiplied into seat gains. More importantly the effects of nonnormality have tended to affect parties differentially. This means that they lead to electoral bias which does not fluctuate with the level of votes, but is a permanent handicap (or asset) to a particular party. This is why nonnormality is closely linked in this chapter with bias. In neither the seats-votes relationship nor bias is the effect of nonnormality very large in Britain and New Zealand. Since the 1950s, the CPDs in South Africa and the USA, however, have become very significantly nonnormal. In these cases (which are discussed in chapter 6), the distortion is so great as to make the normal model, and hence the power laws, inapplicable.

Nonnormality, being a characteristic of the shape of the CPD, naturally reflects the spatial distribution of voters. Hence, much of this section concerns the relationship between the territorial pattern of party support and the degree of electoral bias. The links between the two, that is, the type of nonnormality, is first discussed in theoretical terms.

Any frequency distribution can be described by four basic parameters—mean, variance (or standard deviation), skewness, and kurtosis. The normal distributions, which have been used above as models for CPDs, vary in terms of their mean and standard deviation but have constant degrees of skewness and kurtosis. Hence nonnormality can be measured in two ways—by deviations from a normal distribution's constants in terms of either skewness or kurtosis. The CPD in figure 4.1(a) has a skewness value of +0.30 and a kurtosis value of −0.12, illustrating two independent divergences from normality which is represented by parameter values of zero in each case. Skewness and kurtosis are precisely defined in the subsequent sections, where both concepts are directly related to the partisan and nonpartisan biases. At this stage it is only necessary to understand that they represent two separate types of nonnormality.

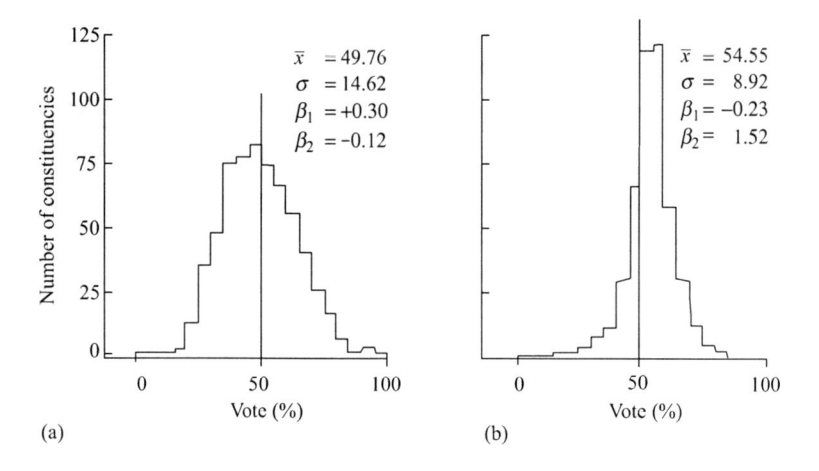

(a) $\bar{x} = 49.76$, $\sigma = 14.62$, $\beta_1 = +0.30$, $\beta_2 = -0.12$

(b) $\bar{x} = 54.55$, $\sigma = 8.92$, $\beta_1 = -0.23$, $\beta_2 = 1.52$

Figure 4.1: *CPDs for (a) Labour Party, 1970; (b) Liberal Party 1906*

The approach adopted in the subsequent discussion is rather informal, relying on diagrams followed by quite extensive empirical illustration. The informal approach will be introduced by briefly considering the effect of variations in the variance of the CPD before nonnormality is specifically treated. Hence the initial discussion repeats previous findings but sets them into an electoral bias framework whereby they link with the ensuing arguments.

Changes in the variance of the normal CPD merely reflect how much the distribution is spread about its mean. This in turn relates to the size of the nonpartisan bias described above. The variance affects the stability of an electoral system where a stable election is defined as one in which a given swing in votes occasions only a relatively small swing in seats. The more stable the election in terms of seats changing hands, the lower the nonpartisan bias. The influence of the variance on the stability of election results depends on the strength of the party under consideration as reflected in its mean constituency vote. The range over which the mean can vary may be partitioned into sections:

(1)	(2)	(3)	(4)	(5)
Variance does not effect bias	Lower variance gives greater stability	Higher variance increases stability	Lower variance gives greater stability	Variance does not effect bias
0		50		100

Mean percentage of vote

With a mean value in the region of 50% [section (3)] a large variance implies that there are fewer seats close to 50%. There are thus fewer 'marginal' seats to change hands with a small swing to either party. A small variance, in contrast, means that a large number of seats will change hands [see figure 4.2(b)]. When the means are more extreme [sections (2) and (4)], the relatively extensive spread of large variance distributions leads to a situation where a small swing causes a larger number of seats to change hands as compared to small variance distributions [figures 4.2(a) and 4.2(c)]. There is also a section of the range where the mean is so extreme [sections (1) and (5)] that none of the constituencies falls on the other side of the 50% threshold.

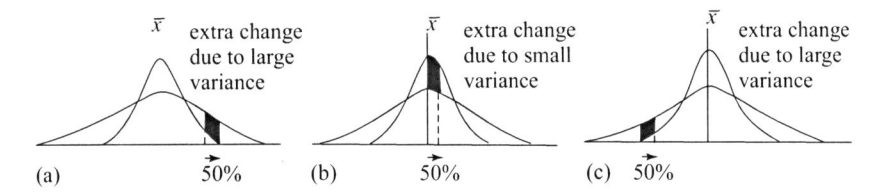

(a) $\bar{x}$ extra change due to large variance — 50%

(b) $\bar{x}$ extra change due to small variance — 50%

(c) $\bar{x}$ extra change due to large variance — 50%

Figure 4.2: Effects of changes in variance on the stability of election results

When the mean is near 50%, a small variance causes a small swing to result in a large number of seats changing hands. For more extreme values of the mean vote proportion, a large variance has this effect. The differences due to variance are shaded black.

A concrete example may clarify the argument above. If an initial mean of 50% for a party is assumed, then the effect of a 1% swing of voters to that party will depend on the variability of the party's voter proportion distribution. There are two extreme cases. Where the standard deviation is a minimum of 0%, an even swing of 1% changes a confused situation with a tie in every constituency into a total victory with one party winning every seat. This is clearly highly unstable. At the other extreme a mean of 50% and a maximum standard deviation of 50% constitutes a distribution where the party wins all the votes in half the seats and no votes in the other half. In this case an even swing of 1%, or indeed of 49%, for or against the party will not change the result from a stalemate. This is clearly a very stable situation. These two particular extremes illustrate the general point that the degree of variability of a voter proportion distribution is directly related to the stability of the election result. All normal distributions, on the other hand, are associated with seats-votes relationships which take the form of power laws (figure 2.9) whereby the exponent is inversely related to the variance. This has previously been derived as

$$k \approx \frac{0.4}{\sigma},$$

so high values of k are associated with instability and high levels of nonpartisan bias (when V is near 50%) and low values of k are associated with stability and low levels of nonpartisan bias.

4.3.1 Nonnormality 1: skewness

The asymmetry of a frequency distribution is measured by its 'skewness'. This measure is based on the third (cubed) moment about the mean and is defined as

$$\beta_1 = \sum \frac{(V_i - \overline{V})^3}{\sigma} \qquad . \tag{4.2}$$

β_1 is zero for any symmetric distribution (including the normal distribution), positive skewness indicates a distribution with the mode to the left of the mean, and negative skewness indicates a distribution with the mode to the right. In the simple two-party situation the CPDs of the two parties are simple mirror images of one another. This means that a positively skewed distribution for one party implies a negatively skewed distribution for the other. Partisan bias is directly related to the level and direction of skewness of a particular voter proportion distribution. This statement can be illustrated with a simple example.

If a mean vote of 50% is assumed, a slightly positively skewed distribution can be seen to be disadvantageous. Large numbers of excess votes are produced in the high tail, with many wasted votes in the large number of constituencies that are lost with just under 50% of the vote [figure 4.3(a)].

malapportionment, nonuniform swing, and nonnormality | 69

On the other hand, with a negatively skewed distribution and a 50% mean the opposite effect results with fewer excess votes in the high tail and fewer wasted votes in close defeats [figure 4.3(b)].

The spatial distribution of voters among constituencies from which these two situations derive is as follows. Positive skewness occurs where the general level of support among constituencies varies about some value below 50% and the mean is boosted by a small number of constituencies where the party has very high levels of support. The negative skewness occurs in the opposite of this pattern with general level of support varying about a value slightly above 50% plus a small number of constituencies where the party is virtually unsupported. This situation seems to fit the patterns of Labour and Conservative support in Britain illustrated in figure 4.1(a).

At this stage it should be emphasised that the partisan effect of skewness is dependent on the mean and variance of the voter proportion distribution. This point can be illustrated by returning to the idea of partitioning the range of mean values, this time between sections in which the effects of skewness differ. The case of negative skewness will be considered first. Five sections of the range of the mean percentage of votes can be identified:

(1)	(2)	(3)	(4)	(5)
No partisan bias	Negative partisan bias	Positive partisan bias	Negative partisan bias	No partisan bias
0		50		100

Mean percentage of vote

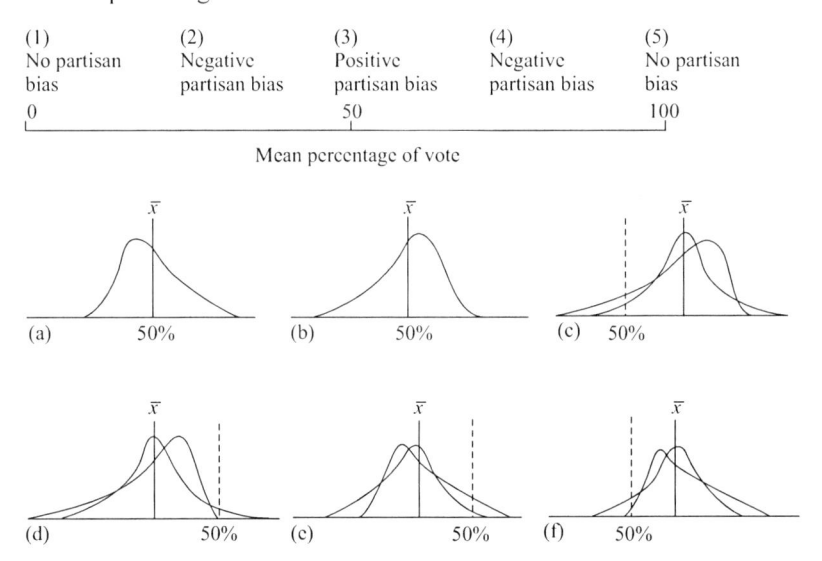

Figure 4.3:   Effects of changes in skewness of the CPD on electoral bias

When the general level of support varies around 50%, a slight positive skewness (a) leads to a large number of votes being wasted, whereas a slight negative skewness (b) means that few votes are wasted in marginal constituencies. Negative skewness can be a disadvantage for both a majority party (c) and a minority party (d). Positive skewness, on the other hand, is an advantage for both majority (e) and minority (f).

Section (3) relates to the situation already described and illustrated in figure 4.3(b). Negative skewness can be a disadvantage for a majority party [section (4)] because the relatively large left-hand tail builds up the number of losing constituencies below 50%. This is illustrated in figure 4.3(c) where we compare the latter case against a symmetrical distribution which produces only nonpartisan bias. For a minority party negative skewness can be a disadvantage [section (2)] because of the small right-hand tail leading to relatively few winning constituencies above 50% [figure 4.3(d)]. At extreme values of the mean [sections (1) and (4)] the skewness can have no effect where a party is winning or losing all the seats in any case.

So far, only the interaction of skewness with the mean has been considered. Differences in variance can be accommodated into the previous discussion by simply noting that the location of the 'boundaries' between the various sections is a function of the level of variance in the distribution. In general, large variances tend to locate the boundaries near the two ends of the range and small variances produce boundaries near to 50%. Thus with small variances sections (1) and (5) can become very large, while with large variances these two sections can disappear.

In the case of positive skewness, the situation is the reverse of the above. The five sections in the range of the mean now have the following effects:

(1)	(2)	(3)	(4)	(5)
No partisan bias	Positive partisan bias	Negative partisan bias	Positive partisan bias	No partisan bias
0		50		100

Mean percentage of vote

The situation for section (3) has previously been described and illustrated in figure 4.3(a), while sections (2) and (4) are illustrated in figures 4.3(e) and 4.3(f) respectively. In these cases the small left-hand tail and the large right-hand tail are found to have distinct advantages. Once again extreme values of the mean can result in no partisan bias in sections (1) and (5). If variance is introduced into the argument, the findings for negative skewness are repeated, with the location of section boundaries depending on the distribution variance.

The electoral bias in the seats-votes relationship with skewed distributions can also be illustrated by the cumulative CPD. This is shown for the positive case in figure 4.4(a). A cumulative standard normal CPD curve is also shown in figure 4.4(b) for comparative purposes. In fact the curve for the skewed distribution produces an asymmetric pattern unlike any previous considered in chapter 2 (figure 2.5). Notice, in particular, that the curve does not pass through the central point at 50%, 50%. In fact this is another way of illustrating the partisan bias. Despite a mean constituency proportion of 50%, in more than half of the constituencies, the party wins less than half of the vote and hence loses. Since the CPD is not symmetrical, however, the argument summarised in figure 2.3(b) (page 17) does not apply and the cumulative CPD does not define the seats-votes curve in this case.

Clearly partisan bias of the sort discussed in the previous section may be directly related to the nonnormality of the party's CPD. It will be shown in section 4.4 that Labour's 1970 CPD [figure 4.1(a)] is positively skewed and that this is directly reflected in the bias against the party as recorded in table 4.9.

4.3.2 Nonnormality 2: kurtosis and bimodality

The kurtosis of a distribution is a general measure of the shape of distribution in terms of peakedness through flatness to a U-shaped pattern. It is defined as

$$\beta_2 = \left[\frac{(V_i - \overline{V})^4}{\sigma^2} \right] - 3 \qquad (4.3)$$

For a normal distribution $\beta_2 = 0$. When $\beta_2 > 0$ the distribution is more 'peaked' than normal (with compensating thick tails) and is said to be leptokurtic. When $\beta_2 < 0$ the distribution is flatter than normal (but with deficiencies in the tails) and is said to be platykurtic. It is thus a measure of the pattern of a distribution about its mean which is independent of the spread as measured by the variance.

The level of kurtosis in a CPD will obviously directly affect the seats-votes relationship since it concerns the central portion of the distribution where seats change hands. It will in some ways have similar types of effects as the variance in terms of electoral stability. This can be easily

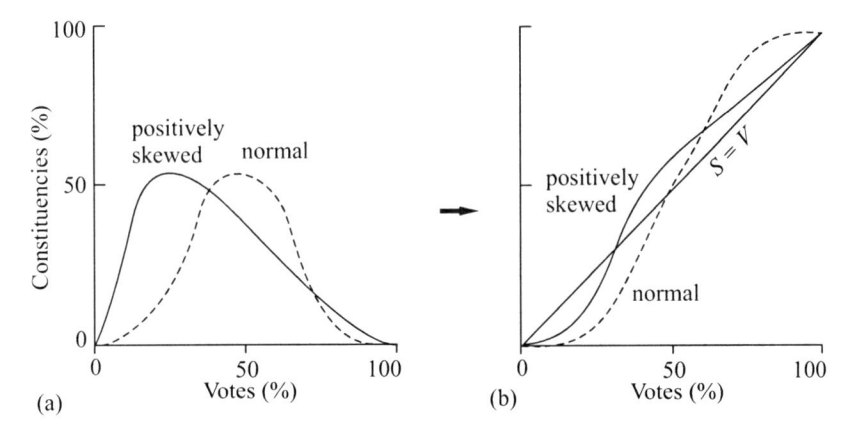

Figure 4.4: Positively skewed CPD (a) and cumulative CPD (b)

illustrated in the case of leptokurtosis. For two CPDs at two elections with the same variance, if one is leptokurtic while the other is normal, the leptokurtic distribution will have more marginal seats and hence be more unstable. Hence this particular nonnormality will produce a seats-votes relationship which is equivalent in some ways to a normal distribution with a lower variance. Platykurtosis will have the opposite effect in counteracting the influence of variance.

In figure 4.1(a) the Labour CPD is almost exactly normal (it is very slightly platykurtic) so instead the kurtosis effect is illustrated in figure 4.1(b). This shows the Liberal CPD for 1906, which has a kurtosis value of +1.52. This nonnormality, coupled with the low variance, produced the highly unstable electoral situation reflected in the Liberal landslide of that year. The contrast between figures 4.1(a) and 4.1(b) is discussed more fully in the next section.

The cumulative CPD for the leptokurtic case may also be used to illustrate the accentuated instability. This is illustrated in figure 4.5 alongside a standard normal CPD with an equivalent level of variance. The excess marginals in the leptokurtic CPD are reflected in the increased steepness of the slope of the curve at its centre. Notice that the excess marginals are balanced by additional safe seats at either end, with fewer constituencies in the middle ranges on either side of the centre.

The platykurtic case has been dealt with in chapter 2 in the discussion of a V-shaped CPD [figures 2.4(d) and 2.5(d)]. In practice this case is of special interest where the platykurtosis reflects a bimodal distribution. All such distributions (including that of the USA) cannot be modelled adequately by power 'laws'. Instead the seats-votes relationship must be derived directly from the CPD. Given any particular CPD it is possible to fit algebraic functions such as to provide a description of the seats-votes relationship although it is not proposed to pursue that line of enquiry here. The most obvious approaches for developing such functions are the

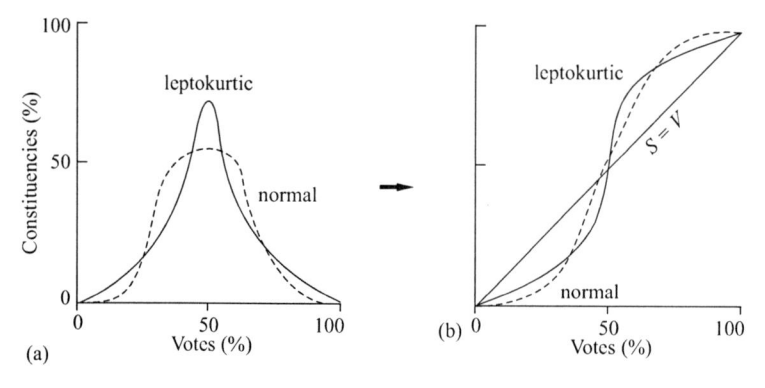

Figure 4.5: Leptokurtic CPD (a) and cumulative CPD (b)

following:

1 A quadratic function could be fitted to the critical central section of the CPD lying between the two modes.

2 It may be possible to treat bimodal distributions as combinations of two unimodal, normal distributions, and if so the seats-votes relationship will be given by the sum of two power laws.

3 A flexible distribution used in other applications is the beta distribution. In this case tables are available once the parameters are estimated. The statistical properties of the distribution are described in Rahman (1968) and the use of the distribution in the present context is outlined by Quandt (1974).

Our treatment of such distributions will be informal, involving empirical description using the kurtosis for New Zealand elections in the next section and discussion of the more extreme US and South African cases in the chapter on decisionmaking in electoral districting.

4.3.3 Empirical studies of constituency proportion distributions

The statistical analysis of CPDs has provided new tools for empirical studies of elections. Hence the aggregate analyses of elections introduced in the last section can now be supplemented by more informative constituency-level analysis. This is illustrated in turn by British and New Zealand elections.

British CPDs

The discussion of statistical parameters of voter proportion distributions suggests a very different treatment of parties depending on whether or not they win approximately half the vote. The empirical analysis begins therefore by informally identifying 'major' and 'minor' parties. The former win approximately half the vote and so are potential government parties whereas the latter win a relatively small proportion of the vote. We shall consider the minor-party case first since the contrasts in types of minor party in British elections have been very great and thus neatly illustrate the relationship between a party's voter proportion distribution and its treatment by the electoral system.

For the analysis of minor-party distributions the party vote will be computed as a proportion of the total vote and uncontested seats treated as either 0% or 100%. Note that this produces a mean value for the distribution which may be quite different from the party's proportion of the overall vote. The existence of uncontested seats is a particular problem for this type of analysis since the overall party vote will not necessarily accurately reflect the party's support in the country. Unfortunately, prediction of a party's vote in constituencies in which it had no candidate leads to all sorts of problems, including having to readjust the votes of parties who did put up candidates. Such modification of the election data requires detailed knowledge of individual constituencies and has not been attempted here. Rather, both a party's overall vote proportion and the mean value of its distribution are used as complementary measures which between them give us a reasonable indication of a party's level of support. Hence the treatment of minor parties is not as rigorous as it could be, but does avoid detailed study of individual constituencies at this stage. Fortunately uncontested seats are much less a problem in recent elections involving major parties, so the subsequent analyses of major parties can be more rigorous.

Minor parties have, by definition, distributions with a low mean value. Since the distribution range is restricted (that is, from 0% to 100%) it follows that a large variance must be accompanied by a relatively high level of positive skewness. Hence the effects of variance and skewness are compounded in the minor-party case. In order to win seats a minor party needs a distribution with a large variance and positive skewness, and with CPDs one reinforces the other. The variance element of this situation will initially be emphasised since this has the most direct interpretation in terms of the spatial pattern of support.

A minor party requires a distribution with a large variance because it can only win seats where its constituency vote is much higher than its overall vote. This large variance will be represented spatially by an uneven pattern of support which may be territorially concentrated. In fact, small parties which represent essentially regional interests are favoured by plurality elections. This can be easily illustrated by contrasting the pre-1920 Irish Nationalist Party with the more recent efforts of the Liberal Party. Figure 4.6(a) shows the distribution of the Irish National Party for the January 1910 election. In this election the Irish Nationalists won eighty-two seats, all but one located in Ireland. This extreme peripheral concentration is reflected in a U-shaped distribution with a very large variance. The nationalists won only 1.9% of the vote, partly because no vote was recorded in the majority of the seats, and where they won they were often unopposed. Thus in this case the mean value of the distribution is a much better indicator of the party's voting strength. In fact with support estimated at approximately 12% of UK votes, the Irish Nationalists won 12% of the seats in Parliament. Such proportionality is to be expected where a party's support is almost totally separate from all other parties' support. Quite simply the party wins all seats and almost all votes in its 'territory' and none elsewhere. This is one situation where a plurality system produces proportional representation. However, it is a limiting case; as a minor party's vote becomes more mixed with other votes its performance declines sharply. Hence this 'PR' type result can be contrasted with treatment of the modern Liberal Party with its nationwide support. Figure 4.6(b) shows the 1970 election distribution of the Liberals. The much smaller variance reflects a more even pattern of support. In this case a mean value of nearly 9% produced only 0.9% of the seats in Parliament. The modern Liberal Party is the classic case of a party that has been badly treated by the plurality electoral system.

malapportionment, nonuniform swing, and nonnormality | 75

This treatment is *not* just because it is a minor party, it is also due to the fact that its support is spread relatively evenly over the whole country. The Liberals are, in a sense, penalised for being a nationwide party. The penalty is large negative biases producing an inability to become a permanent, significant parliamentary force.

The early electoral history of the Labour Party falls somewhat between the extreme concentration of the Irish Nationalists and the nationwide character of the Liberals. The first election which the Labour Party fought in strength was in 1906 when twenty-nine seats were secured, largely because of preelection arrangements with the victorious Liberal Party (Pelling, 1967). In 1909 the Miners' Union joined the Labour Party, thus delivering to the party what was to become a concentrated core of support. This can first be seen in the January 1910 election when Labour's total of seats rose to forty. The CPD in this case [figure 4.6(c)] shows a rather high variance and skewness, although not as large as the Irish Nationalist's parameters for the same election. Thus with 8% of the vote, Labour was able to win 6% of the seats, recording only a small overall negative bias of 2% despite their small proportion of the overall

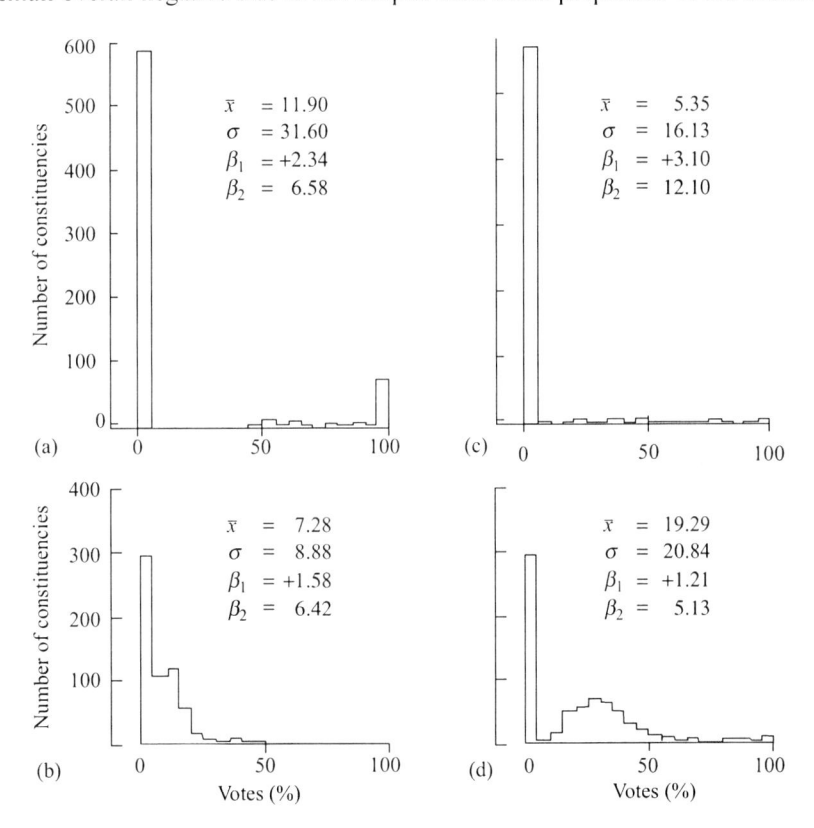

Figure 4.6: CPDs for minor parties: (a) Irish Nationalists, January 1910; (b) Liberals, 1970; (c) Labour, January 1910; (d) Labour, 1918

vote (which is normally associated with large negative nonpartisan bias). The spatial pattern of the constituencies where Labour obtained over 50% of the total vote does not show the extreme concentration of the Irish Nationalists, but does have a distinct clustered pattern. Two types of constituency are represented; the English and Welsh coalfield constituencies and a small number of constituencies that show Labour beginning to win the support of the inner-city working class. It is this concentrated pattern of support in just a few constituencies that enabled a viable Parliamentary Labour Party to develop before the First World War.

The development of the Labour party from minor-party to major-party status represents the changeover in British elections from essentially Conservative-Liberal contests to Conservative-Labour contests. Since the Conservatives appear in both sets of elections it seems plausible to hypothesise that the Labour Party simply displaced the Liberals by taking over their support. This sort of argument is supported by the fact that regions of traditional Liberal support, such as Wales and Scotland, were to become strong Labour areas. However, analysis of the CPDs suggests a very different interpretation. The changeover to Labour represents a change of dominant cleavage reflected in elections. Thus Conservative -Labour contests are different in kind from Conservative-Liberal contests. Resulting differences in pattern of support for the major parties will be directly reflected in the CPDs.

CPDs from both types of election contest (in 1970 and 1906) are shown in figure 4.1. The most noticeable feature of this diagram is the stark contrast between the 1906 and 1970 distributions. The statistical parameters confirm a visual assessment. In 1906 the standard deviation is low and kurtosis high, compared with 1970. This one diagram shows the immediate cause of the Liberal's landslide win in 1906. The narrow, peaked distribution only has to move a little along the votes axis to produce a major changeover of seats. In 1906 the whole peak moved past the 50% point on the two-party vote axis and hence precipitated a landslide. Notice that the Liberals won less than 55% of the two-party vote by constituencies. This simple diagram suggests why the elections before the First World War were such unstable affairs. In contrast, the relative stability of post-1945 elections would seem to require a somewhat higher standard deviation. The 1970 distributions exhibit this property. These two pairs of distributions reflect two different cleavages operating in the British electoral system, rather than a spatial redistribution (relative to constituencies) of the same kinds of supporters.

How typical of their respective types of contest are these two pairs of distributions? To answer this question, the contrasting cleavages need to be illustrated by more than just this single electoral comparison. First, the present cleavage can be considered in a little more detail with analysis of Conservative-Labour contests over seven other elections since 1923. Second, Conservative-Liberal contests are considered in elections where the Liberals have been an electoral force in terms of votes if not seats. Finally, these same elections are considered as if they were Labour-Liberal contests by omitting the Conservative vote. Although there has never actually been all Labour-Liberal contest for government, the results of this analysis are interesting as a prelude to our later consideration of three-party contests. In the subsequent discussions the distributions will not be illustrated but simply represented by their parameters.

Table 4.3 shows the parameters of eight Conservative voter proportion distributions each based on the two-party Conservative-Labour vote. (Standard deviations from table 2.2 are repeated here for completeness.) The eight elections may be viewed as three sets — (1) 1923, 1924, and 1929 when the Liberals were still an electoral force; (2) 1955, 1956, and 1970 from the period when the two main parties dominated elections; and (3) the 1974 elections when the Liberals staged a remarkable revival in terms of votes if not seats. Thus elections under sets (1) and (3) can be viewed more properly as three-party contests and will be analysed as such in chapter 5. However, in all elections studied, Labour and Conservatives *do* win the vast majority of seats so that in terms of parliamentary power they are two-party contests.

To begin with, the middle set of elections of almost complete two-party dominance will be considered. Two features are of particular note. First the kurtosis is very small, indicating very little divergence from normality. Second, however, the distributions are clearly not 'normal' but are negatively skewed, especially in 1955 and 1970. This is the reflection of the Labour Party's positively skewed distribution in these elections, which is part of the legacy of its past. Quite simply Labour strongholds in the coalfield and inner-city constituencies are more numerous than similarly safe Conservative seats. Hence the mean of Labour's distribution is drawn towards this extreme tail of many wasted votes. This is the

Table 4.3: Statistical parameters for Conservative voter proportion distributions (versus Labour)

Election	n^a	$\bar{x}$	σ	β_1	β_2
1923	352	53.09	14.58	0.28	−0.19
1924	427	59.43	13.99	0.12	−0.34
1929	532	51.24	18.01	0.01	−0.69
1955	623	51.61	14.93	−0.29	−0.12
1966	623	45.81	14.60	−0.05	−0.14
1970	623	50.24	14.62	−0.30	−0.12
1974 (February)	623	50.50	16.47	0.03	−0.68
1974 (October)	623	47.21	17.28	−0.06	−0.86

[a] n is number of contests; $\bar{x}$ is constituency mean; σ is standard deviation; β_1 is skewness; β_2 is kurtosis.

classic case of electoral bias due to the form of the voter proportion distribution. In the next section it will be shown that Labour suffered a negative partisan bias in 1955 and 1970 and this skewness property of the distribution is the immediate cause. The effect for 1970 can be clearly seen on figure 4.1 where the mode of the Labour distribution is firmly below the 50% point although the mean is only just below 50% at 49.8%.

This 'built-in' bias against Labour as a major party is a well-known occurrence. For example, Butler (1963, page 196) has written of the 1950 and 1951 elections:

"To secure a majority over the Conservatives the Labour Party needed to get two per cent more of the vote than them, or to put it the other way round, the Conservatives stood to win more seats than the Labour Party even though they polled as much as two per cent—or about 500,000 votes—behind them in the popular poll."

This is the cause of Labour 'losing' the 1951 election as the most popular party in the country. Rydon (1957, page 61) has noted this phenomenon in Australia and New Zealand as well as in Britain and feels that it is "an almost inevitable feature resulting from the concentration of Labour votes in industrial areas". In other words Labour parties are penalised because of the geographical distribution of their support. A similar penalty befell the United Party in South Africa (with important political consequences) in 1948, 1954, and 1958 when they lost elections as the most popular party in the country. Such bias is only 'inevitable' in the context of plurality-type elections, of course.

This asymmetric relationship between the Conservative Party and the Labour Party has not always existed. In the set of 1920s elections the Conservative distribution was positively skew. However, these distributions are based on far fewer contests, with the strongholds of each party not being contested by the other party. This means that the relatively more common safe Labour seats do not appear in these distributions, which only treat constituencies where both parties put up candidates. However, in 1923, in particular, Labour was putting up candidates for the very first time in some constituencies and this is reflected in many Conservative 'safe' seats with respect to Labour, hence producing the negative skewness. By 1929, when there were far more Conservative-Labour contests and the latter party was more established, this skewness disappears.

One very interesting feature of table 4.3 is the similarity between the 1929 distribution and the two 1974 distributions. They combine high standard deviations with hardly any skewness but marked platykurtosis. Thus the 1974 elections are, in this statistical sense, a move back to the position of 1929. The variance is no longer of cube-law proportions and the skewness does not operate against Labour as in 1970. It is noteworthy that in both 1929 and February 1974 Labour gained fewer votes than the Conservatives while winning more seats. What seems to be happening in these 'good' years for the Liberals is that they take a disproportionate number of votes from Labour in the relatively safe Conservative seats (see Steed, 1974, for tactical voting in the February 1974 election by Labour supporters). This has a two-fold effect in terms of the relationship between Labour and Conservative votes. First, it produces more 'very safe' Conservative seats relative to Labour thus balancing Labour's safe seats and producing a symmetric distribution. Second, this increase in 'safe' seats in terms of the two-party vote leads to an increase in variance or standard deviation. The increase in stability in terms of seat turnover implied by the increased variance is supported by the notable decline in kurtosis. However, the reorganisation of the CPDs produced by a good Liberal performance is largely concentrated away from the marginal seats and it is doubtful whether there has been any notable increase in stability for the small swings of vote typical of most electoral changes.

All of the elections from 1923 can be seen in retrospect as Conservative-Labour contests, but this was certainly not so clear to the participants in the 1920s and the Liberals also made a strong bid for parliamentary power in the two 1974 elections. In both these sets of elections the Conservative and Liberal vote can be considered to produce Conservative-Liberal contests in the same way as the 1906 election has already been dealt with. Although the results are in a sense 'artificial' in that Labour votes are ignored, this method should reproduce the character of the Conservative-Liberal political cleavage, especially in the 1920s, which is not so far removed from the 'real' Conservative-Liberal contest of 1906. The results of this exercise are shown in table 4.5 (below) for the Conservative distributions.

The Liberal-Conservative cleavage was reflected in 1906 by a very small standard deviation. This feature is maintained through all the CPDs in table 4.4 and represents a major contrast with table 4.3. Low variance reflects potential instability in Liberal-Conservative contests, which was in fact operative before the First World War. However, there are major changes in the pattern since 1906. Most notably the Conservative distribution has become highly negatively skewed, partly no doubt

Table 4.4: *Statistical parameters for Conservative vote proportion distributions (versus Liberals)*

Election	n	$\bar{x}$	σ	β_1	β_2
1906	478	45.45	8.92	0.23	1.52
1923	367	54.47	10.75	0.21	0.20
1924	269	64.45	11.64	−0.19	0.94
1929	469	58.40	13.16	−0.71	0.75
1974(F)	521	62.76	8.46	−0.93	2.85
1974 (O)	619	66.40	9.50	−0.97	2.93

because of the smallness of the Liberal vote even in these 'good' years. This is the reflection of the Liberals' positive skewness, which is a feature of all minor-party distributions as previously noted. Although values of over +0.9 for skewness are high, this represents a massive decline in skewness since the 1970 election, when it stood at +1.58 with the Liberals as more clearly a minor party.

Another feature of the Liberal-Conservative cleavage pattern is the leptokurtosis which reinforces the low variance in making contests potentially unstable. The high kurtosis value for 1906 is maintained as positive kurtosis throughout all of these elections, with the leptokurtosis feature becoming particularly noticeable in the 1974 elections. We can summarise the present Liberal-Conservative cleavage as being based on the traditional low-variance, leptokurtic CPDs of 1906 which favour the Conservatives as the dominant party in these two-party contests. The new feature of positive skewness of the Liberal distribution is not enough to counteract the low variance to any great degree.

Finally a Labour-Liberal cleavage can be postulated. As noted, there has never been a real Labour-Liberal contest for parliamentary power and in some ways the Liberals may be said to have helped nurture the early Labour Party. However, the 1920s elections and the two 1974 elections can be analysed as Labour-Liberal contests by ignoring the Conservative vote. The results of such an exercise are shown for Labour distributions in table 4.5. There is a further change in the variance of the distributions. In this case the standard deviations are consistently high, rivalled only by the Conservative-Labour contests of 1929 and 1974 in table 4.3. This indicates that there is more polarisation in Labour-Liberal contests than in Liberal-Conservative contests. The high standard deviation indicates that there are areas where one party or the other does relatively very well at the expense of the other. This contrasts with the Liberal-Conservative situation. The consistent negative skewness of the Labour distributions reflects Liberal success in Conservative seats where Labour does particularly poorly. In terms of Liberal-Labour contests the Liberals have more 'safe' seats away from the mean than Labour. Although this feature does illustrate the artificiality of this analysis it does also reflect the possibilities

Table 4.5: Statistical parameters for Labour vote proportion distributions (versus Liberals)

Election	n	$\bar{x}$	σ	β_1,	β_2
1923	300	51.47	16.13	−0.41	0.08
1924	265	52.00	17.97	−0.21	−0.40
1929	470	55.44	18.51	−0.42	−0.73
1974 (F)	521	59.26	16.02	−0.58	−0.05
1974 (O)	619	67.67	16.54	−0.79	0.03

that this analysis is probing. For instance if the Liberals were able to replace the Conservatives as a major party it *is* highly likely that these Conservative constituencies would become relatively safe Liberal seats. What this exercise tells us is that Labour-Liberal contests would be much more like the Conservative-Labour cleavage than the earlier Conservative-Liberal cleavage.

These CPD analyses suggest that it is the Labour Party which is determining the type of cleavage that operates in British elections. This relatively new party is explicitly based on economic-class interests and this forces its opponents, Conservative or Liberal, to likewise become an economic-class party in the pattern of their support. Thus it is incorrect to suggest that the Labour Party simply replaced the Liberals. Despite Labour becoming strong in several traditional Liberal regions, the geographical pattern of support is more locally polarised where Labour is a major party. The geographical pattern of Conservative support, and Liberal support when viewed against Labour, is one of rural and middle-class constituencies to contrast with Labour's hold on urban working-class constituencies and the coalfields.

The discussion so far has dealt with minor and major parties separately, so the Labour Party has been viewed from two different perspectives. This will now be used as the basis for sketching a simple temporal model of the growth of a party from minor-party to major-party status.

The lesson of this section so far is that a party's success depends to some extent on the pattern of its support. It follows that Labour's achievement in moving from minor-party to major-party status was due in part to the geographical distribution of its supporters. This fact can be generalised into a developmental model of electoral bias as follows.

1 A concentrated core of support is the geographical condition for the success of a minor party. Without such a core no minor party can achieve any initial legislative representation. This situation existed for Labour before the First World War and is represented by the January 1910 CPD previously discussed (figure 4.6). At this stage, there is little or no bias and the party wins seats roughly in proportion to votes.

2 The next stage is to spread from these cores and this involves putting up candidates in less certain areas. The result is increasing electoral bias as many more votes are won but these do not produce a return in terms of seats. This is represented for Labour by the 1918 election where they only won sixty seats but, as their distribution shows (figure 4.6), they were beginning to make a much wider impact. From contesting seventy-eight and fifty-nine seats in the two 1910 elections, they jumped to contesting 359 seats in 1918. They were then in a position of having consolidated their core and were attracting support from beyond this core. However, this new support was not concentrated enough or large enough to win many seats at the time. The result was that the party suffered negative electoral bias reflecting these many

wasted votes. In 1918 Labour won 22.2% of the vote but won only 8.5% of the seats, thus recording a large bias of −13.7%. This was the initial penalty Labour had to pay for becoming a national party.

3 Although Labour only won sixty seats in 1918 they were second in seventy-eight seats, so the stage was set for the next step in their emergence. By 1922 Labour was the second party in Parliament, winning 154 seats, including many more working-class urban constituencies to add to the earlier core. From that time onwards Labour has always been a major party. The initial challenge produced a series of three-party election contests which, with the plurality law, tended to give unstable results. This is reflected in the 1920s elections where small swings in votes produced major changes in Parliamentary representation. These elections are analysed more fully in chapter 5.

4 With the return to largely two-party contests the geographical pattern of support again becomes important. Emergence from a concentrated core was an advantage to the minor party but this same core now becomes a disadvantage. This core of support is now represented as the extreme tail in a negatively skewed distribution of constituency proportions as previously shown for 1970 (figure 4.1). This core holds many wasted votes, with the result that the party now typically suffers from partisan electoral bias as has been shown.

This sequence of events is presented as a schematic diagram in figure 4.7. The Labour Party's record from 1910 to 1974 is set alongside this development model for illustrative purposes. From 1945 to 1970 cube-law predictions have been added to illustrate the negative partisan bias for each election except 1970 (see discussion of the distribution effect in the next section).

The developmental model explicitly links the pattern of party support with the emergence of a new party. It is clearly based on just one case study and so it is necessary to ask how general it is. It obviously only relates to parties similar in nature to the British Labour Party. Such parties must have a core of support but must also have an attraction which allows them to spread their support. Clearly, other working-class-based parties have these properties, and Labour Parties in Australia and New Zealand might be expected to have experienced a similar pattern of development. More recently the New Democratic Party in Canada may yet match this pattern. Other types of party will not fit the model. Thus parties representing rural interests will not be able to spread and become 'national' parties. Hence the demise of Social Credit in New Zealand. In Australia the Country Party has had to ally with the Liberals to become an electoral force. The model clearly depends on the type of party being studied. In fact it relates directly to what has become the major modern transformation of electoral politics—the emergence of the economic-class cleavage as the dominant feature of elections (Lipset and Rokkan, 1967).

malapportionment, nonuniform swing, and nonnormality | 83

Recent British elections have seen the rise of a core-periphery cleavage to challenge economic class. The periphery has been represented by Nationalist Parties in Scotland and Wales. These can be treated as minor parties in the way the earlier Irish Nationalists have been previously considered. Clearly, like the Irish Nationalists, they win no electoral support outside their territory and hence may be considered geographically concentrated in support. This allowed them to win more seats in October 1974 than the Liberal Party, which polled far more votes overall in Britain. Hence this is another classic case of the advantages of geographical concentration. However, there is an alternative way of viewing this Nationalist success. If we treat them in terms of just Scottish and Welsh constituencies then an entirely different pattern emerges.

At their own 'national' scale, both the Scottish Nationalist Party (SNP) and Plaid Cymru (PC) become major parties. In table 4.6 they are both treated as major parties in the manner of the previous analyses. Thus SNP is analysed as if it is competing with Labour and Conservatives in Scottish constituencies and PC is treated in the same way for Welsh constituencies. The contrasting pictures emerge. The most obvious difference is in the mean values showing how much stronger the SNP is

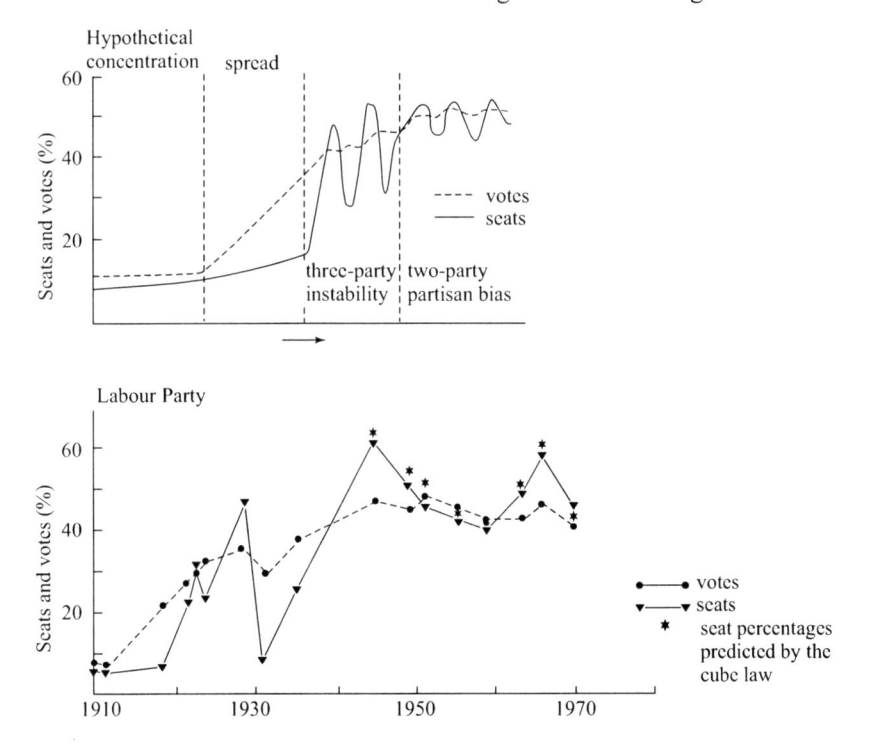

Figure 4.7: A developmental model of electoral biases

compared with PC. However, the differences go further than simple levels of support. The SNP two-party contests produce variance values not unlike cube-law requirements although it is of interest that the variance with Labour is larger than the variance with the Conservatives. This suggests a rather greater degree of separation between supporters of SNP and Labour than between SNP and Conservatives although the difference is not large. It also indicates that within Scotland the SNP's appeal is not evenly successful but varies at a level similar to the two original parties. In this sense it is different in kind from the spatially even, 'nationwide', support pattern of the Liberals in Britain as a whole. In the case of Wales the opposite pattern of two-party contests emerges. PC produce a cube-law-type level of variance with Labour as opponents but their variance with Conservatives is extremely large. This indicates a high degree of separation of support between PC and the Conservatives. In fact PC support is less evenly spread over its territory than that of the SNP. This is consistent with Taylor's (1973) discussion of PC as essentially a cultural defence party in contrast with the SNP's more genuine nationwide credentials.

What this analysis shows is that both nationalist parties have developed with a geographically uneven pattern of support within their territories. This was necessary to win seats. A more even pattern of support (like the Liberals) would be unproductive for an initially small party although such a pattern allows a major party totally to dominate its territory (for example, Irish Nationalists). Both parties are planning to spread out from their major areas of support, but with one or two exceptions (for example, the Outer Hebrides) their cores of support are not as strong as Labour's early constituencies. This means that, on the one hand, they can be more easily removed from Parliament with a small swing against them. On the other hand they will not suffer the electoral bias of Labour if they consolidate and become one of two major parties in future elections in Scotland and Wales.

New Zealand CPDs
The standard deviations for CPDs covering seven recent New Zealand elections were presented in table 2.3 and were briefly discussed in

Table 4.6: Statistical parameters for the nationalist vote proportion distributions, October 1974 election

Contest	n	$\bar{x}$	σ	β_1	β_2
SNP versus Labour	71	47.98	16.27	0.90	−0.15
SNP versus Conservative	71	56.03	14.26	0.10	−0.48
PC versus Labour	36	18.24	14.42	1.50	1.44
PC versus Conservative	36	34.84	24.78	0.52	−0.91

chapters 2 and 3. The other parameters are added in table 4.7. There are two surprising features of this table. First, although the positive skewness expected of Labour Parties is clearly apparent in 1957 when Rydon was writing, there is a definite trend towards increasing negative skewness for Labour. Hence, on the basis of the previous arguments, this Labour Party should have been relatively favoured over recent elections. This can be assessed by using prediction techniques previously developed. The normal model using the actual standard deviations is used in table 4.8. (Actual standard deviations are used to take into account the fact that they are systematically lower than those for the cube-law model.) As expected, the 1957 result reflects the positive skewness of Labour's CPD, and negative residual is recorded. Subsequently the negative skewness has tended to produce a positive residual for Labour as predicted. There are exceptions, however, specifically in 1972. This residual against Labour is recorded in a winning year. Hence both negative biases are recorded in the two years when Labour won the elections. This feature seems to be more important than the changing skewness. It relates to the main component of nonnormality in New Zealand CPDs, the kurtosis.

Table 4.7: *Statistical parameters for Labour vote proportion distributions in New Zealand, 1957–1975*

Election	$\bar{x}$	σ	β_1	β_2
1957	50.9	11.2	+0.22	–0.94
1960	46.3	11.6	+0.06	–0.92
1963	46.7	12.6	–0.00	–0.91
1966	46.8	12.9	–0.17	–0.79
1969	48.0	11.9	–0.18	–0.55
1972	52.6	11.4	–0.23	–0.76
1975	44.3	10.8	–0.32	–0.42

Table 4.8: *Predictions based on a normal distribution and partisan bias, New Zealand Labour Party, 1957–1975*

Election	Actual seat proportion, S	Prediction[a], $\hat{S}$	Residual $(S - \hat{S})$
1957	0.513	0.532	–0.019
1960	0.395	0.377	+0.018
1963	0.408	0.397	+0.011
1966	0.408	0.401	+0.007
1969	0.461	0.433	+0.028
1972	0.563	0.591	–0.028
1975	0.375	0.298	+0.077

[a] Based upon actual standard deviations from tables 2.3 and 4.7.

Table 4.7 shows a consistent pattern of platykurtic CPDs. Such flat distributions imply fewer marginal seats than a normal distribution. This is the reason why Labour tend to do relatively well as a losing party in table 4.8 in comparison with the normal predictions. The bias for Labour merely reflects the platykurtic nature of the CPD. This works against them as a winning party and accounts for the negative bias in 1957 and 1972.

The evidence of tables 4.7 and 4.8 would seem to suggest that for New Zealand CPDs the most important parameter is β_2 and the use of the normal model is now of doubtful validity for New Zealand elections despite earlier suggestions to the contrary (Kendall and Stuart, 1950). This is confirmed by visual inspection of the CPDs in figure 4.8. The platykurtosis is directly reflected in bimodal distributions. An explanation for such CPDs is presented in chapter 6, and figure 4.8 will be discussed in the argument of that chapter.

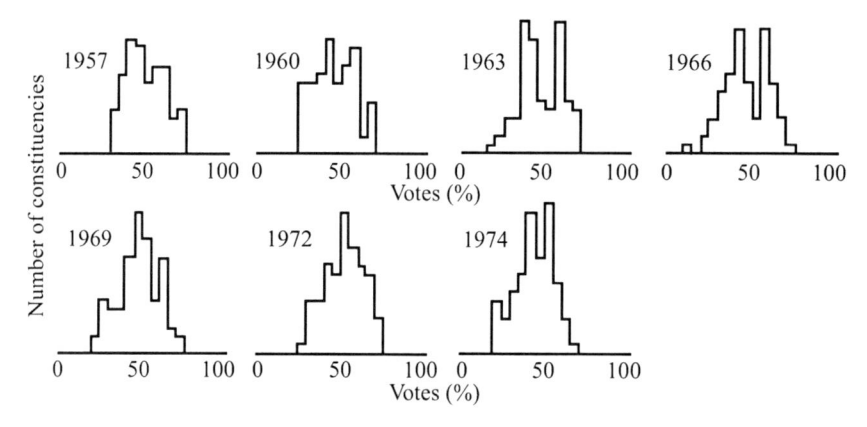

Figure 4.8: CPDs for the Labour Party in New Zealand elections, 1957–1975

4.4 The components of electoral bias

This book is about the seats-votes relationship and in particular the differences that occur between vote proportions and seat proportions for parties. This has been informally defined as electoral bias and has underlain the discussion of much that has gone before. In this final section of the chapter, electoral bias is brought out from the background into the forefront of attention. This can be done because it is now possible to show how each influence on the seats-votes relationship contributes to bias. In other words it is possible to decompose total bias into its constituent parts. [For an alternative algebraic approach see Brookes (1959; 1960) and Johnston (1976a; 1976b).]

First it is necessary formally to define the dependent variable. If the proportion of votes won by a party is denoted as (V) and the proportion of seats as (S) then electoral bias (B) is

$$B = S - V. \tag{4.3}$$

One reason for the difference between S and V will relate simply to whether the party in question wins most votes. Plurality elections typically produce a 'winner's bias'. Such differences may be termed *nonpartisan bias* since they accrue to either party, depending only on who wins most votes. The cube law is a particular case predicting known levels of nonpartisan bias. This is used as a standard here, but any other applicable power 'law' (or alternative symmetric function dependent upon the CPD) would suffice, if the CPD was not that which underlies the cube law. Nonpartisan bias is due to a *distribution effect* in the sense that excess votes of the winning party are distributed in such a way as to ensure a disproportionate share of the seats for that party. This distribution effect was the subject matter of the last chapter. However, this is not the only type of distribution effect. Butler and others have shown that there are partisan biases in addition to the cube-law-based nonpartisan biases. Such partisan biases may be due to the malapportionment effect identified above or there may be a partisan distribution effect. This will occur where one party's votes are distributed among constituencies in such a way that they win fewer seats than their opponents for similar levels of the vote. The most common form of this partisan distribution effect occurs when one party has its support highly concentrated in some areas, as described for left-wing parties above. This obviously produces a large number of wasted votes which contribute nothing to the process of gaining seats. These overlapping relationships may be shown as follows:

$$\underbrace{\underbrace{\text{winner's (or loser's) bias}}_{\text{nonpartisan bias}} + \overbrace{\text{partisan distribution bias}}^{\text{distribution effect}} + \underbrace{\overbrace{\text{malapportionment bias}}^{\text{malapportionment effect}}}_{\text{partisan bias}}}$$

The three individual biases add up to the total electoral bias *(B)*. By measuring each source of bias the relative importance of malapportionment and other causes of bias can be assessed for a given election. A description of how this can be achieved is followed by an application of the method to two British elections.

First the initial malapportionment effect in the election result is identified. This is achieved in the same way as previously described by computing the mean constituency vote proportion, which we can interpret as the predicted vote proportion ($\hat{V}$) under the assumption of no malapportionment. The malapportionment effect (M) then becomes predicted vote ($\hat{V}$) minus actual vote (V), that is

$$M = \hat{V} - V. \tag{4.4}$$

The sign of M is a direct reflection of party advantage, so parties which tend to win large constituencies suffer a negative malapportionment effect.

This leaves the distribution effect *(D)* as

$$D = B - M, \quad (4.5)$$

incorporating both partisan and nonpartisan elements.

The next problem is how to separate the nonpartisan (D_N) and partisan (D_p) elements of *D*. This is achieved by employing the cube law (or equivalent function). In elections for which it is appropriate the cube law gives a clear set of predictions regarding winner's bias so that for any proportion of the vote a proportion of the seats (*S*) can be predicted. Hence if $\hat{S}$ denotes predicted seats nonpartisan bias can be estimated as

$$D_N = \hat{S} - \hat{V}. \quad (4.6)$$

The predicted vote based on equal constituencies is used so that the measure does not compound this nonpartisan effect with malapportionment. D_N is therefore the bias which is expected from the cube law operating in a system of equal-size constituencies, that is, after malapportionment has been taken into account.

Finally the discrepancy between the cube-law prediction and the actual seat result can be used to define the partisan distribution effect. That is,

$$D_p = S - \hat{S}. \quad (4.7)$$

Thus, if a party receives a proportion of the votes of 0.55 with no malapportionment, it expects to win a proportion of 0.65 of the seats but if it gains only 0.60 then the partisan distribution bias would be –0.05; that is, the party receives less than it might expect as the election winner. In this case the total bias is +0.05, made up of a nonpartisan bias of +0.10 counteracted by a partisan bias of –0.05.

The three components of our electoral bias have now been defined. These may be written together as follows:

$$M = \hat{V} - V, \quad D_N = \hat{S} - \hat{V}, \quad \text{and} \quad D_p = S - \hat{S}.$$

This simple set of equations can be easily shown to be consistent with the initial notion of electoral bias as being the sum of these three components:

$$B = D_N + D_p + M \quad (4.8)$$
$$= (\hat{S} - \hat{V}) + (S - \hat{S}) + (\hat{V} - V)$$
$$= S - V.$$

All predictions cancel themselves out and we are left with the original definition of electoral bias.

This approach can be illustrated by analysing two elections in England showing contrasting malapportionment effects. The English Boundary Commissioners reported in 1954 and their districting proposals were used for five elections from 1955 to 1970. In their proposals they purposely made the rural constituencies smaller than urban constituencies by an

malapportionment, nonuniform swing, and nonnormality | 89

average of 4000 voters. This clearly suggests a partisan malapportionment effect for the Conservatives in the 1955 election. However, in the ensuing years it was the inner urban constituencies which lost most population so that by the 1970 election Labour were winning the smaller constituencies (Rowley, 1975a; 1975b). Hence the bias resulting from malapportionment should be reversed for these two elections. An electoral bias analysis on the 1955 and 1970 elections for English constituencies is carried out to illustrate this change and further to put the malapportionment effect into a quantitative perspective alongside other effects.

The electoral-bias analysis for 1955 and 1970 is set out in table 4.9. This table calibrates the bias from the point of view of the Labour Party since this was the overall disadvantaged party at both elections. For the sake of clarity the relevant values can be abstracted from table 4.9 and expressed in the same form as equation (4.8). In both years the Labour Party suffered an overall bias of just over 5%. This can be decomposed as follows:

$$B = D_N + D_P + M$$
$$1955 \ -0.057 = -0.029 -0.019 -0.009$$
$$1970 \ -0.054 = -0.048 -0.008 + 0.002$$

Although the absolute degree of bias was closely similar in the two years, the composition can be seen to have varied widely. In 1970 the nonpartisan effect, which exaggerates a votes gain by cube-law magnitudes, accounted for almost 90% of the overall bias, while in 1955 it accounted for only half. The increase in the level of nonpartisan bias to 1970 reflects the slight change in votes (which was then magnified). The increase in the importance of nonpartisan bias is also due to the declining levels of partisan bias. The malapportionment effect changed in the expected manner from negative to positive, while the partisan distribution effect declined significantly over the period although it remained negative. This indicates the erosion of Labour stronghold constituencies in which thousands of votes had traditionally been wasted. The period was one in

Table 4.9: *Electoral bias with respect to the Labour Party in England, 1955 and 1970*

		1955	1970
V	proportion of the two-party vote	0.481	0.477
S	proportion of seats	0.424	0.423
B	electoral bias	−0.057	−0.054
$\dot{V}$	mean constituency proportion of vote	0.472	0.479
M	malapportionment effect	−0.009	+0.002
D	distribution effect (residual)	−0.048	−0.056
$\dot{S}$	predicted proportion of seats (cube law)	0.443	0.431
D_N	nonpartisan bias	−0.029	−0.048
D_P	partisan distribution effect	−0.019	−0.008

which coalmining declined rapidly in many areas with consequent loss of population and changing occupational structure. Also it was a period which saw a considerable flight of population from the old inner-city areas of the conurbations. In short, concentrations of Labour voters were being dispersed both at the city scale and at the regional scale.

It is ironic to note that the redrawing of constituency boundaries in Britain has traditionally had the effect of restoring the bias against Labour to its maximum levels. The negative malapportionment effect in 1955 was artificially created, and increased the more 'natural' negative, partisan distribution effect. As time goes on, out-migration from Labour constituencies reduces or reverses the malapportionment bias, but after fifteen years or so the Boundary Commissioners step in to restore what time has healed. The irony was especially acute in 1970 when the Labour Government refused to allow redistricting before the impending election in order not to impair its chances of winning. This refusal, which was inadvertently the fair course of action, was roundly condemned by commentators, most of whom presumably did not realise that redistricting has the effect of restoring bias rather than removing it.

This type of decomposition can be conducted for almost any (plurality) election although the equivalent to the cube law may have to be selected with care. In countries where gerrymandering, or other processes, have produced a highly irregular CPD it may not, however, be meaningful to produce a predicted seat proportion on the basis of some simple seats-votes relationship. In South African elections for instance most constituencies are not contested, and a seats-votes relationship is virtually meaningless since hardly any seats are exchanged when there are realistic degrees of swing.

In elections which are applicable, the method provides interesting insights into the nature of the biases inherent in the plurality system. These prove to be more complex than one would guess given the apparent simplicity of the system. Even so, these biases are only those which occur in two-party contests. With more than two parties the scope for bias is greatly increased, and the plurality system on occasion surpasses itself in the erratic way in which it relates seats to votes. Three-party elections are the logical next place to venture in this exploration of plurality elections, but first a brief summary on the status of the cube law in two-party contests.

This chapter can be summarised as follows:

(1) Malapportionment will occur in all elections but its influence may be avoided in modelling (or measured in empirical studies) by using the mean of the CPD as the effective vote.

(2) Nonuniform swings will occur in all elections but where the variation is small and random or linearly related to party support the effect on the CPD is minimal.

(3) Nonnormality in CPDs is reflected in skewness, which produces partisan bias, and kurtosis, which is associated with bimodal distributions leading to highly stable electoral situations.

(4) Finally these effects can be brought together with the normal models of the previous chapter to identify the components of electoral bias within any single election. It is in this final section that the approach adopted here departs most significantly from Tufte's criticism quoted at the beginning of the chapter. Interestingly enough, while he was "disposing of the cube law" as merely British 'political folklore', Taagepera (1973) was asserting that "the cube law has been the only political science law that looks like a physics law". Clearly folklores and physics are incompatible. The view taken here lies between these extremes. Tufte (1973) clearly shows that the cube law does not possess the universality of a physics law—to expect otherwise is naive. It has been shown in this chapter, however, that divergences from model predictions need not be used merely to condemn a model, but may be used constructively to further understanding of the processes involved.

chapter five | three-party elections

One of the most restrictive assumptions of the last two chapters was that elections should be contested by only two parties. It has been shown that the seats–votes relationship in two-party elections can be adequately characterised and accounted for, and the time has now come to widen the discussion to three-party contests. With the exception of the USA, all the countries considered here have well-established minor parties. In the last chapter it was shown, in a nonformal manner, how and why such minor parties fare so badly in plurality elections when it comes to winning seats. However, the only treatment of minor parties so far has been in terms of 'artificial' two-party CPDs. Although the results produced in such exercises may prove interesting, a formal methodology is required to treat multiparty situations as a distinct type of election separate from the simple two-party case.

In this chapter the frequency-distribution approach is retained and extended to deal with three-party elections. To begin with, it should be noted that percentages of party vote can no longer be based upon the two-party vote. In figure 5.1 the CPDs of the four major Canadian parties in 1974 are shown, based upon total (four-party) vote. This change in computation of the party vote means that the 50% winning threshold employed in the previous modelling no longer applies. In figure 5.1 some seats are won in constituencies within all class intervals over 30%. The inapplicability of the 50% winning post means that it is no longer easy to devise a simple function relating seats to votes. Consequently this question is left to appendix 2 where the modern

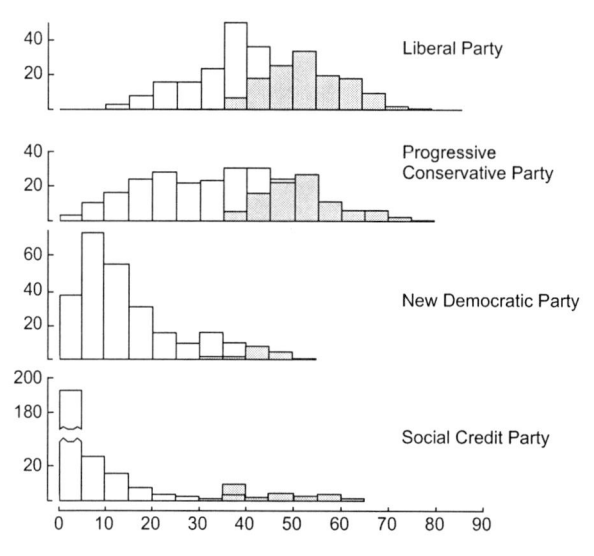

Figure 5.1: CPDs for Canadian parties, 1974. Constituencies won by a party are shaded

Canadian situation is considered further. It is, however, possible to describe the mechanics of the seats–votes relationship in three-party elections. This is the prime aim of this chapter. Although such description naturally helps in the prediction of seats, prediction is not the focus of attention, since the emphasis is on clarity rather than on precision. Empirical application of the approach is presented in the final section, where some predictions are tested but the examples remain illustrative rather than rigorous evaluations.

5.1 The three-party seats-votes relationship and the election triangle

It has been suggested above that three-party contests are far more complicated than 'simple' two-party elections. Although distortions may arise, the dominant effect in two-party elections is one of regularity. The simple world of two parties is not mirrored in the three-party case. With three parties instability is the order of the day, and description of the relationship between seats and votes is consequently a more hazardous undertaking. An example of the extremes which can arise is provided by Canadian elections in the 1930s. Table 5.1 shows how the Liberal Party declined in popularity between 1930 and 1935, with the astonishing result that its proportion of seats rocketed from 37% to over 70%. Three-party elections, it seems, can enter the realms of fantasy, making the bias of the cube (or similar) law seem a very tame affair.

Three-party elections are not always as unstable as in the case above, but they do have unpredictability among their major characteristics. In British elections there have been two periods in which three parties have gained significant proportions of the vote. The first was in the 1920s, coming to a sudden end with the formation of the National Government in 1931. The second has appeared since 1970 with the reemergence of the Liberal Party after over forty years of decline and insignificance. The four elections during the 1920s (table 5.2) saw a steady rise in the Labour share of the vote. This orderly progression was accompanied by an erratic performance in terms of seats. A knowledge of the Labour vote alone gives little guide to the number of seats won. As in the Canadian example, the performance of the other two parties has as much or even more influence on the seats proportion as does a party's own

Table 5.1: *Seats and votes in the Canadian General Elections, 1930 and 1935*

	1930		1935	
	votes (%)	seats (%)	votes (%)	seats (%)
Liberal	45.5	37.1	44.9	70.6
Conservative	48.7	55.9	29.6	16.3
Other parties	5.9	6.9	25.4	13.1

Source: Spafford (1970)

success in terms of votes. The Conservative seats are also unpredictable, declining by 14% between 1922 and 1923 despite a virtually identical share of the popular vote. The simple cube law is of course useless in this context, based as it is on a 50% winning post.

After the UK election of 1931 a long period ensued until 1970 in which elections were essentially two-party affairs. The first and last elections of this period are given in table 5.2, and for each of the two main parties the cube law predicts the outcome in seats reasonably well. The new three-party situation (in England at least) of the 1974 elections has the Liberals running a share of the vote close to 1924 proportions, but with a seat proportion which stubbornly refuses to rise by more than nominal amounts and which resembles the levels of the two-party era more than those of the 1920s. Has the nature of the three-party contest changed after an interlude of half a century or is this another manifestation of three-party instability? Such questions can be answered by constructing election triangles.

Table 5.2: Seats and votes in British three-party elections
Source: Butler and Sloman (1975)

	Labour		Conservative		Liberal	
	votes (%)	seats (%)	votes (%)	seats (%)	votes (%)	seats (%)
Three-party						
1922	29.5	23.1	38.2	56.1	29.1[a]	18.9
1923	30.5	31.1	38.1	42.0	29.6	25.9
1924	33.0	24.6	48.3	68.1	17.6	6.5
1929	37.1	46.8	38.2	42.4	23.4	9.6
Two-party						
1931	30.6	8.4	(67.0[b])	(90.0[b])	0.5	0.7
1970	43.0	45.6	46.4	52.4	7.5	1.0
Three-party						
1974 (F)	37.2	47.1	38.2	47.1	19.3	2.2
1974 (O)	39.6	50.2	36.0	43.6	18.4	2.0
1979	36.9	42.2	43.9	53'4	13.8	1.7

[a] National Liberal plus Liberal; [b] National Government.

5.1.1 Election triangles

The single most important tool in the analysis of three-party elections is the election triangle. This is a simple and effective device, but one which has not seen widespread use in political science[1]. In our context the

---

[1] Since undertaking this research on three-party elections we have become aware of several other suggestions that a triangle should be used, and one other application. Strangely, none of the suggestions or applications have come from mainstream electoral research. Indeed the origin has usually been those with some mathematical training, despite the simplicity of the idea. The earliest suggestion known to us, was made by D Ibbetson in the discussion following the reading of Berrington's paper to the Royal

triangle is a straightforward graph, or system of Cartesian coordinates, as shown in figure 5.2. The triangular shape results from the fact that since the votes of the three parties have to sum to one hundred, only a triangular region of the plane is relevant. The constraint that votes sum to one hundred is the reason why three parties can be depicted on a two-dimensional graph. In other words, there are only two *independent* variables, the votes for the third party are determined by the performance of the other two parties. The scale of votes for the third party bisects the right angle of the triangle. At the origin the third-party scale is at 100%, and the value declines towards the top right-hand corner of the page. Any point on the hypotenuse represents a zero vote for the third party (the vote percentage of the other two parties varies along the hypotenuse, which is equivalent to a single scale for two-party elections).

The result for any constituency can be represented by a point marked in the triangle. The outcome of the contest in each constituency can be read from the graph if the latter is divided into three 'victory regions'. If a constituency lies inside the 'victory region' of party A for instance, then this means that party A wins in that constituency. These regions, drawn in figure 5.3, intersect at the point where each party gains one-third of the vote, and are constructed by drawing lines to the 50% points on the two axes, and back to the midpoint of the hypotenuse.

The triangle is illustrated in figure 5.4 with the Canadian election of 1974. Canadian elections are notoriously difficult to analyse owing to

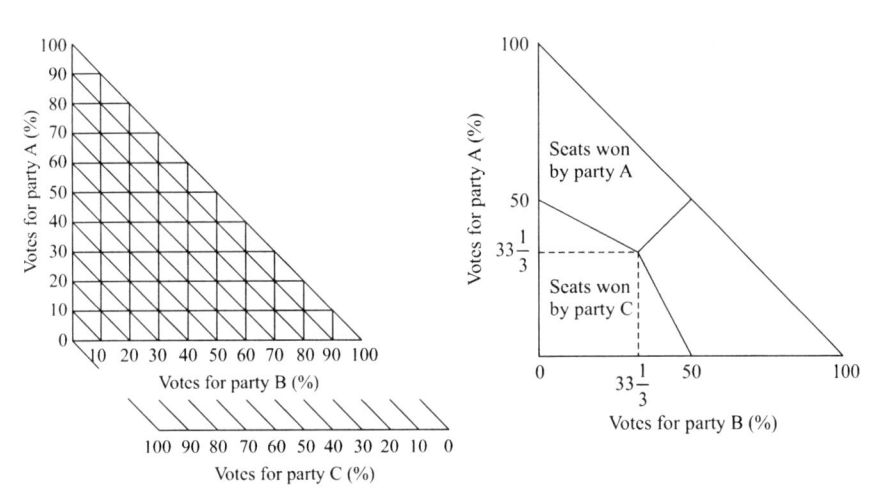

Figure 5.2:   The election triangle

Figure 5.3:   Victory regions of the electoral triangle

Statistical Society in 1964 (Berrington, 1964, page 55). A more recent application is in the context of measuring swing: Upton and Farlie (1974). These and other authors tend to use an equilateral triangle. In our case, however, we have used a right-angled triangle from the beginning, because of the properties of the Cartesian graph, and this has proved a considerable aid in subsequent analysis.

the multiplicity and regionality of parties. In figure 5.4 the votes of each of the three main parties, Liberal, Progressive Conservatives, and New Democrats, are expressed as proportions of the three-party vote. As an added refinement, the seats won by the fourth party, Social Credit, are identified with a distinct symbol. The share of the vote gained by Social Credit is not identified but it can be seen that victories occur in those constituencies in which the Liberals are clearly the second party, and in which the New Democrats pick up only a tiny fraction of the votes. The great diversity of party composition in constituencies partly reflects the strong regional tendencies in Canadian elections, and as a result the points are widely spread across the triangle. The analyses begin, however, by modelling the situation of a third party with an even pattern of support across constituencies; refinements are subsequently made to reflect situations such as that depicted in figure 5.4.

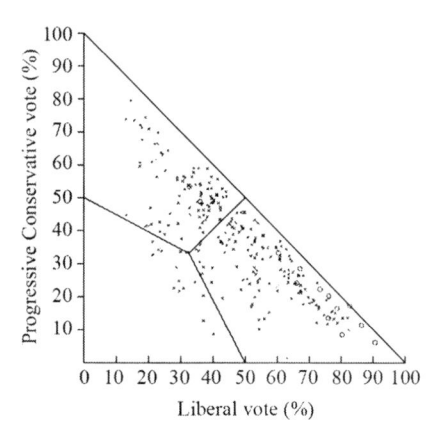

Figure 5.4. The election triangle for Canada, 1974
× constituencies won by Liberals, Progressive Conservatives, or New Democrats;
○ constituencies won by Social Credit; the New Democrat vote increases from 0% at the hypotenuse to 100% at the origin.

5.2 The case of nationally uniform third-party vote

In many ways the simplest of all three-party electoral situations is found where the third-party obtains a uniform proportion of the vote in each constituency. A uniform swing (the absolute difference of the vote proportion between two elections) to (or from) the third party can be depicted on an election triangle as a movement of the two-party CPD perpendicular to the hypotenuse. If at the first election the third party obtains no votes in any constituency, then all constituencies lie along the hypotenuse. A swing of 10% to the third party would result in a movement of each constituency from the hypotenuse to the third party's 10% line (which is parallel to the hypotenuse).

As a starting point a two-party election may be considered. In this case the constituencies form a (one-dimensional) frequency distribution which lies along the hypotenuse. A uniform swing to the third party entails a rigid movement of this distribution in a direction perpendicular to the hypotenuse. (Imagine a frequency distribution cut out of cardboard, and standing vertically on the page on which the triangle is drawn.) As the distribution moves towards the origin, none of its area enters the victory region of party C until 33.3% of the overall vote has been captured. This is the case in which a party which has 33.3% minus one vote in every constituency will win no seats.

The more interesting and less obvious results occur when the 33.3% threshold is passed, and the distribution begins to move into the party C victory region. The technical problem is to calculate what proportion of the area lies within this region. To do this the form of the distribution must of course be specified, and in this chapter the normal distribution which underlies the (two-party) cube law is retained, that is a normal distribution with a standard deviation of 0.137. It is possible to use other distributions, but this is a choice applicable to several electoral situations. The electoral situation being described is thus one in which a two-party contest, adequately described by the cube law, is transformed into a three-party contest by the emergence of a new party with geographically uniform support. The position would be not too unlike that in Britain in the 1970s with the reemergence to prominence of the Liberals, or of New Zealand elections during the postwar period with Social Credit as the third party.

5.2.1 Equal attraction rates

Assume that the cube-law distribution is initially centred at the point (0.5, 0.5) where party A has half the aggregate vote, party B also has half, and party C has none. Also let us begin with the case in which party C attracts votes evenly from parties A and B, which means that the centre of the distribution moves at right angles to the hypotenuse (along line OF on figure A3.1, page 223). To avoid confusion later it should be noted that the direction of movement of the *centre* of the distribution reflects the attraction rate from the other parties, while the relation of the base of the distribution to the hypotenuse reflects the relationship between party C votes in each constituency and the strength of one (or both) of the other parties. The current assumption of spatially uniform swings means no association between the strength of party C and the strength of other parties. The lack of association in turn implies that the base of the distribution remains parallel to the hypotenuse (no matter where the centre of the distribution may be).

The relationship between seats and votes for party C is given by:

$$S_C = \begin{cases} 2\left[\Phi\left(\frac{3V_C - 1}{2\sigma}\right) - 0.5\right], & V_C \geq 0.333, \\ 0, & V_C < 0.333, \end{cases} \quad (5.1)$$

where

S_C is the proportion of the seats and
V_C is the proportion of votes for party C as before,
Φ is the normal integral (values obtained from table 2.1),
$\sigma = 0.137$.

Since votes are attracted equally from the other parties, the attraction of seats is symmetric and the relation for the major parties is simply

$$S_A = S_B = \frac{(1 - S_C)}{2}$$

The derivation of equation (5.1) is described in appendix 3.

The graph of equation (5.1) in figure 5.5 shows that party C gains seats at an extremely rapid rate after attaining the 33.3% threshold. With 37% of the aggregate vote, party C is the single largest party in the parliament, and with 40% enjoys an absolute majority over the combined forces of the other parties. This graph illustrates the extreme delicacy of three-party elections when one of the parties has a very even spread of support. Small fluctuations in the aggregate votes in the range close to 37% lead to wild changes in the distribution of seats.

The degree of instability depends on the degree of spatial uniformity of support for one of the parties. A very high degree of uniformity is improbable in a political system which has a class-based cleavage because of the way in which socioeconomic forces spread the voters, but can arise if the cleavage is not class-based. The British Liberal Party has managed to cross class boundaries in gathering support (perhaps partly because it serves as a vehicle for the protest votes of temporary defectors from the major parties). If this type of support can be maintained beyond the 33.3% threshold then something akin to the situation depicted in figure 5.5 will arise. The Liberal Party may in fact have approached closer to sudden power than is commonly realised since at least one opinion poll showed support running at 30% a mere week before the election of

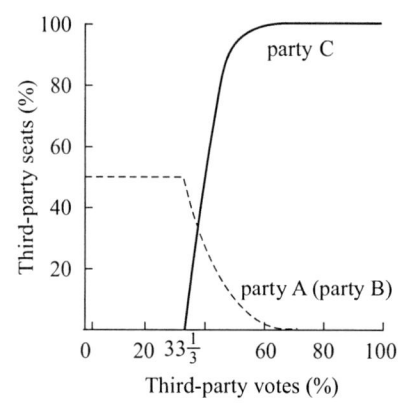

Figure 5.5: The seats–votes relationship for a third party with equal attraction

February 1974 [reported on Independent Television News (ITN), February 1974]. The long-term levels of Liberal support, as reported by the opinion polls, are graphed in figure 5.6. A less probable hypothetical example might be a women's party. If one assumes such a party to be independent of social class the spatial distribution of support might be extremely even. Finally, a similar situation can materialise if a major party in a two-party system splits or collapses in some way which leaves the remaining party with a relatively (even if not absolutely) evenly spread support. This is the situation which underlay the very large fluctuation in party fortunes in the Canadian elections of the 1930s quoted above (table 5.1).

The assumption of exactly uniform support is not realistic given the prevailing nature of politics in plurality systems, and it is important to modify it in the direction of reality. This will be attempted below, but first the question of differential attraction rates will be tackled. The calculation of the seats–votes relationship for differential attraction is much easier if spatially uniform support is assumed for party C. The refinement of nonuniform support can then be applied in similar ways to cases of both equal and unequal attraction.

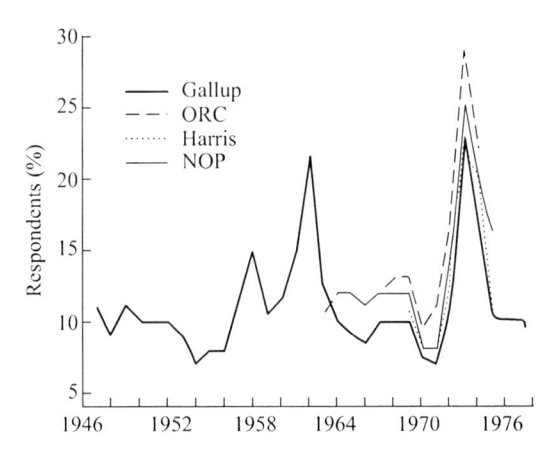

Figure 5.6: Liberal support as measured by opinion polls, 1946–1975. Source: Butler and Sloman (1975)

5.2.2 Unequal attraction rates

Assume that a third party emerges by capturing an equal proportion of the vote in each constituency, but does so while attracting votes differentially from the other two parties. If the third party attracts votes from parties A and B in the ratio 1 : 2 then we can define an attraction ratio as

attraction ratio = smaller attraction rate : larger attraction rate = 1 : 2.

Now consider the following three situations:

	Party A	Party B
Constituency 1	70	30
Constituency 2	50	50
Constituency 3	30	70

If the third party manages to win 45% of the votes in each of the above hypothetical constituencies with an attraction ratio of 1 : 2 from parties A and B, then the third party will take 21% of party A's vote in constituency 1, 30% in constituency 2, and 50% in constituency 3. This means that the conversion of voters from party A (or party B) to the third party (party C) is inversely related to the local strength of party A.

Although this appears an unlikely situation it is not all that unrealistic when it is remembered that, as noted in the last chapter, swings between elections are unexpectedly unrelated to local levels of support, at least in the UK. A swing of 5% away from a party is as likely to occur in a constituency where a party gains 25% of the vote as in one where it gains 75%, despite there being three times as many potential defectors in the latter. The situation in this case can be thought of as an extension of the processes discussed by Butler and Stokes (1974) in the context of uniform swing. A plausible process might be one in which defection to the third party is greatest where local reinforcement of party support is weakest, that is, in constituencies with low levels of initial support. Our purpose is not, however, to argue that such an eventuality is likely to occur. It remains a hypothetical situation, but one where it is nevertheless interesting to investigate the relationship between seats and votes.

The seats–votes equation in this case is given by:

$$S_C = \begin{cases} \Phi\left[\dfrac{(2k+3)V_C - 1}{2\sigma}\right] - \Phi\left[\dfrac{(2k-3)V_C - 1}{2\sigma}\right], & V_C \geq 0.333, \\ 0, & V_C < 0.333, \end{cases} \quad (5.2)$$

where, as before,

S_C, V_C are the aggregate seat and vote proportions won by the third party,

σ is the standard deviation of the two-party CPD of the major party (0.137 in this case),

Φ is the normal integral (from table 2.1),

$k = \tan(\frac{1}{4}\pi -$ attraction ratio).

The derivation of equation (5.2) is described in appendix 4.

The seats–votes relationship is graphed in figure 5.7. The relationships are shown for two parties, the emerging third party (party C) which soon becomes the dominant force, and also for the party (party A) from which fewest votes are attracted. The battle for dominance is a contest between these two parties since the other, formerly major, party becomes eclipsed extremely rapidly as party C gains votes beyond the 33.3% votes threshold. (The seats won by party B can be inferred from figure 5.7. The 1 : 1 line for party A is the best that party B can achieve. Other attraction rates lead to a more steeply declining curve between 33.3% and 50% of votes.)

Several points stand out from the graph. First, an emerging third party gains seats most rapidly by taking votes from the other parties in equal amounts. (As with the case of equal attraction no seats are won with less than a third of the overall vote.) Attraction ratios of less than 1 : 1 lead to a less rapid accumulation of seats, although for ratios greater than 1 : 2 the difference is very slight. However, when votes are drawn very predominantly from only one of the two opposition parties the rate of accumulation of seats is markedly slower. None of this makes a great difference to the point at which absolute or partial majorities are won. An attraction ratio of 1 : 4 gives a majority over all parties at 42.5% of the aggregate vote. This can be compared with just under 40% when the ratio is 1:1, and 50% when it is almost 0:1. If all the votes are drawn from only one party then an absolute majority is technically never reached. Instead a tied two-party contest results.

The point at which party C becomes the single largest party is even less sensitive to the attraction ratio. A ratio of 1 : 1 gives this result at 37.5% of the vote, while a ratio as low as 1 : 4 leads to the same position at 40.5% of the vote. The full effect of attraction ratios on the points at which an absolute majority is won, or largest-party status is reached, is shown in figure 5.8.

All of the results thus far assume an exactly uniform level of support for party C. Before relaxing this assumption a final refinement can be added.

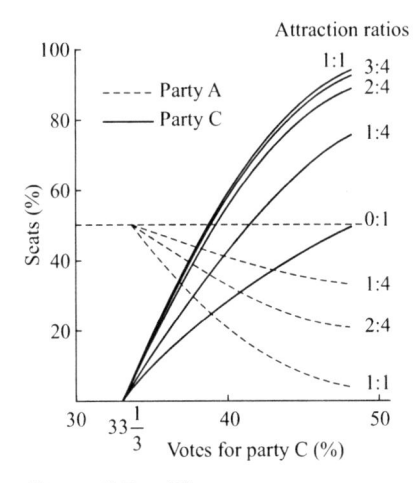

Figure 5.7: The seats–votes relationship for varying attraction rates

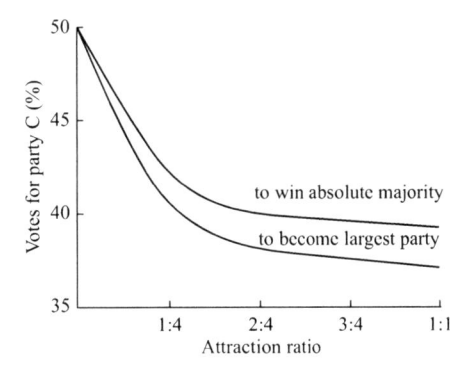

Figure 5.8: Votes required for a third-party to become the largest party and win an absolute majority

The situation in which parties A and B are not equally balanced between themselves results in the following equation:

$$S_C = \frac{+3)V_C - (1-d)}{2\sigma} - \Phi\left[\frac{(2k-3)V_C - (1+d)}{2\sigma}\right], \quad (5.3)$$

where $d = \frac{1}{2}(V_A - V_B)$ and $V_C \geq 0.333$.

The derivation of this equation follows lines similar to those above and will not be included. Unless the difference between the strength of party A and that of party B is large, the conclusions reached above are not significantly affected and no further discussion is necessary. Equation (5.3) gives the most general relationship between seats and votes for a third party with uniform support. To make further progress it is necessary to examine the relationship when support levels are not identical in all constituencies.

5.3 Nonuniform levels of third-party support

There are many ways in which support levels can diverge from the position of strict uniformity in all constituencies. This is the same as saying that there are many, indeed an infinite number, of different possible patterns of support across constituencies. The variety of patterns can, however, be classified into two types. Those in which support for party C is related to the level of support for the other parties, and those in which it is not. Both of these types will be examined in this section, along with some discussion of regional variation in support which may contribute to either of the two types but because of its importance merits specific attention.

5.3.1 Independent variable support for the third party

When support for party C is unrelated to the local strengths of the other parties this implies that party C votes are distributed independently of the strength of the other parties. For any given level of support for parties A and B there will be a range of support levels for party C, although the average must always be the same or else party C support would no longer be independent of the other parties. (This is not strictly true, but is the simplest case in which third-party support is unrelated to the strengths of the other parties.) There is thus a distribution of support levels for party C, and this has the same mean, although not necessarily the same variance, at any level of support for the other parties.

The situation can be illustrated by the 1957 election in New Zealand, shown in figure 5.9. In this case support for the third party (Social Credit) averages out at close to 5% no matter what local vote is achieved by the Labour Party or the National Party. The constituency proportions do vary, however, although the variation is slight in comparison to Canadian elections for instance (figure 5.4). In New Zealand the three-party seats–votes relationship might be quite well approximated by the equations given in previous sections, but a more variable third-party performance would need a modified approach.

Variable third-party support can be modelled within the triangle framework through the use of a two-dimensional frequency distribution. This means that in addition to a distribution parallel to the hypotenuse, there is a distribution perpendicular to the hypotenuse at every point along the one-dimensional CPD. If the frequency distributions were both normal then a three-dimensional representation would be a solid bell-shaped object (either round or elongated) standing up on an election triangle. In the New Zealand case the object is very elongated indeed, resembling a ridge rather than a bell. This is because the variance of distribution for (either of) the two major parties is much greater than the variance of the third-party distribution. The variance of the distribution for Labour in 1957 was for instance 0.013, compared to 0.0005 for Social Credit.

The relationship between seats and votes is obtained by calculating the proportion (volume) of the two-dimensional distribution which lies within the party C victory region for any level of aggregate votes. Although the concept is little different from before, the mathematics of two-dimensional distributions are more complex and it will not usually be possible to provide formulae for the relationship when nonuniform support is assumed. It is, however, possible to construct graphs based on approximate rather than exact methods. (The approximations themselves can be made as accurate as necessary, although the work involved may increase greatly. The construction of figure 5.10 is described in appendix 5.) In doing so below only the case of even attraction ratios will be examined directly.

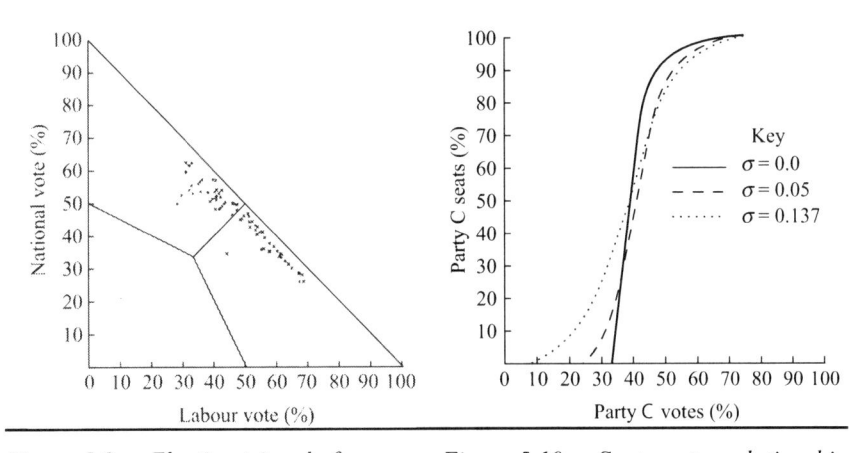

Figure 5.9: Election triangle for New Zealand, 1957. Social Credit vote increases from 0% at the hypotenuse to 100% at the origin

Figure 5.10: Seats–votes relationship for third party with variable levels of support

Uniform levels of support across constituencies for party C result from a CPD for party C which has a standard deviation of zero. The seats–votes relationship consequent upon this was illustrated in figure 5.5 and is repeated in figure 5.10. The other relationships are also shown in figure 5.10 for comparison. One corresponds to a CPD for party C with a standard deviation of 0.05. This implies a relatively even geographical spread of support and in fact 0.05 was chosen because it is close to the standard deviation of the CPD for the British Liberal Party in the 1974 elections. The other case corresponds to a standard deviation of 0.137. This is the variance underlying the cube law, and indicates a geographical spread of support which would be typical of a major party in almost any of the countries discussed in this book. In this case third-party support is as widely spread as support for the major parties, and an actual example approaching this situation would be the three-party system prevailing in Britain in the 1920s. Modern Canadian elections have a third party with widely spread support, and in this case the seats-votes curve would be near the 0.137 curve on figure 5.10.

As will be seen below, this model is not yet as realistic as is feasible, but the previous paragraph is meant to give an indication that in the relationships described in figure 5.10 a close approximation to real electoral situations is being approached. With a CPD standard deviation of 0.05 for example, indicating only moderately varying support, seats begin to be won in significant numbers with 25% of the aggregate vote. These seats are largely those which are marginal between the major parties and in which the third party gains higher than average levels of support. For a third party which is increasing its support over time they would be the vanguard of an incipient army of seats.

After gaining 30% of the total votes the gain in seats becomes very rapid, reaching about 17% with one-third of the vote. The most important difference between completely uniform and moderately varying levels of support is thus the number of seats gained up to 33.3% of the vote. With completely uniform support across constituencies no seats are won below this votes threshold whereas with a moderate spread (CPD standard deviation of 0.05) 17% are gained. In the British parliament this would amount to 108 seats out of 635 and is clearly of significance. The more important thresholds now become 25% of the vote, at which only a handful of seats would be won, and 30%, at which thirty-five seats would be gained in Britain, marking the takeoff point. With more than one-third of the total vote, the number of seats won by party C does not greatly differ between uniform and 'moderately varying' support. In both cases the increase in constituency victories is very rapid indeed, with party C becoming the single largest party at 37% to 38% of the vote and achieving an absolute majority of seats at just under 40%.

When levels of support vary geographically by as much for a third party as for the other parties the seats–votes relationship is that depicted in figure 5.10 for $\sigma = 0.137$. Since a third party cannot simultaneously have a normal CPD and a high standard deviation for very low proportions of the total vote, only the curve above about 25% of the vote is of concern here. With 25% of the vote party C would win under 15% of the seats, rising to one-third of the seats with one-third of the vote. After this momentary point of proportional representation the seats victories accrue fairly rapidly and once again an absolute majority is won with under 40% of the total vote. On the assumption of even attraction from the other parties, party C becomes the largest single party with one-third of the vote, but in this situation with three evenly balanced parties the seats proportions are very unstable. Slight gains or losses of total votes will have very large repercussions in terms of seats. A swing from party C to the major parties (equally) of only 3% could result in change from being marginally the largest single party, to a situation in which party C trailed behind the other parties by over 120 seats (in the case of the British Parliament of 635 seats).

The general points to be drawn from figure 5.10 are the following:

(1) The more geographically variable is the third party's support, the lower is the proportion of the total vote needed to win significant numbers of seats. A geographic spread similar to that of the modern Liberal Party in Britain would begin to win seats at about 25%. With the New Zealand Social Credit Party the figure would be close to 30%.

(2) The more evenly spread is the support for the third party, the more rapidly are seats gained once the initial threshold is passed.

(3) The status of 'single largest party' is reached with a lower proportion of the vote the greater is the geographic spread of support, although the difference is slight: that is, from 33.3% to 38% of the vote over the ranges of geographic spread considered here.

(4) The position of obtaining an absolute majority of seats is reached with close to 40% of total votes, almost irrespective of the degree of geographic spread.

The seats-votes curves in figure 5.10 relate solely to the case where a third party attracts votes evenly from both of its rivals. It is not proposed to construct similar diagrams for attraction ratios other than 1:1, since the form of the relations can be clearly seen through comparing figures 5.7 and 5.10. From figure 5.7 it was noted that attraction ratios as low as 1 : 2 produced curves little different from the case of equal attraction. This will also be true when third-party support levels vary in an independent manner. The 0.05 and 0.137 curves would be slightly less steep if attraction rates were as low as 1 : 2, but this would make only a marginal difference to the points at which largest-party status or an absolute majority is reached. With low attraction rates, reflecting support gathered largely from only one of the rival parties, the difference between the 'uniform support' and 'varying support' relationships will be wider but still not large. The curves for varying support will begin to increase earlier than for uniform support, but will be initially less steep, only converging again as the votes total approaches 50%. None of the conclusions about the effects of differential rates of attraction of votes are materially altered by changing the nature of third-party support from geographically uniform to geographically variable.

5.3.2 Third-party support related to major-party strength

It seems likely on a priori grounds that the level of support for a third party might be related in some way to the strength of one or both of the major parties. The reasons might be that a third party attracts voters from the other parties in proportion to their strength. This will produce a relationship between third-party support and major-party strength as long as the attraction ratio is not equal to 1:1. Alternatively, the local balance of power between the two major parties may have a strong influence on the support of the third party. A third party which has the function of acting mainly as repository for the temporary protest votes from major-party supporters may find its strength lower in constituencies which are marginal between those major parties. In this case the major-party defectors defect less eagerly when there is a strong possibility of thereby delivering the seat to the main rival party. As will be seen below there is evidence that this process occurs in British and New Zealand elections, although not necessarily for the reasons given above. (An alternative explanation of the same phenomena might be tactical voting by major-party supporters in constituencies where their party has no chance of victory.)

A contrasting situation may occur when a third party is not of the protest-vote type. In this case third-party support may be higher in the marginal constituencies of the major parties because in these constituencies the threshold for victory is lower and there is more chance of victory. In these constituencies apathy borne of perpetual defeat is easier to dispel both in party organisations and in individual voters. There is evidence in figure 5.11 that in Canada in 1972 support for the New Democrat Party was strongest where the Liberals and Progressive Conservatives were most evenly matched. Once again the reasons for this pattern of support are not necessarily, those given above. However, the above points do suggest the interesting possibility that the pattern of support for the third party may be used to differentiate those parties which largely attract protest votes from those with a more soundly based support. Other criteria such as temporal fluctuations in total votes for the third party should be capable of the same type of discrimination, and it would be valuable to examine whether the two factors lead to the same conclusion.

There are a potentially large number of ways in which votes for third-party candidates can be related to the strength of one or both of the other parties. The simplest and also probably the most realistic relationships are linear. This means that V_c increases (or decreases) in some fixed proportion with V_A or F_B, with perhaps the addition of a constant percentage of votes as well. This linear form is illustrated by line ab on figure A6.1 (page 228). All constituencies are assumed to lie somewhere along this line, and in this case the vote proportion gained by party C (measured along the party C scale, OF) is low when V_A is high, and conversely is high when V_A is low. The fact that ab is a straight line rather than some other curve reflects the fact that we are hypothesising a linear relationship. The line ab can be described algebraically as

$$V_C = \alpha - \beta V_A,$$

meaning that votes for party C decline in proportion β as votes for party A increase, with the addition of α votes whatever the value of V_A. The constant α gives the value of V_C when V_A is zero.

This section is concerned solely with linear relationships, although other cases would involve little extra difficulty. Even when attention is confined to linear relationships there are still a large number of possibilities. Instead of selecting an arbitrary range for analysis, the method will be outlined in appendix 6, and a particular case derived from the position of the modern Liberal Party in Britain will be analysed in the empirical applications of section 5.4.

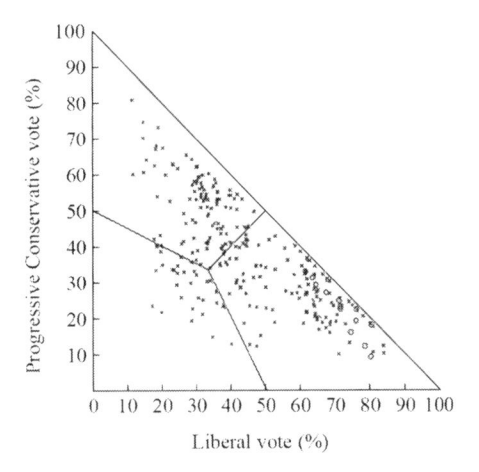

Figure 5.11: Election triangle for Canada, 1972
× constituencies won by Liberals, Progressive Conservatives, or New Democrats;
○ constituencies won by Social Credit; New Democrat vote increases from 0% at the hypotenuse to 100% at the origin.

5.3.3 Regional variation in third-party support

Regionally based minor parties are a relatively common occurrence and it seems appropriate to make some comments on the way in which regional variations in support levels would affect the conclusions reached earlier in this chapter. Since there are a variety of types and degrees of potential variation it is only possible to generalise by taking cases.

A first possibility is that there may be significant but small differences between widely defined areas. As long as these areas include a wide range of constituency types, then the regional differences will usually be lost in the general variation between constituencies. In the British Elections of 1974 there was evidence of generally higher support for the Liberals in the South of England compared with the North. This was partly due to greater support in Conservative-held constituencies, which are proportionately more numerous in the South, but whatever the cause, the result is the triangle shown in figure 5.12 for the October 1974 election. This regional component of the Liberal votes pattern may be taken care of in any analyses incorporating variable and linearly related types of variation.

If the divergence between widely defined regions were to be very marked then two separate clusters of constituencies would emerge on a diagram like figure 5.12 instead of one. Any analysis would then have to treat the regions separately. Examples of marked regional differences are naturally most common when the third party has a nationalist or regionalist complexion. An extreme case was the Irish Nationalist Party in Britain prior to the formation of Eire. Virtually all constituencies in what is now Eire were won by the Irish Nationalists (between 1885 and 1918), most of them unopposed, because of the great majorities which would have accrued to them had any other party decided to contest the seats. Elections in Britain prior to 1922 consisted of two contrasting systems. In Great Britain a two-party contest prevailed in which seats and votes could be adequately related via a power law. These constituencies would be along the hypotenuse of the electoral triangle. Most of the Irish constituencies in contrast would be clustered in the bottom left-hand corner of the triangle. Any sensible analysis of the overall relation between seats and votes in this period would have to treat the two 'regions' separately.

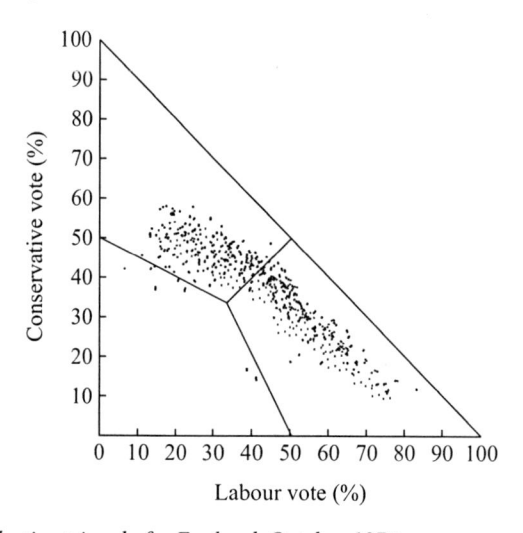

Figure 5.12. Election triangle for England, October 1974.

Variations from the national average which occur in narrowly defined areas can potentially cause different problems since there is less likelihood of a wide range of constituency types occurring within the area. In this case, high (or low) levels of support for the third party may occur in constituencies dominated by only one of the two main parties. Such occurrences can be encompassed within the range of techniques outlined above, depending on the exact nature of the regional variation. One likely case is that where the *variance* of third-party support increases with the strength of the relevant major party. This may occur for nonregional reasons and constitutes a plausible occurrence. The analysis of this case is not undertaken here, but could be worked out along the lines adopted in this chapter.

One final type of regional variation can be dealt with quite simply. This is where a small number of constituencies show extreme levels of support for a third party. In Britain the 'Celtic fringe' areas contain such constituencies. Where the number is very few as in Britain, they are easy to count into the analysis separately.

5.4 Empirical applications

In this section the general approaches of frequency distributions and triangular graphing are applied to elections in Britain and New Zealand. The theoretical modelling of the previous sections has progressed from the simplistic unreal assumption of uniform third-party support through to consideration of a variety of types of nonuniform levels of third-party support. These latter cases enable the theory to be related to actual election results. The purpose of this section is to give an indication of how the methods described above may give insights into the ways in which plurality voting treats political parties in the three-party case.

5.4.1 Three-party elections in Britain

At the beginning of the chapter (in table 5.2) two series of three-party elections in Britain were identified. It was noted that the electoral outcomes were very different, with the Liberals faring far worse in winning seats in the 1974 elections compared with the 1920s. This contrast in third-party fortunes is reflected in the election triangles for the two series of elections as illustrated in figures 5.13 and 5.12 for 1929 and October 1974 respectively. In the 1929 triangle the main feature is the variability or spread of the Liberal vote whereas the October 1974 triangle is notable for the distinctive linear relationship between Liberal and Conservative voting levels. Hence these two sets of elections will be used to illustrate the first two types of nonuniform third-party support identified in the previous section — variable independent support and linearly related third-party support. The third type of nonuniform third-party support, that of regionally based parties, will then be briefly considered by using the Nationalist Parties as the third parties in Scotland and Wales.

The transformation of British elections from largely Liberal–Conservative contests to triangular Liberal–Conservative–Labour contests was extremely rapid. As noted in chapter 4, the burden of contesting most seats as a new force initially meant a large negative bias for Labour, typical of the plurality system, but the split in the Liberal Party aided the transition to major-party status. During most of the 1920s, elections were fought by three large parties, all of which were fully national and bidding seriously for governmental power. This is an unusual occurrence in countries using the plurality system, but with the analysis of this chapter it is possible to treat it as a simple extension of any three-party election.

The development of the three-party system had a strong influence on the spread of support for the three parties. Since the Conservative Party and the Liberal Party had a degree of class-based support previous to the emergence of Labour (which was even more strongly class-based) all three parties had similarly uneven degrees of spread of support across constituencies. In each case the variance of the CPD was similar to that underlying the cube law (0.137). The wide spread of support can be seen in figure 5.13, the election triangle for 1929.

The elections of 1918 and 1922 were complicated by the existence of a national coalition in the former and a serious split in the Liberal Party covering both. The elections of 1923, 1924, and 1929 were truly three-party affairs and in each case the aggregate vote for the three major parties was in excess of 93% of the total. The results of these elections are repeated in table 5.3 alongside predictions derived from the graph in figure 5.10 for $\sigma = 0.137$. The predictions are crude ones based on the assumption of evenly balanced major parties which is built into figure 5.10. A more serious analysis would develop the model further to allow for unevenly balanced major parties. In addition no account is taken of

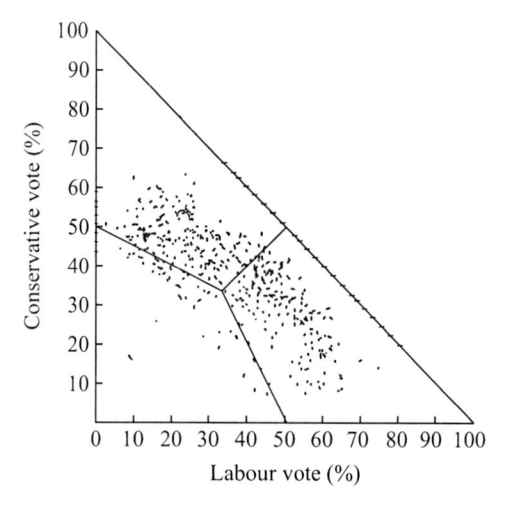

Figure 5.13: Election triangle for Britain, 1929; Liberal vote increases from 0% at the hypotenuse to 100% at the origin

differences between parties in total numbers of candidates, of unopposed returns, or of the complex variations in types of two-party constituency contest. Despite these apparently overwhelming difficulties the model predicts the third-party (Liberal) seat proportion tolerably well, with an average discrepancy between observed and predicted seat proportions of 1.8%. The reasons for this are that the variances of the CPDs are well approximated, and the imbalance between major parties has little effect on third-party seats within the narrow ranges experienced in these elections. Also, uncontested seats were normally those in which there was little chance of victory, and hence these have little direct effect on the seats–votes relationship within narrow ranges of vote changes. Differences in total numbers of candidates do, however, affect the total vote percentages, and this will have introduced some error into the predictions. This point is discussed in appendix 2.

The relationship between Liberal votes and Liberal seats can be obtained from figure 5.10. The decline in votes of 11.9% between 1923 and 1924 was accentuated to 18.8% in terms of seats, an exaggeration effect of approximately one and one-half. This occurs because the slope of the line (for $\sigma = 0.137$) in figure 5.10 is approximately 1.5 in the relevant range. The subsequent recovery in votes of 5.8% up to 1929 was only met with an equal (5.7%) recovery in seats. The multiplier in this case was unity and not one and one-half. The reason once again can be seen from the graph, which has a slope of approximately one in the votes range 17% to 24%. The plurality system treated the Liberals unfairly, exaggerating their decline but not their recovery. The underlying reasons were of course the mechanisms underlying the seats–votes relationship, namely the combination of the rules of the plurality system, and the degree of spread of support for the three parties across constituencies.

The seat predictions for the Labour Party and the Conservative Party are included in table 5.3 but only for the sake of completeness. They are not serious predictions because for figure 5.10 evenly balanced major

Table 5.3: Three-party elections in Britain, 1923–1929
Source: Butler and Sloman (1975); predictions are from figure 5.10.

Year	Party	Votes (%)	Seats (%)	Predicted seats (%)
1923	Conservative	38.1	42.0	(47.0)
	Labour	30.5	31.1	(25.0)
	Liberal	29.5	25.9	22.5
1924	Conservative	48.3	68.1	(78.0)
	Labour	33.0	24.6	(33.0)
	Liberal	17.6	6.5	6.0
1929	Conservative	38.2	42.3	(47.0)
	Labour	37.1	46.8	(44.6)
	Liberal	23.4	9.6	11.0

parties were assumed, which was not the case except in 1929 (when the best prediction is obtained). The percentages do not necessarily even sum to one hundred, and the deviation from a sum of 100% increases with the difference between major parties in votes percentage. Reasonable prediction of Conservative and Labour seats would require a modification of the model, which has not been undertaken here. The *general* nature of the seats–votes relationship for major parties in the 1920s can, however, be inferred from the analysis of this chapter. The accentuation in seats for any change in percentage of votes is maximised if the major parties remain equally balanced, but is lowered only slightly if the performance of these parties diverges. From figure 5.10 it can be seen that the maximum slope of the line (for $\sigma = 0.137$) is approximately 2.5, and this maximum operates throughout the range in vote percentages from 30% to 50%. Between 1923 and 1929, the changes in Conservative and Labour proportions of the vote were both accentuated by about this proportion. The Conservative change was negligible, but Labour increased its vote by 6.6% and its seats by 15.7%, that is, by a multiple of 2.4 times the change in votes. The changes between 1923 and 1924 cannot be explained in this way, principally because of the great changes in numbers of candidates fielded by the parties, and in particular the slump in number of Liberal candidates. It would be a simple matter to make allowance for potential votes in uncontested seats to improve the predictions but this is not the principle concern here and has not been done.

Analyses employing figure 5.10 assume that the level of support for the third party is independent of support for one or both of the major parties. This is clearly not the case in figure 5.12 for October 1974. The salient characteristics of this distribution are that:

(a) The Liberal vote is unrelated to Labour strength in those constituencies won by Labour, and the distribution of the Liberal proportions has a low standard deviation of only about 0.05.

(b) In constituencies won by the Conservative Party (or in which the Conservatives were second to the Liberals), the Liberal vote increases with Conservative strength. The relationship can be described as approximately

$$V_{lib} = \alpha + \tfrac{2}{3}(1 - V_{lab}),$$

where α is the average Liberal vote proportion in Labour-held constituencies minus 0.33. In the October 1974 election α was approximately -0.15. Also the standard deviation of the distribution of Liberal votes is higher in Conservative-held constituencies, being close to 0.09.

It is necessary to calculate the seats–votes relationship for the Liberals in two separate exercises, one for seats in which Labour dominates the

Conservatives and one for the converse of this. The two results can then be combined to obtain an overall relationship for the Liberals[2].

The seats–votes relationship depicted in figure 5.14 is based on the October 1974 election in England. The calculations assume the variance values outlined above, and also assume that the Labour Party and the Conservative Party each would have exactly half of the seats when the Liberal vote is small (say less than 10%). These magnitudes are all close to the real values; they are approximated and not exact, since the purpose is illustration rather than precise prediction. Nevertheless the relationships shown on figure 5.14 are likely to be good guides to the position currently prevailing in England.

The graph shows that the Liberals will begin to win seats with around 15% of the total votes. In actuality a handful of extreme results, partly

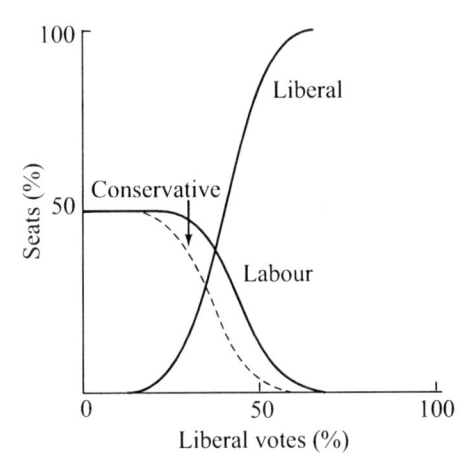

Figure 5.14: The seats-votes relationship based on the English election of October 1974

[2] The determination of the average Liberal vote in Conservative-held seats needs some mention here. On the assumption of an even initial division of seats between Labour and Conservatives, the Liberal vote proportion V_{lib} is an average of the vote in Labour-held seats and in Conservative-held seats. In the latter case there is half of a normal distribution lying along the line $V_{lib} = \alpha + \frac{2}{3}(1 - V_{lab})$. The mean in this dimension is taken as

$$\int_0^3 z \exp\left(-\tfrac{1}{2}z^2\right) dz = 1 - \exp\left(-\tfrac{9}{2}\right) = 0.99 \approx 1.0,$$

that is, the mean value lies at approximately one standard deviation (0.09) along the line $V_{lib} = \alpha + \frac{2}{3}(1 - V_{lab})$ from the dividing line between Labour and Conservative victories. This value of 0.09 allows us to establish where this mean lies along the V_{lib} axis. If the intersection between $V_{lib} = \alpha + \frac{2}{3}(1 - V_{lab})$ and this dividing line is designated δ then this is also the average Liberal vote in Labour-held seats, that is, it is the point where the long axes of the two bivariate half-distributions meet. Using Pythagorean theorem the mean vote in Conservative seats is δ + 0.05 along the V_{lib} scale. V_{lib} itself is the average from the Labour-held and the Conservative-held seats respectively, that is, $V_{lib} = \frac{1}{2}(2\delta + 0.05) = \delta + 0.025$. Hence for any value of V_{lib} the mean Liberal vote is $V_{lib} + 0.025$ in Conservative-held seats and is $V_{lib} - 0.025$ in Labour-held seats.

in the 'Celtic fringe' of Devon and Cornwall mean that a few seats are won with less than 15% of the votes. The model used here is not designed to take account of these unusual cases, and they make very little difference to the overall relationship. The gain in seats becomes very rapid after 25% of the total votes are won. This gain is chiefly at the expense of the Conservative Party, and the Liberals would replace the latter as main opposition party with 34.5% of the total vote. At this point where all three parties are fairly evenly matched *in votes* the division of *seats* would be:

    Labour 44%,   Liberal 28%,   Conservative 28%.

As usual in three-party elections the division of seats would be very unstable. A further small Liberal gain in total votes, bringing the party up to 37%, would lead to the Liberals replacing Labour as the largest single party. The Conservative Party would at this point be reduced to only 22.5% of the seats. At 40% of the vote the Liberals would have an absolute majority over both parties. Labour would form the main opposition with a third of the seats and a much-reduced Conservative Party would retain only the status of a minor party.

In all of this discussion of 1974 the figures have referred only to England. In Scotland, Wales, and Northern Ireland the third parties tend not to be the Liberals and separate analyses are necessary. If the simple, although rather unrealistic, assumption that the electoral situation in these countries remained unchanged from that in October 1974 is made, then there would be approximately an extra 10% of seats for Labour, 5% for the Conservatives, and less than 1% for the Liberals. This would entail a somewhat wider gap between the Labour and Conservative curves on figure 5.14, and also a small shift to the right for the Liberal curve. Since over 80% of the constituencies are in England, however, most of the above conclusions would be applicable to Britain as well as England. The points at which the curves intersect would be placed a little further to the right but the differences would be small.

A more philosophical question is whether a relationship like that in figure 5.14 is of any predictive value. This would entail assuming such things as a continuing small geographical variation in Liberal support as Liberal votes increased, and fixed relationships between Liberal strength and Labour strength and between the Liberals and Conservatives. There is scope for much argument on these points, but as an indication of what might have happened in 1974, figure 5.14 probably has a good deal of validity. The graph of Liberal support over time (figure 5.6) shows that Liberal support is by no means always consigned to the regions of great negative bias with under 20% of the total vote. A continuation in the surge of popularity seen at the beginning of 1974, instead of the fallback which has occurred, would have left a very different political position in Britain from that which actually exists today. Whatever the situation, however, the techniques outlined above permit insights to be gained into the seats–votes relationship. The assumptions used above are illustrative, but others more appropriate perhaps to existing or changing circumstances can be built in.

The analysis of the two contrasting three-party situations in the 1920s and 1974 allows an answer to be given to the query posited at the beginning of this chapter—has the nature of the three-party contest changed after an interlude of half a century? The answer most definitely seems to be yes. The Liberal Party has been transformed from a situation with support which was highly variable over constituencies and unrelated to the strength of other parties to one with relatively uniform levels of support linearly related to the Conservative vote (in Conservative-held seats).

As mentioned previously, regional third parties are represented in an extreme form by Irish Nationalist parties before 1921. However, the newest phenomenon of British elections is the return of nationalist parties as a force to be reckoned with despite the considerable setback of 1979. The most important has been the Scottish Nationalist Party (SNP), emerging by February 1974 to a position in Scotland similar to that of the Liberals nationally. The traditional bias against minor parties with fairly uniform support (in this case within Scotland) was avoided for two reasons. First the SNP have a marked tendency to gain most support in the strongholds of the major parties, indicating either well-developed tactical voting or more probably that the SNP has acted as a vehicle for protest voters. More importantly the SNP has shown an ability to do extremely well in a small number of seats. It is these victories against the main pattern of their support which have allowed a small but proportionate, and critically important, degree of parliamentary representation. Figure 5.15 shows, however, that by October 1974 the SNP reached a position where the extreme victories could easily pale into insignificance beside a mass of seats won through a rise in the general levels of support. Labour, which has had a majority of Scottish seats for much of this century, was likely to suffer the greatest loss had the SNP tide continued to roll in.

The contrast between Scotland and Wales, which is reflected in the different degrees of devolution debated by Parliament, is made clear by figure 5.16. This diagram from the October 1974 election is also closely representative of the February election. In both cases support for the Welsh Nationalist Party, Plaid Cymru, was low and evenly spread except for three constituencies which the party narrowly won. A strong upsurge in support towards the 33% threshold could lead to a dramatic turn in future but up until now Plaid Cymru have shown little evidence of raising their general support above the level of the merely hopeful. Without a further upsurge in support Plaid Cymru appears set to remain a permanent minority. This is a status which some parties maintain over long periods without fragmentation or dissolution. One such party is Social Credit in New Zealand, which is discussed in the following section.

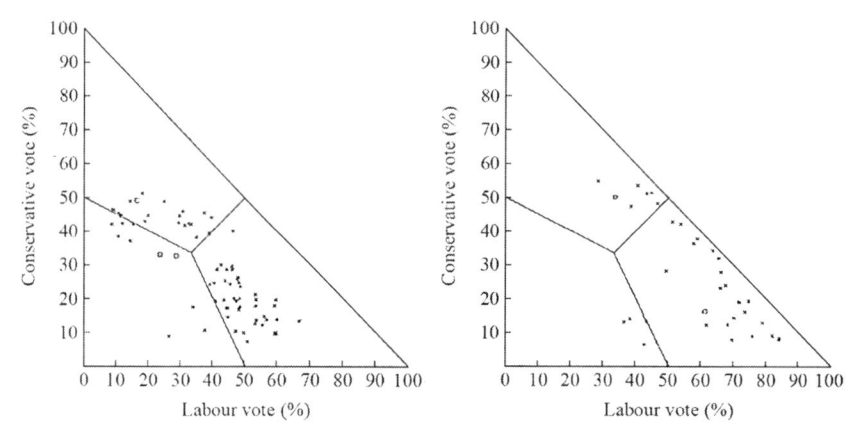

Figure 5.15: Election triangle for Scottish constituencies, October 1974 × constituencies won by Labour, Conservatives or Scottish Nationalists; ○ constituencies won by Liberals; Scottish Nationalist vote increases from 0% at the hypotenuse to 100% at the origin.

Figure 5.16: Election triangle for Welsh constituencies, October 1974 × constituencies won by Labour, Conservatives, or Plaid Cymru; ○ constituencies won by Liberals; Plaid Cymru vote increases from 0% at the hypotenuse to 100% at the origin.

5.4.2 A permanent minority: Social Credit in New Zealand

The electoral situation in New Zealand has had many parallels with Britain since the war. The two-party contest based upon a class cleavage is supplemented by a third party with a relatively uniform pattern of support. For Conservative–Labour–Liberal in Britain read National–Labour–Social Credit in New Zealand. The two systems diverged in the early 1970s, however, with the Liberal upsurge of 1974 contrasting with a fallback in Social Credit support in 1975 in New Zealand. In this section Social Credit is briefly considered as a case study of a party, in a three-party system, which has no realistic chance of becoming a governing party.

The position in the 1957 election in New Zealand, previously described in figure 5.9, remained broadly the same through the elections of 1960 and 1963. The singular significant difference was the detachment of one constituency from the main mass to the brink of victory, which was achieved as Social Credit's first seat in 1966. The ability of an occasional circumstance or candidate to thrust a third party to victory in one, or occasionally more, seats occurs in other countries, and is reminiscent of the Orpington constituency in the case of the British Liberals in the 1960s.

The best election for Social Credit occurred in 1966, and the relevant triangle is shown in figure 5.17. In addition to the general upsurge in popularity, two facts stand out. First, there is the marked tendency for Social Credit to pick up more of the vote where the Labour Party or the National Party was strongest and least in constituencies which were marginal between the major parties. It has been argued above that this pattern of support indicates either tactical voting by major-party supporters hoping to oust their main rivals, or else the third party receiving votes which are more protests against the major parties than expressions of heartfelt approval for the third party itself. In this case the tactical hypothesis is probably untenable since Social Credit were relatively far removed from winning in almost all seats. A similar argument could be levelled against the protest-vote hypothesis. In this case several constituencies would have come close to Social Credit victories if levels of support had been as high in the (major-party) marginals as in Labour or National strongholds. Although it is unlikely that Social Credit could have actually won seats even under this assumption the possibility may have been enough for the major parties to retain the loyalty of their supporters in marginal constituencies.

The second characteristic of the 1966 election was a slight tendency for Social Credit votes to increase more strongly with increasing Nationalist strength than with increasing Labour strength. This pattern has similarities once again with the British Liberal Party, although with the Liberals the tendency is much stronger. In both countries the third party appears to overlap politically more with the right-wing party than with the left-wing party, making the former more vulnerable to any upsurge in third-party popularity.

The direct association between support for Social Credit and the strength of the major parties has implications for the seats–votes relationship if the party should ever attain the vote threshold necessary to

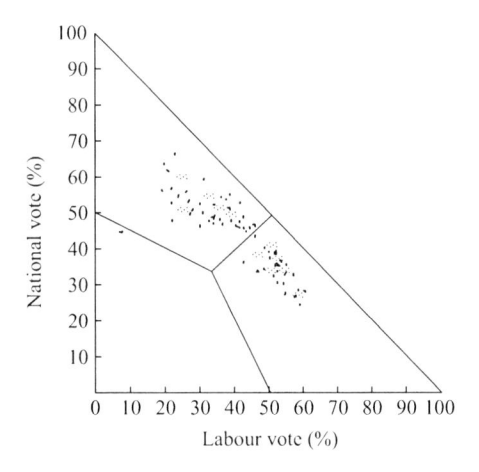

Figure 5.17. Election triangle for New Zealand, 1966: Social Credit vote increases from 0% at the hypotenuse to 100% at the origin.

begin winning seats in significant numbers. On the assumption that the association between major-party and third-party strengths remains similar to that of 1966, then a Social Credit upsurge would begin to win votes with about 27% of the aggregate votes. This is a formidable threshold. It is similar to that facing the British Liberals, and as in Britain it may in itself be enough to prevent any third-party breakthrough. If such a breakthrough should occur, however, then the transformation in fortune would be dramatic. The particular configuration of support for Social Credit would make the seats–votes curve almost vertical above 35% of the votes, with a very steep slope of about six. In terms of figure 5.12 the curve would have, at the lower end, a form similar to that for $\sigma = 0.05$. By 35% in votes, however, it would approximate the line for $\sigma = 0.0$. Hence 35% of the vote would gain only 20% of the seats, but 38% in votes would gain 40%, and 39.5% would secure an absolute majority of seats for Social Credit. If a relatively even attraction of votes from the major parties is assumed, then Social Credit would itself become the strongest party, with 37.5% of the votes.

The prospect of forming a government with an absolute majority of seats but under 40% of the votes will probably seem remote to a party which has never attained even half this figure. The reality of life for Social Credit is one in which not only is there bias against it for being an evenly spread third party, but even worse the bias will tend to increase rather than decrease with increasing popularity unless at least 30% of the aggregate votes can be won.

After 1966 the advance of Social Credit did not continue, and instead the party returned to its pre-1966 levels of support. This is a further indication that its additional popularity in 1966 did not consist of genuine support. The decline in support occurred in almost all constituencies, with the greatest declines in the major-party strongholds, which had previously seen the greatest gains. In a handful of cases Social Credit retained its 1966 levels. These again demonstrate how outstanding circumstances or candidates can make a difference in a small minority of seats. In this case the 1966 successes brought the party into local prominence. All of the cases were seats held by the National Party, and in which Labour was particularly weak. In Labour-held seats nothing, it seems, could prevent the return to pre-1966 conditions, and even in 1969 there was no indication that Social Credit had made any inroads. By 1975 the situation was in almost all respects virtually identical to that in 1957, as far as Social Credit was concerned. The only difference was the presence of two outliers of Social Credit strength. In these constituencies, both of which were National strongholds against Labour, Social Credit gained between 30% and 40% of the votes. Once again there is a parallel with the tiny minority of 'Celtic fringe' and other constituencies which form outliers of strength for the British Liberals.

This account of New Zealand elections has concentrated almost exclusively on the third party. As far as the major parties are concerned elections in New Zealand are two-party contests. The National and Labour parties win virtually every seat in each election and the seats–votes relationship may be approximated by the cube law as discussed in chapter 4. Hence, just like in England, the plurality system has converted a three-party contest in votes into a two-party contest in seats.

5.5 Conclusion: three-party elections, the Achilles heel of the plurality system

In chapter 2 it was concluded that the seats–votes relationship depended directly upon the spatial distribution of voters. A class-based cleavage, acted upon by the forces controlling residential location, forms a spatial distribution of party support for major parties which results in the accentuating biases that are a commonplace feature of our electoral system. In this chapter the seats-votes relationship in three-party elections was found to be just as dependent on the geography of support. There is, however, a vital difference between two–party and three-party elections. Third parties are more likely than major parties to draw support in a way which cuts across class lines. The result can easily be a spatial distribution which is relatively uniform.

It is this uniform distribution which highlights the central weakness of the plurality system. The weakness is the fact that electoral stability, measured in the seats–votes relationship, is a function of the spatial distribution of voters. It is the 'accident' of class-based residential patterns which allows two-party systems to perform tolerably. A reasonably strong third party with spatially even support will lead to greatly exaggerated consequences of any shift in votes.

In actual elections this weakness tends not to have materialised in its most unstable form despite the evidence of instability at the beginning of this chapter. In the Canadian and British (1920s) examples the third parties had relatively uneven support which served to damp down the fluctuations attendant on any voting change. The reasons why the inherent dangers of three-party instability remain submerged are an interesting example of the way in which systems can preserve their structure. The mechanism in this case is the enormous electoral bias which acts against weak third parties, underplaying their real success in attracting support and lowering the ability of such parties to attain real power. Even if a breakthrough were achieved, it seems likely that the two-party structure would be quickly reinstated, since the instability would tend towards the virtual annihilation of one of the three parties.

Despite these mechanisms it is by no means impossible that an extreme example of three-party instability will in fact emerge. Britain and New Zealand at present seem the most probable victims, but national third parties with even support are probably capable of emerging elsewhere.

It is somewhat paradoxical that perhaps the best example of electoral instability known to us occurred in a dominantly two-party system, that of Britain at the beginning of the century (as long as the Irish Nationalists are discounted). The lack of a fully class-based cleavage led to a more even distribution of major-party support than is the case today, with the result that elections could easily lurch from landslide to landslide as in 1900 and 1906, discussed in the last chapter. In this case the preventive mechanisms were not operative, nor was the instability as great as would result in Britain at present if the Liberals were to regain part of their former strength.

The analysis of this chapter has shown how a theoretical investigation can reveal the nature of the plurality system. This approach is more effective in this sense than any empirical study could hope to be, limited as it is by what has occurred in the real world as opposed to what could potentially happen. The work above has concentrated on technical questions, and a good deal of application of the results remains to be undertaken. It is our hope that others will accept the challenge to develop and apply the work.

chapter six | decisionmaking in electoral districting

Our analyses so far have assumed the constituencies or electoral districts to be simply 'given'. However, in every election considered above, the actual voting has been preceded by some decisionmaking agency deciding who belongs to which constituency. In plurality elections somebody has to divide the map of the country into a required number of districts. As suggested in chapter 1, this procedure may have direct implications for the final election result. Elections can be 'won' even before the electorate votes, as Elbridge Gerry so skilfully illustrated many years ago. Here we have the most obvious reason why it is the US elections which are most unlike cube-law predictions in Tufte's analyses reported in figure 1.3. Clearly a gerrymanderer with very detailed voting records can produce almost any CPD he wishes; a normal distribution will presumably only emerge where such a distribution is in line with the interests of the gerrymanderer. In this situation the cube law exists, or does not exist, at the whim of the districting decisionmaker.

The practice of gerrymandering has stimulated a small literature on electoral districting in geography (Sauer, 1918; Bunge, 1966; Orr, 1970) but until recently this has not been concerned with electoral outcomes. In contrast American political scientists have amassed a huge literature concerning alleged gerrymanders and illustrating gross malapportionment (see, for example, the essays in Jewell, 1962). The reapportionment revolution has stimulated a further large extension of this literature as lawyers and political scientists have discussed and debated the string of Supreme Court decisions through the 1960s and into the 1970s. Despite the quantity of literature on this theme, the existing approaches to studying electoral districting have been severely criticised. Pulsipher (1973) suggests that "the contentious might argue that the only non-obvious result of these studies of malapportioned legislature was a misallocation of the scarce scholarly resources of political science". Even Dixon (1971) has gone so far as conceding that "The reapportionment revolution caught everyone unprepared—judges, political scientists, lawyers, political philosophers". One reason for this situation is the lack of a comprehensive framework within which districting decisions may be viewed. It is the purpose of this chapter to present just such a framework and to show how it can be used to throw fresh light on the relation between different types of decisionmaking body in the US and in other countries. This will allow consideration of the work of neutral Boundary Commissioners in Britain alongside gerrymanderers in American state legislatures. First, however, it is necessary to identify the various types of decisionmaking bodies which appear in the realm of electoral districting.

6.1 Types of districting agencies

The rules for electoral districting vary between countries, as briefly described in chapter 1, and there are many different ways in which such procedures may be classified into general types of decisionmaking activity. However, American political scientists now seem to be generally agreed that the most relevant criteria to use in considering the decisionmakers relates to their underlying motives. A simple three-fold typology of decisionmaking agencies has come to be widely used which identifies partisan, nonpartisan, and bipartisan districting agencies. Each type will be considered in turn.

6.1.1 Partisan decisionmaking

Gerrymandering is largely associated with American political life although there are, in fact, numerous examples of partisan districting in Canada (Dawson, 1935), Britain (Seymour, 1915), Northern Ireland (Robinson, 1970), and Argentina (Little, 1974), and France has even had its "age of gerrymandering" (Campbell, 1958). None the less, the vast majority of gerrymandering at least within economically developed nations has occurred, and continues to occur, in the USA and we will concentrate on American examples in our discussion here.

Griffith (1907) has documented the early history of partisan districting and numerous more recent examples can be quoted of accusations of gerrymandering. New York State, for example, has been described fairly recently as "a two-party state with a one-party legislature" (Tyler and Wells, 1962) because of the practice of the Republican majority in the Albany legislature to discriminate against Democratic voters. It is possible to continue quoting particular examples of gerrymandering but at this stage it is more relevant to attempt assessment of the prevalence of partisan districting in the USA. A reasonable guide to the general importance of gerrymandering in the USA can be obtained through Sickels's (1966) study of House of Representatives elections in larger states (those with at least ten seats) between 1946 and 1964. In the initial part of his study, Sickels concentrated on the party at each election that won over 50% of the state vote. These parties were then divided into two groups—parties controlling the state legislature and hence having the power to gerrymander the congressional district boundaries and those parties without this power. He then compared each type of party in terms of its seats-votes relationship. His results are displayed in figure 6.1 and their interpretation is quite striking. Remember that all parties shown on this graph 'won' their elections in terms of votes but very often those without the power to gerrymander 'lost' in terms of seats. Clearly gerrymandering flourished in the USA in the period immediately prior to the reapportionment revolution.

In chapter 4 it was shown that in Sickels's subsequent analysis the importance of malapportionment in this electoral bias was minimal. The implication is that the gerrymandering suggested by figure 6.1 was not based on discriminatory malapportionment but was due instead to the location of boundaries with respect to party voters. Sickels (1966) has therefore concluded "that the constitutional limitations on variations in size will not have much effect on the drawing of district lines for the benefit of the party in control of the state legislature". Clearly, for the American system, the eradication of malapportionment can only be considered an initial step in achieving Chief Justice Warren's basic aim of "fair and effective representation".

Some observers have taken this argument even further. Dixon (1971) for instance accuses the reapportionment revolution court rulings as having produced "a gerrymanderer's paradise". He criticises the courts for acting under the influence of what he terms "the equal numbers–equal representation fallacy". He illustrates this fallacy with the 1969 court ruling in *Wells v Rockefeller*. This ruling disqualified a plan for New York congressional districts because they involved population deviations of 6.6% from the state average. However, the plan had been agreed by both parties in both houses of the state legislature and was only opposed by the objection of one voter. None the less, he won his case and while the case was pending, the Republicans gained control of the legislature, so the decision gave them the opportunity to use their new power to gerrymander. This they did so that they were able to gain two new seats in the 1970 election (Baker, 1971). Democratic leaders made a legal challenge but the new plan, with a maximum deviation of only 490 persons (0.10%), was quite acceptable to the courts despite its generally accepted partisan nature. Clearly strict population criteria do not prevent gerrymandering, but conversely may increase opportunities for partisan districting. Furthermore, court acceptance on population-equality grounds will give a legitimacy to a discriminatory plan. In this situation, reform of distribution can be seen to be potentially counterproductive in terms of reform of representation.

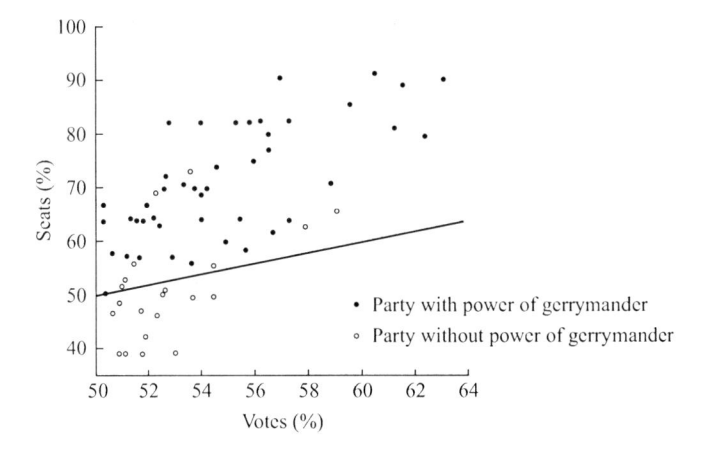

Figure 6.1:   Seats, votes, and the power to set district boundaries in US elections

If strict population controls do not prevent gerrymandering, what of the other two constraints in the traditional trilogy—compactness and contiguity? Probably because of the origin of the term gerrymandering, compactness criteria have traditionally been viewed as safeguards against partisan districting. Schwartzberg (1966), for instance, infers that gerrymandering may be avoided by strict arithmetic control on levels of district compactness. However, this is merely a further fallacy, what Dixon (1968) terms "the myth of compactness", to complement the equal numbers fallacy. As he puts it, "a rigid compactness-contiguity rule shifts attention from the realities of party voting to mere physical geography". Gerrymandering may or may not be related to odd-shaped districts; it all depends on the underlying pattern of party votes and the skills of the districting agency. Baker (1971), for instance, notes that the Republican 1969 plan for New York was generally more compact than the previous joint effort despite its alleged partisan nature. It seems that the Republicans exploited both the equal numbers-equal representation fallacy and the myth of compactness in their skilful partisan districting.

Dixon (1968) sees the problem of gerrymandering as reducing to one of proof in a strict legal sense. Political accusations aside, it is very difficult to prove gerrymandering in the same way as malapportionment. With the latter abuse there is a standard—equal-population districts— against which the court can compare a complaint. With partisan districting it is not clear what the standard districts should be. Thus, whereas degree of malapportionment may be easily measured, degree of gerrymandering is a much more difficult notion. Hence, where the courts have had to consider accusations of gerrymandering, they have been much less forthright than with the malapportionment cases. The key case arose again in New York in *Wright v Rockefeller* (1964) where the plaintiff argued that the division of Manhattan into four congressional districts was designed to discriminate against black voters. However, black politicians gave evidence of support for *both* sides in the case, some arguing that a very safe black district ensured black representation despite wasted votes, while others preferred a more even pattern of black voters among districts so that blacks would have some control over more than one congressman. The court found against the alleged gerrymander on grounds of lack of proof (Dixon, 1968). Although subsequent cases have proven 'racial gerrymandering' with multiseat districting (Baker, 1971), there remains no judicial curb on partisan districting on party political lines.

What conclusions can be drawn? Sickels has shown that gerrymandering was flourishing before the reapportionment revolution and the suggestion is that it will continue to flourish despite of, or even because of, court involvement in electoral districting. As Dixon (1971) notes, the courts have become "prisoners of their own logic". The result is, as Baker (1971) sees it, that "the decade of the 1970's holds the potential for having the most extensive gerrymandering in the nation's history — an ironic capstone to the previous decade that accepted one man, one vote, as a constitutional principle". He somewhat ruefully adds that "if widespread partisan gerrymandering replaces malapportionment as a major electoral problem, the reapportionment revolution will have won a hollow victory indeed".

6.1.2 Nonpartisan decisionmaking

While American reformers may agree on their dislike for explicitly partisan districting, they are not agreed on what type of agency should replace the state legislature. Perhaps the most obvious reform is to take the districting out of the hands of the politicians and to use a neutral or nonpartisan body like the British Boundary Commissions. In America this proposal has been closely associated with the suggested introduction of electronic computers as aids in districting. The following discussion will largely draw upon the debate surrounding nonpartisan computer districting.

The most straightforward argument for replacing politicians in the realm of electoral districting came from Vickrey (1961) in a paper ambitiously titled "On the prevention of gerrymandering". In this paper he argued that in the absence of clear criteria on what is a fair set of districts, we should instead aim for "some kind of procedural fairness". Hence "the elimination of gerrymandering would seem to require the establishment of an automatic and impersonal procedure for carrying out a redistricting". This summarises the essence of the nonpartisan computer districting school of thought. Vickrey suggests an algorithm for carrying out such districting but the development of computer districting came from elsewhere.

The best-known work on computer-aided districting comes from CROND Inc (Computer Research on Non-partisan Districting), who describe themselves as "a group of civic minded engineers" (Weaver, 1970). Their algorithm was first presented in 1963 (Weaver and Hess, 1963) and is now available in the form of a do-it-yourself manual for civic groups. The algorithm uses only population and locational data and attempts to maximise population compactness while maintaining an equal-population constraint. Thus there is no consideration of party fortunes, as partisan districting is replaced by automatic computer-generated districting under 'citizen control'. Quite simply, population and geographical data are fed in and the computer produces the required number of districts.

The limitations of this approach were soon noted following extravagant claims for his own algorithm by Forrest (1965) that "since the computer doesn't know how to gerrymander ... the electronically generated map can't be anything but unbiased". This statement was immediately challenged by Appel (1965) and the nonpartisan debate had begun. The CROND group have not been so naive in their use of the term nonpartisan, Weaver (1970), for instance, pointing out that "the term, non-partisan, is used to refer to the procedure used, not to the result". However, the implication of their work is often otherwise: Weaver has produced a manual with the title *Fair and Equal Districts* although we are told that proportionality in terms of seats is only 'hopefully' approximated.

Dixon (1968) has termed these arguments "the myth of a non-partisan cartography". He argues that "all districting is gerrymandering. ... To be brutally frank, whether or not there is a gerrymander in *design,* there normally will be some gerrymander in *result."* Thus, a nonpartisan approach offers no certain approach to any theoretically desirable electoral outcome. A computer program may produce a solution that approximates proportional representation or it may produce an ideal gerrymander for one party over another. A nonpartisan approach treats each of these possibilities as equally desirable as long as nobody has conscientiously designed such outcomes. Seen in this light, the logic of the nonpartisan argument is very weak indeed: The political payoffs do not simply go away when you ignore them.

Computer districting came to the fore with the aftermath of the reapportionment revolution. However, it should not be seen as in any way comparable in importance. Despite statements that "electronic computers are in wide use, helping to solve districting problems" (Congressional Quarterly Service, 1966) and predictions that all electoral districting will be carried out by computers in fifty years' time (Boyd, 1965), the practical use of computers in districting has been minimal. The relatively large literature has remained in the realm of what might be. After the 1970 census, for instance, every state with more than one congressman was redistricted but the Congressional Weekly Reports mention only two uses of computers. Other evidence of applications can be found from other sources but the total political use (rather than technical demonstration) remains small (Weaver, 1970; Nagel, 1972). There is no example of electoral districts designed by the CROND group ever having been adopted, for example. Their original applications were for New Castle County, Delaware and the Delaware legislature itself, and both of their plans were totally rejected. Similarly, Forrest's plans for New York were considered "totally unusable". The only exception to this dismal record of application is the Iowa Redistricting System developed by Liittschwager (1973), which involves a sophisticated version of Vickrey's original algorithm. However, although the approach is itself nonpartisan, the reasons for its political acceptance may well have been partisan. Thus for Iowa's legislative districts, Liittschwager (1973) notes that "computer-aided plans were prominent in about 70% of the districts recommended by the Iowa Subdistricting Commission and subsequently passed by the Iowa legislature". Such partial acceptance of computer plans is obviously a potentially dangerous procedure allowing a legislature to choose those parts of a plan it prefers and to discard parts that are less politically satisfying. Liittschwager had further success in helping draw Iowa congressional districts after the 1970 census. In this case, eleven computer plans with very small largest/smallest population deviations were produced; ranging from 1.0020 to 1.0053. However, the legislature chose the plan with the largest deviation and slightly modified it so that the ratio was raised to 1.0065. Such a solution remains well within court guidelines. However, this solitary practical success for nonpartisan computer districting hardly lives up to the impersonal, automatic ideal with which Vickrey started. As Weaver (1970) has pointed out, CROND has only received requests for help from parties *not* in power.

Nonpartisan districting need not involve computers, of course. Richard Morrill a prominent geographer was made a Master of Court in Washington after a legislative stalemate over the districting issue in 1974. Since he was given only a month to produce legislative districts, he was only able to experiment briefly with computers. His final solution was a purely manual one. However, his instructions were explicitly nonpartisan in nature. The court barred him from using any political data and he was also instructed to have no contact with any officials of the political parties. The philosophy behind the Washington Court's instructions are not all that far removed from the thinking that underlies the setting up of neutral Boundary Commissions in Britain and Commonwealth countries. These bodies are nonpartisan agencies *par excellance* and hence they qualify for all the criticisms that have been levelled at the nonpartisan computer districting school. The main contrast lies in their practical application; districting solutions of boundary commissions have a very high level of acceptance throughout the world and the partisan nature of some of their results was illustrated in chapter 4. In a practical sense, therefore, criticisms of the nonpartisan approach are much more important when transferred across to the field of neutral commissioners. They use what Dixon (1971) calls "the three monkeys policy—speak no politics, see no politics, hear no politics". He prefers the term 'innocently partisan' to nonpartisan. Nagel (1965) is equally scornful of this approach, which he dismisses as "only nonpartisan in the sense that it is unpredictable as to which party it will favour". Nonpartisan districting is adequate for reform of distribution; it has little or nothing to offer in terms of reform of representation.

6.1.3 Bipartisan districting

After completing his districting exercise in Washington, Morrill was able to point out that his neutral solution lay midway between partisan Democrat and Republican proposals in terms of electoral effects (Morrill, 1973). Given the court's rules, such an outcome was purely fortuitous. Morrill implies that this outcome is a desirable result; if this is the case, then it seems fair to ask why such a solution was not designated as the purpose of the exercise. This would have ensured such a solution rather than relying on chance. This type of argument is typical of the bipartisan school of thought in electoral districting. This admits of the political sensitivity of electoral districting and proposes that districting solutions should be the result of bipartisan negotiations so that both majority and minority parties in a legislature influence the outcome.

The bipartisan approach is associated with the computer algorithm developed by Nagel (1965; 1972). This is a simple boundary heuristic which swaps border base units (counties, wards, etc) between districts and assesses whether such changes improve the districting pattern. Improvement may be assessed in several ways and may include voting data either to assess the results or as criteria for improving a solution. One possible way of improving a solution is to aim for proportionality between votes and seats. Obviously, such a criterion can only be applied where voting data form part of the input and so is only possible with a bipartisan approach.

One feature of the Nagel algorithm is that it disturbs existing patterns much less than other algorithms do. This is because an existing pattern of districts can form the input to the algorithm so that the final solution will be based in part on the existing solution. Other algorithms start afresh and take no account of previous districts, so they are correspondingly more revolutionary. This is one reason why nonpartisan algorithms have had little practical success. This bipartisan algorithm on the other hand is much more acceptable to politicians, especially incumbents. Furthermore, the explicit incorporation of voting data also directly coincides with the politicians' direct interest in the districting outcome. As Nagel has pointed out, it is wholly unreasonable to expect politicians to sacrifice their political careers at the random whim of a computer, as nonpartisan districting expects. Nagel's bipartisan approach is first and foremost a politically realistic approach to the introduction of computers into electoral districting. However, actual use of this algorithm has again been limited. Most examples reported by Nagel (1972) relate to just one side in a districting battle using the flexible nature of the algorithm to produce partisan solutions. Since these users have been minority parties, it follows that the computer-produced results have not had much influence on the final outcomes. However, one interesting example Nagel quotes is that of the Lawyer's Committee on Civil Rights under Law who have prepared plans for Mississippi and Virginia which give blacks proportional representation.

Dixon (1968) follows Nagel's lead in advocating a bipartisan approach to the problem of redistricting. He identifies the bipartisan solution as a way of sidestepping the issue of proving partisan gerrymandering in the courts. Dixon (1971) advocates the use of Bipartisan Commissions consisting of members of both parties to produce districting plans. He lists several advantages over partisan and nonpartisan approaches, in particular the way in which the approach is forced to "focus on the realities of political representation and will inevitably include a strong presumption of representative fairness", thus lessening the possibility of court litigation in the matter. Since 1973, court decisions have come to reflect Dixon's views as more latitude in population criteria has been allowed for bipartisan considerations (Knight, 1976).

Of course, the bipartisan approach to drawing electoral districts predates the use of computers in this field. Dixon (1971) notes that 'informal' bipartisan agreement has been quite common in the past. Where there is a legislative stalemate between houses in a state legislature and the governor, then either the issue goes to court or else a bipartisan agreement has to be made. In Washington the former path was taken, resulting in Morrill's nonpartisan plan. However, there are strong pressures to avoid the unpredictability of a court plan, so compromise would seem to be the most likely outcome of such situations. Mayhew (1971) has described such districting practice as bipartisan gerrymandering. The reintroduction of the term gerrymandering brings an image of smoke-filled rooms with politicians carving up the state to protect their own interests, this time involving dealing between both parties. This suggests a completely different view of bipartisan districting. Mayhew argues that this approach will tend to produce safe seats with very few marginal seats. This will be directly reflected in the voter proportion distribution and will have major implications for the seats-votes relationship. The evidence suggests that bipartisan gerrymandering is coming to dominate the American political scene.

Kendall and Stuart (1950) presented the CPD for the 1944 congressional elections and showed that, if the ten southern states are omitted, the distribution is unimodal with a standard deviation of 13.2%, which is close to British elections. This interprets American elections as reflecting two cleavage patterns, a one-party South and a more typical two-party contest elsewhere. However, when American elections are viewed over a longer term, it is found that the 1944 election is merely part of a general trend towards more dispersed distributions. Stokes (1967) presents distributions for 1874, 1914, and 1958 congressional elections and shows how the proportion of 'swing' districts (45% to 55%) has declined from 48% through 30% to 24%. Tufte (1973) has subsequently found that this trend has culminated in a bimodal distribution. His histograms clearly show the gradual development of a bimodal pattern about the centre of the distribution (figure 6.2). Whereas the 1948 distribution has

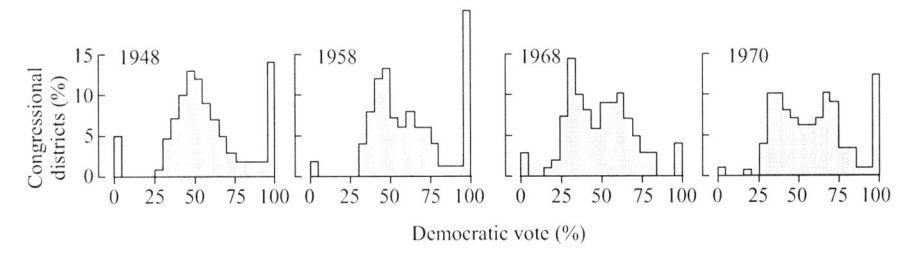

Figure 6.2: Postwar changes in US congressional CPDs (redrawn from Tufte, 1973)

a single central mode, by 1970 the centre is clearly bimodal reflecting a deficiency of 'swing' seats. Tufte (1975) has subsequently shown the same effect within particular states using cumulative CPDs. Figure 6.3 shows changes between 1950 and 1970 for Michigan and Pennsylvania congressional districts which indicate a fundamental change in the seats-votes relationship.

Tufte explains this bimodality in terms of Mayhew's bipartisan gerrymandering. If Tufte is correct it seems that the enormous amount of redistricting that accompanied the reapportionment revolution of the 1960s has had its most profound electoral effect in enabling the trend towards bipartisan gerrymandering to gather speed. In fact, many recent apportionment acts have been simply described as 'Incumbent Survival Acts' (Tufte, 1973, page 552). Noragon (1973) presents further evidence of this process. In a study of congressional districts before and after forced redistricting, Noragon computes a net loss of twenty-eight marginal districts.

The electoral implications of this process are clear. There are fewer marginal districts, so elections are much more stable events. After 1970 in Michigan, for instance, a 12% swing against the Democrats would have entailed no loss of seats (figure 6.3). Quite simply, voters have less effect on the outcome of elections. Tufte (1973) notes nationally how the Democrats in 1970, and the Republicans in 1966 and 1968, both won a

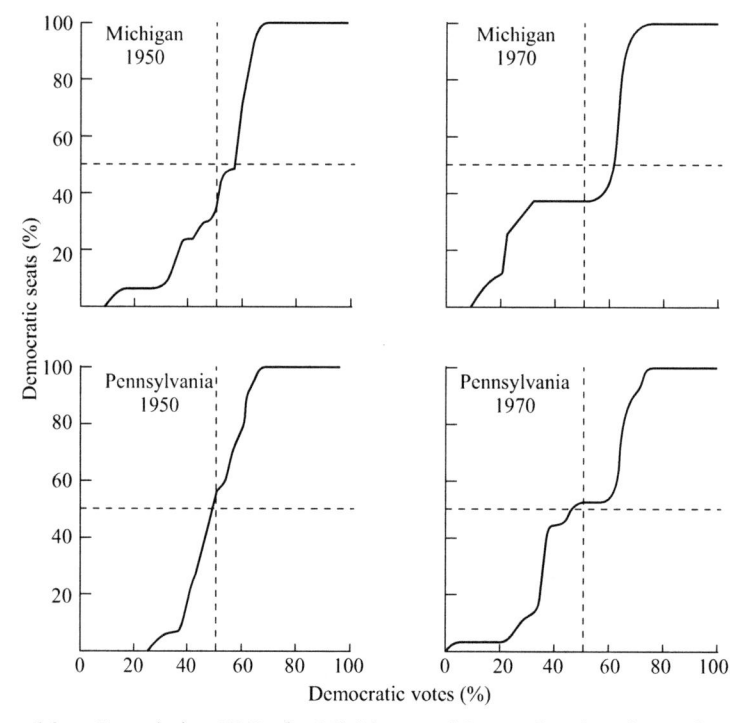

Figure 6.3: Cumulative CPDs for Michigan and Pennsylvania (after Tufte, 1975).

substantial swing in the popular voting which was not reflected in substantial changes in Congress. However, the best example of this effect is probably the 1974 election. In this case, the Watergate affair meant a large swing to the Democrats and they were hoping for a two-thirds House majority. However, the bimodality of the central range of the CPD thwarted them. The distribution in contested seats is shown in figure 6.4. The swing to the Democrats has clearly moved the distribution along so that the 'safe' Republican core is in danger. However, the swing only involved the central portion of the distribution where seats are few. Hence, the Democrats did not win their two-thirds majority despite a landslide in votes. Bipartisan gerrymandering, it seems, protected the Republican party in their hour of need. The geography of election boundaries ameliorated the electoral effects of Watergate. There can be no clearer example of the influence of the spatial organisation of elections on the operation of the Democratic system in countries using plurality laws.

Clearly the bipartisan proposals of Nagel and Dixon, even if considered superior to a nonpartisan approach, provide as many new problems as solutions to old problems. Simple bipartisan agreement omits one important group from consideration: the voters. An unconstrained bipartisan approach will lead, and has led, to a decrease in the power of voters to affect elections. Thus, any Bipartisan Commission would seem to require nonpartisan citizen representation as a watchdog to protect the role of the voter in elections. A compromise position which admits to some role for a nonpartisan check on politicians in their districting decisionmaking would seem to be indicated.

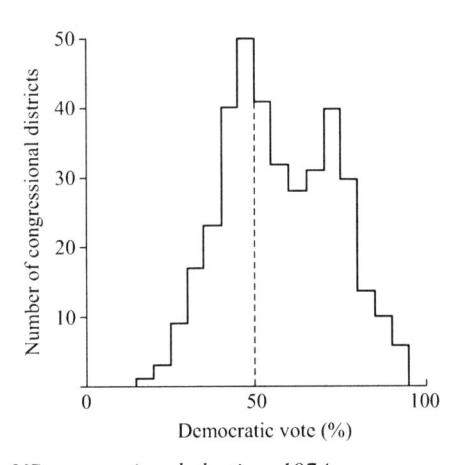

Figure 6.4: CPD: US congressional election, 1974

6.1.4 Beyond the USA

Up until this point, this chapter has reflected the literature on decisionmaking in electoral districting so that it has been almost solely concerned with American elections. In chapter 1, however, American elections were merely identified as one end of a spectrum of varying degrees of political involvement in the districting procedure. In the following discussion other countries will be considered in the light of recent changes in American districting[1].

The most notable feature of modern American elections is the bimodal CPD which, it has been argued by Tufte, reflects bipartisan political districting. Hence the discussion has continued to be concerned with CPDs, albeit in a less formal way than in previous chapters. It is now possible to identify two ways in which a bimodal CPD can be produced: (1) where the districts are smaller than the mosaic of party voter clusters (figure 3.1) and (2) by bipartisan gerrymandering. (Alternative explanations of bimodal CPDs are given in appendix 7.) In most of the national elections considered here, it seems highly reasonable to assume that the former situation does not obtain. Hence bimodal CPDs may be used to infer political involvement in the districting procedure.

In chapter 1, British districting practice was identified as being at the opposite end of the spectrum from that of the USA since it included minimum political involvement. This argument is substantiated by the British CPDs, which have been shown to be closest to normality, with no indications of bimodality appearing at all. This is not strictly true of the other countries that use the plurality election law. In the same chapter New Zealand was identified as having political involvement in the districting by the inclusion of party nominees on the districting commission. This rule seems to be enough to have produced a bimodal CPD for the New Zealand elections discussed in chapter 4. Notice that in figure 4.8 the bimodality is particularly pronounced after the districting following the 1960 census, as reflected in the 1963 election CPD. Hence this seems to be a simple explanation for New Zealand's CPDs being different from British CPDs despite the political and cultural similarities between the two countries.

In chapter 1 it was also noted that whereas Canada had set up neutral boundary commissions in 1964, their results were subject to modification by MPs within Parliament. From the previous discussion it would seem that such direct political involvement might once again produce bimodal CPDs. Canadian elections are, of course, multiparty affairs but the methods employed in chapter 4 to derive two-party contests may be

---

[1] The discussion below continues to be concerned solely with the five countries using plurality laws, identified in chapter 1. However, it is of interest to note that perhaps the most explicit examples of electoral districting to incorporate consideration of electoral outcomes can be found in British colonies in the 1940s and 1950s (P J Taylor, 1973). In Mauritius (Smith, 1960), Ceylon (Tinkler, 1956), and Malaya (Laponce, 1957), for instance, colonial boundary commissions were required to consider ethnic patterns in drawing constituency boundaries so as to avoid plurality elections discriminating against minority groups. This seems to have been the only way in which the 'Westminster model' could become acceptable in a culturally plural society.

used in this context to see if bimodality does occur. Figure 6.5 shows the CPDs for the Liberal Party on the assumption of simple two-party contests against their rivals for government, the Progressive Conservatives. The result is that, once again, distinct bimodal CPDs emerge. This evidence for political involvement is less convincing than that for New Zealand since other important party considerations, involving the New Democrats in particular, are not taken into account. Nevertheless the two major parties do totally dominate the Canadian parliament in terms of seats so that political involvement should be most clearly reflected in relations between Liberals and Progressive Conservatives. Hence the CPDs do seem to indicate clear evidence of continuing political involvement in electoral districting despite the major change in procedure set out in the 1964 Act.

This leaves just South African elections to be considered. In chapter 1 the possibility of political involvement in the districting procedure was left an open question. A stage in the argument has now been reached when South African elections can be assessed. This is such an interesting and important example that it warrants a section to itself.

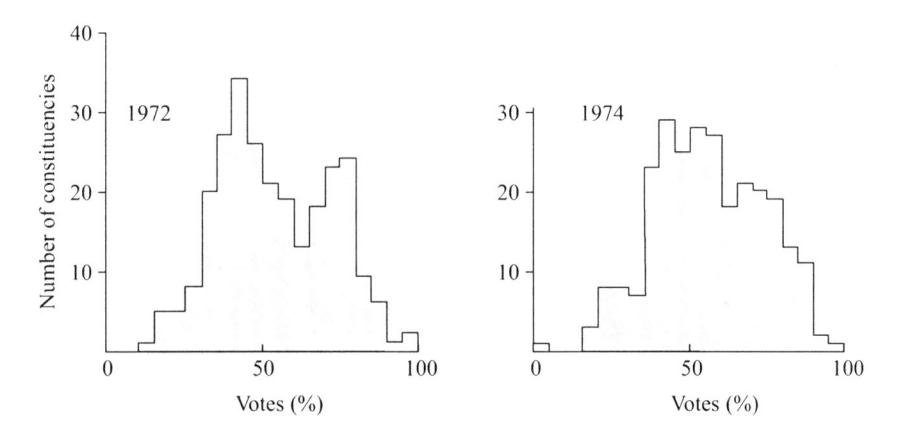

Figure 6.5: CPDs for the Canadian Liberal Party

6.1.5 The question of South African elections

It was argued at the end of chapter 3 that the standard form of the CPD will be that of the normal distribution. As long as constituencies are larger than the residential clusters of like-minded party supporters we would expect to discover this type of CPD unless gerrymandering or some other distorting element was a major influence.

In South Africa the CPD proves to be far from normal. The two-party distribution for the United Party in the 1974 election is shown in figure 6.6. Over half of the constituencies were uncontested by both major parties, and most of these were won by the National Party. The minority of contested seats form a highly skewed distribution with a mode at close to a United Party proportion of 35%. An interelection swing of 10% between the major parties, which would be large by comparison with the UK, would lead to only six or eight seats changing hands. This small number would have almost no effect on the permanent majority held by the Nationalists, which in 1974 was seventy-one seats over all opposition parties.

South African elections are clearly not real contests at all. There has been virtually no chance of the United Party (or any other opposition party) winning. The electoral bias can be partially seen in the discrepancy between vote proportions and seat proportions (table 6.1) but even this is not a good measure of bias in cases like this, since the failure to win no matter what will have a demoralising effect on the supporters of the disadvantaged party. The United Party did not win the elections of 1948, 1952, and 1956 despite having an estimated majority of the votes in each year. Since then its position has become increasingly hopeless and the current position is that it has been disbanded.

Mass democracy has a fragility which is usually concealed by the stability of the few countries using this form of government. The major parties must

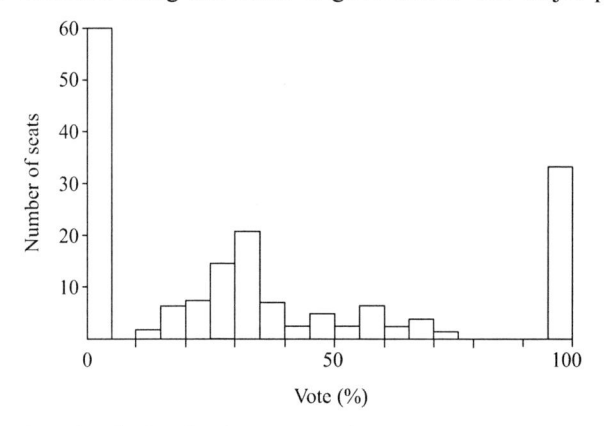

Figure 6.6: CPD for the South African United Party, 1974

Table 6.1: Electoral bias in South African elections. Sources: Heard, 1974; South Africa Yearbook (1977)

	United Party (% of total) actual votes	estimated votes[a]	seats	Actual bias (1)–(3)	Estimated bias (2)–(3)
	(1)	(2)	(3)	(4)	(5)
1948	50.9	53.3	47.3	–3.6	–6.0
1953	50.2	54.7	40.9	–9.3	–13.8
1958	43.3	50.1	35.3	–8.0	–14.8
1961	37.6	–	32.7	–4.9	–
1966	37.3	–	24.4	–12.9	–
1970	37.4	–	29.6	–8.8	–
1974	32.1	–	25.1	–7.0	–

[a] Estimated by Heard (1974), making allowance for uncontested seats.

decisionmaking in electoral districting | 135

for instance have approximately balanced strength and be capable of changing places. South Africa is not really a democracy in this sense and might more accurately be described as a one-party state which holds ritual elections. How has this situation come about? Is it the result of the particular socioeconomic structure and social geography of South Africa's white population, or is it alternatively the result of deliberate and massive gerrymandering?

One way in which gerrymandering can potentially be identified is to examine changes in the degree of electoral bias over time. In South Africa this is not easy because so many constituencies are uncontested. In over half the constituencies there are not even ritual elections! The only indication of voting strength comes from the unrepresentative minority of constituencies which both major parties choose to contest. Also we should repeat the point made above that continual defeat, even with a majority of votes, is very likely to reduce the strength of the United Party; that is, the elections reduce the strength of a variable which they are supposed to measure.

The degree of electoral bias in postwar elections is shown in table 6.1. The actual bias for the United Party changed from positive to negative up to 1948 despite an increase in the proportion of votes. Since 1948 the bias has been continuously large and negative. The problem has not traditionally been the United Party's inability to win votes, indeed Heard (1974) estimates that until 1958 they were the major party in votes. Instead there is some element in the South African electoral system which has consistently worked against the United Party whatever its success in the polling booths.

A more practical way of attempting to decide whether the cause is gerrymandering or 'natural' factors is to examine the CPD for the 1948 election. This was the first South African election won by the National Party, and if gerrymandering is important it is likely to have occurred since 1948. The CPD for 1948 is displayed in figure 6.7. Aside from the uncontested seats the distribution is approximately normal although somewhat skewed. It is certainly closer to normality than the CPD of the 1974 election. The interpretation is slightly, although not significantly, confused by the fact that the National Party did not contest forty-six seats.

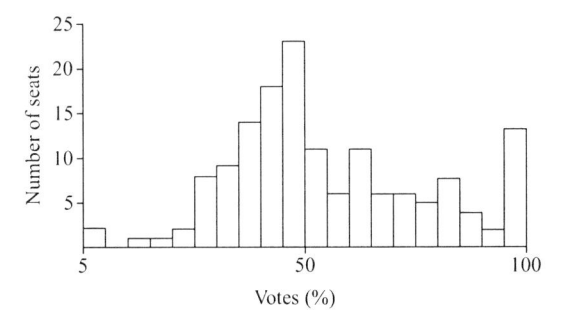

Figure 6.7: *CPD for the South African United Party, 1948*

Eleven of these were not contested by any opposition party, while in the remainder the United Party were opposed by a mixture of minor parties and independent candidates. A direct comparison with the 1974 election would involve calculating a CPD for the two-party vote, but it is in fact more representative to use the CPD for total votes (as shown in figure 6.7). The turnout was only slightly below average in seats not contested by the Nationalists. Since National Party supporters were more likely to vote for minor parties or independents than for United Party candidates it is reasonable to view such constituencies as producing a fair indication of United Party support. Some of the independents were actually thinly disguised Nationalists and attracted large votes. One was the future Prime Minister B J Vorster. The wide spread of the 1948 CPD (with a standard deviation of 18%) and the skewness to the right both probably reflected those aspects of white South African society which are unusual in the context of the English-speaking democracies. The relatively high spread of the CPD reflects the greater than usual separation of the supporters of the major parties. The predominantly Afrikaans support of the National Party was largely concentrated in rural areas at this period, while the English speakers on whom the United Party was based were largely urban dwellers. Not too much should be made of the separation of the two sets of supporters, however, since the spread of the distribution is no greater than for major parties in Canada or in UK elections with significant Liberal intervention.

The separation of the supporters probably has more effect on the skewness of the distribution. There was an excess of constituencies (compared with a normal distribution) in which the United Party gained over 70% of the votes. These were urban constituencies, and the concentration resembles, and exaggerates, the concentrations of working-class voters in urban or coalfield constituencies in other countries.

The results of the particular social geography of early postwar South Africa were thus to produce a high spread and positive skewness in the CPD. Neither effect was large enough significantly to differentiate South African elections from those in other countries. A power function of the cube-law type, but with an exponent closer to two than to three, would have given a reasonable approximation to the seats-votes relationship. No such function would suffice in modern South African elections, so what has changed since 1948?

There are three obvious possibilities for consideration, although other factors may also be at work.

(1) The United Party may have given up contesting many constituencies in which it loses election after election, resulting in a 'distorted' nonnormal CPD.

(2) The urbanisation of the Afrikaans-speaking population may have altered the relationship between constituency boundaries and the geography of National Party support in such a way as to produce a nonnormal CPD.

(3) The nonnormality may have resulted from changes in the way boundaries were drawn by the South African Delimitation Commission. Each of these possibilities can be considered in turn.

(1) The first possibility seems an unlikely explanation because the United Party did contest a considerable number of seats in which they subsequently won less than 30% of the (two-party) votes. If we assume that the sixty-one seats uncontested by the United Party were less likely to be gained than the seats which they did contest and failed to win, then the lack of normality cannot be due to the uncontested seats. The reason is that the sixty-one uncontested seats would (by assumption) have attracted less than about 30% of the two-party votes. Also the thirty-four seats which were uncontested by the Nationalists would have been won by the Unionists with over 50% of the vote. When these magnitudes are viewed in conjunction with figure 6.6, it is clear that the uncontested seats would if contested be more likely to produce a bimodal distribution than a unimodal distribution of the normal type.

(2) The second possibility is more complex. In 1948 the great majority of Nationalist supporters were living in rural areas. Since then a strong urbanisation process has occurred so that by 1974 a clear majority of Afrikaans speakers were living in urban areas. This means that a dramatic change occurred in the electoral geography of South Africa and the question is whether or not it altered the CPD in the manner observed in figures 6.6 and 6.7. On the face of it this seems unlikely since urbanisation seems more likely to reduce rather than increase the physical separation between the two sets of party supporters. A reduced degree of separation would in turn tend to reduce rather than increase the spread of the CPD. However, it is possible that in this case the language and cultural differences led to greater separation within the cities than had formerly existed in the urban-rural split.

A major research project would be needed to decide this issue completely, but it is possible to make some progress by examining the case of Johannesburg alone. This is possible by using the figures quoted in table A.1 of Hart and Browett (1976). In 1970 the Afrikaans speakers constituted 27% of the population of Johannesburg, and the Hart and Browett figures show how the Afrikaans speakers were distributed over 203 census tracts in the city. This distribution is described in table 6.2. The positively skewed distribution indicates a less than even pattern of Afrikaans speakers in Johannesburg. Nevertheless these figures do not support a hypothesis of extreme ethnic separation in the city. Although a degree of residential segregation undoubtedly exists, the figures also show some mixing of the two groups in a large number of census tracts.

This frequency distribution of areas of Afrikaans-speaking people is only one aspect of the spatial distribution. The other is the relative position of these areas; that is, do these census tracts group together on the ground to form relatively larger clusters of ethnic groups? An examination of figure B.8 in Hart and Browett (1976) shows that Afrikaans speakers are concentrated in the southern and western sectors of Johannesburg. Even so, the pattern exhibited is not greatly dissimilar in concentration to that found for social-class segregation in other countries such as Britain. Certainly the overall degree of segregation at either the intracensus-tract or intercensus-tract scale lends relatively little support to the view that the pattern of votes is responsible for the modern South African CPD. This is despite the fact that South African constituencies are quite small and therefore closer in scale to the residential/voter mosaic and that the voting itself seems to be more polarised [closer to 80 : 20 than the UK's 70 : 30 ratio of support from 'natural' support groups—see Peele and Morse (1974)]. Although it is difficult to come to exact conclusions concerning the effects of urbanisation on the South African CPD on the evidence we have available to us, it is reasonable to argue that it does not indicate the extreme levels of segregation that would be necessary to generate on its own the degree of separation of voters represented by the modern CPD in figure 6.6.

(3) Finally, it is possible to examine the possibility that the South African districting agency has artificially produced a CPD which causes a permanent bias against the United Party. This is done in two ways. First the rules governing the districting process can be examined to see if this possibility is likely. Second, subjective evidence on gerrymandering can be introduced.

As outlined in chapter 1 constituency boundaries are redrawn by a judicial Delimitation Commission after each census. The three judges forming the commission are appointed by the state President and regulate their own procedure. They construct the boundaries on five criteria (Carter, 1958),
(1) recognising community of interest,
(2) taking account of physical communications,
(3) taking account of physical features,
(4) taking account of existing boundaries,
(5) taking account of population density, with scope to vary the size of constituencies by up to 15% from the average if necessary.

Table 6.2: The distribution of Afrikaans speakers in Johannesburg, 1970. Source: Hart and Browett (1976)

Afrikaans speakers (%)	Census tracts (%)
0–17.3	48.3
17.3–33.7	21.2
33.7–50.0	13.3
50.0–66.3	6.9
66.3–82.7	5.9
82.7–100.0	4.4

The degree of political involvement is apparently quite strong despite the judicial composition of the Commission. In the 1953 delimitation for instance both major parties submitted boundary plans which were largely adhered to by the Commission (Carter, 1958, page 153). This was possible because the parties concentrated their plans on their own strongholds.

The Delimitation Commissions appear to have emphasised two of the five criteria. The criterion of population density has consistently been used to make rural constituencies smaller than their urban counterparts. This has the effect of giving the National Party a built-in advantage, but not one which explains the greater part of the pro-National bias. In a detailed submission to the 10th Commission in 1953 A Suzman, arguing against malapportionment, estimated that it had provided a six-seat advantage for the Nationalists in 1948 (Carter, 1958, page 152).

The second point of emphasis may concern the criterion of community of interest. Carter (1958, page 154) judged that the distinguishing feature of the 1953 Commission (which was the first postwar one under a National government) was "upon securing the greatest degree of identity among members of a constituency". Again, in reference to the 1958 election Carter (1963, page 492) states, "increasingly South African delimitations are separating National Party and United Party supporters into different constituencies so that fewer are won by narrow margins". This may feasibly have been a conscious intention, but it may also have been an unconscious consequence of the urbanisation discussed above. Carter, however, judges that both factors were operative (Carter, 1958, page 154). A discussion of the delimitation rules does not conclusively indicate that electoral bias was artificially created, although the " 'community of interest' criterion makes this a possibility".

Finally, there is some subjective and circumstantial evidence to consider. For example Stanley Uys, a notable South African journalist, "blamed the disasterous delimitation for the size of the United Party's defeat" in 1958 (Heard, 1974, page 83). The previous delimitation had abolished seven seats of which five had been held by the United Party, and had created seven new ones, of which the United Party won only two. In contrast the delimitation in 1953 was generally considered to have been neutral by the United Party press in the context of the 1953 election (Carter, 1958, page 152). On a more ominous note Farquharson quotes an ex-Nationalist Party official saying that, having won in 1948, some Nationalists were intent on securing future victories by whatever means (Farquharson, 1959).

What can be concluded about the effects of the districting agency upon the outcome of South African elections? First it is not possible to prove intentional gerrymandering. Proof of intent is an elusive matter at the best of times, and in this case there are alternative factors which could have led to the dramatic change in the CPD. The issue cannot be settled here and what is needed is a careful study of changes in the spatial distribution of National voters and changes in the constituency boundaries.

Needless to say this would be a laborious task. What can be said, however, is that the districting procedure is clearly responsible for the huge bias which typifies South African elections. The responsibility stems from the elementary fact that it is possible to draw boundaries in such a way as to avoid the excesses. The successive Delimitation Commissions have produced an electoral framework, whether knowingly or not, which makes a mockery of democracy. Even if the impersonal forces of socioeconomic change are the root cause of the bias (and this is still not clear), the choice exists to acquiesce in the consequences or alternatively to counteract them. All of this is not, however, to say that the responsibility lies with the actual members of the Delimitation Commissions. Their brief does not include the criteria of ensuring fair elections. In this case the responsibility lies with the Government since it does have the power to amend the terms of reference of the Delimitation Commission. This power has not been used and the reason is presumably not unconnected with the fact that the National Party (which would lose from any reform) had been in office since 1948.

6.2 A statistical framework

The precondition for gerrymandering, partisan or bipartisan, is that there should be a range of alternative districting solutions which produce a variety of electoral outcomes for the same level of party votes. This allows a choice in districting which implies a choice in the electoral outcome. From what population of all possible solutions are such choices made? This question leads directly into consideration of the statistical basis of districting.

All districting agencies can be viewed as having the same basic task of choosing one districting solution out of the many possible. This is the context within which the gerrymander thrives. It is also the context within which the computer, Boundary Commission, or any other agency has to operate. It is a statistical context in that there is a population of feasible solutions from which just one has to be chosen. As such, it can become the basis of both empirical and theoretical research set in a truly comprehensive framework (Pulsipher, 1973; Taylor and Gudgin, 1976b). It is the purpose of the remainder of this chapter to set partisan, nonpartisan, and bipartisan districting within this statistical framework.

6.2.1 Constituencies as combinatorial structures

The number of ways an electorate of several million can be divided into a given number of constituencies is truly astronomical. In practice, however, individual voters are not themselves grouped to form constituencies but rather some small areal units form the basis of the aggregation. In Britain these base units consist of wards within cities and local-authority areas elsewhere. In America, base units vary from city blocks through to counties, depending on the population density. In each case, the problem can be viewed simply as combining n base units to form k constituencies such that each base unit is in one and only one constituency. The problem is identical to the region-building problem discussed by Cliff et al (1975) and their work is drawn upon in what follows.

Now that the districting problem has been explicitly specified the number of possible districting solutions can be derived. The number of base units in constituency i will be defined as f_i so that

$$\sum_{i=1}^{k} f_i = n, \qquad (6.1)$$

and further the number of constituencies which comprise j base units will be denoted g_j so that

$$\sum_{j=1}^{n} g_j = k \qquad (6.2)$$

This means, for instance, that in a division of four base units into two constituencies of one unit and three units, respectively, $f_1 = 1$, $f_2 = 3$ so that $f_1 + f_2 = 4 = n$, and $g_1 = 1$, $g_3 = 1$ so that $g_1 + g_3 = 2 = k$.

Given this information, the total number of different ways n base units can be grouped into k constituencies is given by

$$a = n! \bigg/ \left[\prod_{i=1}^{k} (f_i!) \prod_{j=1}^{n} (g_j!) \right] \qquad (6.3)$$

Thus, in the simple example above

$$a = \frac{4!}{3!1!1!1!} = 4,$$

which means that there are four possible ways of forming two constituencies from four base areas so that one has three base areas and the other has one. In fact, in this simple case it is possible to enumerate all possible solutions. Let the base areas be denoted A, B, C, and D, then the four solutions are (A, BCD), (B, ACD), (C, ABD), and (D, ABC). Cliff et al (1975) give a table illustrating many such simple examples and go on to show how the total number of solutions for n and k for all possible f_i and g_j can be calculated. Their conclusion is that as n increases, the number of possible solutions grows 'explosively'.

In the electoral districting problem, not all possible solutions for given n and k are equally feasible. In the simple example above, it might obviously be queried why one constituency is seemingly three times larger than the other in terms of base units. Most electoral districting operates under some type of equal-size constraint, however lax in practice. In fact, all of the rules incorporated in the electoral laws described in chapter 1 represent constraints on the number of possible solutions. Many of the vast number of possible solutions that we would derive, using Cliff et al's unconstrained approach, would be disqualified as sets of constituencies for violating one or more rules. It is possible, therefore, to interpret rules for districting as constraints on the possible number of *feasible* solutions. In a very direct sense rules do restrict the gerrymanderer in terms of his range of choice, but if the range of choice remains relatively large, the restrictions of the rules are irrelevant in practice.

The equal-size constraint in electoral districting can be approximated by restricting the f_i s and g_j s within the Cliff et al approach. Although actual size rules relate directly to population and voters, equality of base units per constituency forms a rough surrogate for this finer level of equality where base units themselves are approximately equal in numbers of voters. On this assumption all constituencies should consist of $n/k = j$ base units, and $g_j = k$, that is, all constituencies have the same number (j) of base units. The number of equal-size solutions is given by

$$a = \frac{n!}{k[(n/k)!]k!} \qquad (6.4)$$

Thus, if $n = 8$ and $k = 2$,

$$a = \frac{8!}{(2 \times 4!)2!} = 35.$$

This means that there are thirty-five different ways that eight base units can be divided into two equal constituencies of four base units each. Hence, even in this simple problem of $n = 8$, $k = 2$, there are still a large number of feasible solutions to choose from given the equal-size constraint. With larger problems the number of solutions is vastly increased. Two examples below illustrate these considerations. These are concerned with deriving two constituencies from eighteen wards in Sunderland and four constituencies from twenty wards in Newcastle upon Tyne with the use of a base-area-size constraint. In the first case $n = 18$, $k = 2$ and in the second case $n = 20$, $k = 4$, to produce constituencies of nine wards each and five wards each respectively. The total number of such equal-size constituencies is given, for the first case, by

$$a = \frac{18!}{(2 \times 9!)2!} = 24310.$$

However, the twenty-four thousand possible Sunderland solutions are swamped by Newcastle's total number of solutions:

$$a = \frac{20!}{(4 \times 5!)4!} = 490 \text{ million}$$

Clearly with simply an equal-size constraint there remains plenty of scope for gerrymandering.

Of course, equal size is only one of several constraints imposed on districting agencies. The other almost universal requirement is that of contiguity. Cliff et al (1975) consider contiguity constraints in some detail. Unfortunately, patterns of contiguities among base areas are very difficult to generalise about. Cliff et al consider the limiting case of maximum constraint where each base unit is only contiguous with one other base unit. This defines a 'chain' spatial arrangement and is used to define a *minimum* number of possible solutions under contiguity constraints:

$$a = k! / \prod g_j . \tag{6.5}$$

However, when combined with the equal-size constraint, a trivial solution is obtained: $a = k!/k! = 1$, which states that there is only one way of dividing a chain into k equal and contiguous parts, irrespective of n or k. Thus, actual numbers of feasible solutions involving equal-size and contiguity constraints will lie between one and the equal-size-constraint number. The exact number within this very wide range will depend entirely on the particular pattern of contiguities, and must be computed separately for each districting problem.

6.2.2 Algorithms for finding feasible solutions

Nearly all algorithms that have been designed to generate electoral districts in the last decade or so have been heuristic in nature (Cope, 1971). This means that some objective is specified, for instance minimising population differences among districts, and the algorithm iterates among possible solutions, gradually finding better and better solutions in terms of the objective. The final solution will likely be a very good solution in terms of the objectives but it will probably not be the best. This is because heuristic algorithms do not consider all possible solutions. Hence, there is always the likelihood of a better solution among the many not considered.

The major reason for the widespread development of heuristic algorithms is the massive size of a total enumeration of districts. It is for this reason that only two districting exercises have developed a method of considering all feasible solutions. In one case, the problem is relatively small (Shepherd and Jenkins, 1970) and in the other the goal of the research was to develop a method of finding the true optimal solution, which therefore involved assessing all solutions (Garfinkel and Taylor, 1969). The two approaches are very similar. Shepherd and Jenkins's algorithm will be briefly described first.

Shepherd and Jenkins divide the districting problem into two parts. First, feasible constituencies are identified from among possible combinations of base units. Second, these constituencies are allocated to plans so that sets of nonoverlapping, contiguous solutions are produced. The two parts may be termed district generation and plan generation respectively. Both parts involve systematic searches, through base units and feasible constituencies respectively. To produce constituencies, each base unit is combined in turn with each other base unit and sets of base units until all possible combinations have been tried. Feasible solutions are then stored for the next stage. This involves an ordered combination of constituencies to assess which combinations produce valid plans. For instance, a problem with four base units might produce the following six feasible constituencies.

AB AC AD
BD
CD
D

Constituencies which include the first base unit (A) are assessed for plan generation. The first constituency is chosen (AB) and the first base unit not included is noted (C). Other districts are now searched with C as their first base area. There is just one (CD) and it is found that along with AB it covers all base units and there is no overlap. Thus, the first feasible plan is AB, CD. The second constituency (AC) has base area B missing so constituencies beginning with B are searched to find a second feasible plan (AC, BD). The third constituency (AD) also omits B but there is no constituency which includes B and forms a feasible plan with AD. Therefore, there is no feasible plan that includes constituency AD. There are no further constituencies which include A so our search for feasible plans is complete; there are just two (AB, CD and AC, BD). For further elaboration of the algorithm see Shepherd and Jenkins (1970).

Jenkins and Shepherd (1972) apply their algorithm to a problem of defining school electoral districts from twenty-one high school districts in Detroit. Feasible electoral districts were defined by a population constraint (25 000 to 50000 students) and a contiguity constraint. They were able to generate 3154 plans for seven electoral districts, 4087 for eight electoral districts, and 130 for nine electoral districts. With the use of the previous notation, $n = 21$ and $k = 7$ produced 3154 solutions; $n = 21$ and $k = 8$ produced 4087 solutions; and $n = 21$ and $k = 9$ produced 130 solutions. This is with a *combined* size and contiguity constraint. Hence, even in a doubly constrained situation, there are plenty of solutions, implying a wide variety of electoral outcomes.

A modified version of the above algorithm was used for the Sunderland and Newcastle examples mentioned above. In this case, size was defined in terms of base units as previously specified. With an added contiguity constraint, a total of eighty-seven possible solutions of two constituencies was found for Sunderland and a total of 334 possible solutions of four constituencies was generated for Newcastle. Clearly, for both cases the introduction of a contiguity constraint has greatly reduced the numbers of solutions, but these numbers still remain relatively large. There is still plenty of choice for the districting agency.

The Garfinkel and Taylor (1969) algorithm represents a more comprehensive approach. Their feasible districts are constrained in terms of a compactness measure as well as population variability and contiguity. Otherwise their algorithm is similar to Shepherd and Jenkins's, involving district-generation and plan-generation stages once again. One reason for the large number of solutions produced for Detroit was the very lax population constraint. Garfinkel and Taylor vary the strength of their constraints and illustrate the changing numbers of resulting feasible districts. Further details of their algorithm and experiments can be found in Garfinkel and Taylor (1969).

The major limitation with algorithms for finding all solutions is their sensitivity to the size of the problem. Garfinkel and Taylor generate complete sets of solutions for two larger problems than the Detroit example ($n = 26$, $k = 6$ and $n = 37$, $k = 4$), but produced no successful runs for another problem with $n = 55$, $k = 5$, due simply to running out of time on the computer. They advise that their algorithm is only feasible with $n < 40$. Even with faster, larger computers it is clear that the size of the problem increases so rapidly as n increases that generation of all solutions for large electoral districting problems will not be possible within the near future.

Even if all solutions for large problems cannot be generated, an indication of the range of likely solutions is highly desirable. This can be achieved by generating a random sample of all possible solutions, for instance by utilising a modified version of the algorithm presented in P J Taylor (1973). In the latter, random numbers are used to select k base units to act as initial cores for constituencies. Base areas contiguous to cores are now added progressively to build up each constituency. A base area is not added if it brings the constituency above a specified population level. After all base areas have been allocated, a check is made that all districts are contiguous and that constituencies are within the required population range. If these criteria are met, this set of constituencies becomes the first in the sample of feasible plans. Six additional base areas are randomly selected, a new set of constituencies is built up and tested, and so on. The algorithm can be terminated whenever the sample size is considered large enough. Hence very large districting problems can be studied although these may well require relatively small samples. The algorithm has been applied to Iowa to produce sets of six congressional districts from ninety-nine counties (section 6.4.3). This problem is clearly too large for the previous two algorithms. However, it has been possible to generate a sample of 700 feasible districting plans which give a good indication of the range of possibilities for Iowa's congressional districts. All solutions include contiguous districts within a population range of ± 15%. This relatively lax population constraint (by American standards) was necessary to generate sufficient solutions. It will not affect our subsequent discussion using these solutions below.

This section has shown that, although the various rules imposed on districting agencies do reduce the numbers of possible solutions from astronomical levels, there will typically remain large numbers of feasible solutions from which to choose. Partisan, nonpartisan, and bipartisan districting all exist within this single framework (Taylor and Gudgin, 1976b). The next two sections investigate the implications of this range of choice. To begin with, the problem of dividing an area into just two constituencies will be considered.

6.3 The two-constituency case

The two-constituency case is particularly simple because it involves only two possible electoral outcomes. If stalemates are ignored so that a majority party and a minority party are assumed, then the only possible results are two seats for the majority party or one seat for each party. The latter result further requires that the minority party obtains at least 25% of the two-party vote.

6.3.1 Alternative solutions

By using the algorithms described in the last section, it is possible to obtain a range of alternative feasible solutions for any two-constituency problem. The next stage is to relate these solutions to possible electoral outcomes. This can be achieved if party votes can be estimated for each district in order to predict a winner. Thus, in a two-constituency analysis it should be possible to make a statement that out of m possible pairs of constituencies, p pairs provide two seats for the majority party and $(m-p)$ pairs provide one seat each. This would provide an empirical assessment of the range of possible fortunes of each party in any particular districting problem. However, in order to generalise beyond the particular it is necessary to enquire what types of districting solution produce the different outcomes. This, in turn, requires some way of characterising different solutions so that they can be related one to another and to electoral outcomes.

Consider the task of gerrymandering a city into two constituencies for the majority party. In order to carry out this task, city wards have to be combined. The first step is to estimate the probable voting levels of each ward for a 'normal election'. Given these figures, it is possible to experiment with different combinations of wards to provide the majority party with both seats. Ideally, both constituencies should be identical in political character, thus reflecting the party's overall city majority. For instance, if the party's overall city vote is 60%, the best solution for the gerrymanderer is for both districts to have 60% voting for the majority party. Divergences from this case put one constituency increasingly at risk. Hence, the best solution from the point of view of the majority party minimises polarisation between constituencies. Where both constituencies are politically identical, polarisation is zero. This may be measured by the variance of the predicted vote proportions for districts in a given solution. Hence, if both constituencies have a 60% level of support, the variance is zero. Majority-party gerrymandering may be described in statistical terms as minimising the between-district variance.

What about the strategy of the minority party? Gerrymandering for the minority party in the two-constituency case involves trying to ensure an even split of seats. In this case, it is best to make the two constituencies as different as possible. This concedes one constituency to the majority party, which they are sure to win anyway, but attempts to make the other constituency sufficiently different to ensure minority-party representation. Hence, the minority strategy is to produce as much polarisation between constituencies as possible and hence to maximise between-district variance.

It is useful, therefore, to characterise alternative districting solutions in terms of political polarisation which is measured as the between-district variance of a solution. A simple example will help to fix ideas. Suppose there are eight base units (wards) to combine into two constituencies of four wards each. The voting in this electoral area is such that the majority party normally obtains a proportion of 0.6 of the overall vote, although at the ward level its proportion varies from 0.31 to 0.89 as indicated in table 6.3. With no further constraints specified, there are thirty-five ways in which these eight base areas can be combined into two exclusive sets of four. All thirty-five solutions are set out in table 6.3.

Table 6.3 represents the range of choice available to a districting agency for this artificial example. The agency has to choose one out of the thirty-five alternatives. Solution 1 has the highest between-district variance and hence represents the optimum for minority gerrymandering. There are three optimum solutions for majority gerrymandering, on the other hand, as solutions 23, 28, and 32 produce two districts with identical voting predictions leading to zero between-district variance. However, the purpose of measuring alternative solutions in terms of variance is to move beyond consideration of these limiting cases. Since there are variances for all of these solutions, it is possible to produce a frequency distribution to illustrate the overall pattern of polarisation. This is given in figure 6.8. The skewed distribution reflects the fact that there are very many more situations of low polarisation than of high polarisation. In other words, it is easier to gerrymander for the majority

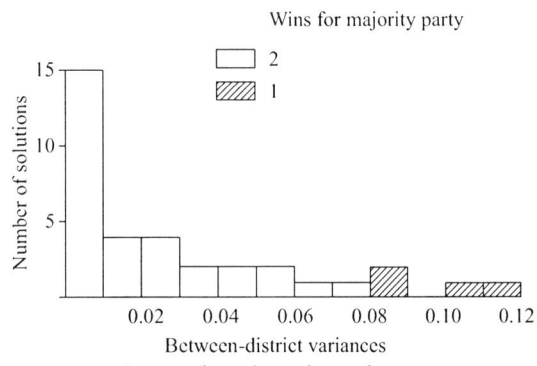

Figure 6.8: Districting solutions for a hypothetical case

party than for the minority party. In fact, as table 6.3 and figure 6.8 show, out of thirty-five possible outcomes, thirty-one predict 2–0 victories for the majority party, and only four involve 1–1 results. The significance of this 'natural' advantage for the majority party will be elaborated below.

Table 6.3: All possible combinations of eight base areas into two 'districts' of four base areas each
Base-area proportions of vote for the majority party are (1) 0.31; (2) 0.47; (3) 0.55; (4) 0.59; (5) 0.61; (6) 0.65; (7) 0.73; (8) 0.89.

Solution	Combinations I	II	x_1	x_2	Result	Between-district variance
1	1234	5678	0.480	0-720	1-1	0.1152
2	1235	4678	0.485	0.715	1-1	0.1058
3	1236	4578	0.495	0.705	1-1	0.0882
4	1237	4568	0.515	0.685	2-0	0.0578
5	1238	4567	0.555	0.645	2-0	0.0162
6	1245	3678	0.495	0.705	1-1	0.0882
7	1246	3578	0.505	0.695	2-0	0.0722
8	1247	3568	0.525	0.675	2-0	0.0450
9	1248	3567	0.565	0.635	2-0	0.0098
10	1345	2678	0.515	0.685	2-0	0.0578
11	1346	2578	0.525	0.675	2-0	0.0450
12	1347	2568	0.545	0.655	2-0	0.0242
13	1348	2567	0.585	0.615	2-0	0.0018
14	2345	1678	0.555	0.645	2-0	0.0162
15	2346	1578	0.656	0.635	2-0	0.0098
16	2347	1568	0.585	0.615	2-0	0.0018
17	2348	1567	0.625	0.575	2-0	0.0050
18	1256	3478	0.510	0.690	2-0	0.0648
19	1257	3468	0.530	0.670	2-0	0.0392
20	1258	3467	0.570	0.630	2-0	0.0072
21	1267	3458	0.540	0.660	2-0	0.0288
22	1268	3457	0.580	0.620	2-0	0.0032
23	1278	3456	0.600	0.600	2-0	0.0000
24	1356	2478	0.530	0.670	2-0	0.0392
25	1357	2468	0.550	0.650	2-0	0.0200
26	1358	2467	0.590	0.610	2-0	0.0008
27	1367	2458	0.560	0.640	2-0	0.0128
28	1368	2457	0.600	0.600	2-0	0.0000
29	1378	2456	0.620	0.580	2-0	0.0032
30	1456	2378	0.540	0.660	2-0	0.0288
31	1457	2368	0.560	0.640	2-0	0.0128
32	1458	2367	0.600	0.600	2-0	0.0000
33	1467	2358	0.570	0.630	2-0	0.0072
34	1468	2357	0.610	0.590	2-0	0.0008
35	1478	2356	0-630	0.570	2-0	0.0072

6.3.2 Constituencies for Sunderland

The above hypothetical example can be extended to cover practical districting situations. However, the example used includes only an equal-size constraint (that is, four base units per constituency) whereas actual districting practice nearly always involves a strict contiguity constraint. This has the effect of disqualifying some solutions as unsuitable. If the pattern of party support among constituencies were random this would not matter since the feasible solutions would simply represent an unbiased random sample of all the possible solutions. However, patterns of party support are typically not random but have a clustered orientation. The positive spatial autocorrelation of the proportions of party support among base areas will mean that like-areas are more likely to be combined, resulting in a bias towards higher variances. Thus, the pattern of party support would seem to operate against the tendency previously noted for aggregation to work in favour of the majority party. Whether this effect is large enough to cancel out the advantage of the majority party will obviously depend on the level of spatial autocorrelation. Since the specific relationship between spatial autocorrelation and the variance from contiguous classes is not known, this question can for the moment only be answered empirically for individual cases. The English borough of Sunderland will be taken as the example of a two-constituency districting problem.

The problem confronting the 1954 Boundary Commissioners when they came to consider Sunderland was to produce two parliamentary constituencies from a set of eighteen wards. This can be translated into a problem of producing two exclusive sets of nine contiguous wards. As previously noted, by using a modification of the Shepherd-Jenkins algorithm eighty-seven alternative solutions to the problem are found.

These alternative solutions can only be politically assessed by using electoral data for wards. Unfortunately, British general election results are not made available for wards and so ward levels of party support have had to be estimated from local-government election results. The resulting values are meant to be illustrative rather than definitive. Local election results have been modified to sum to an overall Labour vote representing a proportion of the vote of 0.585. This coincides with the 1970 level of support for Labour in what was a relatively close General Election. The resulting distribution of variances for the eighty-seven solutions when these estimated voting levels are used, is shown in figure 6.9. This distribution is derived from a voting pattern which is positively spatially autocorrelated; Conservative wards are concentrated into two middle-class areas in the northeast and south of the town (see Robson, 1969). However, this autocorrelation does not prevent the generation of a pattern of variances, most of which are relatively small (figure 6.9). Notice how these possible variances are spread around the particular variance expected for the whole country under cube-law-type conditions (0.019).

The processes operating which tend to produce the overall cube-law-type result are operating here to produce the very many small variances shown in figure 6.9. However, here there are a whole range of possible variances reflecting alternative electoral outcomes. Only one is chosen by the districting agency and it can be seen that it is likely to favour Labour. Out of the eighty-seven solutions, only fourteen allow the Conservatives to win one seat despite their 41% share of the vote. The electoral bias towards the majority party noted in previous chapters at the national scale can be seen here operating at the local level. It is the combination of these local biases that finally results in the nonpartisan bias shown previously to operate at the national scale.

The specific situation which leads to a winner's bias for Sunderland can be easily described since Sunderland's two areas of high Conservative support are separated in most solutions. On their own neither is large enough to outnumber surrounding pro-Labour areas. The Conservatives can only win a seat in Sunderland when their two middle-class areas belong to the same constituency. This is illustrated in the best solution for the Conservatives in figure 6.10(a). For Labour, on the other hand, these two areas need to be separated and outnumbered by Labour territory [figure 6.10(b)]. In simple terms, east-west divisions of the borough tend to allow Conservative representation, north-south divisions let Labour win both seats. There are more ways in which a north-south

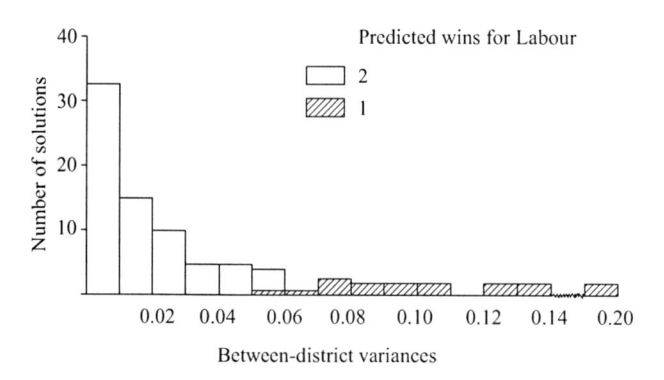

Figure 6.9: Districting solutions for Sunderland

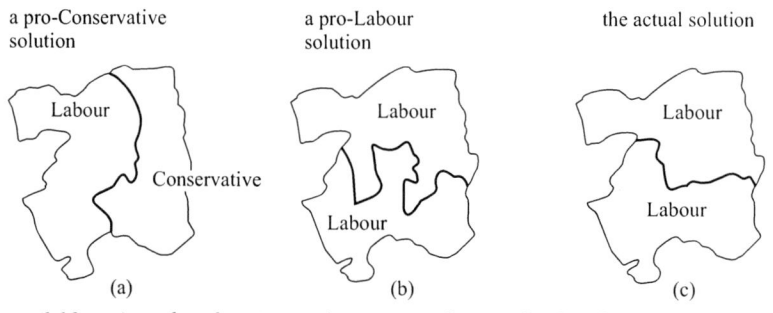

Figure 6.10: Actual and optimum districting solutions for Sunderland

division can be achieved and the Boundary Commission have accepted one of these [figure 6.10(c)].

What effect do changes in the overall level of support have on the electoral implications of Sunderland's eighty-seven solutions? If a uniform swing across wards from the 1970 figures is assumed, it is possible to reassess the solutions for different Labour proportions of the vote. This is illustrated in figure 6.11. At 50% of the vote, all solutions predict one seat each; when Labour wins 64% of the vote, all solutions predict both seats for Labour. There is a fairly steady decline in Conservative successes as the Labour vote increases from 50% to 64%. What this means is that the plurality electoral system allows *no* way in which a minority with up to 36% of party voters can be represented in Sunderland given the spatial distribution of support typical of the Conservatives.

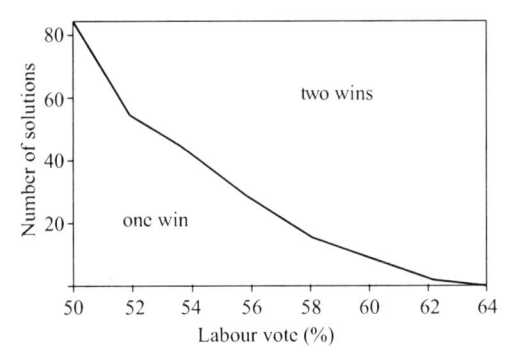

Figure 6.11:   Hypothetical election results in Sunderland for varying levels of votes

6.3.3 Districting decisions of alternative agencies

What are the implications of the above analyses? Basically, the variance distributions can be generalised into two types of solution. These are 'modal' types with small variances and 'tail' types with large variances. By using this dichotomy it is possible to classify districting agencies in terms of the sort of solution they are likely to produce. Eight such agencies are specified in figure 6.12.

The two cases used to introduce our discussion are placed at the top of the lists in figure 6.12. A partisan agency working for the majority party will normally choose a modal solution while a partisan agency working for a minority party will opt for a tail choice. Partisan districting will produce either type of solution depending on who is designing the districts. This is not the case for the other two general types of districting agency. Nonpartisan agencies will not consider electoral outcomes and so their solutions may be considered arbitrary selections from the whole population of solutions. However, since the modal solutions are far more common than tail solutions, it follows that nonpartisan agencies are more than likely to make a modal choice. Consequently the three nonpartisan agencies identified in figure 6.12 are all allocated to the modal column.

In contrast, bipartisan districting will be directly concerned with the political outcomes. However, in this case, fair shares for both sides will require polarised districts, which are the result of tail choices. These considerations lead to the intriguing finding that in the simple two-constituency case it is bipartisan and nonpartisan districting which contrast most acutely in terms of electoral outcomes although both may produce solutions similar in effect to partisan gerrymanderers. Neutral boundary commissions have an effect similar to that of majority-party gerrymandering, and bipartisan commissions will have an effect similar to that of minority-party gerrymandering. In the Sunderland example, the result would have been very similar if the Labour Party had been allowed to gerrymander in a true American style. The use of a nonpartisan agency proved to be no advantage to the underrepresented Conservative minority.

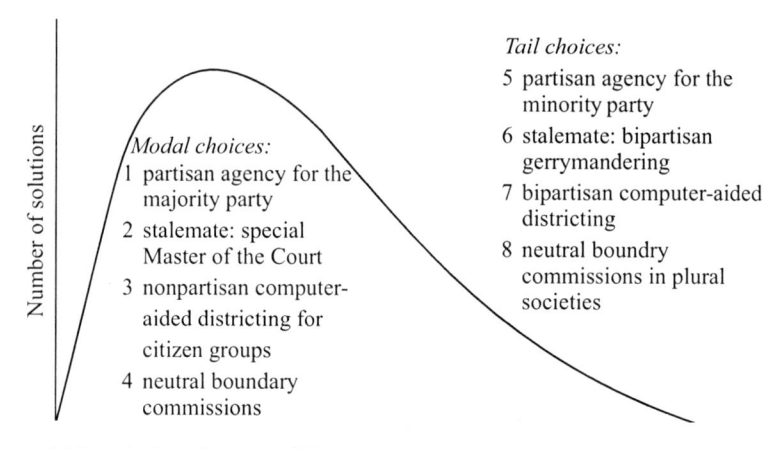

Figure 6.12:   A classification of districting agencies

Modal choices:
1 partisan agency for the majority party
2 stalemate: special Master of the Court
3 nonpartisan computer-aided districting for citizen groups
4 neutral boundary commissions

Tail choices:
5 partisan agency for the minority party
6 stalemate: bipartisan gerrymandering
7 bipartisan computer-aided districting
8 neutral boundry commissions in plural societies

6.3.4 A formal derivation of majority-party bias

The above discussion has illustrated the proposition that most districting solutions will tend to favour the majority party. Specifically the theory is based upon the fact that the two examples show more solutions favouring the majority party than favouring the minority party. In this section this finding is presented more formally.

Each arrangement of base units gives one independent result (the first constituency) and a second result dependent on the first (the second constituency). In statistical terms there is just one degree of freedom. In solution 1 in table 6.3, for example, the first solution gives an electoral outcome of 48% of the vote for the majority party in the first constituency so that it follows that in the second constituency the majority party must win 72% of the vote to produce the overall average of 60%. Hence when plotted against one another on a graph, such pairs of results define a one-dimensional pattern at 45° to the axes (figure 6.13). This space may be divided into different regions corresponding to election results. In the top right-hand quarter the majority party wins over 50% of the vote in both constituencies and hence this is the 2-0 region. In the top-left and bottom-right quarters the majority party wins only one constituency so that these represent two 1 – 1 regions.

The reason for defining regions producing different election results is that if it is possible to specify the distribution of feasible outcomes which lie along the 45° line then the proportion of majority party 2-0 victories can be derived. The distribution of alternative solutions can be considered as equivalent to a sampling situation with a population of n objects (base units) sampled without replacement $j = n/z$ times. Hence a constituency may be considered a sample and the constituency result as the sample mean. Now the distribution of sample means is known to approximate a normal distribution whatever the underlying distribution of population. According to the central limit theorem the distribution of sample means tends towards normality as sample size increases. How quickly normality is achieved by increasing sample size depends on the underlying population, but the convergence is usually quite rapid. Snedecor and Cochran (1967, page 52) show, for example, that samples of five from a rectangular distribution are large enough to produce a normal distribution of sample means. Hence a normal distribution of constituency results may not be all that unrealistic in the present situation.

The standard deviation of this normal distribution of electoral outcomes will depend on the standard deviation of the underlying population of base units and on the sample size (j). The latter will vary for particular districting problems. In the hypothetical example used previously, the standard deviation of the base-area proportions is 0.16 so that the standard deviation of the constituency results will be $0.16/j^{1/2} = 0.08$.

If normality is assumed, it is possible to predict exactly the proportion of solutions favouring the majority party for a particular overall level of vote. This is simply that central part of the normal distribution in the

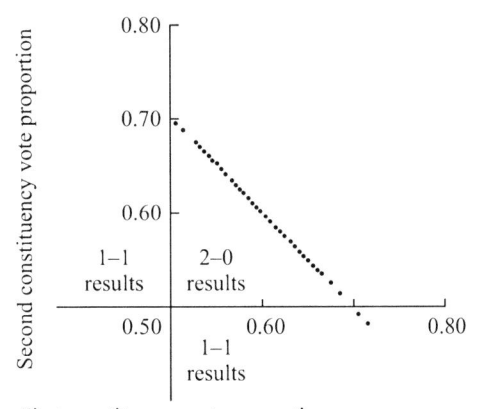

Figure 6.13:   Formal derivation of electoral bias

2–0 win region. This is given by

$$2\left(\Phi\frac{V-0.5}{\sigma}\right)-1,$$

where V is the overall vote proportion and Φ is the cumulative normal distribution function given in table 2.1.

In the hypothetical example this gives an estimate of 0.79, which corresponds to a prediction of twenty-eight 2–0 wins out of thirty-five, compared with the actual number of thirty-one out of thirty-five in table 6.3. In this case the process underlying the central limit theorem is clearly operating for as low a sample size as $j = 4$.

In the Sunderland example not all combinations of nine from eighteen are considered because a contiguity constraint is imposed. Hence the analogy with the sampling experiment will only be strictly equivalent where the pattern of base-area proportions is spatially random. This is known not to be the case in Sunderland. Nevertheless a normal distribution of election results does occur and the above model predicts a proportion of 0.8 for 2–0 victories to Labour, or seventy out of the eighty-seven solutions. This compares with the actual situation of seventy-four out of eighty-seven, so that in this 'real world' example the model operates reasonably well. This suggests that this approach may well be quite robust in the usual situation where vote proportions in base areas are spatially autocorrelated.

Two extensions of the model may be briefly mentioned. First the level of majority-party vote may be varied to produce the pattern of predicted 2–0 victories equivalent to the graph of solutions for Sunderland in figure 6.11. Second, a more complete application would be to extend the method beyond the two-constituency case. The three-constituency case, for example, has two degrees of freedom, so the solutions may be defined in a plane. A bivariate normal distribution model may then be employed to predict the number of solutions lying in the several win regions. It is not proposed to extend this methodology here and cases with more than two constituencies will be treated in the more informal manner of the previous discussion.

6.4 Extensions to more than two constituencies

How far can the surprising classification of districting agencies for the two-constituency case be extended to electoral areas with more than two constituencies? The added complexity of extra constituencies makes direct application of the previous ideas difficult. With more than two possible electoral outcomes, it seems likely that the simple dichotomy between modal and tail choices will not be sufficient to incorporate the extra complexity. The only thing to be sure of in a plurality election is that the party winning most votes must win at least one seat. This means that the number of possible wins for the majority party is the same as the number of seats being contested. With three seats, there are three possible electoral outcomes (3–0, 2–1, and 1–2), with four seats, four solutions (4–0, 3–1, 2–2, 1–3), and so on. In any practical districting situation, all of these possible outcomes may not materialise, but they must be considered in any theoretical argument.

6.4.1 Variance and party fortunes

The two limiting cases identified in the last section were that maximum between-district variance was found to optimise the minority party's position, and that minimum between-district variance was found to optimise the majority party's position. This latter statement is still true where there are more than two constituencies. Clearly, the majority party in theory has its best result where all constituencies are identical and the variance is zero. This will give the majority party a clean sweep of all seats.

What are the electoral implications of maximising between-district variance? The limiting case occurs where party voters are totally separated so that each constituency is 100% for one party. For instance, in a five-constituency situation, a majority's 60% of the overall vote would be concentrated solely in three constituencies with all minority votes in the other two. Notice that the 3–2 result in terms of seats is proportional to the 60–40 vote assumption. Separation of voters and, hence, maximising between-district variance tends to produce proportionality in representation. However, it is known from the skilful deeds of gerrymandered in the past that minority parties can do better than obtain proportionality. Elbridge Gerry certainly surpassed proportionality for his minority party in the original gerrymander in Massachusetts.

The best solution for a minority party is not total separation from majority-party supporters, but rather a solution where minority-party votes are spread among constituencies such that each *just* represents a majority in that constituency. Any further concentration merely produces wasted excess votes. In theory a constituency is won when one party obtains a proportion of 0.5 of the two-party vote plus one additional vote. With v voters and k constituencies, this threshold (t) can be written,

$$t = \frac{0.5v}{k} + 1. \tag{6.6}$$

In constituencies of over a thousand voters, $0.500 < t < 0.501$, although in practice, gerrymanderers would obviously design their districts by predicting a winning threshold much greater than this theoretical t value in order to incorporate a reasonable margin of error (for example $t = 0.55$). In this discussion t will be employed to represent both the theoretical and the practical winning threshold, since the exact value of t does not alter the conclusions. The minority party obtains proportion q of the vote.

From the above assumptions, the distribution of constituency vote proportions for the minority party in its optimum districting solution will have a proportion q/t of the constituencies with proportion t voting for the party, and a proportion $1 - (q/t)$ of the constituencies where the party receives no votes. The variance of the CPD in this optimum districting solution is given by

$$\frac{q(q-t)^2}{t} + \left(1 - \frac{q}{t}\right)q^2 , \qquad (6.7)$$

which reduces to *(tq — q^2)*. This variance compares with the maximum variance based on distributions reflecting total separation, given by

$$q(1-q)^2 + (1-q)q^2 , \qquad (6.8)$$

which reduces to $(q - q^2)$. Thus, the optimum solution for the minority party has a variance of only a proportion of the maximum variance, since $t < 1$. This means that, as the variance increases, the minority party will tend to be favoured until some value (less than the maximum variance) is reached, after which point the advantage to the minority party tends to decline to the position of proportional representation.

Hence, the relationship between party fortunes and between-district variance is not a simple monotonic one. In fact, it can be easily shown that the relationship is by no means stable. A solution where the minority party just fails to win in many constituencies will produce a variance very similar to the variance for the minority party's optimum solution reported above. All that can be asserted is that small variances will favour the majority party; the best solutions for the minority will be associated with some known higher level of variance; and finally, maximum variance implies proportional representation. Although the theory is much less clearcut than in the two-constituency case, there are three types of solutions to look out for in empirical studies.

6.4.2 Constituencies for Newcastle upon Tyne

The Newcastle districting problem is specified as that of producing four parliamentary constituencies from twenty wards. In the Boundary Commission's solution of 1954, a small area outside Newcastle (Newburn) was added to one of the constituencies, but this addition is ignored here. Party voting is estimated for wards in the same way as for Sunderland, so that they relate to Labour's 1970 level of support, 0.58. A total of 337 different solutions were produced such that each constituency consisted of five discrete, contiguous wards. The pattern of the variances is shown in figure 6.14. Like the Sunderland case, there are very many more low variances than high variances in a skewed distribution. However, the electoral outcomes are a little more complicated. In this case, three possible results emerge, 4 – 0 or 3 – 1 to Labour or a 2 – 2 split. Notice that the best results for the majority are among the smallest variances as decisionmaking in electoral districting | 157

in the two-constituency case. In contrast, the best results for the minority are not at the other end of the distribution, but are in the middle range of variances. This is exactly consistent with the above extension of the variance argument into more than two constituencies.

Examples of good solutions for each party are illustrated in figure 6.15. In this case, Labour votes are concentrated in the south (along the river) and in patches (of council housing) in the north, while Conservative support is largely in the north of the city. Hence, the best solution for the Conservatives produces two northern constituencies which they can just win, and two southern constituencies which they lose badly [figure 6.15(a)]. In contrast, the best solution for Labour involves combining northern and southern wards into north-south sectors in which Labour hold a majority [figure 6.15(b)].

The actual solution of the Boundary Commission reflects neither of the above strategies [figure 6.15(c)]. It carves out one constituency in the north for the Conservatives, leaving Labour to win the other three. This result is hardly surprising, given the overall pattern of possible results. In fact, the most noticeable feature of figure 6.15 is the overwhelming dominance of 3 – 1 wins to Labour. This electoral outcome is predicted for fully 256 solutions, which represents slightly over three-quarters of the total. Hence, the Newcastle case is similar to the two-constituency case in Sunderland in this respect; there is one electoral outcome which is the most common among solutions and the Boundary Commission has selected

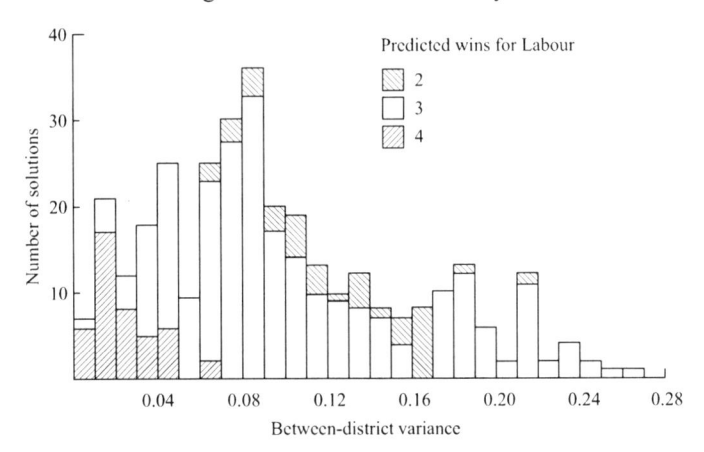

Figure 6.14: Districting solutions for Newcastle upon Tyne

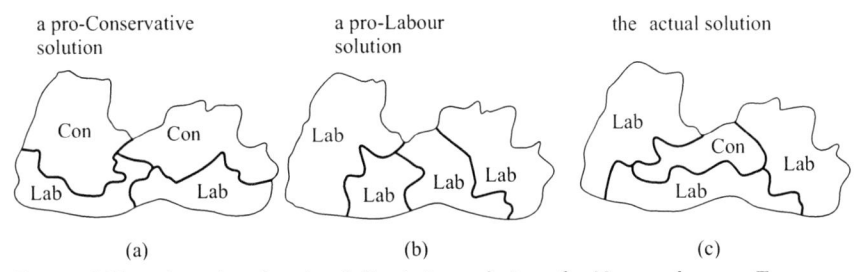

Figure 6.15: Actual and optimal districting solutions for Newcastle upon Tyne

one of these most common solutions. This evidence supports the view of the Boundary Commissioners as merely choosing arbitrarily from the population of possible solutions and hence, favouring the majority party. In Newcastle, Labour's 58% of the vote gives them a 75% share of the seats.

What happens when there is a swing away from a 'normal' year like 1970? Figure 6.16 shows predicted electoral outcomes over the 337 solutions for a Labour vote ranging from 50% to 64%, with the same swing in each ward. This shows that 3 – 1 wins for Labour are the most common result for all Labour percentages from 54% to 64%. An even 2 – 2 split is only most common for 50% and 52%. This shows how quickly the winner's bias begins to operate as a party's vote rises above 50%. Labour's three seats in Newcastle are relatively safe.

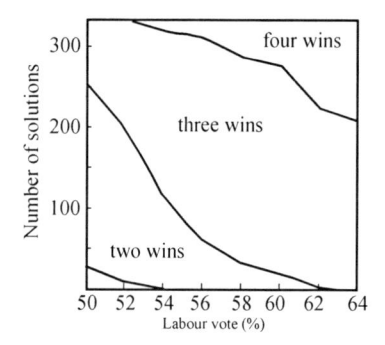

Figure 6.16: Hypothetical election results in Newcastle for varying levels of votes

6.4.3 Congressional districts for Iowa

The results of the 1970 US census showed that the State of Iowa was growing at a slower rate than the US as a whole, and as a result Iowa found itself apportioned only six seats in Congress instead of the seven held since 1960. These seven districts had generally split 5 – 2 in favour of the Republicans. The Democrats were largely concentrated in the few urban counties but they were not a small minority—in 1968 they polled 46% of the vote for example, and the existing districting solution involved a relatively high degree of competition between parties. Four of the seven districts were considered 'swing' districts. This is the situation which had to be converted into a six-district solution.

The redistricting was the responsibility of the state legislature, both houses of which were Republican controlled in 1970 – 1971 and the Republican governor. Thus, the possibility of partisan districting is clearly present. This is reflected in an early suggestion by one group of Republicans who actually produced the perfect population-equality solution [figure 6.17(a)]. Since the 1970 population total for Iowa was an odd number, equal district populations were impossible with an even number of districts. None the less, this Republican solution does have five districts with equal populations (470840) and one district with just a one person difference (470841). This solution meets Supreme Court requirements to the absolute limit, but was one of the most flagrant gerrymanders attempted. It combined pro-Democrat counties in central Iowa into a single heavily Democratic district so that an overall 5 – 1 split in favour of Republicans was confidently predicted. This is surely a classic case of attempting to use population equality to justify a partisan districting solution.

This attempted Republican gerrymander was never seriously considered because it violated county boundaries. The Iowa electoral law insists that congressional districts be made up of whole counties, hence without a court challenge to this law the Republican plan was disqualified at the start. In fact, as mentioned above, the legislature employed Liittschwager's Iowa Redistricting System, which used Iowa's ninety-nine counties as base units. One of the eleven computer solutions was chosen and slightly modified [figure 6.17(b)]. On 1968 levels of support (Republicans 54%) the final plan would give the Republicans a 4 – 2 majority of congressmen.

Although at first sight a 4 – 2 win for 54% of the vote seems to be a good solution for Republicans, seen in the wider perspective of other possible solutions, the result is not so unfair. The algorithm described above for large combinatorial problems was used to produce a sample of 700 six-district solutions and these were evaluated by using the actual county vote proportions for 1968. The distribution of variances is shown in figure 6.18, where it can be seen that 541 of the sample do lead to

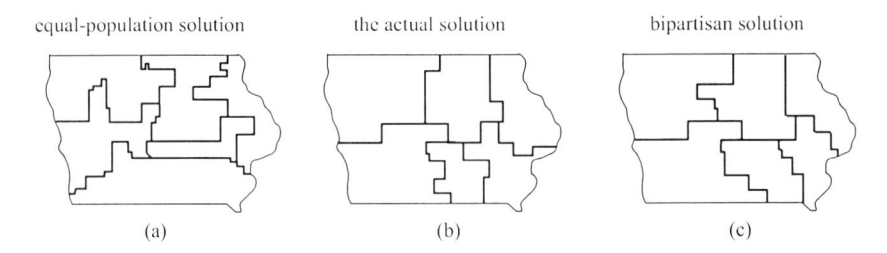

Figure 6.17: Districting solutions for Iowa

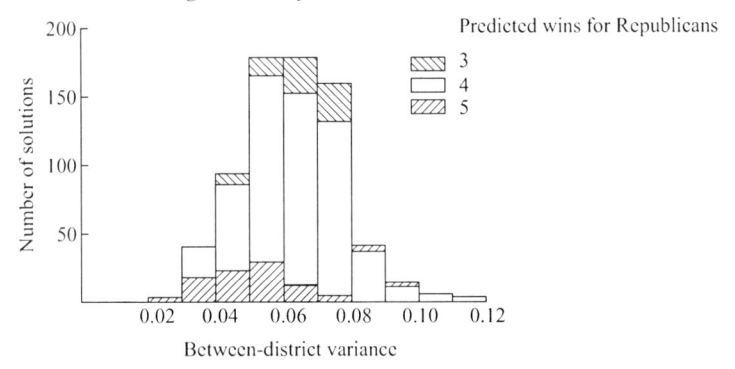

Figure 6.18: Distribution of feasible districting solutions for Iowa

4 – 2 wins for the majority. Hence the final plan is one of the most common

category of electoral outcomes. There are thus two similarities with the two previous British examples; first, there is one particular electoral outcome which occurs in the vast majority of solutions and, second, the actual chosen solution is predicted as producing this most common electoral outcome. This adds weight to the earlier suggestion that partisan and nonpartisan agencies tend to produce similar electoral outcomes.

Of course, the political choice inherent in the American system of districting means that other possibilities may be canvassed. However, the 1970 – 1971 districting solution was certainly not a bipartisan gerrymander, which was so common elsewhere. Republican attempts to gain four seats meant that the districts remained relatively competitive like the preexisting Iowa districts. An alternative bipartisan solution was presented in P J Taylor (1973) [figure 6.17(c)]. This was designed so that a 50 – 50 split in the vote would result in a safe 3 – 3 split in seats. In fact, the smallest majority was calculated at over 19000. Hence, this is a typical bipartisan solution ensuring three seats per party for 'normal' elections. However, elections themselves would become much less interesting events as districts would only change hands in particularly one-sided elections. This solution almost takes elections out of the hands of the voters.

This can be contrasted with the actual solution, which made Iowa one of the few states where the large swing against the Republicans in 1974 did count. All of Iowa's districts lay in the middle of the overall CPD shown in figure 6.4 so that the post-Watergate swing in 1974 produced a 5 – 1 victory for the Democrats. Moreover the result was within 1% swing for a startling 6 – 0 clean sweep. The Democrats achieved this massive victory in terms of seats with just 54% of the vote. Although they cannot be held to have gerrymandered the districting solution of 1970 – 1971, they have been the party that has truly benefited. This is simply a result of their being a majority party in a solution which was not bipartisan. The outcome is clearly unfair, Republican strength of 46% deserves more than one congressman out of six.

The Iowa example demonstrates what was concluded at the end of the first section of this chapter, namely that alternative districting solutions can, in their different ways, be equally unsatisfactory. Is a stable 3 – 3 situation better than possible 6 – 0 landslides?

6.5 Is there a satisfactory districting procedure?

One thing that most political scientists and commentators agree upon is that partisan districting is ethically unjustifiable. For one party to enhance the value of its vote just because they are in a legislative majority is clearly unsatisfactory. However, in this chapter it has been shown that alternative districting procedures create new problems. A nonpartisan approach is sometimes said to reflect integrity but it is also naive and simplistic.

Procedural fairness is not enough, since, as in all other aspects of politics, means and ends cannot be arbitrarily separated. It is little consolation to a party that suffers badly from a particular districting solution that the solution was chosen with no political malice. For the party it is the effect that counts, not the motives of the districting agency.

One type of party that suffers badly from *any* districting solution is the minor party with nationwide support. None of the alternative districting approaches discussed in this chapter in any way help to contribute to solving the problem of this type of minor party. Bipartisan districting can only help a party with either approximately half the vote or specific areas of concentrated support. In any case, it has been shown that a bipartisan approach is almost equivalent to disenfranchising the voters.

What is the solution? If there is no satisfactory way of defining electoral districts, it suggests that the fault lies in the electoral method. Since chapter 2, it has been shown how the relationship between seats and votes in plurality elections is affected by malapportionment, the form of the constituency proportion distribution, types of swing, number of parties, and ways in which the constituencies are defined. All of these 'problems' produce results that are unsatisfactory in one form or another. Can they be overcome 'at a stroke' by changing the electoral system? Chapter 7 attempts to answer this question by considering systems of voting other than plurality elections.

chapter seven | beyond pluralities

This monograph is primarily about plurality elections and the mechanisms involved in translating seats into votes in such elections. The methodology developed in previous chapters provides the basis for an understanding of how plurality elections inevitably tend to produce large electoral biases. This is the reason why so few countries use this system of voting for electing their lower houses. In a sense these countries have been left behind as the rest of the elective democratic world has moved on to proportionally representative ways of electing their representatives. In chapter 1 this was identified as the reform of representation.

Chapter 6 was concerned with electoral reform but only within the context of plurality voting. The conclusion was that modifications of the procedures for drawing constituency boundaries would not overcome this intrinsic property of plurality elections to produce electoral biases. Hence meaningful reform of representation will have to involve a change in the system of voting itself. It is the purpose of this penultimate chapter to look beyond plurality elections and investigate alternative systems of voting. Particular emphasis will be placed upon the spatial organisation underlying these other voting systems, so parts of the methodology developed for plurality elections will be applied in subsequent analyses. The chapter is written from the point of view of the reform of British elections, since electoral reform is currently a 'live' issue in Britain. However, before analysis can begin it is necessary to describe briefly the alternative systems of voting available to reformers.

7.1 Systems of voting

Although proportionality of seats and votes among competing parties was identified as the goal of reform of representation in chapter 1 [equation (1.1)], in practice no system of voting has ever attained perfect proportionality of all parties in an election. Rae (1971) prefers to think of voting systems as lying on a continuum of varying degrees of disproportionality away from the proportional representation (PR) ideal. In this chapter this disproportionality will be measured for each party in an election by computing electoral biases as before, that is party seat percentage minus party vote percentage. The electoral biases resulting from all British elections since 1922 are illustrated in table 7.1. This table shows many of the effects of plurality elections previously discussed. Here it will be used as a 'standard' of disproportionality against which other voting systems can be compared.

The most popular method of electing national assemblies is *the PR list system* (Lakeman, 1974). This involves multimember constituencies, and electors are required to select from among party lists of candidates. Each party then has representatives elected from their lists in proportion to the votes cast for their list. There are a wide variety of such voting systems which allow different degrees of choice for voters within party lists. Nevertheless such voting systems with their emphasis on party organisation have never gained appreciable support among the 'Anglo-Saxon' democracies. This situation may, however, be on the verge of changing. The EEC aim to use a uniform system for the second direct election for the European Parliament due 1984. The UK was the only country to use the first-past-the-post system in the first direct election and will be under pressure to conform in future. A list system will be one of the options strongly considered by the EEC, but since there has never been a major body of support in Britain for list systems this procedure for voting is not considered further here. There are, in fact, three methods of voting that stand out as viable possibilities for change in Britain. These are the alternative-vote system, the single-transferable-vote system, and the additional-member system. Each will be briefly described in turn.

A simple objection to the plurality system is that with more than two candidates, the winning plurality proportion may be less than 50% of the vote. This means that a member is elected by a minority of voters in that constituency. Majority systems of voting have been devised in order to overcome this problem. This can be achieved by instituting two or more ballots so that candidates polling few votes on the first ballot are eliminated and their supporters have a chance to choose a second candidate in the next ballot. This type of system, without actually requiring a majority on the second ballot, operates in France. It is generally considered cumbersome because the same effect may be obtained

Table 7.1: *Electoral biases for British elections, 1922–1979*

Election	Conservative	Labour	Liberal
1922	+17.9	−6.4	−10.2
1923	+3.9	+0.6	−3.7
1924	+19.8	−8.4	−11.1
1929	+4.1	+9.7	−13.8
1931	+21.7	−22.1	−1.1
1935	+16.0	−12.9	−3.0
1945	−6.5	+13.6	−7.1
1950	+4.2	+4.3	−7.7
1951	+3.4	−1.6	−1.5
1955	+4.9	−2.4	−1.7
1959	+8.5	−2.8	−4.9
1964	+4.9	+6.2	−9.8
1966	−1.7	+9.7	−6.6
1970	+6.0	+2.6	−6.5
1974 (February)	+8.8	+10.3	−17.1
1974 (October)	+7.8	+11.0	−16.2
1979	+9.5	+5.3	−12.1

with one ballot using the alternative-vote system. In this case, the alternative-vote system (AVS), the voter indicates his first, second, third, etc preference of candidates. This ranking of votes allows the returning officer to reallocate minor candidate's votes by next preference until a majority candidate emerges. This system of voting is used for the Australian House of Representatives and was very nearly adopted for British elections in 1931 (Butler, 1963).

The *single-transferable-vote system (STV)* is generally considered a method of proportional representation (Rae, 1971) although it does not involve explicit treatment of parties as in the PR list systems. In this system each voter ranks candidates by preference as in the alternative-vote procedure. However, STV uses multimember constituencies so that several different party candidates may be elected for a given district. As in the alternative-vote system minor candidates are eliminated and their votes reallocated on the basis of their next preference. Candidates are declared elected when their total vote (including transferred lower preferences) passes the required quota. This quota is given by

$$\frac{u}{s+1} + 1,$$

where there are s seats in a constituency and a total of v valid votes. This system is used in the lower houses of Ireland and Malta and the upper houses in Australia and South Africa. It is, in a sense, the 'Anglo-Saxon' form of PR and in fact came close to being adapted for British elections in 1917-1918 (Butler, 1963).

The alternative-vote system and STV are the only two reforms of voting that have been seriously canvassed in Britain until recently. However, the 1970s have seen a new voting system being proposed by the Hansard Society. This is *the additional-member system (AMS)*, which is a mixture of pluralities and proportionality. It simply involves electing a proportion of an assembly, say half, by using pluralities in single-member constituencies and then 'topping up' this result with additional members so as to achieve proportionality between overall votes and seats. This system preserves the single-MP-constituency link while also aiming at PR. The unofficial report of the Hansard Society in 1976 recommended a form of AMS for British elections.

Each of these three alternative voting systems is considered in turn in this chapter. The analyses continue to investigate aspects of the spatial organisation but in contexts other than plurality laws. Abolishing plurality voting does not automatically counteract the problems inherent in the spatial organisation of elections. Problems can remain which will cause electoral biases and these need to be understood before any reform gets under way.

The evaluation of the alternative voting systems consists of two separate types of evidence. First, actual uses of the voting method in countries where it has been applied over several elections are considered. In each case a table is produced which shows how electoral biases have affected the three main parties contesting the elections. These tables are identical in layout to table 7.1 and should be directly compared with this first 'electoral bias table'. This type of evidence involves the very considerable problem of translating findings from these countries to Britain. However, this information is supplemented by a second type of evidence consisting of simulations of what would happen in British elections if these alternative systems were employed. This involves the problem of translating votes cast under a plurality system into the form required by an alternative system. The problems involved in using both types of evidence will be dealt with as we proceed.

7.2 Majority systems of voting

A reform of the voting system, replacing plurality voting by majority voting, can be implemented with a minimum of disturbance to the existing electoral machinery. Single-member districts are maintained so that there would be no need to change constituencies or existing arrangements for their periodic revision. All that is required is to change the form of ballot, either to request ranking of candidates to facilitate transferring votes or else to allow voting in a second ballot in constituencies where a majority is not obtained by any candidate to the initial ballot. This ease of implementation of reform is, however, gained at a price. The districting system is maintained and this means that the familiar problems associated with districts reappear under majority systems of voting.

7.2.1 The alternative vote in Australia

One major difference between Australian and British politics since the war has been in the different levels of success of the two country's Labour parties. The British Labour Party has won six out of ten postwar elections while the Australian Labor Party (ALP) has won three out of thirteen postwar elections. This poor record directly reflects the fact that ALP have virtually always suffered from some degree of electoral bias. Table 7.2 shows these biases and they are remarkable in that in each of these elections the ALP was the largest single party. In a plurality election the ALP would expect to gain a winner's bias, in Australian elections this simply does not seem to occur. Hence this forms a major contrast with table 7.1. This is further highlighted by the fact that the ALP consistently does better in terms of votes than its British counterpart. Even in the most recent elections of 1975 and October 1974, respectively, the ALP obtained 3% more of the vote in their landslide defeat than the British Labour Party in their electoral victory! A tendency towards an anti-Labour bias in plurality elections has been previously noted. In Australian alternative-vote elections this bias is maintained and multiplied.

Why should the ALP fare so badly? First the alternative-vote system does not prevent the bias identified for plurality voting operating against Labor. In particular the partisan bias associated with malapportionment and the distribution effect identified in chapter 3 can still occur (Blewett, 1972). One party can still win smaller constituencies in this system and it can also have its vote more effectively distributed among constituencies. Both effects have been measured for Australian elections by Soper and Rydon (1958). They studied the 1949, 1951, and 1954 elections and found malapportionment to be a negligible factor in the bias. However they found the ALP constituency proportion distribution to be positively skewed as indicated by the difference between the mean and the median. The cumulative distribution shows the ALP winning far more constituencies with very large majorities than its rivals. McPhail and Walmsley (1975) briefly compare the 1969, 1972, and 1974 elections and show how the ALP has continued to have larger winning votes than its rivals. Figure 7.1 shows the CPD for the 1974 and 1975 elections, the latter being disastrous for ALP with 44% first preferences producing only 28% of the seats. The positive skewness is again readily apparent in the classic way expected for major Labour parties (1974, $\beta_1 = +0.27$; 1975, ($\beta_1 = +0.91$). Hence it can be stated that the ALP are discriminated against because of the nature of the distribution of its support, as would occur in plurality elections.

The above discussion partially explains why the ALP does badly, but not why it does particularly badly when compared with the British Labour Party. To answer this question it is necessary to go beyond simple distribution effects and consider the interaction of the Australian party system with the alternative-vote procedure. First of all it should be noted that the alternative-vote system differs from a plurality system only in

Table 7.2: *Electoral biases in Australian elections, 1946–1975*
Sources: Hughes and Graham (1968), McPhail and Walmsley (1975), and *Australian Year Book* (1968).

Election	Liberal	Labor	Country
1946	−0.4	−8.0	0.0
1949	+6.1	−7.2	+4.8
1951	+2.7	−5.2	+4.7
1954	0.0	−0.9	+3.8
1955	+6.7	−2.6	+3.7
1958	+10.3	−5.9	+6.3
1961	+3.3	+1.3	+5.4
1963	+5.5	−5.4	+7.5
1966	+9.5	−4.3	+7.7
1969	+2.0	+0.3	+7.4
1972	−1.6	+4.0	+6.6
1974	−3.5	+2.7	+6.5
1975	+10.7	−14.5	+6.9

those constituencies where the leading candidate does not win 50% of the vote. In Australian elections 50% is achieved by one candidate in approximately two-thirds of constituencies. Thus only about one-third of the constituencies require the use of other preferences. Even within constituencies where preferences have to be reallocated, in more than half the cases the original leading candidate (with a plurality) becomes the final winning candidate (with a majority). However, there is ample evidence that the transfer of votes does operate against Labor. Butler (1973), for instance, points out that in the eight elections up until 1972 Labor only once came from second place to win. This contrasts with Liberal and Country Party candidates, who came from second place to win in twelve cases in 1969 and fourteen cases in 1972. These successes were based on both minor-party voters (including Democratic Labor supporters) allocating their preferences against ALP but particularly transfers of votes between the Liberal Party and the Country Party enabled one of them to overhaul the ALP. Thus the ALP was not able to benefit from a division of the non-Labor vote in the way in which they could under a plurality system. These changes between plurality and majority positions occur in only a few constituencies but they are important in an assembly of only 122 seats. Hence here there is an added dimension in the particularly poor performance of the ALP. The requirement of a majority rather than a plurality in constituencies enables the anti-Labor vote to be most effectively used in preventing election of ALP members (Graham, 1962).

The effectiveness of the alternative-vote system in overturning simple pluralities relies on there being reasonably large minority parties. In a pure two-party system of course all pluralities are majorities. This situation is most nearly found in the USA and we can predict that, given the present American party system, the alternative-vote procedure applied to the US Congress would have no effect whatsoever since congressmen are already normally elected by district majorities. Hence the successful

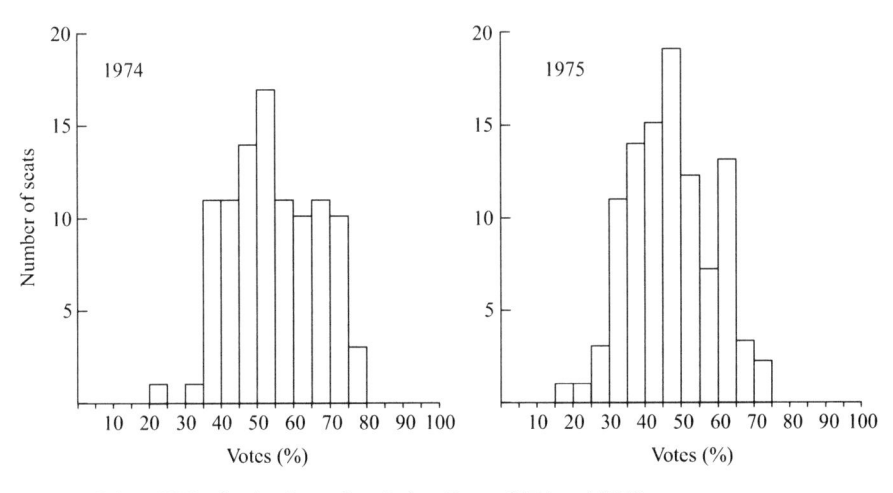

Figure 7.1: CPDs for the Australian Labor Party, 1974 and 1975

168 | seats, votes, and the spatial organisation of elections

operation of the alternative-vote system requires, at the very least, a three-party election situation.

In chapter 5 the electoral triangle was employed as the basis for modelling three-party plurality elections. The same can be used to illustrate the operation of the alternative-vote system. Parties A, B, and C will be considered as before, with party C's vote specified by a notional scale declining from 0° at the hypotenuse to 100° at the lower left-hand corner of the diagram.

Figure 7.2(a) shows the initial division of the triangle into six regions. There are the three outer triangles where one of the three parties obtains a majority of the first count and is returned. We need not consider these cases further. The inner triangle, however, represents the region where no party has an initial majority. One of the three parties has to be eliminated for the second count and so the inner triangle is divided into three quadrilaterals, each defining an elimination region for the three parties.

In each elimination region there are only two possible winners left. Which candidate wins depends on first-preference votes plus the allocation of the eliminated-candidates preferences. Consider party C's elimination region. Let party C's second preferences be γ% for party A and $(100 - \gamma)$% for party B. Then the elimination region can be divided into two by a line from the point where party C votes = 0% (the hypotenuse). The angle θ_γ from the hypotenuse depends on γ such that $\theta_\gamma = 0.9\gamma$. Hence if party C's preferences are evenly split between party A and party B, $\gamma = 50$%, so $\theta_\gamma = 45°$, which evenly divides the elimination region. Similarly if party A's preferences are allocated α% to party B and $(100-\alpha)$% to party C it is possible to define $\theta_\alpha = 0.45\alpha$ as shown in figure 7.2(b). In the same way party B's preferences split β% to party A, $(100-\beta)$% to party C and $\theta_\beta = 0.45\beta$. All three elimination regions can therefore be

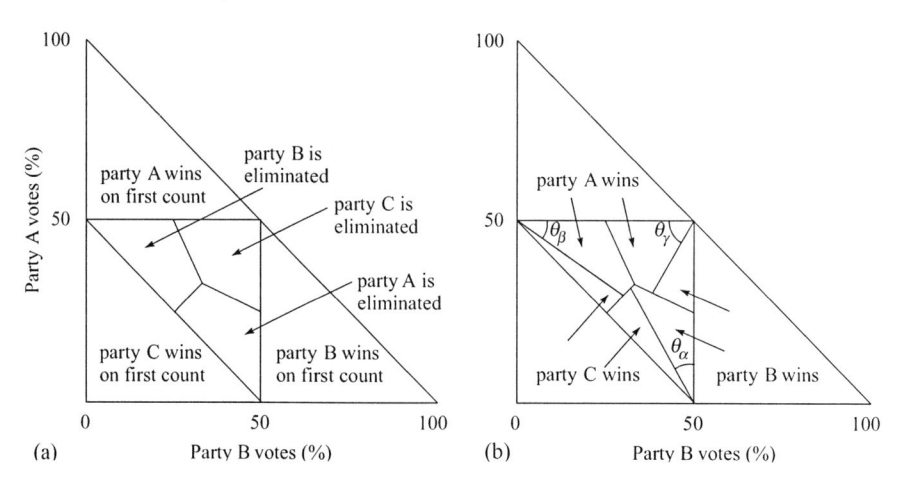

Figure 7.2: Election triangle for the alternative-vote system

beyond pluralities | 169

divided into two and added to the noneliminated parties' initial winning regions.

In the case where $\alpha = \beta = \gamma = 50\%$ the final winning regions are identical to the winning regions in a plurality election. Counting preferences only converts pluralities into majorities. However, differences from plurality elections result from situations when α, β, and γ differ from 50%. In Australian elections, for example, the figures $\alpha = 50\%$, $\beta = 30\%$, $\gamma = 20\%$ (where A is the ALP, B is the Liberals, and C is the Country Party) give the correct final election result for 1975. This produces $\theta_\alpha = 45°$, $\theta_\beta = 13.5°$, and $\theta_\gamma = 9°$. The resulting winning regions are shown on figure 7.3, imposed upon the 1975 elections and depicting the Country Party as the third party. The demise of the ALP compared with the British Labour Party results because it has a much smaller winning region in the election triangle. The alternative-vote system in Australia adds further to the distribution effects which the ALP already suffers as a labour party. Hence, in practice, reform of plurality into majority voting in Australia has not been a form of reform of representation in the sense used in chapter 1: proportionality has in no way been enhanced but rather electoral biases have been added to (Graham, 1962).

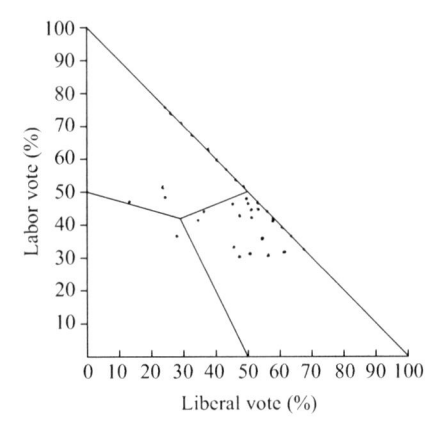

Figure 7.3: *Election triangle for Australia, 1975*

7.2.2 The double ballot in France

France adopted universal manhood suffrage in 1848 and the first ever national election involving a mass electorate was held in that year. Hence while other countries were debating suffrage issues, France was able to experiment with alternative methods of voting. The result is that there has never been a generally accepted method of voting for the French National Assembly and the voting system has itself been an issue in most elections. Since 1848 there have been thirteen major changes in the system of voting as one faction after another has sought to maximise the effectiveness of its vote. Each of these changes has been more radical than any reform legislation in Britain or the USA. However, the changes cannot be interpreted as a sequence of electoral reform evolving into a reform of representation. This can be easily appreciated by noting the variations in the systems adopted in this century:

until 1919	two-ballot majority system,
1919-1927	PR (list system),
1927-1945	two-ballot majority system,
1945-1951	PR (list system),
1951-1958	distorted list system,
1958-	two-ballot majority system.

This yo-yo effect of accepting and then rejecting proportional representation simply reflects what Mackenzie (1958) terms electoral engineering. Recent changes have aimed specifically at 'neutralising' the electoral strength of the Communists.

The success of this electoral engineering can be gauged from table 7.3. The Communists have been slightly favoured by the list system elections except for the 1951 election but have otherwise fared badly under majority system elections, especially since 1958. This contrasts with the Gaullists, who have regularly achieved a major bonus of seats from the electoral system since 1958. The exception of the 1951 election, in which the Communists suffered under a list system, simply reflects the specific design of the electoral law to discriminate against that party despite the use of party lists. In this case the Paris region was organised under a normal PR list system arrangement so that minority parties (non-Left) would be fairly represented while in the rest of the country a multimember majority system operated so that any alliance obtaining over 50% of the vote were allocated all seats. This, of course, generally operated against the Communists, who were generally weaker outside Paris. This law was, not surprisingly, thought to be unfair and the return of de Gaulle in 1958 led to its repeal and the return of the single-member

Table 7.3. *Electoral biases in French elections, 1936–1973*
Source: Criddle (1975).

Election	System	Communist	Gaullist	Socialist
1936	majority	−3.2	–	+4.8
1945	list	+2.3	–	+1.3
1946	list	+1.6	–	+0.7
1946	list	+1.5	–	−1.4
1951	list	−8.5	−2.2	+2.2
1956	list	+1.0	−1.3	+0.6
1958	majority	−16.8	+21.9	−7.1
1962	majority	−13.3	+24.5	−1.3
1967	majority	−7.2	+11.3	+5.6
1968	majority	−13.0	+27.9	−4.5
1973	majority	−6.2	+15.9	+0.4

majority system again. However, the result was to increase the discrimination against the Communists, as table 7.3 shows.

Criddle (1975) identifies two types of cause for the Communist demise, which he terms structural and behavioural. The former cause includes those effects previously identified for simple plurality elections, namely malapportionment and distribution effects. Behavioural causes, on the other hand, are the direct result of the modification of the initial pluralities in the first ballot by the voting in the second ballot. Hence behavioural causes are seen as being a direct result of the particular electoral system. This interpretation is very similar to our previous discussion of the alternative-vote system in Australia, where additional causes of bias have also been identified by going beyond a simple plurality requirement for election.

Criddle (1975) attempts to evaluate these various causes of bias and his findings are briefly presented here. Although he shows that in the last three elections Communists have on average won larger constituencies than Gaullists (1967, 4500 larger; 1968, 5300 larger; and 1973, 4000 larger), the effect of this malapportionment in terms of seats in the assembly has been very small. However, its effect has been important on one occasion. In 1967 Criddle redistributes fourteen seats and finds that the Left would have had a net gain of three to the Gaullists net loss of three. This would have been enough to have prevented the Gaullist election victory with its margin of only seven seats. Nonetheless it is concluded as usual that, generally speaking, malapportionment has not been a major cause of the electoral bias.

Distribution effects are another matter, however. The Communist Party, like all parties of the Left, draws much of its support from urban and industrial regions. This concentration of support makes it particularly susceptible to distribution effects. In 1967, for example, the Communists held 33% of their seats with second-ballot majorities of over 20% compared with only 12% of such majorities for the Gaullists. In 1973 the difference was less marked, 20% and 15% respectively, but this evidence does support the idea that the Communists had the typical left-wing positively skewed CPD producing distribution effects. However, in the French case these effects were enhanced by partisan districting. Departments have been divided in such a way that each main town is broken up and the parts are aggregated with surrounding rural areas. The result has been to separate Communist support so that it is unable to win any seat in the department. This is identical to Louis Napoleon's method of 'controlling' the Left of a century earlier (du Vistre, 1869). It contrasts with the districting of the 1927 law which treated towns as single constituencies, thus allowing some Communist victories in generally hostile rural regions. This is one reason why the bias against the Communists in the majority election of 1936 is so much less than the bias after 1958 (table 7.3).

Finally what of the behavioural effects of the French electoral system? In this case the relatively large number of parties means that most contests are decided on the second ballot since initial majorities are hard to obtain. Hence the second ballot changes the initial plurality results more than alternative votes do in Australia. However, the process leading to extra biases is similar. It relies on a general alliance of parties against the discriminated party. In France bias against the Communists has been greatest where an election has not developed into a simple bipolar situation. In 1958, for example, of the 426 second ballots all but eighty were contested by more than two parties. This resulted in the largest bias against the Communists (table 7.3). However, the 1960s saw the development of the Left alliance again so that for the last three elections 80% of second-ballot contests have been bipolar and the bias against the Communists has been much lower. (1968 reflects a large Gaullist victory so biases will have been increased by a nonpartisan winner's bias.) The very low bias of 1936 similarly reflects the bipolarity of that particular election.

The alliance of the Left has not totally eradicated the behavioural effects, however. The decline in intra-Left second-ballot contests from 210 in 1958 to zero in 1968 and 1973 does not mean that the remaining leftist candidate automatically wins the support of the combined leftist vote. Criddle shows that Socialist second-ballot candidates consistently do better than Communist second-ballot candidates. In 1973, for instance, there were twenty-one occasions when the total leftist vote on the first ballot was over 50% but was under 50% on the second ballot. On fourteen of these occasions the second-ballot candidate was a Communist. Similarly, of the twenty-nine occasions when an initial leftist vote of under 50% was converted to a second-ballot vote of over 50%, only five of these successful candidates were Communists. Hence, even in alliance, Communists do not obtain the full vote they might expect. It has been suggested, for instance, that the Left would have won in 1967 had they put forward more Socialist candidates in place of Communists in the second ballot (Williams and Goldey, 1967).

The conclusions concerning the French form of majority voting are very similar to the conclusions concerning the Australian system. This particular voting method discriminates against the Left above and beyond the bias expected from a plurality election.

7.2.3 A majority-vote system for Britain

Given the conclusion concerning majority-vote systems it may seem unnecessary to illustrate their possible application elsewhere. They do not contribute in the least to any reform of representation as the term was used in chapter 1. However, the working of this type of system in France and Australia has led to suggestions that it is a way of ensuring that Britain's anti-Labour majority do not have to suffer Labour governments continually (Lakeman, 1974). In this section, therefore, the effects of an alternative-vote system on British parliamentary representation is considered to see whether a strong anti-Left bias could be easily introduced.

The effect of using an alternative-vote system for British elections has recently been investigated by Steed (1974; 1975a) and Berrington (1975). The problem they face is to translate votes cast under a plurality system into predicted preferences for an alternative-vote system. Their solution is to make general assumptions concerning this translation so that in each case a range of possible election results using the new system are presented. Despite the resulting imprecision in these predictions, this is the only realistic way of dealing with this problem and their results are presented here. Fortunately the ranges of results produced are consistent in answering questions concerning the relative treatment of the two main parties.

Steed (1974) uses the February 1974 results to investigate what would have happened had an alternative-vote system been used. He postulates six possible ways in which eliminated party votes would be represented in terms of second choices. In four-party contests, 75% of Liberal second choices are assumed to go to the Nationalists and vice versa. Otherwise six alternative situations are postulated, depending on how minor-party and major-party second preferences are distributed. They are summarised in the following table.

	Major parties 80 : 20 to minor parties	Major party 90 : 10 to minor parties
Minor parties 55 : 45 to Conservative	A	B
Minor parties 50:50 split	C	D
Minor parties 55:45 to Labour	E	F

In all cases it is assumed that minor parties will split fairly evenly between major parties whereas major-party supporters will tend to prefer minor parties to their rival major party.

The results of distributing second choices in these six situations are given in table 7.4. This shows relative percentage gains and losses

Table 7.4. *Predicted effects of the alternative-vote system for February 1974 (number of seats)*

Situation	Labour	Conservative	Liberal	Nationalist
A	−26	−20	+37	+9
B	−28	−47	+65	+10
C	−10	−36	+37	+9
D	−12	−63	+65	+10
E	+4	−50	+37	+9
F	+2	−77	+65	+10

Source: Steed (1975a).

compared with the actual (plurality) result. Predictably the minor parties gain while, on the whole, the major parties lose ground. However, notice that Labour do manage to make gains where they obtain a majority of minor-party second preferences. In fact in terms comparing the major parties, these results consistently show Labour to lose fewer seats than the Conservatives. The one exception is situation A and even here this is the closest the results come to giving equal treatment to the two parties. As the parties stand in February 1974, therefore, it seems that the alternative-vote system would help the two minor parties but largely at the expense of the Conservatives.

Berrington's analyses based on the October 1974 results confirm this finding. He postulated four situations:

1. (a) 80% net transfer of Liberals to Nationalists and vice versa,

    (b) 80% net transfer of major to minor party,

    (c) minor parties' second choices split evenly between major parties;

2. as situation 1 but only 40% net transfer of major party to minor party;

3. as situation 2 but with a net overall gain of 2.5% for leading minor party in terms of first preferences;

4. as situation 1 plus minor party net gain from situation 3.

These latter assumptions in situations 3 and 4 concede the point that people would probably vote differently under a new system of elections— if minor parties are seen to gain more seats, voting for them is less of a waste of the vote. Berrington's results are summarised in table 7.5. In each situation minor parties gain and major parties lose. However, it is Conservatives who provide the minor parties with most of their new seats. This is particularly the case in England where Liberals are predicted to take over in many of the seats in which came second in the actual election results. Thus the Conservatives' greater losses occur for the simple reason that they have more seats than Labour where the Liberals are in second place. This peculiar effect of the interaction of distribution of votes with the alternative-vote system produces a distinctive anti-Right bias in British elections in complete contrast to our findings for actual elections in Australia and France. As Berrington notes, his situation 4 has the consequences of putting Labour in a near-Scandinavian situation.

Why do the British predicted results differ so much from actual majority-election results? The answer seems to be in the particular nature

Table 7.5: Predicted effects of the alternative-vote system for October 1974 (number of seats).
Source: Berrington (1975).

Situation	Labour	Conservative	Liberal	Nationalist
1	−28	−53	+41	+38
2	−15	−27	+15	+25
3	−28	−55	+42	+39
4	−34	−112	+101	+43

of the British political parties and their interrelationships. The Liberals are very different from the Country Party in Australia and Labour is very different from the Communist Party in France. The reasons for the anti-Conservative effect can be seen in the election triangle in figure 7.4. Win regions are defined as in Steed's situation C. These assumptions increase the area of the Liberal winning region at the expense of both other parties. However there is a much higher density of constituencies where the new Liberal winning area encroaches on the Conservatives and this produces a disproportionate number of Conservative losses.

Of course, the party system which produces these results is itself a product of a tradition of plurality elections. Whether a series of majority elections would force an anti-Labour alliance to develop is merely a matter of speculation. However, this does seem to be a very good strategy for both the Conservative and the Liberal Party under a majority-vote system and it would result in the anti-Left bias recorded elsewhere.

In conclusion it can be stated that majority voting systems do not improve the representativeness of a parliament. Electoral biases remain and may be magnified. By concentrating on eradicating small pluralities at the *local* constituency level, this reform possibility continues to neglect the relationship between seats and votes at the *national* scale. Hence quite arbitrary national results may occur such as the predicted discrimination against the Conservatives in Britain. Proportionality is not aimed at and is not achieved. The most damning example of its application is in the 1948 Alberta provincial election where Social Credit won every seat with just 58% of the first-preference votes. Any electoral system with a record such as this can no longer be seriously considered by electoral reformers. In recent years electoral reformers have devoted their energies to supporting either STV or the German mixed system of AMS.

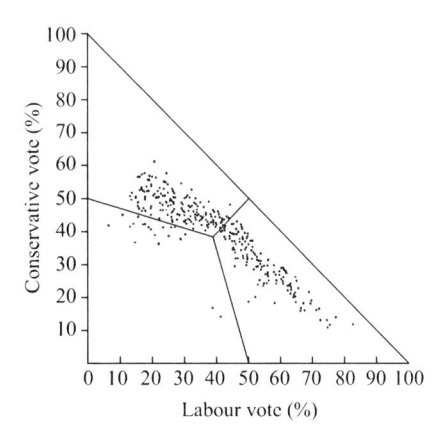

Figure 7.4: Election triangle for England, October 1974

7.3 The single-transferable-vote system

The single-transferable-vote (STV) system is the product of nineteenth century liberal concern for the individual rights of voters in elections. It was in no way developed to produce proportional representation of parties. Nonetheless it has become generally accepted as a method of proportional representation and Rae (1971) shows that in this respect it produces results similar to more direct forms of PR using list systems. Rae's evidence consists of recent Irish elections and we will delve into Irish elections in a little more detail to try to understand why this method should produce party proportionality.

7.3.1 STV in Ireland

The 1921 Treaty creating the Irish Free State specifically guaranteed use of STV for national elections so as to integrate the Unionist minority (O'Leary, 1975). Hence the British House of Commons foisted a system on the Irish which they had only a few years earlier rejected for themselves, and despite attempts to get rid of it, STV has remained the system of voting to the present day. It is by far the major example of the practical use of STV, having been used in eighteen general elections since 1923. [For the introduction of STV to Northern Ireland see Laver (1976).]

Levels of electoral bias in Ireland's eighteen elections are summarised for the three main parties in table 7.6. Clearly the two main parties are consistently overrepresented but not excessively so. Labour, as the smaller

Table 7.6: Electoral biases in Irish elections, 1923–1977
Source: 1923–1973 calculated from O'Leary (1975) with unopposed seats not counted. All biases are based upon first preferences.

Election	Fianna Fail	Fine Gael	Labour
1923	+1.2	+2.0	−2.4
1927 (June)	+2.8	+2.9	+1.9
1927 (September)	+2.6	+1.7	−0.3
1932	+3.7	+2.3	−3.0
1933	+0.3	+1.1	−0.4
1937	+4.3	+0.2	−0.5
1938	+3.0	−0.5	−3.1
1943	+6.3	+0.3	−3.3
1944	+5.6	+1.0	−2.9
1948	+4.0	+1.4	+0.9
1951	+0.3	+2.3	−0.5
1954	+1.1	+2.2	+0.2
1957	+5.1	+0.8	−1.6
1961	+5.2	+0.9	−0.9
1965	+2.6	−1.2	−0.7
1969	+6.0	+0.9	−4.4
1973	+1.4	+2.7	−0.4
1977	+5.3	−0.7	−0.2

party, does much worse but never suffers anything like as badly as the British Liberals (table 7.1). These results are similar to other systems of proportional representation, which in practice always slightly favour large parties over small parties (Rae, 1971).

Despite these largely proportionate results, controversy has still occurred over the organisation of elections. These specifically relate to the spatial division of the country into multimember constituencies. The delimitation of constituencies has always been the responsibility of the Minister of Local Government. This has allowed the governing party a free hand in designing constituencies and has inevitably led to accusations of gerrymandering (Gallagher, 1974). However, in the case of STV, it is not so much the exact positioning of boundaries relative to party voters which has caused controversy, but rather the variations in sizes of constituencies in terms of numbers of seats.

Results can be distorted in two ways by changing the sizes of constituencies. First the production of proportionality is generally facilitated by larger constituencies. Obviously proportionality can only be crudely approximated in a three-seat constituency but can be more accurately reflected in a nine-seat constituency. The only constraint imposed on the Irish government is that there should be one seat per 20000 to 30000 population and that there must be at least three members per constituency. This allows plenty of freedom in spatial organisation (Mair and Laver, 1975). In the initial Electoral Act of 1923, large constituencies were quite common — there were nine constituencies with seven or more members. Since 1947, however, the largest constituencies have had only five members and in the last two distributions (1969 and 1974) nearly two-thirds of districts have been three-member constituencies (Mair and Laver, 1975). Gallagher (1974) analyses all election results from 1927 to 1973 and shows that the smaller the constituencies the larger the average electoral bias. However, these individually large biases, on average 10% for three-member constituencies, cancel one another out when aggregated to national results as shown in table 7.6. Hence the trend towards smaller constituencies does not seem to have had major repercussions on the national results.

The second way in which size of constituency may be manipulated for partisan ends is by relating the size to the electoral strength of a party. In gerrymandering for a party which has a slight majority in a region, three-member constituencies are probably best in order to record a series of 2–1 wins. On the other hand where a party is in a slight minority, four-member constituencies are best since a 2–2 share of seats results in most cases. The strategy is to win as a majority and draw as a minority. Fianna Fail, for instance, are generally stronger in the west and weaker in the east. Their electoral law of 1969 tended to produce three-member constituencies in the west and four-member constituencies in the east. Mair and Laver (1975) particularly discuss the case of Dublin where twenty-seven seats were allocated to six four-member constituencies and one three-member constituency. In the six four-member constituencies in the 1969 election Fianna Fail won two seats each with votes ranging from 34% to 43% while its opponents also won two seats per constituency with between 52% and 61% of the vote.

All of the electoral laws up to 1969 were passed while Fianna Fail were in government. Gallagher (1974) has attempted to discover the degree of partisan manipulation of sizes by directly relating constituency sizes to levels of Fianna Fail support. He argues that the optimum sizes for the party are as follows:

29%-36% of the vote—five members to win two,
36%-46% of the vote—four members to win two,
46%-56% of the vote—three members to win two,
56%-63% of the vote—four members to win three.

For each election following a new electoral law, he finds the numbers of constituencies within each vote range which correspond to the optimum size. Early laws are found not to have significant correspondence between size and vote but in 1969 fully two-thirds of constituencies are of the 'right size' from Fianna Fail's point of view. Thus there does seem to be evidence of partisan manipulation of the spatial organisation in 1969 and this is reflected in Fianna Fail's positive electoral bias in table 7.6, which is the second largest bias recorded in Irish national elections.

In 1974, a year after coming to office, the Fine Gael-Labour coalition revised the constituencies and apportioned Dublin's twenty-seven seats among nine three-member constituencies. This was clearly designed with partisan intentions and it was predicted that the coalition's Dublin representation would increase from fourteen to eighteen (Mair and Laver, 1975). Such a situation has a very familiar ring about it—seats are predicted to change hands irrespective of any change in party voting. As it turned out this gerrymandering was in vain. A large swing of 7% to Fianna Fail in 1977, with up to 10% in Dublin, meant that three-member constituencies were not safe 2–1 wins for the coalition. In fact Fianna Fail won two out of three seats in five of Dublin's new constituencies to finish with a majority of Dublin representatives, fourteen of the twenty-seven in this coalition stronghold. Elsewhere Fianna Fail won two out of three representatives in thirteen of the remaining seventeen three-member constituencies. The large swing to Fianna Fail enabled the party to win more than its usual share of seats in three-party contests and this contributed to the relatively large positive bias for the party in 1977 (table 7.6). This story is not unlike that told of the Iowa Republicans in the last chapter. The moral is the same in both cases: delicate gerrymandering will rebound upon the designers where a large swing of votes overturns expected predictions. Hence the demise of Iowa Republicans in 1974 and the Irish coalition in Dublin in 1977.

Mair and Laver (1975) propose that the decision on size of constituencies should be taken out of the hands of the government and transferred to 'an impartial commission'. Of course a nonpartisan agency will not be able to solve the problem of whether Dublin should have three-member or four-member constituencies. If either size is 'impartially' chosen this will not lessen its partisan effect. The real answer, within the context of STV elections, seems to be to use larger constituencies. This can be done by raising the minimum size to five-member constituencies thus making all three-member and four-member seats illegal. Although the five- and six-member constituencies may be used to discriminate in the same way as three- and four-member constituencies, with these larger districts the margin of error is much finer and the final results will more often be proportional. This is discussed and illustrated by Paddison (1976).

Whatever partisan spatial organisation has been designed for recent Irish elections, the practical effects have been minimal, as a quick glance at table 7.6 confirms. Gallagher (1974) emphasises the disproportionality in the system but even he has to conclude that it produces results far more like a PR list system than a plurality or majority system. However, it is still not clear why an electoral system which does not itself consider parties should produce such proportional results.

Mair and Laver (1975) present several preconditions for proportionality to be achieved with STV. Basically, proportional representation is a consequence of the electoral system and the behaviour of voters and parties. If the voters vote strictly along party lines then STV will tend to produce proportional representation of the parties. Distortions may occur with differential leakage between parties (loss of votes when moving from first to second preferences and beyond) or when parties nominate too many candidates and thus suffer unduly from extra leakage. However, the effects of these distortions, and of constituency-size manipulation, are usually not strong enough to make much difference to the proportionality inherent in the interaction between STV and party voting. The STV method of voting in Ireland has thus been successful, not only in terms of its original intention of integration, but in terms of relatively fair representation of parties.

7.3.2 STV for British elections

The effects of STV on British elections are much more difficult to predict than the effects of the alternative vote. STV not only involves use of preferences but also requires definition of new multimember constituencies. Hence before any predictions can be made, actual voting figures have to be reorganised into a new pattern of larger districts.

Experiments involving a partial reorganisation of constituencies have been reported by Ross (1955) and Berrington (1975). Ross constructed twelve multimember constituencies from fifty-seven original constituencies in different parts of the country. He then aggregated the 1950 election results to produce estimates of first preferences in his twelve constituencies. However, the resulting distribution of seats produced only minor changes. Conservatives had actually obtained twenty-eight seats, Ross predicted twenty-four to twenty-six under STV; Labour had obtained twenty-five seats, Ross predicted twenty-four to twenty-five. The major gain was by the Liberals, who had obtained four seats but were predicted to win six to nine seats.

Berrington (1975) constructed eighteen new multimember constituencies from eighty-eight original constituencies. His predictions of the outcome, using the October 1974 results for first preferences under STV, show larger changes than Ross's. Conservative and Labour representation declines again, from thirty-eight to twenty-nine and from forty-three to thirty-seven, respectively. On this occasion there are two minor parties. Liberals move from four to seventeen seats, Nationalists from three to five. Hence the Liberals benefit much more in this experiment than in the previous one. This is partially due to their far higher vote in 1974 compared with 1950 but direct comparison between the two analyses is impossible owing to their application of STV in different parts of Britain.

Steed (1974) presents predictions for all of Britain using STV based on February 1974 election results. He makes two predictions, the first simply uses February 1974 voting totals as they stand and the second modifies the totals to allow for constituencies where Liberals did not stand and also switches back tactical voting for Liberals to its Labour origins. His results are shown in table 7.7. There are massive gains for Liberals at the expense of both major parties. Notice that under the first assumption the Conservatives would have become the largest party in Parliament as their vote warrants. In fact the proportionality of Steed's results are impressive throughout. This being the case he does not bother to compute STV estimates using October 1974 votes (Steed, 1975a).

These STV predictions all agree that the major parties would lose seats and the minor parties, especially the Liberals, would gain seats. Such findings are to be expected from an electoral system which purports to approximate proportionality. However, it was found in the Irish case that attempts had been made to distort proportionality by using different-sized constituencies. The experiments reported above generally used

Table 7.7: Predictions for STV in February 1974
Source: calculated from Steed (1974).

Party	Vote (%)	Actual seats (%)	Predicted seats (%)	Modified vote (%)	Predicted seats (%)
Labour	38.0	48.3	37.6	38.4	38.5
Conservative	38.8	47.7	39.5	38.0	37.2
Liberal	19.8	2.2	19.7	10.5	21.0
Nationalist	2.6	1.4	3.2	2.3	3.1

larger constituencies than those applied in Ireland. The distribution of sizes used by Ross and Berrington are shown in table 7.8 and Steed mentions "multi-member seats of about five members". Hence there are no estimates of the effect of STV as organised in Ireland with largely three-member constituencies or in fact as organised into relatively large constituencies with eight or nine members each. In order to assess this aspect of the spatial organisation of elections under STV, three experiments have been conducted using different sizes of constituencies. In the first experiment the aim was for 'small' three-member constituencies, in the second for 'medium' five-member constituencies, and in the third for 'large' nine-member constituencies. It is assumed that if Boundary Commissions carried out this task county boundaries would have been maintained where possible, so that some variations in sizes is allowed to accommodate this factor. Nonetheless, strict limits were set in each districting exercise, no small districts could have more than five members, no medium districts could have less than four or more than seven members, and no large districts could have less than five or more than twelve members. The final distributions of sizes are shown in table 7.9. These three different spatial organisations are used to assess scale effects on the operation of STV using both February and October 1974 election results.

Let us begin by considering the predictions obtained with the October results. These voting figures are very suitable for applying to STV because the Liberals contested all but four seats and the Nationalists contested all seats in their territories. Liberal votes in the four constituencies they left uncontested have been estimated by simply giving them the average Liberal vote for their region and type of constituencies (urban/rural). These regions and types are described below. Other party votes in the constituencies were modified to take account of the Liberal 'intervention'. Apart from this very small change to four out of 623 constituencies, the

Table 7.8: Sizes of constituencies (number of members) in STV experiments

Experiment	3	4	5	6	7
Ross (1955)	2	2	6	1	1
Berrington (1975)	0	5	10	3	0

Table 7.9: Sizes of constituencies (number of members) in the spatial organisation experiments

Experiment	3	4	5	6	7	8	9	10	11	12
Small constituencies	139	39	10	–	–	–	–	–	–	–
Medium constituencies	–	16	85	20	2	–	–	–	–	–
Large constituencies	–	–	7	3	14	14	24	12	0	2

actual October results were used for the STV first preferences. For transferring votes of eliminated candidates (1) no leakage within parties was assumed, (2) for between-party transfers minor-party candidates receive 70% of votes transferred, and (3) where all minor-party candidates are eliminated, excess minor-party votes are allocated equally to the two major parties.

The predicted effect of using STV for these different spatial organisations is shown in table 7.10. As before, in all cases Liberals and Nationalists gain seats and the two major parties lose seats. However, there are important differences among the predicted results. Although size of constituency makes little or no difference to the Nationalists, for the Liberals these differences are important. With three-member constituencies there are many occasions where the Liberals are not strong enough to reach the quota of 25% + 1 and so the seats are apportioned 2–1 to the major parties. In this way very many Liberal votes continue to be wasted. Hence the Liberals are underrepresented although not nearly so badly as with the actual plurality result. With medium-size constituencies the required quota declines, with five-member constituencies it is 16.67% + 1, so Liberals are able to obtain representation in almost every English constituency and their level of underrepresentation is accordingly reduced. Finally with large constituencies Liberals do better still and approach proportionality as the quota is small enough to ensure one or more seats in every constituency.

It is instructive to compare these predicted Liberal performances for small constituencies with those of Ireland's third party, Labour. It should be admitted immediately that comparisons are difficult because Labour in Ireland have been in coalition with a major party and the Liberals have not. This will partially explain why Irish Labour does better under STV than the Liberals. Another explanation relates to the spatial distribution of votes of each party. Irish Labour, despite being a minor party, has the usual Labour characteristic of more clustered support. In 1973 the standard deviation of its CPD was higher than those of the two other parties so that despite its overall low percentage of the vote (14%), its

Table 7.10: Voting and representation for different sizes of constituencies, October 1974

Party	Vote (%)	Actual seats number (%)	Predicted seats (STV) small number (%)	medium number (%)	large number(%)
Conservative	37.0	277 44.5	250 40.1	229 36.8	232 37.2
Labour	40.5	320 51.4	284 45.6	274 44.0	265 42.5
Liberal	18.9	13 2.1	64 10.3	95 15.2	102 16.4
National	3.6	14 2.2	25 4.0	25 4.0	24 3.9

variation in vote allowed it easily to exceed its quota in some areas despite the small size of Irish constituencies (Busteed and Mason, 1974). The Liberals' more even pattern of support, however, makes small constituencies more of a problem despite their overall higher level of support than the Irish Labour Party. This is probably the main reason for these British experiments showing a larger effect of spatial organisation than the actual Irish results seem to show (Gallagher, 1974).

Discussion of the Liberals in the experiments emphasises the basic differences between these STV results and the actual outcome. Figure 7.5 shows two different ways of displaying the Liberal vote in October 1974. Figure 7.5(a) shows absolute numbers of voters by regions and by type of constituency (on an urban-rural scale) within regions. From this map it can be seen that Liberals are most common in the urban Southeast and urban North and have lowest numbers in Scotland. Figure 7.5(b) emphasises the relative strength of the Liberals at the constituency level. In this case the strong position of the Liberals in the South and West is emphasised and Scotland no longer appears such a bleak prospect. In figure 7.5(c) the simple geography of Liberal representation after the October election is shown. This map clearly reflects the relative strength of Liberals in figure 7.5(b) and simply seems to ignore the absolute picture of figure 7.5(a). Thus Scotland provides three Liberal MPs, the urban Southeast provides none. These diagrams clearly show how the plurality system distorts the geography of voting into a distinctive geography of representation which may be quite unrelated. The Liberal Party in Parliament may look like a Celtic-fringe party, but the Liberal Party in the country is truly nationwide.

In what way do the experiments suggest that STV would change this distortion? Figure 7.6 shows the three predicted geographies of representation for the Liberals for the different-sized constituencies. It is immediately apparent from all three maps that the patterns of representation are now much more akin to the actual pattern of votes. Even with small constituencies, the Southeast begins to provide many more Liberal MPs so that the earlier predominance of the Southwest is easily overtaken. Notice that in Scotland Liberals actually lose two MPs under the small constituencies. With medium constituencies the extra Liberal MPs largely come from the North. This reflects the fact that the level of Liberal support was generally lower in the North so that they were quite often unable to gain representation with three-member constituencies. However, with medium-sized constituencies Liberals begin to win seats throughout the North. This pattern is consolidated for large constituencies, whose pattern of representation most closely resembles the absolute pattern of votes.

STV would clearly affect the Liberal Party more than simply increasing its MPs. Those MPs themselves would more closely reflect the pattern of Liberal support in the country. This can be shown to be true for the

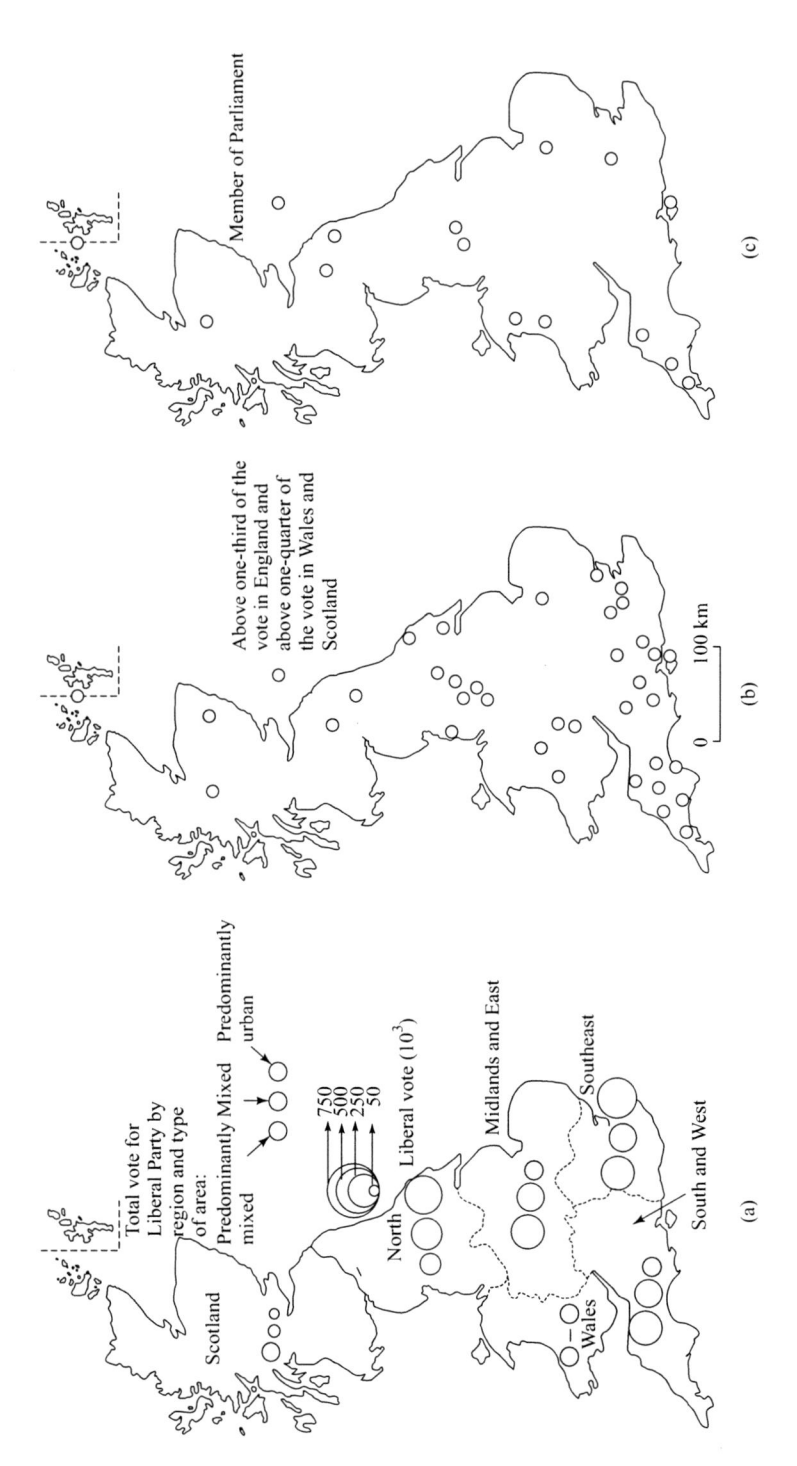

184 | seats, votes, and the spatial organisation of elections

Figure 7.5: The spatial distribution of British Liberal support and success, October 1974
(a) absolute numbers of voters by region and type of constituency; (b) relative strength of the Liberals at the constituency level; (c) the geography of Liberal representation after the election.

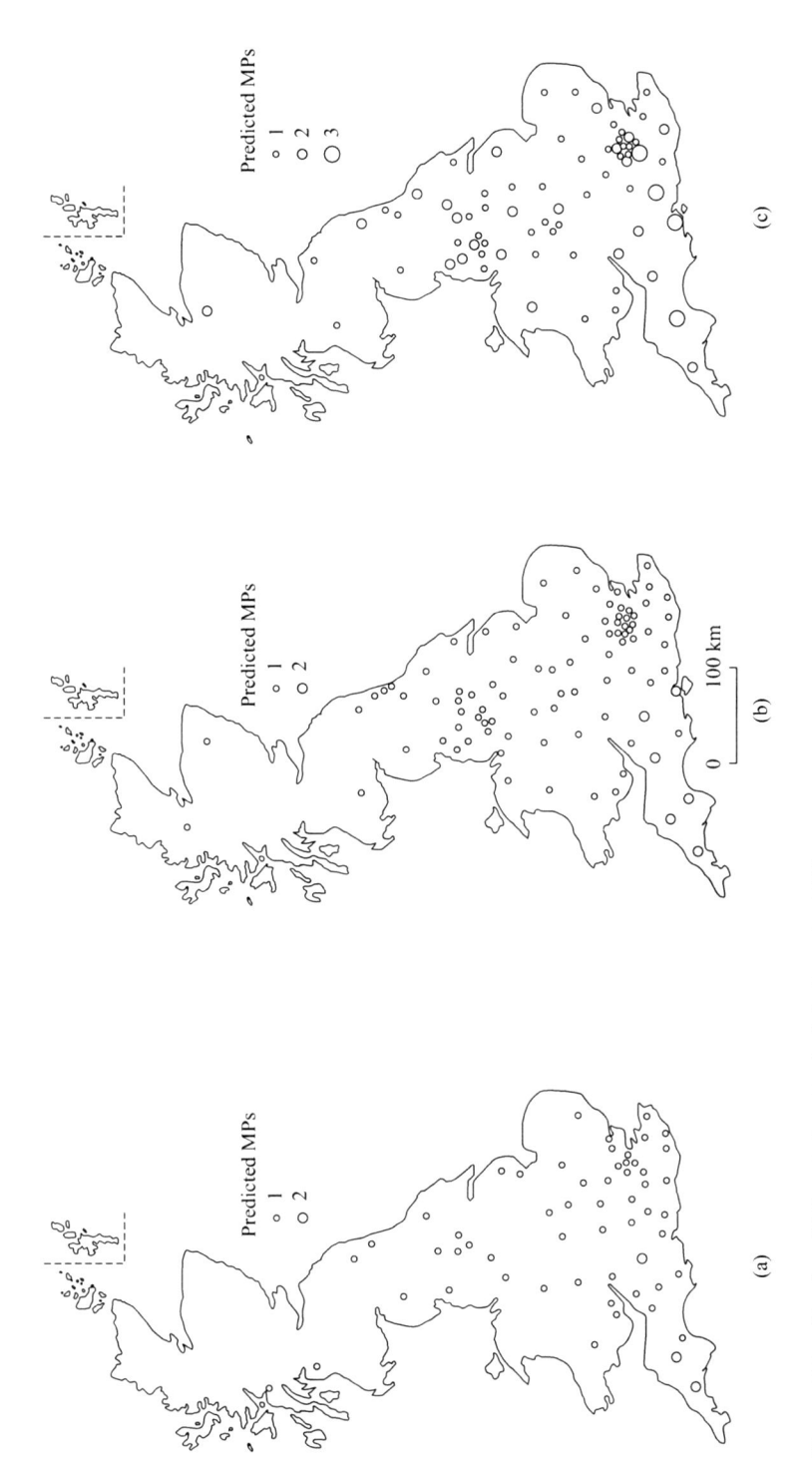

Figure 7.6: Predicted Liberal victories in Britain under STV (a) small constituencies; (b) medium-sized constituencies; (c) large constituencies.

other parties also. Table 7.11 shows the voting pattern, actual seats, and predicted seats for the medium-sized constituencies over six regions and three constituency types. These figures show a redistribution of seats *within* parties. Consider the rural South and West with the urban North. In the first category it is predicted that the Conservatives would lose fourteen seats and Labour would gain seven. In the second category Labour lose eighteen seats and Conservatives gain fourteen. What is happening is that the distortions of representation produced by the plurality system are being eradicated. Plurality elections make Conservatives more rural and Labour more urban in representation than their support would warrant. STV corrects this development so Labour and Conservatives win more seats where they are relatively weak. The result would be that there would be more southern Labour MPs and more northern Conservative MPs. Although the plurality system in Britain does not produce the level of regional party polarisation found in Canada, the geography of representation is a distorted image of the voting pattern, and STV does correct it. Hence our consideration of the October 1974 experiments can be concluded by emphasising that STV produces more proportionality

Table 7.11: Voting and representation by regions and types of constituency, October 1974
The three rows of figures for each region represent percentage vote, actual number of seats, ; and predicted number of seats, in that order. C is Conservative Party, L is Labour Party, Lib is Liberal Party, and N is Nationalist parties.

Region	Type of constituency											
	rural				mixed				urban			
	C	L	Lib	N	C	L	Lib	N	C	L	Lib	N
South and West	44	28	28		45	27	28		41	36	22	
	29	2	2		16	3	2		6	6	0	
	15	9	9		9	5	7		5	5	2	
Southeast	47	29	24		42	36	22		39	43	18	
	35	2	0		18	10	0		49	52	0	
	18	13	8		13	9	6		39	48	13	
Midlands and East	44	35	21		39	43	19		34	51	16	
	33	11	1		16	22	0		6	30	0	
	20	16	9		15	17	6		13	21	2	
North	42	38	20		39	42	19		30	52	18	
	15	11	0		18	22	1		12	84	2	
	12	9	5		15	19	7		28	56	14	
Scotland	26	33	11	31	27	32	8	34	22	45	6	27
	6	12	3	4	5	8	0	7	5	21	0	0
	7	8	2	8	6	6	1	7	5	14	0	7
Wales	26	40	20	15					23	57	13	8
	4	6	2	3					4	17	0	0
	4	6	3	2					4	14	2	1

between parties as constituencies get larger and it also produces a redistribution of representation within parties.

Predicting STV results for the February 1974 election is much more difficult because the Liberals did not contest 106 constituencies. Liberal votes for these constituencies have been derived by assuming an even 'backward swing' over all constituencies from October. Hence Liberal votes are calculated at 3.4% less than their October level, the votes being taken evenly from other parties. The same procedure was used for the one Scottish constituency (Orkney and Shetland) where there was no Nationalist candidate in February. This method will only give a rough approximation of the likely pattern of votes had the constituencies been contested, but it is much better than assuming zero votes. It is assumed the method is adequate given that these results will aggregate together with 'real' results in the STV experiments. Otherwise assumptions are identical to the October experiments.

The February STV predictions will be considered in terms of their differences from the October predictions. [In Irish elections changes in first preferences have not always been very clearly reflected in the changeover of seats (O'Leary, 1975).] Table 7.12 compares the two sets of predictions and specifies the seat changes. The first point to note is that the Liberals do much better in these experiments than in the earlier ones. Even with small constituencies they win over a hundred seats. This is because their higher level of support allowed them to share more three-member constituencies with the two major parties. Hence it is at this scale that we find the largest change from October. With medium-sized constituencies the result is very similar to Steed's predictions (table 7.7) although the two analyses are based on slightly different voting figures and different constituencies.

The overall seat changes are remarkably consistent with the changes in the pattern of votes between February and October. Steed (1975a) shows that in gross terms Conservative support only fell very slightly (–0.4%) while Labour gain (+3.6%) was complemented by the Liberal loss (–3.4%). Table 7.12 shows that Labour are the main winners of seats and Liberals the main losers with Conservatives being the most stable. The Conservatives actually gain five seats with small constituencies and this reflects the

Table 7.12: Party representation and change by size of constituency, February-October 1974

Party	Small F	O	change	Medium F	O	change	Large F	O	change
Conservative	245	250	+5	242	229	–13	238	232	–6
Labour	267	284	+17	245	274	+29	244	265	+21
Liberal	101	64	–37	119	95	–24	125	102	–23
Nationalist	10	25	+15	17	25	+8	16	24	+8

'tactical' advantage they have in three-member constituencies where Liberals just fail to reach the required quota in October. Hence apart from the experiment with small constituencies where Liberals lose to Labour and Conservatives, the STV experiments do illustrate how seat changes reflect vote changes. Table 7.13 details this effect by illustrating predicted changes by region and type of constituency for the medium-sized constituency experiment. In all categories changes in vote are closely paralleled by changes in seats.

This discussion concludes with the view that as well as working in Ireland in practice, STV seems also to work in Britain in theory. In all experiments STV is far more proportional in its results than the actual plurality results, to the great benefit of the Liberal Party. Minor arbitrary distortions remain with small constituencies, illustrating the possible influence of the spatial organisation but these are largely eradicated when medium or large constituencies are used. However, it should be remembered that these good performances were found under simple theoretical conditions and in practice party alliances or differential preference leakages might cause further distortions. Nonetheless it does not seem unreasonable to suggest that STV would in practice be as successful in Britain as its actual application has been in Ireland.

7.4 A mixture of pluralities and PR

It has long been realised that some of the resistance to proportional representation can be overcome if certain elements of the plurality system are maintained. In particular, the single-member constituency with its direct link between member and constituents is highly prized by defenders of the plurality system. Hence it had been suggested as early as the 1910 Royal Commission (Lakeman, 1974) that proportional representation should be achieved by using present voting arrangements based on single-member constituencies with seats being allocated by using the aggregate of constituency votes over the country as a whole. The Danish Parliament seems to have been elected on this type of basis in 1915 in its transition from the original plurality system to the present PR list system (Lakeman 1974). However, the only country where a 'mixed system' has been used for a series of elections has been the Federal Republic of Germany (FRG) since the last war. It was first used in the British zone, reflecting British parliamentary influence combined with German experience of PR in the Weimar Republic, and was adopted for the Federal elections of 1949. It is perhaps ironic that it is this system which has now found particular favour among proponents of electoral reform in Britain (Hansard Society, 1976). The German system and its application will be briefly described before turning to the possibilities of its use in Britain.

Table 7.13: Changes in voting and predicted representation by regions and types of constituency, February–October 1974 (%). The three rows of figures for each region represent vote change, predicted seat change, and actual seat change.

Region	Type of constituency											
	rural				mixed				urban			
	C	L	Lib	N	C	L	Lib	N	C	L	Lib	N
South and West	0.0	+1.8	−1.8		0.0	+3.0	−3.0		−1.1	+2.7	−1.6	
	0	+1	−1		0	0	0		0	0	0	
	0.0	+3.0	−3.0		0.0	0.0	0.0		0.0	0.0	0.0	
Southeast	+0.3	+3.6	−3.9		+0.2	+2.7	−2.9		+0.1	+3.9	−4.0	
	−1	+3	−2		0	0	0		−1	+7	−6	
Midlands and East	−2.7	+8.1	−5.4		0.0	0.0	0.0		−1.0	+6.9	−5.9	
	+0.4	+2.7	−3.1		+0.1	+3.0	−3.1		−1.5	+4.1	−2.6	
	0	+1	−1		−1	+2	−1		0	+5	−5	
	0.0	+2.2	−2.2		−2.6	+5.2	−2.6		0.0	+13.9	−3.8	+13.9
North	−0.4	+4.0	−3.6		−0.7	+3.1	−2.4		−0.5	+4.3	−3.8	
	0	0	0		−2	+3	−1		−3	+7	−4	
	0.0	0.0	0.0		−4.9	+7.3	−2.4		−3.1	+7.1	−4.0	
Scotland	−6.6	+0.4	−4.7	+10.7	−5.9	+1.0	−4.1	+9.0	−6.9	+1.0	−4.3	+10.2
	−2	0	−1	+3	−1	0	0	+1	−2	0	−1	+3
	−8.0	0.0	−4.0	+12.0	−50	0.0	0.0	+5.0	−7.7	0.0	−3.8	+11.5
Wales	−1.9	+2.2	−2.3	+2.2					−1.8	+4.0	−1.9	−0.4
	0	−1	0	+1					0	+1	−1	0
	0.0	−6.7	0.0	+6.7					0.0	+4.8	−4.8	0.0

7.4.1 The 'mixed system' in the Federal Republic of Germany

The German system of voting derives from a specially constituted Parliamentary Council of 1949. They proposed that 60% of members be elected in constituencies by pluralities and the remaining 40% be elected from party lists to achieve proportionality on a land (regional) basis. In 1953 the system was modified so that only 50% were to be elected for constituencies. Further each elector was given two votes, one to cast for a constituency candidate and one to cast for a Land party list. Finally in 1956 the qualification for parties to share in the allocation of additional members proportionally was settled on. In order to be awarded Land seats a party either has to obtain 5% of the list votes on a federal basis, or it has to have won three seats in the constituencies. This rule disqualifies very small parties from obtaining entry to the Bonn parliament.

This mixed system of voting has been used in eight elections since 1949 and the resulting electoral biases for the three main parties are shown in table 7.14. The disqualification of minor parties produces most of the electoral bias in this table. Minor-party votes are not counted in the proportional allocation of extra seats, so the parties receiving seats obtain slightly more than their overall proportional vote would warrant. This was more important in the earlier elections when the major parties were less dominant than today. However, since 1961 the three main parties have obtained 94% of the total vote or more—in 1972 and 1976 they obtained over 99% of the total vote.

A second cause of bias can be found in the distribution of votes among the Lander. If a party is very strong in a Land, it may win more seats in the constituencies alone than it is entitled to overall with its proportion of the Land vote. Such extra seats are not taken away but remain with the party as a bonus. Hence parties with strong Land concentrations of support may obtain more than their proportional share of seats in that Land. With only 60%, and later 50%, of seats allocated on a constituency basis, such bonuses are relatively rare but they did occur in 1949 (two seats), 1952 (three seats), 1957 (three seats), and 1961 (five seats)

Table 7.14: *Electoral biases in West German elections, 1949–1972*
Source: Roberts (1975).

Election	CDU-CSU	SDP	FDP
1949	+3.6	+3.4	+1.0
1953	+4.7	+2.2	+0.4
1957	+4.1	+2.2	+0.5
1961	+3.2	+1.9	+0.6
1965	+1.8	+1.4	+0.4
1969	+2.7	+2.5	+0.2
1972	+0.5	+0.6	−0.1
1976	+0.6	+0.5	−0.1

(Hansard Society, 1976). However, with the 'diffusion' of the main parties throughout the state (Laux and Simms, 1973), such levels of concentrated support no longer seem to exist so that there have been no bonus seats since 1961. Even the traditional strength of the Bavarian wing (CSU) of the Christian Democrats has not led to bonus seats as the Social Democrats have increased their support in Southern Germany. Elsewhere the German constituency elections tend to operate in a manner similar to that of British elections. Table 7.15 shows the parameters of the Social Democrats CPD's for 1972 and 1976 as two-party contests against the Christian Democrats (CDU). Notice the slight negative skewness, which is unusual for a leftwing party, but otherwise the CPD is quite normal. The variance is particularly low and this is consistent with the larger constituencies (150000 voters). From chapter 2 it is known that a variance of 10% implies a gradient of four at the 50% vote mark on the cumulative normal distribution so that the constituency part of German elections roughly corresponds to a 'quartic' power law. However, the rapid changeover of seats with small changes of votes that this implies is unimportant since resulting biases are corrected in the regional 'topping up' procedure. In conclusion the eradication of very small parties and bonus seats (despite the use of large constituencies) means that the most proportionate election results discussed in this book occurred in Germany in 1972 and 1976.

The West German electoral system does seem to have justified the hopes of its proponents in producing both proportionality in results while preventing multiplication of parties. Nonetheless, dangers of manipulation must be recognised. The bonus seat anomaly does provide a loophole for producing nonproportionality. This can be exploited by two parties in alliance. If the weaker of the two parties advises its voters to vote for candidates of its ally in the constituency contest then that party might easily win more than its proportionate share of seats overall. However, the lesser party in the alliance will not lose any seats since its constituency votes would probably be wasted in the plurality method anyway. However, if the supporters cast their votes for the party's Land list, it will still receive seats in proportion to its true strength. On the other hand, the major party in the alliance can expect no extra seats at the Land allocation so that its supporters' votes for its party list are wasted. If they switch their second vote to their ally's party list, then the ally

Table 7.15: *Parameters of the Social Democrat (versus Christian Democrat) CPD for German elections, 1972 and 1976*

Election	$\bar{x}$	σ	β_1	β_2
1972	52.71	9.50	−0.44	+0.06
1976	49.24	9.36	−0.30	+0.06

will receive far more seats than its true level of support would warrant. Between them both parties could, in this way, obtain far more seats than their combined vote would warrant. Hence the German mixed system does not ensure proportionality, proportionality still relies on the behaviour of parties and voters.

In practice most voters in German elections have supported the same party with both of their votes. However, split voting has occurred in the past (Birke, 1961) and may still be important. The Free Democrats (FDP) have consistently done better in the Land voting, presumably because their supporters regard votes for FDP as being wasted at the constituency level. In fact, since 1961 FDP have not won any constituency seats. However, in 1972 their constituency vote was only 4.8% compared with their Land vote of 8.4%. Hence there seems to be clear evidence of tactical voting, albeit on a minor scale. Notice, however, that this tactical voting does involve putting FDP beyond the 5% threshold for obtaining their proportionate share. Since the Social Democrats (SDP) are in government coalition with FDP, it is clearly within their interest to maintain FDP support above 5% and the rise in the FDP fortunes in 1972 may have been due to some SPD tactical voting. This is supported by the fact that FDP's revival was in terms of Land votes only (Hansard Society, 1976).

It can be concluded that, in practice, the West German electoral system does approach proportionality and that it has improved in this respect. Nonetheless, opportunities do exist for manipulation of the system with tactical voting and there is some evidence that this practice is growing.

7.4.2 Additional members for the British parliament

Current interest in the West German electoral system has led to suggestions for its modification for adoption in Britain and to predictions of the effects of the modifications. Suggested alterations centre on the double-voting procedure, the operation of the minimum threshold and the proportion of constituency seats. By allowing voters only one vote each, for both constituency candidate and regional party lists, the system is simplified and the more extreme manipulations described previously become impossible. By applying a 5% minimum threshold at the regional level, representation is ensured for regionally based parties such as the SNP and Plaid Cymru who do not poll 5% overall. Finally, by employing a higher proportion of constituency seats, the size of constituencies may not grow too large under this system for the same overall size of Parliament. Each of these three modifications forms part of the Hansard Society's (1976) report's recommendations.

Before the Hansard Society report had been published, there had been predictions on the effects of the additional-member system of voting. Using February 1974 results, Steed (1974) illustrated possible results from such a system, first with the 5% threshold operating nationally and, second, with it operating regionally. This alteration in the rules largely effects the SNP and Plaid Cymru, as table 7.16 shows. Also shown on this table are results with the assumption of Liberal candidates in all seats and no tactical voting by Labour. In all cases the electoral bias is relatively small, particularly where regional minimum thresholds are employed.

Steed (1974) does not indicate the proportion of constituency seats to additional seats. Berrington (1975) presents an example based on 400 (63%) constituency MPs and 235 additional members. His results are similar to Steed's in terms of electoral biases and the effect of changing the basis of calculating the threshold. However, the Hansard Society report recommends 480 constituency seats (75%) in a 640 member House of Commons. This is a higher proportion that that ever used in Germany and introduces the possibility of bonus constituency seats. Let us consider how this might work.

Constituency members will continue to be elected by a simple plurality so that the processes described in previous chapters will continue to operate at this stage. This means that the vast majority of constituency MPs will belong to the two main parties, especially the winning party. If it is assumed that these seats will be apportioned in the cube-law manner, then the number of bonus constituency seats can be predicted. Let V_M be the proportion of the overall vote going to the two major parties, V_A be the proportion of the vote of one of the two major parties, party A, so that (V_A/V_M) is the party's proportion of the two-party vote. Further let there be a proportion S^c of all seats allocated to constituencies. Of these constituency seats let minor parties win a proportion S_m^C. From the cube law it is known that the proportion of constituency seats won

Table 7.16: *Predictions using additional-member system, February 1974*
Source: Steed (1974)

Party	Vote (%)	National threshold	Bias (%)	Regional threshold	Bias (%)
Seats with actual voting					
Conservative	38.8	249	+1.2	244	+0.4
Labour	38.0	244	+1.2	239	+0.4
Liberal	19.8	127	+0.6	124	+0.1
Scottish National	2.0	2	–2.0	13	+0.1
Plaid Cymru	0.6	1	–0.6	3	–0.6
Seats with modified voting					
Conservative	38.0	243	+1.0	239	+0.4
Labour	38.4	246	+1.1	241	+0.3
Liberal	20.5	131	+0.5	129	+0.2
Scottish National	1.8	2	–1.8	11	0.0
Plaid Cymru	0.5	1	–0.5	3	–0.5

by the party will be given by

$$S^c_A = \frac{(V_A/V_M)^3}{3(V_A/V_M)^2 - 3(V_A/V_M) + 1}(1 - S^c_m), \qquad (7.1)$$

so that the proportion of all seats won in just this first stage is given by

$$S_A = \frac{(V_A/V_M)^3(1 - S^c_m)}{3(V_A/V_M)^2 - 3(V_A/V_M) + 1} S^c . \qquad (7.2)$$

Now if $S_A > V_A$ then party A will have won more seats in the first stage than its proportional overall vote entitles it to. Hence bonus seats result and electoral bias is produced.

Table 7.17 shows predictions of seat proportions computed from equation (7.2) with $S^c_m = 0.04$ and $V_M = 0.75$ as in the October 1974 election. Three types of voting arrangements are considered, the current German situation with $S^c = 0.5$, the original German situation with $S^c = 0.6$ and the Hansard Society proposals for Britain with $S^c = 0.75$. Clearly the more seats allocated to constituencies the more chance of bonus seats. This is shown in table 7.17. In all predictions for $S^c = 0.75$ the seat proportions are above the specified vote levels so that bonuses and electoral bias would be produced. Otherwise bonus seats only occur in one other situation in the table. Whereas proportionality is almost achieved with AMS in German elections the Hansard Society's proposals by no means guarantee such good results for British elections. Even with only 40% of the overall vote, a major party would win more than its proportionate share of seats at this first stage of the election. As the vote rises, the number of bonus seats would become quite marked and the system would be relatively disproportionate in terms of seats and votes.

This means that even Labour's weak showing (40% for a winning party) in October 1974 would lead to a small (3%) bonus of constituency seats at the overall national scale. If seats were awarded at a regional scale, Conservatives would have more than their proportionate share of seats in the Southeast (42.1%), Southwest (43.1%), and East Anglia (43.8%) while Labour would win bonus seats in East Midlands (43.1%), West Midlands (43.9%), Yorkshire (46.9%), Northwest (44-6%), North (49.9%),

Table 7.17: Predictions of overall seat proportions derived from constituency elections only [computed from equation (7.2)]

Proportion of constituency seats (S^c)	Proportion of total vote (V_A)				
	0.40	0.45	0.50	0.55	0.60
0.50	0.29	0.37	0.43	0.46	0.47
0.60	0.35	0.44	0.51	0.55	0.57
0.75	0.43	0.56	0.64	0.69	0.71

and Wales (49.5%). Liberals would not win any bonus seats anywhere, of course. These predictions based on a cube-law relationship suggest that a very high proportion of constituency seats perpetuates electoral biases as major parties continue to be overrepresented in their regions of strong support. Some of this regional bias will be cancelled out when seats are aggregated at the national level but Labour will probably tend to benefit overall. Hence the ironic finding that the Hansard Society report's recommendations would replace one system that has tended to penalise Labour for its geographical concentration of support at constituency level with another system which rewards Labour for its regional concentrations.

The additional-member system is illustrated here by simulating a British election with half the seats allocated to constituencies and additional members allocated by home countries, England, Scotland, and Wales (Northern Ireland is not considered here). Table 7.17 shows that this will not produce bonus seats. Furthermore October 1974 voting figures can be easily used in the simulation with $S^c = 0.5$ since constituency results may be combined in pairs to form new larger AMS constituencies (with one triple in Scotland). The result is 311 constituencies, 258 in England, eighteen in Wales, and thirty-five in Scotland. The constituency MPs elected for these districts are shown in table 7.18 along with the additional members needed to produce proportionality. The simulated electoral biases are very small and such an election could fairly claim to have produced proportional representation.

AMS is the most successful electoral system for minimising electoral bias that has been considered here. This seems to be true both in practice in Germany and in theory in Britain. Biases can be produced but these may be easily avoided to produce both constituency MPs and proportional representation.

Table 7.18: Predicted results using AMS for October 1974

Party	Vote (%)	Constituency MPs	List MPs	Total	Electoral bias
Conservative	36.7	122	108	230	+0.3
Labour	40.2	181	71	252	+0.3
Liberal	18.8	1	117	118	+0.2
SNP	2.9	7	11	18	0.0

7.5 Conclusions: electoral engineering

The conclusions to be derived from consideration of alternative voting systems are presented in table 7.19. The biases all relate to actual or predicted results based on October 1974 voting figures. The alternative-vote results are Steed's (1975a) 'average' findings for this system of voting, the STV results are from the 'medium-sized constituency' experiment, and the AMS results are from the 50-50 experiment. It is clear that any change benefits the Liberals at the expense of the two major parties. However, it is AMS which, not surprisingly, produces the most proportionate results. It is this latter system, therefore, which can fairly claim fully to produce a reform of representation. If this system were adopted for British elections it would constitute the final stage in the path to electoral reform traced in chapter 1.

This all seems very simple and straightforward but, in practice, problems in electoral politics are never quite so easy, and the additional-member system has not been without its critics even in Germany. In 1967 the Minister of the Interior appointed an advisory committee of academic experts (seven professors) to review the voting system and they recommended the adoption of plurality elections of the British type. Similarly in Ireland STV has come under attack, and as recently as 1959 a referendum to substitute a plurality system for STV only just failed, with 48% voting for the change. Hence both of these countries have not been too far removed from emulating France and rejecting a proportionate system for a disproportionate procedure. The path to electoral reform is certainly not a smooth one.

All proposals and counterproposals concerning electoral reform are ultimately based on alternative theories of parliamentary representation. At the core of all such theories are questions relating to the purpose of elections and the relationship of the legislature to the electorate. Chapter 1 used as a basis the view that the purpose of elections is to produce a legislature that reflects the opinions of the electorate, specifically through political parties. The resulting reform of representation is at variance with other theoretical bases. The major alternative relates to the view that elections are simply a means of producing governments. Hence the major result of an election does not relate to proportionality but simply to which party won and whether they have a majority with which to govern. With this theory a system of voting which does not normally produce a single majority party in the legislature has failed in its major purpose. The proposers of the changes to the electoral systems of Germany and Ireland, for instance, emphasised the need for one-party majorities to avoid multiparty coalition governments. If this theory of

Table 7.19: Electoral biases under different systems of voting, October 1974

Party	Actual (plurality)	AVS	STV	AMS
Conservative	+7.8	−0.1	+3.1	+0.3
Labour	+11.0	+7.5	+5.1	+0.3
Liberal	−16.2	−10.4	−8.6	+0.2
Nationalist	−1.3	+3.9	+0.4	0.0

parliamentary representation is held then the electoral reform discussed above is a blind alley.

This does not mean that the results above are necessarily of little or no interest to opponents of electoral reform. Since all discussion of electoral systems is based on some underlying theory of representation, it follows that proposals for either change or no change can equally be considered electoral engineering. Quite simply, a theory of representation gives a purpose to elections which the proposed voting system is designed to implement. The question that arises is how good is the engineering, does the voting system do as it is intended. All laws have two types of result, intended effects and unintended effects. The analyses help clarify how far the former effects have been or will be achieved and what unintended effects have arisen or will arise. The importance of understanding electoral laws in this very basic sense is highlighted by the example given by Steed (1975b) that some MPs supported the 1885 British reforms because they thought that single-member plurality elections would help achieve proportional representation. Clearly it is no longer possible to make such an error but *all* effects must be understood before any electoral engineering is attempted.

Although never explicitly designed with any particular purpose in mind, the plurality system now has the intended effect of producing simple one-party government based upon two-party competition. Although this is not always the case with plurality elections, the overall record in this sphere is impressive (Rae, 1971). Hence for the electoral engineers who prefer no change, plurality elections are successful in their major purpose. However, there are many unintended effects which have been described in previous chapters and which still require careful consideration. Plurality systems favour some parties over others in a quite arbitrary manner depending on the pattern of their support. Plurality systems have the equally arbitrary effect of polarising representation compared with the patterns of support. In Britain and New Zealand this occurs on an urbanisation dimension, in Canada it threatens the integration of the state, and in the USA it maintains the 'solid South' as an aftermath of the Civil War. Furthermore, plurality systems have the unintended effect of not really counting everybody's vote when allocating representatives. Every election produces millions of wasted votes. Some voters can vote at every election during their lives without having any effect whatsoever. This happens to all voters who constitute permanent minorities — Labour supporters in Sussex or Conservatives in Durham for example. It is surprising how high the turnout is in plurality elections given this lack of any real participation which is often involved.

Supporters of the plurality method of voting need to consider whether their goal of 'stable' government can still be achieved in the context of reform which eradicates these arbitrary effects. The results above show that majority-type voting systems are no solution since they share these arbitrary effects.

One country that has employed an explicit electoral law to produce 'stable government' is Greece. Table 7.20 shows votes and seats proportions for the November 1977 Greek election along with the electoral biases that resulted. These biases have a familiar pattern to them, with larger parties gaining at the expense of smaller parties, but they are in fact different in kind from our previous examples. The biases are specifically created by the electoral law. A list system in multimember constituencies is used which enables some minority-party representation but there is also a topping-up process, with additional seats given to parties obtaining over 25% of the vote. Hence the biases in table 7.20. This is an electoral law which explicitly incorporates the idea of stable government being the preferred outcome of an election. It is a piece of conscious electoral engineering in the same way as other list systems produce PR.

This Greek electoral law is consistent with the theory of representation loosely adhered to by proponents of plurality elections but explicitly sets out to produce a situation favouring one-party government in a largely two-party parliament. However, it remains arbitrary in application of the crucial 25% vote threshold for bonus seats. A more satisfactory arrangement is to relate seats to votes through explicit incorporation of a seats-votes function into the electoral law. This may be achieved by using an additional-member system in which the topping-up procedure produces a desired seats-votes relationship that need not be the proportionality produced in German elections. In Holland, for example, it has been proposed that a 'square law' be adopted for allocating seats to parties from list votes (Theil, 1972). In Britain the cube law might be used in allocating additional members. Elections would then be consistent in the sense that the votes-seats relationship would be deterministic, not probabilistic as is currently the case and as has been modelled above.

Hence the interesting conclusion is that an additional-member system is the best electoral arrangement for *both* major theories of representation. The additional members ensure that all votes count and give the system a flexibility to produce exactly the seats-votes relationship that is agreed

Table 7.20: *Votes, seats, and election biases in the 1977 Greek election*

Party	Votes (%)	Seats (%)	Electoral bias
New Democracy	41.85	57.67	+15.72
Pasok	25.33	30.67	+5.34
Democratic Centre	11.95	5.00	−6.95
Communist	9.36	3.67	−5.69
National Rally	6.82	1.67	−5.15
Eurocommunist	2.72	0.67	−2.05
Neo-Liberals	1.08	0.67	−0.41

upon. Hence all arbitrary unintentional effects may be abolished and the debate can become directly concerned with theories of representation and not with their partial reflections in voting systems. The additional-member vote system is simply the most reliable tool available for the respectable electoral engineer: it takes the geography out of elections.

chapter eight | concluding comments and summary

The essential criticism of the plurality system of elections is the way in which seats won fail accurately to mirror votes gained. The reason for the problem is the territorial basis of the system, whose main characteristic is that the aggregate result depends on the individual constituency contests where the winner takes all no matter how slender his local support. The adherence to single-member constituencies is based on the idea of local representation, an idea which van den Bergh (1955) considers:

> has been out of date for over a century and which is essentially unsuitable for our modern democracy. This idea which is feudal in origin still partly fits into the sphere of the limited monarchy. Democracy, however, demands representation of ideological-political currents, and these recognise no local boundaries. In the light of modern conceptions, the system of single member constituencies represents an inadequate and clumsy attempt at building a twentieth century political system on medieval foundations.

The moral is that proportionality in elections at the aggregate, national, level requires that the voting system be designed with national as well as local considerations in mind. Even at the local scale the first-past-the-post system has problems. In what sense for instance does an MP of one political party represent constituents whose views on most issues are diametrically opposed. Would it not be better to give constituents a choice of representative? Nevertheless it is problems of electoral bias at the national scale (the discrepancy between vote proportion and seat proportion) which are more important.

In the preceding chapters bias was described as being one of several types. Winners' bias accentuates the advantage of the party gaining most votes. In most plurality systems the multiplier converting votes swings into seats swings is between 2.5 and 3.0. Conversely a common feature of plurality elections is a savage bias against minor parties. The British Liberal Party can for example win 18% of the vote but only 2% of the seats. The multiplier determines the responsiveness of parliamentary composition to shifts in voting preference. In Britain at the turn of the century the multiplier was larger than at present and consequently there was a tendency for elections to lurch from landslide to landslide despite quite moderate shifts in the strength of support for the two main parties. Not all plurality elections exhibit winners' bias, however, and in South Africa even quite large swings in voting have almost no impact on the number of seats won by each party.

The second type of bias is caused by the relative overconcentration of supporters of one party into stronghold constituencies. The consequence of numerous wasted votes largely afflicts left-wing parties since their support tends to be most concentrated. As a result, plurality (and related) elections tend to display an anti left-wing bias which occasionally manifests itself in the left-wing party winning most votes but nevertheless losing the election. Nowhere can this have had more important consequences than in South Africa, where the foundations of Apartheid were laid in a decade during which the National Party won successive elections despite gaining fewer votes than its main rival.

The final source of bias is the least important but is paradoxically probably the best known. This is malapportionment, or the differences between parties in the average number of total voters per constituency. However, the possibility of malapportionment emphasises an additional weakness. Since territoriality, and hence boundaries, are at the heart of the plurality system, it is possible to alter the outcomes of elections by changing the boundaries. Although gerrymandering generally has a bad name (with good cause), it has on occasions been used purposively to prevent the permanent submergence of minorities. Yet its less altruistic uses are more widespread than is often realised, especially in the USA. In all countries someone has to fix the boundaries and even neutral agencies can favour one party over another, in ways which are sometimes described as being 'innocently partisan'.

The aim of this volume has been to explain why and how these problems arise in plurality elections. At the end of a lengthy and rather technical analysis it is appropriate to take stock of what has been achieved. The main findings concern the way in which the seats-votes relationship reflects the spatial distribution of party support. This work, described in chapter 2, extends the analysis of Kendall and Stuart (1950) to show how many forms of spatial distribution can be converted in mathematical equations linking seats and votes. The equations which occur in practice tend to be simple, often predicting that the ratio of seats gained by two parties is the ratio of their votes raised to some power.

As is well known the latter power has often been found to be the cube, that is, the seats ratio equals the cube of the votes ratio. The reason for this relationship has, however, presented a mystery to those who do not see why the same seats-votes relationship should recur in countries whose political structure, and scale and organisation of elections differ widely. Some, like Tufte, have objected that the exponent is not generally exactly three and may be nearer to two, but more importantly that there is no theoretical underpinning for the cube law. These objections have caused Tufte to reject the cube law, declaring that

> ... the cube law has appeal because it is one of those charming, harmless, story-explanations that so often embellish perennial celebrations—like Santa Claus or the Easter Bunny. It should be left at that (Tufte, 1974, page 211).

Although Tufte is correct in rejecting the cube as a universal generalisation with law-like qualities, he is wrong to suggest that matters should rest there. The cube and related ratios have a strong theoretical underpinning, and demonstrating this fact is the burden of chapter 3. The mystery of the cube law can be restated by asking why the support for the major parties should be spatially distributed in such a way as to produce a cube, or similar, ratio. The answer is relatively simple although a little subtle. Constituencies can be viewed as samples from the overall population of voters, containing mixtures in different proportions of supporters of each party. These supporters are clustered on the ground because party allegiance largely reflects social class and because different social classes usually live in distinct areas. The form of the overall distribution of constituency proportions depends on just how strongly clustered are party supporters relative to the size of constituencies. It was shown that the multiplier linking seats to votes can be obtained from a relatively simple equation in which the variables describe the size, spatial concentration, and political homogeneity of social-class clusters. The characteristics of such clustering are controlled by the socioeconomic forces governing residential segregation, and these forces are reasonably similar among the industrial nations which use the plurality system. Hence the similarity in the seats-votes relationship.

The parameters of the above equation are not easy to measure in a general sense, but in this study a test case was performed within a single city—Newcastle upon Tyne—and the values obtained produced a multiplier very close to that of the cube law. This equation is in many ways the key result of the study, pointing as it does to the heart of the link between seats, votes, and the spatial distribution of voters.

The remaining findings in the work were concerned with extending the applicability of the seats-votes work, and in modifying the basic model in the direction of reality. Some of the modifications provide measures of such things as the relative concentration of support in party strongholds, measures which permit a simple yet effective decomposition of electoral bias into its three components. In another modification interelection swings which vary between constituencies were considered. This section (4.1) produced the surprising conclusion that if swings are random, and not related to the strength of party support (which is broadly the case), then the seats-votes multiplier will diminish over time.

Extensions of the seats-votes work include an analysis of the mechanics of three-party elections, and of the practice and consequences of gerrymandering. In the former case a quantified model was developed to predict three-party seats from a knowledge of the votes. (As in all sections of this work prediction of the votes themselves is left aside as being a different issue.) The main results showed precisely how the spatial distribution of third-party support governs both the votes threshold at which seats begin to be won, and also the rate at which they are subsequently gained. Several countries have third parties with support which is relatively evenly spread across constituencies, and it is these which the plurality system tends to punish most mercilessly for their electoral weakness. What is perhaps not generally realised is how rapidly the weakness could potentially change to strength. With 25% of the votes such a party will win almost no seats, but with a further 10% or so, it soon becomes the most powerful single party. The seats-votes multiplier for these third parties is large (around six) once the critical threshold is attained. The three-party analysis is a flexible one and can show for example why contests between three powerful parties, as in Britain in the 1920s, produce such unstable results.

Gerrymandering is a topic in which some conclusions are relatively obvious; majority-party gerrymanderers must for instance concentrate opposition strength to pile up large numbers of wasted votes. However, in section 6.1 the notion of gerrymandering was placed where it belongs, within the broader context of electoral districting. In chapter 6 the drawing of any one set of boundaries is seen as merely one outcome from the entire set of feasible districting solutions. When this is done it becomes obvious that most solutions will favour the majority party. Hence neutral Boundary Commissioners who do not explicitly take note of party advantage are likely to select a configuration of boundaries which favours the local majority party.

The paradoxical solution emerges that neutral Boundary Commissioners are likely, by the law of averages, to act in the same way as would a gerrymanderer acting for a local majority party. In effect the British Boundary Commissioners gerrymander for Labour in the inner cities and for the Conservatives in most other areas. Although the attendant biases cancel themselves out to a large, although not complete, extent in aggregate, the result is a greatly distorted pattern of representation. Labour becomes a party of urban MPs, and the Conservatives a party of rural, small town, and suburban MPs, although in both cases these form caricatures of the parties' bases of support. The Boundary Commissioners are not to be particularly blamed for this state of affairs, it is more an almost inevitable outcome of the plurality system. One might also note in passing that the Liberal Party in Britain has a similarly distorted pattern of representation. The widespread support for this party is mirrored distortedly by a small band of MPs largely from the Celtic and island fringes.

The biases which are inherent in plurality elections can in theory be avoided by the adoption of proportional representation. In practice, Anglo-Saxon nations have chosen to continue with territorially based elections which van den Bergh finds so archaic. The alternative-vote, single-transferable-vote, and additional-member systems are all quite strongly based on constituencies, although in the latter two cases there are attempts to counteract the plurality biases. This is done either by loosening the one-member, one-constituency relationship (in STV) or by topping up the constituency seats in such a way as to move towards proportional representation. The discussion of these ideas in chapter 7 brings together ideas and work which will already be familiar to many political scientists, although they are set within the framework of the analyses in previous chapters, to bring out fresh insights. The main new conclusion shows how proportionality in AMS elections depends upon specific combinations of constituency and additional members. The suggestion made by the Hansard Society to have 75% of constituency MPs in British elections is shown to be too high, and to produce biases for the majority party in the same way as do unmodified plurality elections. The moral to be drawn echoes the theme running through all of these concluding remarks: too strong an adherence to territorially based elections will lead to disproportionate elections.

As a final point we can emphasise the methodological lessons which may be drawn from this study. The work has demonstrated to us the relative power of abstract modelling over empirical investigation as a method of investigating systems or processes. This is something long recognised by economists, but not practised widely in the other social sciences. The power derives from a concentration upon the major, and often inevitable, links in the system. In the case of elections a seats-votes relationship must follow from the relative numbers of marginal and nonmarginal contests. These in turn are a direct reflection of the spatial distribution of voters, and in particular of the size of clusters of voters relative to the size of constituencies. Each of these links can be seen by looking hard at the nature of plurality elections. Having got this far it is not difficult to translate the system into mathematical terms in the form of process generating a probability (frequency) distribution.

The important feature is that each step can be made by logical analysis, and one step follows logically from another. In contrast some others have tried to account for the seats-votes relationship by empirical methods, generally based on fitting regression lines to actual election data in the hope of revealing something of general importance (Dahl, 1956; Tufte, 1973). The weakness in this approach is that it is essentially descriptive and there is no logical place to go after the first step. A leap of imagination is required, but of all mental commodities imagination is unfortunately the one in shortest supply. In essence, the key is to model the process (or in this case the system) rather than the patterns which occur empirically. This has been the approach followed throughout this study in looking firstly at two-party elections, then at three-party elections, and finally at electoral districting. It has in our view paid dividends in a way unlikely to occur with an empirical investigation. Although the penalites of being abstract may be initially onerous it is usually possible to work back towards reality, and this is certainly the case with plurality elections.

appendix 1

Alternative approaches to explaining the cube law

The existence of a relationship which is both tightly defined (unlike so many in the social sciences) and unexplained has attracted researchers from far and wide. Several branches of the social sciences are represented by those taking up the challenge of explaining the cube law. In this appendix three of the most direct attempts are reviewed. These are those of March — better known for his work in behavioural economics, Taagepera, and the game theorists Sankoff and Mellos. Other work on the cube law which involves differing approaches to modelling rather than explanation as such (for example, Thiel, 1970) is not reviewed.

March's behavioural rationalisation

March (1957) began by reviewing the empirical evidence for the cube law from the UK and the explanations advanced in Kendall and Stuart (1950) to account for it. His own explanation is based on behavioural considerations. In this account we will first review March's criticisms of the Kendall and Stuart approach (on which chapter 3 is based), and then assess March's own explanation.

March rejects Kendall and Stuart's Markov approach for two reasons. The first is that "the level of correlation between successive drawings is ... improbably extreme". The second, and "perhaps more important", is that the level of correlation necessary to result in the cube law varies from country to country with the size of constituency. In section 3.2 we demonstrated, at least to our own satisfaction, that a spatial interpretation and some modifications to the simple Markov model overcome these problems.

March leaves the Markov approach at this point and turns to the Lexian alternative. He points out correctly, in apparent contrast to Kendall and Stuart, that the form of the resulting distribution depends almost entirely on the arbitrarily selected distribution of constituency mean proportions. Although this is enough in itself to reject the Lexian approach as an ultimately useful one, March views this as only a partial disadvantage, and bases his objections to it on three further points.

(1) It does not explain why CPDs should be normal in the UK and poisson in the USA (1928–1954). (The poisson distribution is similar to the normal distribution except that it is slightly skewed, and for the same mean as the normal has its mode at a slightly lower value.)

(2) This scheme depends on equal-size constituencies, and yet US Senate elections 1928–1954 approximate to the cube law despite their notoriously varied constituency sizes.

(3) The Lexian scheme reflects the geographical distribution of voters, and yet distributions based on the same districts differ between those for congressional elections and those for presidential elections in the same year.

Although the Lexian approach needs no defence since it is inapplicable as a working explanation, it is illuminating to discuss March's objections. In the case of point (1) the observed poisson distribution is an artificial creation resulting from March's consideration of contested seats only, and his definition of a contested election as being one in which the major party wins less than 90% of the vote. In the period considered, 1928 to 1954, the USA essentially had two electoral cleavages. One was a two-party system based largely on social-class, covering most of the country. The other, a hangover from the Civil War, was a virtual one-party system in the Southern States. Since the cube law is only relevant to the former type of cleavage, the Southern States must be considered separately. Kendall and Stuart excluded the ten Southern States which returned only Democratic congressmen from their analysis of the 1944 congressional election, and found that the CPD had "a form closely resembling the British type" with "a standard deviation close to the value required by the law of cubic proportion". March's procedure removes some of the Southern seats, but leaves enough to produce a distribution slightly skewed to the right, which thence resembles the poisson distribution. A cutoff point at 75% or 80% instead of 90% would remove all or most of the skewness and bring a return to normality!

The second objection is of little importance. The assumption of constituencies of uniform size is adhered to for analytic convenience. Constituencies of nonuniform size would, however, make little difference unless the sizes were strongly related to the level of the constituency proportions. The third point is more important and merits a closer examination. March is hypothesising a set of voters with fixed voting intentions with regard to the two parties. Two elections in the same year should produce very similar frequency distributions, whereas, in fact, those for congressional elections typically had a variance half as large again as those for presidential elections. However, it is difficult to assume that the different nature of the elections had no influence in deflecting voters from their strict party allegiance. At the very least, the presidential contests are much more nationally oriented events than congressional elections. As such the swings between successive presidential elections should be more uniform across constituencies than are swings in congressional elections where local issues add to the national influences. As outlined in section 4.1, nonuniform swings between elections result in higher variances than do uniform swings.

March's own suggestion for explaining the existence of the cube law involves two behavioural processes, one at the *inter*constituency scale, the other at the *intra*constituency level. In the former case, parties are supposed to bargain, with policies offered to electors, for control of constituencies. Since each party will aim at a low majority, this process will produce, according to March, a low-variance, peaked, unimodal distribution around 50% of the vote. Although bargaining with potential voters is undoubtedly a feature of elections, this bargaining is more a national than a local feature. In the UK it is certainly true that Members of Parliament have little local power, and party policy is aimed largely at national groups. Indeed, politics is so 'nationalised' that even in local elections national issues play a major role.

It is not easy to translate this process from the national to the local level, particularly in UK politics. It may be argued that parties can design policies most likely to appeal to voters in marginal constituencies. This, however, presupposes the existence of the marginal constituencies which the process is supposed to be accounting for. It is possible to suppose that this process modifies frequency distributions which owe their existence principally to the spatial distribution of voters who have relatively unchanging propensities to support one or the other of the parties. Even this suggestion, however, is ruled out by the uniformity of election swings across constituencies within the UK. Presumably, if policies were designed specifically to woo voters in marginal constituencies, then these constituencies should show greater swings. Alternatively, two parties both attempting the same ploy may cancel each other out, and thus not affect the frequency distribution. However the problem is approached, it seems most unlikely that March's process operates in the UK. If it does not explain the cube law for the UK, then it cannot be considered a general explanation. Since the empirical regularity of the cube law transcends national boundaries, arguments based on particular circumstances which may not hold generally would seem to be a nonstarter.

The *intra*constituency process assumes that the probability of an individual's switching parties is a linear function of the pressure exerted on him by other individuals to do so. The pressure exerted equals the number of supporters times the logarithm of the size of majority (or minority) in the constituency. The latter element describes the probability that party supporters do not vote either because their party has little chance of winning, or because their party has little chance of losing. March argues that this process will produce a bimodal distribution of constituency proportions, with few constituencies near 0.5 and modes near 0.4 and 0.6. This result, however, depends on some underlying distribution of constituency proportions—presumably that produced by the *inter*constituency process. Unless the latter is accepted, the bimodal distribution is ruled out, at least in the form described by March. We can note, moreover, that March offers only the vaguest of empirical support for this process.

March combines the two distributions, having weighted them equally, and asserts that the combination of a bimodal distribution with a trough at 0.5 and a unimodal one with a sharp peak at 0.5 will produce something akin to a normal distribution. March adds arbitrarily selected parameters to his distributions and arrives at the correct 'cube law' variance. The only explanation offered in support of the parameters is the assertion that they are "not unreasonable". Finally, March uses his model to account for the difference between the normal distributions of UK elections and the poisson, distributions of US elections. This explanation, however, merely returns to the definition of uncontested seats, and it is this, and not the processes themselves, which causes the difference between the two countries.

March outlines two processes, neither of which is supported with any real empirical evidence. From these he constructs, in a relatively informal way, frequency distributions but has no way of deriving their parameters and hence their exact shape. Finally, he combines the two distributions with equal weightings, offering no reason to explain why the two processes should have equal force. This combination of tenuously argued circumstances leaves the reader in a position in which, at best, he says "maybe" and, at worst, says that the underlying processes carry little conviction and hence the rest of the argument fails.

One positive point is that the article points up the assumption underlying all of the probability models of section 3.2 to the effect that individuals with relatively fixed support propensities exist. These individuals are allocated to constituencies by socioeconomic forces and the rest follows quite easily. If such voters are not the norm, and instead most are 'floating voters', reacting to the issues of the day, then the reasoning of section 3.2 fails. However, intensive studies, most notably that of Butler and Stokes (1974), reveal that for most voters in the UK at least, the political allegiance tends to be fixed early in life and to remain similar in all elections. March emphasises the power of political parties to influence voters, and thus looks at a very different aspect of the political process, and one which is likely to be more important in the USA where swings between elections are normally much larger than elsewhere (Burnham, 1975). In our terms, such political bargaining and pressures influence the mean of the frequency distribution, that is, its location on the votes axis, and swings between elections, but not the shape of the distribution, including the variance. We assert that the shape of the distribution is determined by the processes outlined in section 3.4, whereas the location and changes of location of the distribution are matters to be explained by political scientists and are not dealt with in this book.

Taagepera's communicaton theory

Taagepera's explanation of the cube law is described in two parts in separate publications (Taagepera, 1972; 1973). The argument in its barest form is that the requirement for members of the national assembly to communicate efficiently both among themselves and with constituents leads to a cubic relationship between the size of the assembly and the number of voters. The latter relationship governs the exponent in the power-law formula leading to the cube law of elections. The communication part of the argument is based on the following assumptions.

1. It is most efficient for assembly members to divide their time and efforts equally in communicating with constituents and fellow assembly members.
2. Communication with a constituent takes an equal amount of time and effort as communication with a fellow assembly member.
3. The 'politically active' constituents include half the population. A different measure of political activity is a country's adult literate population.

Using these assumptions and using simple measures of maximum numbers of interpersonal links, Taagepera calculates that:

$$A = P^{1/3}, \qquad (A1.1)$$

where A is the number of assembly members and P is the politically active population. Taagepera also shows that the empirical relationship between assembly size and population is not far removed from equation (A1.1) for over a hundred national assemblies in the mid-1960s. He makes no attempt to calibrate the relationship formally for the somewhat unconvincing reason that "a purely empirical fit to the situation around 1965 is not likely to apply to any other period except approximately" (Taagepera, 1972, page 387).

The theory and the facts are in approximate agreement, however, and Taagepera continues, in the second paper, to link the size of assembly with the cube law. This is achieved firstly by hypothesising that the exponent k in the power law formula is a function of the assembly size, and the total number of voters, that is,

$$\frac{S}{1-S} = \left(\frac{V}{1-V}\right)^{n(\bar{V},\bar{S})} \qquad (A1.2)$$

where S and V are the seats and votes respectively won by a party in a two-party election, $n(\bar{V}, \bar{S})$ is some function of the total votes $(\bar{V})$ and total seats $(\bar{S})$.

He then considers a two-stage process in which voters elect sub-representatives who themselves elect the assembly members. Each stage is related by an expression of the form of equation (A1.2), and the function n is the same for both stages. This leads indirectly to the expression

$$n(\bar{V}, \bar{S}) = \frac{m(\bar{V})}{m(\bar{S})}$$

where m is some function.

For informal reasons Taagepera decides that m is the logarithmic function:

$$m(\bar{V}) = \log(\bar{V}), \; m(\bar{S}) = \log(\bar{S}).$$

By using equation (A1.2) it can be seen that

$$n(\bar{V}, \bar{S}) = \frac{\log[S/(1-S)]}{\log[V/(1-V)]}.$$

Hence, according to Taagepera,

$$n(\bar{V}, \bar{S}) = \frac{\log(\bar{V})}{\log(\bar{S})},$$

but from the communication analysis

$$\frac{\log \bar{V}}{\log \bar{S}} = 3$$

if votes are equated with the politically active section of the population.

This completes the explanation for the appearance of the cube law in elections for national assemblies, and it is shown that in the countries which are examined in this book (with the exception of South Africa) that $\log \bar{V}/\log \bar{S}$ takes values of between 2.7 and 3.3. Finally the cube law is generalised to cover elections at a variety of scales ranging from labour union branches to US presidential elections. This is done by showing that the exponent of equation (A1.1) remains approximately equal to $\log V/\log S$ in a number of empirical examples covering the full range of electoral scales.

This account is brief and does less than justice to Taagepera's ideas, but the more important thing in the present context is to assess their validity, and the links between them and the explanation for the cube law given in chapter 3.

There are two problems with the communication section on the size of assembly. The first is that the assumptions are not necessarily the most plausible from a British vantage point, although they may be relevant for other political systems, and Taagepera makes no attempt to defend them. Second, the facts do not particularly appear to support the theory. In the developed noncommunist countries to which multiparty elections are most applicable the relationship between the logarithm of politically active population and the logarithm of assembly size appears to be closer to quadratic than cubic (Taagepera, 1972, page 392). Again Taagepera makes no attempt rigorously to compare the theory with the observations. Despite these shortcomings the empirical findings do remain and in accounting for them in communication terms Taagepera is likely to be on the right lines.

The second part of the argument contains the fascinating result that $\log \bar{V}/\log \bar{S}$ has a value which is close to three in most of the English-speaking democracies which use the plurality system. It is surely correct to draw the conclusion that some connection exists between this ratio and the seats-votes relationship described by the cube law or similar power laws. It is easy to demonstrate, however, that a cubic exponent does not necessarily follow when $\log \bar{V}/\log \bar{S}$ has a value of three. The latter value has been relatively stable in US congressional elections in recent years while the exponent in equation (A1.1) has been steadily declining. In South Africa the relationship between the size of assembly and the number of voters has not altered very radically in the postwar period, although the exponent has declined from being greater than two in 1948 to almost zero in 1974.

These examples illustrate the fact that for any given numbers of constituencies and voters it is possible to rearrange the boundaries or to effect other changes to produce a variety of values for the power-law exponent. The latter depends on the variance of the CPD, which itself is influenced by the number of constituencies relative to the number of votes. The exact positioning of the boundaries may be a very considerable additional influence.

In conclusion it is probably true that communications influence the size of assemblies relative to the numbers of voters. The latter relationship in turn does influence the variance of the CPD and hence the exponent in equation (A1.1). However, the way in which the links are drawn by Taagepera between the communications considerations and the cube law contains important weaknesses. In deriving the expression $n(\bar{V}, \bar{S}) = \log V/\log \bar{S}$, for instance, Taagepera does not explain why he uses an unrealistic two-stage process, and does not defend the assumption that the same function $n(\bar{V}, \bar{S})$ applies to both stages. The use of a logarithmic function in the derivation of the cube law is unconvincingly argued. Taagepera appears to have identified some interesting relationships in political representation, but has not in our view succeeded in drawing formal links between them.

A game-theoretic approach

Sankoff and Mellos (1972) investigate the form of seats-votes relationship which would result from a nationally-based contest between two political parties. In this contest the parties must allocate their resources (measured as total votes) to each constituency in secret amounts. The party allocating most resources in any particular constituency wins the seat. If total votes are distributed in a ratio $V/(1-V)$ between the parties and both try to maximise their gains, then this contest can be analysed by using game theory. Sankoff and Mellos undertake such an analysis and calculate that if the parties adopt optimal or near optimal strategies, then the average seats-votes relationship will be given by $S = (3V-1)/2V$. The graph of this function is zero at a votes proportion of $\frac{1}{3}$ and rises monotonically through $\frac{1}{2}$ at $V = \frac{1}{2}$ to 1 at $V = 1$. The slope of the curve at $V = \frac{1}{2}$ is two.

This is a rough although not particularly close approximation to the cube-law curve, and Sankoff and Mellos show how an additional assumption of a hard core of voters in each constituency would increase the slope of their curve at $V = \frac{1}{2}$. This increase would tend to give a better approximation to the cube law.

This derivation is most interesting for the way in which it demonstrates how a process of interparty competition at constituency levels could generate a seats-votes relationship not too far removed from those observed in reality. The analysis is unlikely to constitute an actual explanation of the cube law (or similar 'laws') because the basic process assumed is not very applicable for highly nationalised elections in which the power laws are still found to be applicable. Moreover, the greater the need to invoke a hard core of voters who are not influenced by the parties' tactics at constituency level, the closer the approach comes to that adopted in chapter 3. Nevertheless, even if the assumptions are not realistic under current conditions the analysis is of considerable value in showing what conclusions follow from the assumptions, and it should be noted that Sankoff and Mellos are not claiming that the assumptions are realistic. As noted with March's theory there is a need to investigate further the ways in which parties gain votes in differing proportions across constituencies. The Sankoff and Mellos result, however, leads to the important conclusion that it may make relatively little difference to the seats-votes relationship whether voters have fixed party allegiances, or votes which can be swayed by parties' disposition of their resources across constituencies.

appendix 2

Functional relationships between seats and votes in multiparty elections

It was stated at the beginning of chapter 5 that it is not easy to devise a simple equation relating seats to votes for more than two parties. However, several authors have attempted to devise such a relationship, and in this appendix their work is assessed and where appropriate is extended. Because multiparty elections are a more significant feature in Canada than in other countries using the plurality system, all of the discussion on multiparty seats–votes relationships involves Canadian elections.

Qualter's multiparty equation

Qualter (1968) introduces two new elements into the modelling of the seats-votes relationships. The first is a generalisation of the two-party cube-law equation:

$$S_i = \frac{V_i^3}{\sum_{i=1}^{n} V_i^3},$$

where S_i is the proportion of seats for party i and V_i is the proportion of votes for party i. Hence the two-party equation $S_i = V_i^3/(V_1^3 + V_2^3)$, used in chapter 2, takes the following form in the three-party case:

$$S_i = \frac{V_i^3}{(V_1^3 + V_2^3 + V_3^3)}.$$

No reasons are advanced for this form of generalisation. The equation in this form does not provide a good empirical fit for Canadian elections, and Qualter introduces his second innovation to improve matters. Since party support in Canada is complex, with strong regional elements, Qualter divides each election into a number of component types of contest. Constituency contests involving only Conservatives and Liberals form one type of contest, for instance, while those involving Conservatives, Liberals, and Progressives form another. Over the period 1921 to 1962, twenty-six different combinations are identified (omitting parties polling less than 10% in any constituency).

The generalised cube-law equation is applied separately to each type of contest, and the predicted numbers of seats are summed to give an overall prediction for any one election. For elections between 1921 and 1965, this procedure 'predicts' the number of seats won by the victorious party within a margin of about plus or minus 5% of its actual seat total. The predictions for losing parties are less good, but nevertheless provide an indication of the division of seats between parties which is reasonable given the complexity of Canadian elections.

Qualter's procedure has the merit of providing a functional relationship for seats and votes in a multiparty election, but it has the following drawbacks.

1. The procedure is more complicated than the two-party cube law, since it requires votes proportions for different types of contest. Nevertheless it is not too difficult to calculate these, or even to estimate them in advance.
2. The procedure is an example of 'blind modelling'. It models the results but not the process producing those results. No insights are gained on the mechanisms linking seats and votes in multiparty elections, and in particular no reasons are given for the form of equation which is used.
3. As indicated in chapter 2 the exponent in power-law equations reflects the spread of the underlying constituency proportion distribution. Since Qualter adopts the same cubic exponent for all parties, and since the cubic exponent reflects a CPD standard deviation of close to 0.13, the generalised cube-law equation is only directly applicable to parties with normal CPDs having this standard deviation. This point can be illustrated for three-party elections in which each party contests all seats. In this case the predicted number of seats for a third party in elections where the other parties are evenly matched in votes is as follows:

Votes (%)   20 30 40 50
Seats (%)   6 24 54 81

These figures can be compared directly with figure 5.1, which is based on the techniques of chapter 5. It can be observed that the predictions are extremely close to those where $\sigma = 0.137$ (figure 5.1 assumes the major parties to have this standard deviation also).

Hence, the generalised cube-law equation can be seen to be a special case, applicable only to elections in which all parties have normal CPDs, each with a standard deviation close to 0.13. Figures 5.4 and 5.11 show how this special condition is approximately fulfilled by the three largest parties in modern Canadian elections. In British elections, however, this is not the case since the Liberals have much more evenly spread support across constituencies than their major-party rivals. Table A2.1 shows how the generalised cube-law equation predicts seats to within an average of plus or minus 6% for major parties (which have roughly applicable CPDs)

Table A2.1: Seats in British elections predicted by the generalised cube-law equation

Party	February 1974 predicted	February 1974 actual	October 1974 predicted	October 1974 actual
Labour	268	301	317	319
Conservative	289	297	249	277
Liberal	57	14	36	13
Nationalist	9	9	21	14
Other	1	2	1	0

but overpredicts Liberal votes by factors of three and four. This overprediction is a consequence of the small standard deviation of the Liberal CPD.

A general seats-votes equation

Qualter's cubic equation applies only to a special case, and in this section a more general equation is derived. The suggested form of this for three-party elections is either

$$S_i = \frac{V_i^k}{\sum_{\substack{j=1 \\ j \ne i}}^{3} V_j^h + V_i^k}, \quad i = \{1, 2, 3\} \tag{A2.1}$$

or

$$S_i = \frac{V_i^k}{V_i^k + V_{j(1)}^l + V_{j(2)}^m}, \quad i = \{1, 2, 3\}, \tag{A2.2}$$

where $j(1)$ and $j(2)$ refer to parties other than party i.

The second of these equations is similar in form to Qualter's except that the exponents are variable for each party. The principle in both cases is each exponent reflects the standard deviation of the CPD for the relevant party.

Equation (A2.1) is derived as follows. If V_1 and V_2 are two random variables representing the votes gained by the two major parties, then the votes gained by the third party (V_3) is also a random variable. Also in a three-party election

$$V_3 = 1 - (V_1 + V_2).$$

If V_1 and V_2 are normally distributed with variances σ_1^2 and σ_2^2, respectively, then V_3 is also normally distributed, with variance σ_3^2, where

$$\sigma_3^2 = \sigma_1^2 + \sigma_2^2 + 2\operatorname{cov}(V_1, V_2)$$

where $\cos(V_1, V_2)$ indicates the covariance of V_1 and V_2 (that is, it is a measure of correlation between V_1 and V_2).

Since V_3 is normally distributed, we know (from chapter 3) that a power-law equation with exponent k reflecting σ_3^2 will give a good representation of the seats-votes equation, that is

$$S_3 = \frac{V_3^k}{(V_1 + V_2)^k + V_3^k} \tag{A2.3}$$

(Although this discussion is couched in terms of a third party, party 3, the principle is the same for any of the three parties.) Equation (A2.3) is, however, incomplete for three-party elections because the 'winning post' is not fixed at 50% as in two-party elections. In fact the 'winning post' in individual constituency contests varies between $33\frac{1}{3}\%$ and 50%. Equation (A2.3) must be altered to allow for this complication.

The election triangle analyses of chapter 5 demonstrated that the average 'winning post' percentage depended on the spread of the CPDs of the three parties. Hence it is necessary to introduce exponents into equation (A2.3), which vary between parties. The new equation thus takes the form:

$$S_3 = \frac{V_3^k}{(V_1 + V_2)^h + V_3^k} \quad . \tag{A2.4}$$

It is relatively easy to show that the average 'winning post' percentage varies with h and k (which in turn reflect the spread of the CPDs). If the average 'winning post' is defined as the votes percentage at which exactly half the constituencies are gained by any one party as its overall vote increases from 0% to 100%, then

$$0.5 = \frac{V^k}{(1+V)^h + V^k}, \tag{A2.5}$$

where V represents the votes % for any one party, and $(1 - V)$ is the votes % for the remaining two parties.

With a little manipulation it can be shown that the 'winning post' percentage V is given by:

$$V = (1 - V)^{h/k}.$$

This equation has to be solved iteratively, but the important point is that V depends on h/k, that is, on both h and k.

Equation (A2.2) can be derived from equation (A2.1) in the following manner. Working again in terms of the third party, we get from equation (A2.1):

$$S_3 = \frac{V_3^k}{(V_1 + V_2)^h + V_3^k} \quad . \tag{A2.6}$$

This is the same as

$$S_3 = \frac{V_3^k}{V_1^l + V_2^m + V_3^k} \tag{A2.7}$$

as long as $(V_1^l + V_2^m) = (V_1 + V_2)^h$. It is difficult to set general conditions for this equality to hold, but progress can be made in cases where $V_1 = V_2$ and $l = m$. These restrictions would be approximately true in British elections where there are two more or less evenly matched major parties whose CPDs have very similar degrees of spread.

In this case it can be shown that:

$$l(m) = \frac{k \log V_3 - \log 2}{\log V_1} \tag{A2.8}$$

or

$$l(m) = h + \frac{(h-1)\log 2}{\log V_1}. \tag{A2.9}$$

Although the exponent h in equation (A2.6) can be derived directly from the CPD standard deviation (as outlined in chapter 3), no such simple relationship appears to hold for the other exponents. For practical purposes:

$$k = \frac{0.399}{\sigma_3}$$

and

$$h = \frac{k \log V_3}{\log(1 - V_3)}.$$

To illustrate these ideas we can note that the British Liberal Party in the 1974 elections had a CPD with a standard deviation of approximately 0.05. Hence

$$k = \frac{0.399}{0.05} \approx 8.$$

In chapter 5 it was estimated that the Liberal Party would win half the seats at $V_3 = 0.4$. Hence

$$h = \frac{8 \log(0.4)}{\log(0.6)} = 14.3.$$

Although, these exponents are strictly only applicable at $V_3 = 0.4$, an application of equation (A2.1) with these exponents predicts third-party seats tolerably well. For third-party vote percentages of 20%, 30%, and 40%, equation (A2.1) predicts 0%, 10.7%, and 49.4% of the seats respectively. A comparison with figure 5.10 (for $\sigma = 0.05$) shows comparable seat percentages of 0%, 8%, and 45%. Equation (A2.1) with the parameters derived above, or alternatively equation (A2.2) with parameters calculated as in equations (A2.8) or (A2.9), provides a passably good approximation to estimates derived in chapter 5. Given the effort required to produce the estimates in chapter 5, such an approximation is very convenient.

Finally, it can be noted that equations (A2.1) and (A2.2) do not provide an accurate estimate of the actual number of seats won by the British Liberals in the 1974 elections. The prediction in both cases is zero seats whereas the actual numbers won were fourteen in February and thirteen in October. These actual numbers cannot be predicted by using any of the methods described in this book, or indeed by using any method other than a great deal of local knowledge immediately prior to the elections.

These seats are largely idiosyncratic victories won against the main tide of events affecting the great majority of Liberal candidates.

Casstevens and Morris's decomposed system

Qualter introduced two new elements in devising his predictive procedure. Of these the disaggregation into separate types of contest is undoubtedly an aid to greater accuracy in election prediction, although his generalised cubic equation proves to be a special case. Casstevens and Morris (1972) add a further refinement by introducing the concept of 'a share of a seat'. In each individual constituency the contestants are awarded shares of the seats in proportion to their individual shares of the votes gained in that constituency. The shares can then be summed over all constituencies to get a predicted total number of votes for each party. The shares are awarded by using a generalised equation of the type introduced by Qualter.

Casstevens and Morris assert that if the exponent in the equation is allowed to increase and become large (but not to vary between parties), then in two-party contests any degree of accuracy can be obtained. In practice this is tautological, however, since a large exponent converts the winning party's vote proportion (which must be greater than 0.5) into a value arbitrarily close to unity. The losing party similarly has its proportion transformed to a value arbitrarily close to zero. In other words, a large exponent awards one seat to the winning party in each constituency. This is not of much predictive value. A second assertion is that a cubic exponent "is the smallest integer power which satisfactorily approximates the number of seats won by a political party over a political system". No reason is given for this assertion, neither is the term 'satisfactorily' defined.

The procedure thus involves assigning shares to parties in each constituency by using Qualter's generalised cubic equation. Although the authors show that the procedure provides a reasonable prediction of seat proportions in three multiparty Canadian elections, it is possible to show that it is based on erroneous foundations and should not be used generally. The problem can be illustrated in the two-party context. The procedure of assigning shares is reasonable only if constituencies are symmetrically distributed around 50% of the votes, that is, only if there is a symmetric CPD centred on 50%. In this case the share assigned to a winning party in one constituency when added to its losing share in the 'mirror image' constituency sums to one whole seat. A seat won with 75% of the votes has for instance a 'mirror image' constituency in which only 25% of the votes are gained. Using the generalised cube-law equation we get the following shares assigned:

Vote proportion	Share of seat
(a) 0.75	$0.75^3/(0.75^3 + 0.25^3) = 0.96$
(b) 0.25	$0.25^3/(0.75^3 + 0.25^3) = 0.04$
	1:00

In this way, one seat is assigned for every constituency in which a party gains over half of the votes. Since these are the seats it actually wins, the prediction exactly matches the reality.

The problem arises when the CPD is not symmetric about 50%. Imagine, for example, a symmetric CPD centred on 40% instead of 50%. Those constituencies in which the party gains more than 50% of the votes can still be matched with their 'mirror images about 50%' to assign one whole seat in each case. The sum in this case is still identical with the number actually won. However, this procedure does not exhaust the list of constituencies in which less than 50% of the vote is gained. There are extra constituencies which are assigned a (minority) share, but which do not correspond to any seat actually won. The sum of these extra shares forms a residual bias which will distort the prediction. The problem is most serious in respect of those seats in which the vote proportion is close to, although below, 50%. These attract relatively large 'shares' and contribute most to the overall prediction bias. As Casstevens and Morris themselves note, the technique can be very sensitive to the number of marginal constituencies.

Hence the decomposed system contains an inherent error which will render it inapplicable for most cases. Even without this defect it is difficult to see what its utility would be since it requires knowledge of the votes proportions for each party in every constituency. Although prediction is only one function of electoral modelling, it is not easy to see that this approach adds much to understanding the seats-votes relationship either, despite the interesting concept on which it is based.

Spafford's regression approach

The approach to seats prediction adopted by Spafford (1970) is based on simpler principles than those considered above. He derives regression equations which link a party's share of the seats in an election to three other factors. These are:

1 that party's share of the votes,
2 the numbers of candidates put up by the party or by other parties,
3 the variation in the size of constituencies.

Of these the last is of relatively minor significance and will not be considered further. Although other authors have regressed seats on votes, Spafford appears to be the first to apply the method to multiparty elections or to include additional variables.

Spafford analyses Canadian elections between 1921 and 1965. For the Conservative Party he obtains an equation in which the seat proportion increases with the Conservative vote proportion and the number of minor-party candidates. The number of Conservative candidates and the relative performance in larger constituencies are additional (negative) factors, although have much less influence. The explanatory power of this equation is high ($R^2 = 0.94$), and it is interesting to note that the coefficient for the vote-proportion variable is 2.9; very close to the 3.0 which would fit a cube-law equation. The effect of minor-party candidates is such that the Conservatives could afford to lose 1% of the votes for every additional fifty-three minor-party candidates and still gain the same number of seats. A similar equation is derived for the Liberal Party although its explanatory power is lower ($R^2 = 0.90$). Finally, for the minor parties in aggregate the independent variables are the minor-party vote proportion and the number of minor-party candidates. The latter variable has a negative coefficient, and the whole equation has an R^2 value of only 0.72.

What these equations essentially do is to relate the seat proportion to the *effective* vote proportion. The intervention of minor parties lowers the threshold needed to win a plurality in any one constituency and hence a lower proportion of votes can be as effective as a higher proportion in contests without minor-party candidates. For accurate prediction this approach is probably as good as any, but most particularly in respect of parties which gain from the intervention of minor parties. As a predictive device, the main shortcoming is the imposed linearity of the relationship between seat proportion and vote proportion. Although a linear relationship holds approximately for small deviations of the vote from 50%, some power of the vote proportion would provide a better overall predictive variable. Again the regression approach models the results and not the processes producing those results. It fails to provide much insight into these processes, although if prediction is the only aim then this is not a drawback except insofar as the specification of relationships between variables depends on an understanding of the processes.

Finally, Spafford's approach is applied in an unamended form to British elections between 1922 and 1974, omitting 1931 when there was a coalition of the major parties. In the following equations S denotes the seat proportion and V the vote proportion, as usual, while N indicates the number of Liberal and Nationalist candidates. The results were as follows:

Conservative Party

$$S = 1.81\,V + 0.02N - 35.03, \qquad R^2 = 0.60;$$
$$(0.53)\quad(0.02)$$

Labour Party

$$S = 1.78V + 0.04\,N - 43.70, \qquad R^2 = 0.89.$$
$$(0.19)\quad(0.007)$$

The figures in brackets are standard errors and indicate that all of the relationships are statistically significant except for that of the number of minor-party candidates in the Conservative equation. Only the equation for the Labour Party has reasonably high predictive power, and as with the Canadian Conservatives an increase of fifty in the number of minor-party candidates would enable the same number of seats to be won with a drop in the vote proportion of 1%. The coefficient for the vote variable is very similar for the two parties. The reason that this coefficient is close to 1.8 rather than 3.0 reflects the considerable spread of vote proportions over this long period. With a wide spread the linear form of relationship takes an average over what is in reality a cubic relationship and thereby reduces the slope.

appendix 3

Derivation of the seats-votes relationship: uniform support and even attraction

The base of the constituency proportion distribution (CPD) is marked on figure A3.1 by the line ab. The line AC has the equation

$$z = \tfrac{3}{2} V_c,$$

where V_c is the line OF (the votes axis for party C scaled from zero at F to one at zero), and z is the line DE (the hypotenuse of the triangle) scaled from zero at E to one at D.

The proportion of ab lying within OACB for $V_c \geq 0.333$ is given by
$$2(z - 0.5),$$
that is,

$$2(\tfrac{3}{2} V_c - 0.5) = 3V_c - 1.$$

The proportion of the CPD corresponding to the section of ab within OACB is given by:

$$2\left[\Phi\left(\frac{3V_C - 1}{2\sigma}\right) - 0.5\right].$$

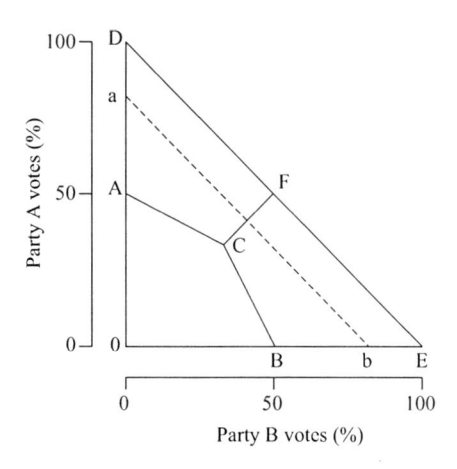

Figure A3.1: Election triangle for uniformly distributed third-party support

appendix 4

Derivation of the seats-votes relationship: uneven attraction from major parties

The case of unequal attraction can be described, in the context of an election triangle as follows. The constituency proportion distribution (CPD) is a univariate distribution which always lies along a line parallel to the hypotenuse (due to the assumption of uniform support for party C). In figure A4.1 the CPD is depicted by the line which contains the points a, b, and c. This is an illustrative case in which party C has gained a proportion of the vote corresponding to bF/OF. (At this level of support note that some of the CPD lies along the axes OD and OE.) In the case of equal attraction the centre of the CPD moves along the line OF, but with unequal attraction it moves along some line starting at F and ending at some point either on OD or on OE. If party B is the party from which *fewer* votes are attracted by party C, and the centre of the distribution moves along the line FG, for example, then

attraction ratio $= \tan \alpha$.

In the derivation below it is convenient to use the 'attraction constant', defined as

$$k = \tan(45° - \alpha).$$

The technical problem is to calculate the proportion of the CPD which lies within the victory region of party C, that is within OACB. In the case illustrated in figure A4.1 this is the portion of the CPD lying between a and c. The procedure used here is to obtain expressions for the lengths of ab and bc, as before, and project the points a, b, and c back onto DE along lines parallel to FG. The area of the CPD between f and d can then be calculated as if the CPD lay along the DE axis. This apparently convoluted procedure simplifies the mathematics.

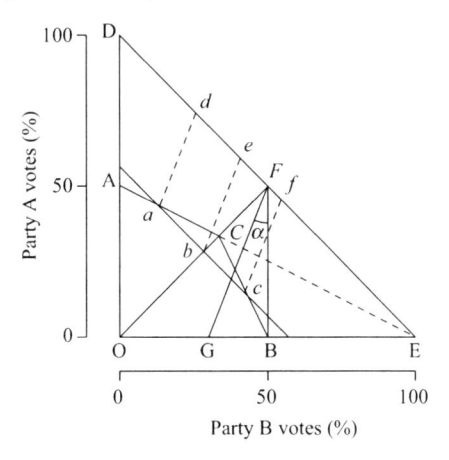

Figure A4.1: Election triangle for uneven attraction rates

Let V_C, the aggregate vote obtained by party C, be the length Fb. Also, let z be a variable scaled from one to zero along DE (in this case F = 0.5). Then a point on the line AE is given by $z = \frac{3}{2} V_C$ as before, and the length ab is

$$z - 0.5 = \tfrac{3}{2} V_C - 0.5.$$

The lines ad and be are assumed to be parallel and hence

$$de = \tfrac{3}{2} V_C - 0.5.$$

Since be is parallel to FG, $\angle Fbe = (45° - \alpha)$ and thus

$$ef = \tan(45° - \alpha)bF$$

$$= kV_C.$$

Hence

$$Fd = Fe + ed$$

$$= kV_C + \tfrac{3}{2} V_C - 0.5.$$

The area of the CPD along Ed is given by

$$\Phi\left[\frac{(k + \tfrac{3}{2})V_C - 0.5}{\sigma}\right].$$

Similarly,

$$Ff = (k - \tfrac{3}{2})V_C,$$

and the area of the CPD along Ef is

$$\Phi\left[\frac{(k - \tfrac{3}{2})V_C - 0.5}{\sigma}\right].$$

The required area is that lying along ab, or equivalently along df, and this is given by

$$\Phi\left[\frac{(2k + 3)V_C - 1}{2\sigma}\right] - \Phi\left[\frac{(2k - 3)V_C - 1}{2\sigma}\right]$$

where σ is the standard deviation of the CPD.

appendix 5

Construction of figure 5.10

The two new seats-votes curves on figure 5.10 were calculated by using approximations. The need in each case was to calculate the proportion of the two-dimensional distribution lying within the victory region for party C for any given position of the centre of the distribution (that is, for any level of total votes). This was achieved by constructing, in half-standard-deviation intervals, the ellipses corresponding to the distribution with $\sigma_1 = 0.137$, $\sigma_2 = 0.05$ and the circles corresponding to the distribution with $\sigma_1 = \sigma_2 = 0.137$. For a range of values for total votes the area of each successive half-standard-deviation ellipse (or circle) segment lying within the victory region was calculated by graphical means.

This area was expressed as a proportion of the total area in each segment, and weighted by the proportion of a bivariate normal distribution lying within the segment. The segments of concern here are the areas lying between successive concentric ellipses (or circles). For instance, the area between the ellipse with radii of one standard deviation and that with radii of one-half standard deviation equals the area of the outer ellipse (radii = σ) minus the area of the inner ellipse (radii = $\frac{1}{2}\sigma$). Since the area of an ellipse is $ab\pi$ where a is the short radius and b is the long radius, the segment areas for successive intervals of $\frac{1}{2}\sigma$ are given by

$$\tfrac{1}{4}\pi(2k+1)\,\sigma_1\sigma_2,$$

where k is the radius of the inner ellipse (or circle) expressed in terms of standard deviations.

For example the area in the segment lying between the two concentric ellipses with radii equal to $\frac{1}{2}\sigma$ and σ respectively is

$$\tfrac{1}{4}\pi(2.1+1)\,\sigma_1\sigma_2 = \tfrac{3}{4}\pi\sigma_1\sigma_2.$$

The weights, or areas under the two-dimensional curve, for successive intervals of $\frac{1}{2}\sigma$ are given by

$$\exp(-\tfrac{1}{2}k^2) - \exp[-\tfrac{1}{2}(k-\tfrac{1}{2})^2],$$

where k is as defined above.

This procedure working in coarse intervals of $\frac{1}{2}\sigma$ is only approximate but is adequate for the purposes to which it is put in this study. For more accurate results sources are available which bypass the need for graphical methods. The area under a circular bivariate normal curve lying within a given radius r is given by $P = 1 - \exp(-\tfrac{1}{2}r^2)$. (See Owen, 1956; 1962, page 170; Zelen and Severo, 1960.)

appendix 6

Derivation of equations for linear relations between third-party support and the strength of other parties

Although it is most realistic to combine linearly related third-party support with the independent-variable case described above, this is not done in deriving the general equations for reasons of analytic simplicity. As before, the addition of a variable component will change the basic relationships in predictable ways.

The method used here is similar to those of previous cases. It is necessary to calculate the lengths dc and ce on figure A6.1 for any length cF (on the assumption that the line ab will move across the graph with the centre of the frequency distribution fixed on the track OF). This is done by expressing the lines ab, AE, and BD as linear equations in relation to the two axes ED and a line parallel to OF centred on E. The various points of intersection (d, c, e) can be established and the distances dc and ce subsequently worked out.

The three equations are:

line ab: $V_C = \alpha + \beta(1 - V_A)$;

line AE: $V_C = \frac{2}{3}(1 - V_A)$;

line BD: $V_C = \frac{2}{3} - \frac{2}{3}(1 - V_A) = \frac{2}{3}V_A$.

Note that, as the line ab moves across the graph, α changes but β is assumed to be fixed. The intersection between ab and AE occurs at the point

$$\left(\frac{3\alpha}{2-3\beta}, \frac{2\alpha}{2-3\beta}\right).$$

The intersection between ab and BD occurs at the point

$$\left(\frac{2-3\alpha}{2+3\beta}, \frac{2\alpha+2\beta}{2+3\beta}\right).$$

The point C is given by

$$\left(\frac{1}{2}, \frac{2\alpha+\beta}{2}\right).$$

From these the distances dc and ce are:

$$dc = \left[\left(\frac{2\alpha}{2+3\beta} - \frac{2\alpha+\beta}{2}\right)^2 + \left(\frac{3\alpha}{2-3\beta} - \frac{1}{2}\right)^2\right]^{1/2};$$

$$ce = \left[\left(\frac{2\alpha+2\beta}{2+3\beta} - \frac{2\alpha+\beta}{2}\right)^2 + \left(\frac{2\alpha}{3\beta+2} - \frac{1}{2}\right)^2\right]^{1/2}.$$

The distances dc and ce are now established for any α and β, that is, for any linear relationship. The use made of dc and ce will depend, however, on the values of α and β. Four separate cases exist:

(1) if $V_C = \frac{1}{2}(2\alpha + \beta) < \frac{1}{3}$, then $S_C = 0$;

(2) if $V_C = \frac{1}{2}(2\alpha + \beta) < \frac{1}{3}$, and $\beta > \frac{2}{3}$, then $S_C = \Phi(dc)$;

(3) if $V_C = \frac{1}{2}(2\alpha + \beta) > \frac{1}{3}$, and $\beta < \frac{2}{3}$, then $S_C = \Phi(dc) + \Phi(ce)$;

(4) if $V_C = \frac{1}{2}(2\alpha + \beta) > \frac{1}{3}$, and $\beta < \frac{2}{3}$, then $S_C = \Phi(ce) + 0.5$.

(Cases where $V_C = \frac{1}{3}$ or $\beta = \frac{2}{3}$ involve a number of tied constituencies and can be ignored in practice.)

The graphs for various values of α and β are not drawn here, but it can be said that for low values of the proportional coefficient β, the curves for S_C will closely resemble those on figure 5.10. Since votes are being drawn differentially from the two major parties the point at which 'major-party status' is reached by party C will be somewhat higher than the $S_C = \frac{1}{3}$.

A further refinement can be added to the above equations if we assume that the coefficient β itself changes as party C gains in total votes. This is a reasonably realistic assumption, and it can be built into the equations by replacing β with $f(V_C)$. A likely contender for the function is $\beta = kV_C$, where k is some constant. In this case kV_C would replace β in the equations.

Finally, it may be necessary to deal with situations in which V_C has a different relationship with V_A in those seats won by party A compared with those won by party B. In these cases two different lines (corresponding to ab) have to be dealt with separately. The principle is, however, just the same as that when only a single line is involved. The combination of two linearly related support levels is illustrated for the modern Liberal Party in section 5.4.

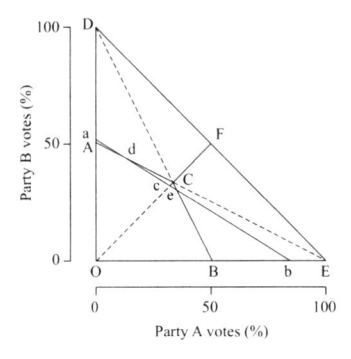

Figure A6.1:   Third-party support related to major-party strength

appendix 7

Alternative explanations of bimodal CPDs

In chapter 7 bimodal CPDs were interpreted as reflecting structural changes in the electoral process, what has been termed bipartisan gerrymandering. This interpretation follows Tufte's (1973) analysis of the falling 'swing ratio' (change in percentage seats for a 1% change in votes) in recent American elections. Tufte's conclusions, however, have come under increasing criticism as the present research has proceeded and hence these alternative explanations of bimodal CPDs are discussed here and briefly related to the arguments in chapter 7 and previous chapters.

The initial criticism of Tufte's bipartisan gerrymandering argument was by Burnham (1974), who argued that the changing American CPD was due to behavioural rather than structural causes. Quite simply voters were becoming less identified with political parties, as indicated by increasing numbers of 'independents' for instance, so that they were more predisposed to vote for the incumbent congressman irrespective of party. This rise in incumbency voting as opposed to party voting would clearly produce a bimodal CPD. Burnham's emphasis on incumbency voting was foreshadowed by earlier work by Erikson (1972) and Mayhew (1971). The latter suggested that incumbency voting was due to increased resources made available to congressmen, with which they could become familiar to and hence woo their district's voters. Subsequently Fiorina (1977) has suggested that incumbency voting is related to the changing behaviour of congressmen, as they are more willing to concentrate on local issues—take on an 'errand boy role'— in order to get reelected. Whatever the cause of the rise of incumbency voting, it has been generally accepted as a new feature of American politics since about 1964. Thus even Tufte (1974; 1975) in his comments on this debate has conceded the existence of this new feature. The question is whether the 'discovery' of incumbency voting behaviour enables researchers to replace the bipartisan gerrymandering interpretation of bimodal CPDs.

The researcher who has been most conclusive in dismissing bipartisan gerrymandering is Ferejohn (1977). He follows Erikson (1972) in dividing states between those that had been redistricted by certain dates and those which had not. He then argues that, if the process of bipartisan gerrymandering were operating, the number of competitive districts should decline in redistricted states but not in states where districts remained unchanged. He is able to show that competitive districts declined in comparable amounts in both types of states. He then concludes that 'redisricting has no influence at all' since the decline in competitive districts is a general phenomenon which can only be explained by a general shift in behaviour, such as incumbency voting.

The major problem with this argument is that it has rather narrowly set out to disprove the bipartisan gerrymandering interpretation *as a process operating alone*. If, as is generally conceded, incumbency voting as a real feature of recent American congressional elections, then it is necessary to consider whether bipartisan gerrymandering has operated in conjunction with this changing behaviour to produce the bimodal CPDs. From this viewpoint Ferejohn's data can be given an alternative interpretation by considering if it is consistent with *incumbency voting operating alone*. If incumbency voting is the sole change operating, then we would expect it to be much weaker in states that have redistricted. In these states links between congressman and voters will have been broken on several occasions, depending on the degree of boundary changes. Hence similar levels of decline in competitive districts in redistricted states and other states is not necessarily consistent with incumbency voting being the sole cause of the bimodal CPD. This leaves the bipartisan-gerrymandering process to account for at least part of the decline in competitive districts in states where redistricting occurred. Hence it is not unreasonable on the basis of the evidence presented to argue for both incumbency voting and bipartisan gerrymandering jointly contributing to the production of the modern American bimodal CPD.

Of course this matter cannot be completely settled without detailed case studies of redistricting practices and changes in voting at the local district and state level. It may be mentioned here, however, that the existence of bimodal CPDs in other countries with some political interference in the boundary drawing (South Africa, New Zealand, and Canada) plus the lack of bimodality in countries with nonpartisan districting procedures (Britain, and also Australia and West Germany in chapter 7) gives further general weight to the existence of a structural basis to bimodality in CPDs.

Finally it may be mentioned that incumbency voting provides a particular type of nonuniform swing situation which can be investigated by developing the modelling procedure described in chapter 4.

references

Alford R R, 1963 *Party and Society* (Rand McNally, Chicago)
Appel J S, 1965 "A note concerning apportionment by computer" *American Behavioural Scientist* 7 36
Baker G E, 1966 *The Reapportionment Revolution* (Random House, New York)
Baker G E, 1971 "Gerrymandering: privileged sanctuary or next judicial target?" in *Reapportionment in the 1970s'* Ed. N W Polsby (University of California Press, Berkeley) pp 121–142
Bergh G van den, 1955 *Unity in Diversity* (Batsford, London)
Berrington H, 1964 "The General Election of 1964" *Journal of the Royal Statistical Society, Series A* 128 17–66
Berrington H, 1975 "Electoral reform and national government" in *Adversary Politics and Electoral Reform* Ed. S E Finer (Anthony Wigram, London) pp 269–292
Birke W, 1961 *European Elections by Direct Suffrage* (Sythoff, Leyden)
Blake D E, 1972 "The measurement of regionalism in Canadian voting patterns" *Canadian Journal of Political Science* 5 55–81
Blewett N, 1972 "Redistribution procedures" in *Australian Politics: a Third Reader* Eds H Mayer, H Nelson (Cheshire, Melbourne) pp 295–300
Boyd W J D, 1965 *Changing Patterns of Apportionment* (National Municipal League, New York)
Brookes R H, 1959 "Electoral distortion in New Zealand" *Australian Journal of Politics and History* 5 218–223
Brookes R H, 1960 "The analysis of distorted representation in two party, single member elections" *Political Science* 12 158–167
Brown P, Payne C, 1975 "Election night forecasting" *Journal of the Royal Statistical Society, Series A* 138 463–498
Bunge W, 1966 "Gerrymandering, geography and grouping" *Geographical Review* 55 256–263
Burnham W D, 1974 "Communication" *American Political Science Review* 68 207–211
Burnham W D, 1975 "The United States: the politics of heterogeneity" in *Electoral Behaviour* Ed. R Rose (Free Press, New York)
Busteed M A, Mason H L, 1974 "The 1973 General Election in the Irish Republic" *Irish Geography* 7 97–106
Butler D E, 1951 *The British General Election of 1950* (Macmillan, London)
Butler D E, 1952 *The British General Election of 1951* (Macmillan, London)
Butler D E, 1955a "The redistribution of seats" *Public Administration* 55 125–147
Butler D E, 1955b *The British General Election of 1955* (Macmillan, London)
Butler D E, 1963 *The Electoral System in Britain since 1918* (Oxford University Press, London)
Butler D E, 1973 *The Canberra Model* (Macmillan, London)
Butler D E, Sloman A, 1975 *British Political Facts 1900–1975* (Macmillan, London)
Butler D E, Stokes D E, 1974 *Political Change in Britain* (Macmillan, London)
Campbell P, 1958 *French Electoral Systems and Elections Since 1789* (Faber and Faber, London)
Campbell R V, Knight D B, 1976 "Political territoriality in Canada" *Canadian Cartographer* 13 1–10
Carter G M, 1958 *The Politics of Inequality: South Africa since 1948* (Praeger, New York)
Carter G M, 1963 *The Politics of Inequality: South Africa since 1948* (Thames and Hudson, London)
Casstevens T W, Morris W D, 1972 "The cube law and decomposed system" *Canadian Journal of Political Science* 5 521–532

Chambers W N, 1967 "Party development and the American mainstream" in *The American Party Systems* Eds W N Chambers, W D Burnham (Oxford University Press, New York)
Cliff A D, Haggett P, Ord J K, Bassett K, Davies R, 1975 *Elements of Spatial Structure* (Cambridge University Press, London)
Congressional Quarterly Service, 1966 *Representation and Reapportionment* (US Government Printing Office, Washington, DC)
Cope C R, 1971 "Regionalization and the electoral districting problem" *Area* 3 190–195
Cox K R, undated "The spatial evolution of national voting response surfaces: theory and measurement" DP-9, Department of Geography, Ohio State University, Columbus
Crewe I, Payne C, 1976 "Another game with nature: an ecological regression model of the British two-party vote ratio in 1970" *British Journal of Political Science* 6 43–81
Criddle B, 1975 "Distorted representation in France" *Parliamentary Affairs* 26 154–179
Dahl R A, 1956 *A Preface to Democratic Theory* (University of Chicago Press, Chicago)
Dawson R M, 1935 "The gerrymander of 1882" *Canadian Journal of Economics and Political Science* 1 197–221
Dixon R G, 1968 *Democratic Representation: Reapportionment in Law and Politics* (Oxford University Press, New York)
Dixon R G, 1971 "The court, the people and one man, one vote" in *Reapportionment in the 1970s* Ed. N W Polsby (University of California Press, Berkeley) pp 7–46
Edgeworth F Y, 1898 "Miscellaneous applications of the calculus of probabilities" *Journal of the Royal Statistical Society* 61 534–544
Erikson R S, 1972 "Malapportionment, gerrymandering, and party fortunes in congressional elections" *American Political Science Review* 66 1234–1245
Farquharson R R, 1959 "South Africa, 1958" in *Elections Abroad* Ed. D E Butler (Macmillan, London)
Feller W, 1968 *An Introduction to Probability Theory and Its Applications* volume 1 (John Wiley, New York)
Ferejohn J A, 1977 "On the decline of competition in congressional elections" *American Political Science Review* 71 166–176
Finer S E (Ed.), 1975 *Adversary Politics and Electoral Reform* (Anthony Wigram, London)
Fiorina M P, 1977 "The case of the vanishing marginals: the bureaucracy did it" *American Political Science Review* 71 177–181
Forrest E, 1965 "Apportionment by computer" *American Behavioural Scientist* 7 23, 25
Gallagher M, 1974 "Disproportionality in a proportional representation system: the Irish experience" *Political Studies* 23 501–513
Garfinkel R S, Taylor H, 1969 "Optimum political districting by implicit enumeration technique" *Management Science* 16 495–512
Graham B D, 1962 "The choice of voting method in Federal politics, 1902–1918" *Australian Journal of Politics and History* 8 164–182
Griffith E C, 1907 *The Rise and Development of the Gerrymander* (Scott, Foresman, Chicago)
Gudgin G, Taylor P J, 1974 "Electoral bias and the distribution of party voters" *Transactions, Institute of British Geographers* 63 53–73
Hacker A, 1964 *Congressional Districting* (The Brookings Institute, Washington, DC)
Hansard Society, 1976 *The Report of the Hansard Commission on Electoral Reform* (The Hansard Society for Parliamentary Government, London)
Hart J, Browett J G, 1976 "A multivariate spatial analysis of socio-economic structure of Johannesburg, 1970" OP-11, Urban and Regional Research Unit, Johannesburg

Heard K A, 1974 *General Elections in South Africa, 1943–1970* (Oxford University Press, London)
Holden B, 1974 *The Nature of Democracy* (Macmillan, London)
Hughes G A, Graham B D, 1968 *A Handbook of Australian Government and Politics, 1850–1964* (Australian National University Press, Canberra)
Jackson W K, 1962 "The electoral framework" in *New Zealand Politics in Action: The 1960 General Election* Eds R M Chapman, W K Jackson, A V Mitchell (Oxford University Press, London) pp 3–12
Jenkins M A, Shepherd J W, 1972 "Decentralizing high school administration in Detroit: an evaluation of alternative strategies of political control" *Economic Geography* 48 95–106
Jewell M E (Ed.), 1962 *The Politics of Reapportionment* (Atherton Press, New York)
Johnston R J, 1976a "Parliamentary seat redistribution: more opinions of the theme" *Area* 8 30–34
Johnston R J, 1976b "Spatial structure, plurality systems and electoral bias" *Canadian Geographer* 20 310–328
Kendall M G, Stuart A, 1950 "The law of cubic proportions in election results" *British Journal of Sociology* 1 183–197
Knight B B, 1976 "The states and reapportionment: one man, one vote reevaluated" *State Government* 49 155–160
Lakeman E, 1974 *How Democracies Vote* (Faber and Faber, London)
Laponce J A, 1957 "The protection of minorities by the electoral system" *Western Political Quarterly* 10 318–339
Laux H D, Simms A, 1973 "Parliamentary elections in West Germany: the geography of electoral choice" *Area* 5 161–171
Laver M, 1976 "On introducing S.T.V. and interpreting the results: the case of Northern Ireland, 1973–1975" *Parliamentary Affairs* 29 211–229
Lewis P W, Skipworth G E, 1966 "Some geographical and statistical aspects of the distribution of votes and recent general elections" miscellaneous paper 32, Department of Geography, University of Hull, Hull, England
Liittschwager J M, 1973 "The Iowa redistricting systems" *Annals, New York Academy of Science* 219 221–235
Lipset S M, Rokkan S (Eds), 1967 *Party Systems and Voter Alignments* (Free Press, New York)
Little W, 1974 "Electoral aspects of Peronism" *Journal of Inter-American Affairs* 7 267–283
Lyons W E, 1969 "Legislative redistricting by independent commissions" *Polity* 1 428–459
McKay D H, Patterson S C, 1971 "Population equality and the distribution of seats in the British House of Commons" *Comparative Politics* 4 59–76
Mackenzie W J M, 1958 *Free Elections* (Allen and Unwin, London)
McPhail I R, Walmsley D, 1975 "Government" in *Atlas of Australian Resources* second series (Department of Minerals and Energy, Canberra) (booklet)
Mair P, Laver M, 1975 "Proportionality, P.R. and S.T.V. in Ireland" *Political Studies* 23 491–500
March J G, 1957 "Party legislative representation as a function of election results" *Public Opinion Quarterly* 11 521–542 [reprinted in Lazarsfeld R F, Henry N W (Eds), 1958 *Readings in Mathematical Social Science* (Free Press, New York)]
Mayhew C, 1976 *The Disillusioned Voter's Guide to Electoral Reform* (Arrow Books, London)
Mayhew D R, 1971 "Congressional representation: theory and practice in drawing the districts" in *Reapportionment in the 1970s* Ed. N W Polsby (University of California Press, Berkeley) pp 249–285

Morrill R L, 1973 "Ideal and reality in reapportionment" *Annals, Association of American Geographers* 63 463–477
Nagel S S, 1965 "Simplified bi-partisan computer districting" *Stanford Law Review* 17 863–899
Nagel S S, 1972 "Computers and the law and the politics of redistricting" *Polity* 5 77–93
Noragon J L, 1973 "Redistricting, political outcomes, and the gerrymandering of the 1960s" *Annals, New York Academy of Science* 219 314–333
O'Leary C, 1975 "Ireland: the north and south" in *Adversary Politics and Electoral Reform* Ed. S E Finer (Anthony Wigram, London) pp 153–184
Orr D M, 1970 *Congressional Redistricting: The North Carolina Experience* (University of North Carolina Press, Chapel Hill)
Owen D B, 1956 "Tables for computing bi-variate normal probabilities" *Annals of Mathematical Statistics* 27 1075
Owen D B, 1962 *Handbook of Statistical Tables* (Addison-Wesley, Reading, Mass)
Paddison R, 1976 "Spatial bias and redistricting in proportional representation systems: a case study of the Republic of Ireland" *Tijdschrift voor Economische en Sociale Geografie* 67 230–240
Peele S, Morse S J, 1974 "Ethnic voting and political change in South Africa" *American Political Science Review* 68 1520–1541
Pelling H, 1967 *The Social Geography of British Elections, 1885–1910* (Macmillan, London)
Pulsipher A G, 1973 "Empirical and normative theories of apportionment" *Annals, New York Academy of Science* 219 234–241
Qualter T H, 1968 "Seats and votes: an application of the cube law to the Canadian electoral system" *Canadian Journal of Political Science* 1 336–344
Quandt R E, 1974 "A stochastic model of elections in two-party systems" *Journal of the American Statistical Association* 69 315–324
Rae D W, 1971 *The Political Consequences of Electoral Laws* (Yale University Press, New Haven, Conn.)
Rahman N A, 1968 *A Course in Theoretical Statistics* (Griffin, London)
Roberts G K, 1975 "The Federal Republic of Germany" in *Adversary Politics and Electoral Reform* Ed. S E Finer (Anthony Wigram, London) pp 203–222
Robinson A, 1970 "Londonderry, Northern Ireland: a border study" *Scottish Geographical Magazine* 86 208–221
Robinson A D, 1967 "Class voting in New Zealand" in *Party Systems and Voter Alignments* Eds S M Lipset S Rokkan (Free Press, New York)
Robson B T, 1969 *Urban Analysis: A Study of City Structure with Special Reference to Sunderland* (Cambridge University Press, London)
Rogaly J, 1976 *Parliament for the People* (Maurice Temple-Smith, London)
Rokkan S, 1970 *Citizens, Elections, Parties* (Mckay, New York)
Ross J F S, 1955 *Elections and Electors* (Eyre and Spottiswoode, London)
Rowley G, 1970 "Elections and population change" *Area* 3 13–18
Rowley G, 1975a "The redistribution of parliamentary seats in the UK: theories and opinions" *Area* 7 16–21
Rowley G, 1975b "Parliamentary seat redistribution elaborated" *Area* 7 279–281
Rowley G, 1975c "Electoral change and reapportionment: prescriptive ideals and reality" *Tijdschrift voor Economische en Sociale Geografie* 66 108–120
Rydon J, 1957 "The relation of votes to seats in elections for the Australian House of Representatives, 1949–54" *Political Science* 9 49–61
Sankoff D, Mellos K, 1972 "The swing ratio and game theory" *American Political Science Review* 66 551–554

Sauer C O, 1918 "Geography and the gerrymander" *American Political Science Review* 12 403–426

Schwartz M A, 1974 "Canadian voting behaviour" in *Electoral Behaviour: A Comparative Handbook* Ed. R Rose (Free Press, New York) pp 437–480

Schwartzberg J J, 1966 "Reapportionment, gerrymanders, and the notion of compactness" *Minnesota Law Review* 50 443–452

Seymour C, 1915 *Electoral Reform in England and Wales* (Oxford University Press, London)

Shepherd J W, Jenkins M A, 1970 "Decentralizing high school administration in Detroit: a computer evaluation of alternative strategies of political control" *Proceedings, Conference on Inter-disciplinary Research in Computer Science, Winnipeg* (Computer Science Association of Canada)

Sickels R J, 1966 "Dragons, bacon strips and dumbells—who's afraid of reapportionment?" *Yale Law Review* 75 1300–1308

Simeon R, Elkins D J, 1974 "Regional political cultures in Canada" *Canadian Journal of Political Science* 7 397–437

Smith T E, 1960 *Elections in Developing Countries* (Macmillan, London)

Snedecor G W, Cochran W G, 1967 *Statistical Methods* 6th edition (Iowa State University Press, Ames)

Soper C S, Rydon J, 1958 "Under-representation and election prediction" *Australian Journal of Politics and History* 4 94–106

Spafford D, 1970 "The electoral system of Canada" *American Political Science Review* 64 168–176

Steed M, 1969 "Callaghan's gerrymandering" *New Society* 13 996–997

Steed M, 1974 "The results analysed" in *The British General Election of February, 1974* Eds D E Butler, D Kavanagh (Macmillan, London) pp 313–339

Steed M, 1975a "The results analysed" in *The British General Election of October, 1974* Eds D E Butler, D Kavanagh (Macmillan, London) pp 313–339

Steed M, 1975b "The evolution of the British electoral system" in *Adversary Politics and Electoral Reform* Ed. S E Finer (Anthony Wigram, London) pp 35–53

Stokes D E, 1967 "Parties and the nationalization of electoral forces" in *The American Party System* Eds W N Chambers, W D Burnham (Oxford University Press, New York) pp 182–202

Taagepera R, 1972 "The size of national assemblies" *Social Science Research* 1 385–401

Taagepera R, 1973 "Seats and votes: a generalization of the cube law of elections" *Social Science Research* 2 257–275

Taylor A H, 1973 "The electoral geography of Welsh and Scottish nationalism" *Scottish Geographical Magazine* 93 44–52

Taylor P J, 1973 "Some implications of the spatial organization of elections" *Transactions, Institute of British Geographers* 60 121–136

Taylor P J, Gudgin G, 1975 "A fresh look at the Parliamentary Boundary Commissions" *Parliamentary Affairs* 28 405–415

Taylor P J, Gudgin G, 1976a "The myth of non-partisan cartography: a study of electoral biases in the English Boundary Commission's redistribution for 1955–1970" *Urban Studies* 13 13–25

Taylor P J, Gudgin G, 1976b "The statistical basis of decisionmaking in electoral districting" *Environment and Planning A* 8 43–58

Taylor P J, Johnston R J, 1979 *Geography of Elections* (Penguin Books, Harmondsworth, Middx)

Thiel H, 1970 "The cube law revisited" *Journal of the American Statistical Association* 65 1213–1219

Thiel H, 1972 *Statistical Decomposition Analysis* (North-Holland, Amsterdam)

Tinkler I, 1956 "Malayan elections: electoral pattern for plural societies?" *Western Political Quarterly* 9 258–282

Tufte E R, 1973 "The relationship between seats and votes in two-party systems" *American Political Science Review* 67 540–554

Tufte E R, 1974 "Communication" *American Political Science Review* 68 211–213

Tufte E R, 1975 "Determinants of the outcomes of midterm congressional elections" *American Political Science Review* 69 812–826

Tyler G, Wells D, 1962 "New York: constitutionally republican" in *The Politics of Reapportionment* Ed. M E Jewell (Atherton Press, New York) pp 221–247

Upton G, Farlie D, 1974 "Swings and roundabouts: the representation and interpretation of voting changes in three party elections" Department of Mathematics, University of Essex, mimeo

Uspensky J R, 1937 *Introduction to Mathematical Probability* (McGraw-Hill, New York)

Vickrey V, 1961 "On the prevention of gerrymandering" *Political Science Quarterly* 76 105–111

Vistre J du, 1869 "Les circonscriptions electorates" *L 'Illustration, Journal Universal* 53 265–266

Ward N, 1967 "A century of constituencies" *Canadian Public Administration* 10 105–122

Weaver J B, 1970 *Fair and Equal Districts* (National Municipal League, New York)

Weaver J B, Hess S W, 1963 "A procedure for nonpartisan redistricting" *Yale Law Journal* 73 288–308

Williams P, Goldey D, 1967 "The French General Election of March 1967" *Parliamentary Affairs* 20 206–221

Zelen M, Severo N C, 1960 "Graphs for computing bi-variate normal probabilities" *Annals of Mathematical Statistics* 31 619

index

Additional-member system (AMS) 164, 188–195, 196, 198–199
Alford R R 6, 7
Alternative-vote system (AVS) 163–164, 165–169
Appel J S 125
Argentina 122
Australia 3, 4, 78, 82, 164, 165–169, 230

Baker G E 9, 123, 124–125
Bergh G van den 200
Bernoulli trials 32
Berrington H 95, 173, 174, 179–181, 193
Bimodal distributions 72–73, 86, 129–131, 132–133, 229–230
Binomial distribution 32
Birke W 192
Blake D E 7
Blewett N 166
Boundary Commissions (Britain) 8–9, 88–90, 125, 127, 149–151, 157–158
Boyd W J D 126
Britain [see also Boundary Commissions (Britain), Conservative Party (Britain), Labour Party (Britain), Liberal Party (Britain), Scottish Nationalist Party, Plaid Cymru]
  changes in voting pattern (swing) 59–60
  constituency proportion distribution 38, 46–47, 63–64, 73–84, 90–91, 132
  development of party support 81–83
  electoral bias 88–91, 163
  electoral districting 8–9, 122, 132, 230
  electoral reform 2, 3, 163–164, 172–175, 179–188, 192–195, 197
  organisation of elections 4
  regionally based parties 20, 108
  seats-votes relationship 14, 21, 42, 215–216
  social cleavage in voting 6
  three-party elections 93–94, 99, 104, 106, 109–116
Brookes R H 57, 86
Browett J G 137–138
Brown P 13
Bunge W 121
Burnham W D 209, 229
Busteed M A 183
Butler D E 8, 54, 59, 60, 78, 94, 99, 100, 164, 167, 209

Campbell P 122
Campbell R V 7
Canada [see also New Democratic Party, Liberal Party (Canada), Progressive Conservative Party, Social Credit Party (Canada)]
  basis of party support 7, 82, 106
  constituency size 38
  constituency proportion distribution 38, 104
  election triangle 107
  electoral districting 10, 122, 132–133
  electoral reform 3
  malapportionment 58
  multiparty elections 92–93, 95–96, 99, 214–222
  organisation of elections 4
  regional integration 197
  seats-votes relationship 214–222, 230
  voting swings 60
Carter G M 138–139
Casstevens T W 219–220
Central limit theorem 153
Chambers W N 6
Christian Democratic Party (CDU) (Germany) 190–192
Cliff A D 141–143
Cochran W G 153
Communist Party (France) 170–172
Computer districting 125–127, 143–145
Conservative Party (Britain)
  additional-member system 193–195
  alternative-vote system 173–175
  basis of support 6
  constituency proportion distribution 77–80
  electoral bias 3, 163
  in Newcastle upon Tyne 49–52, 157
  prewar elections 79–80
  seats-votes relationship 94, 104–116, 215, 221–222
  single-transferable-vote system 180–188
  spatial distribution of support 84, 108
  in Sunderland 149–151
  three-party elections 109–116
  wasted votes 3
Constituency proportion distribution (CPD) 14–17, 31, 38, 46–47, 52, 67–73
Cope C R 143
Country Party (Australia) 82, 166–169
Cox K R 5

Crewe I 6
Criddle B 170, 171
CROND Inc 125–127
'Cube law' 26–30, 31, 54–55, 91, 121, 201–202

Dahl R A 204
Dawson R M 122
Delimitation Commission (South Africa) 137–140
Democratic Party 6, 12, 20
Denmark 3, 188
Diggle P 42
Dixon R G 121, 123, 124, 127, 128–129
Double-ballot voting system 163, 169–172

Edgeworth F Y 31, 38
'Effective vote' 56–59
Election triangle 94–96, 169
Electoral bias 57–58, 70–72, 81–84, 86–91, 118, 162–166, 169–174, 176, 190–192, 198
Electoral reform 2–4, 162, 197
Elkins D J 7
Erikson R S 229

Farlie D 95
Farquharson R R 7, 11, 139
Feller W 35
Ferejohn J A 229–230
Fianna Fail 176–178
Fine Gael 176–178
Fiorina M P 229
Forrest E 125
France 2, 3, 4, 122, 163, 169–172
Free Democratic Party (FDP) (Germany) 190, 192

Gallagher M 177–179, 183
Garfinkel R S 143–145
Gaullist Party 170–172
Germany (Federal Republic) 188–192, 196, 230
Gerrymandering 121–125, 135, 152
Goldney D 172
Graham B D 167, 169
Greece 198
Griffith E C 122

Hacker A 9
Hansard Society 164, 188, 191, 192, 193–195

Hart J 137–138
Heard K A 7, 10, 58, 134, 139
Hess S W 125
Holden B 1

Iowa 126–127, 145, 158–160
Ireland 3, 5, 164, 176–179, 182–183, 187, 196
Irish Nationalist Party 5, 6, 20, 74–75, 108

Jackson W K 9
Jenkins M A 143–144
Jewell M E 9, 21
Johnston R J 57, 86

Kendall M G 21, 26–28, 31, 46, 86, 129, 201, 206–207
Knight B B 7, 129
Kurtosis 66, 71–72, 85–86

Labour Party (Australia) 78, 82, 165–169
Labour Party (Britain)
    additional-member system 193–195
    alternative-vote system 173–175
    basis of support for 6, 110
    comparison with Australian Labour Party 165
    constituency proportion distribution 66, 69, 75, 80–81
    electoral bias 78–79, 81–82, 89–90, 163
    electoral history 75–76, 81–82
    in Newcastle upon Tyne 49–52, 156–158
    seats-votes relationship 12, 25, 94, 110–114, 215, 221–222
    single-transferable-vote system 180–188
    spatial distribution of support 3, 77
    in Sunderland 149–151
    three-party elections 108, 110–114
    wasted votes 3
Labour Party (Ireland) 176–178, 182–183
Labour Party (New Zealand) 6, 12, 78, 82, 85–86, 102–103, 116–119
Labour Party (South Africa) 7
Lakeman E 3, 11, 162, 173, 188
Laux H D 191
Laver M 176, 177–179
Lexian model 33–35, 206–207
Liberal Party (Australia) 166–169

index | 239

Liberal Party (Britain)
  additional-member system 193–195
  alternative-vote system 173–175
  Celtic fringe 109, 114
  constituency proportion distribution 66, 72, 74–75, 79–81, 104
  election triangle 97, 110
  electoral bias 75, 109–115, 163
  electoral history 109–110
  in Newcastle upon Tyne 49
  seats-votes relationship 94, 104–105, 109–114, 215, 218
  spatial distribution of support 6, 108–109
  three-party elections 97–99, 109–112
  variation in votes 99
  wasted votes 3
Liberal Party (Canada) 7, 92, 93, 96, 106, 107, 133, 221
Liittschwager J M 126, 159
Lipset S M 82
Little W 122
Lyons W E 10

Mackenzie W J M 170
Mair P 177–179
Malapportionment 55–59, 87, 89
Malta 164
March J G 206–209
Mason H L 183
Mayhew D R 129, 229
McKay D H 8
McPhaill R 166
Mellos K 212–213
Morrill R L 127
Morris W D 219–220
Morse S J 7, 138

Nagel S S 126, 127, 128
National Party (New Zealand) 6, 102–103, 116–119
National Party (South Africa) 7, 11, 133–140, 201
New Democratic Party 7, 82, 92, 96, 106, 107
New York 122, 123–126
New Zealand [see also Labour Party (New Zealand), National Party (New Zealand), Social Credit Party (New Zealand)]
  basis of party support 6, 82, 197
  constituency size 38–39

New Zealand (continued)
  constituency proportion distributions 14, 20–21, 42, 45–47, 63, 84–86, 102–103, 132, 230
  election triangle 117
  electoral bias 78, 85–86, 118
  electoral districting 9, 132
  electoral reform 3
  organisation of elections 4
  seats-votes relationship 42, 45–47, 102–103, 117
  three-party elections 102–103, 106, 116–119
  voting swings 60, 63
Newcastle upon Tyne 48, 49–51, 142, 144, 156–158
Noragon J L 130
Normal distribution 20–26, 31

O'Leary C 176, 187
Orr D M 121
Owen D B 226

Paddison R 179
Patterson S C 8
Payne C 6, 13
Peele S 7, 138
Pelling H 75
Plaid Cymru (PC) 83–84, 115–116, 173–174, 180, 182, 186, 193
Plurality system 3–4, 11
Political party systems 5–6
Progressive Party (South Africa) 7
Progressive Conservative Party 7, 92, 96, 106, 107, 122, 220–221
Proportional representation 1, 3, 4, 18, 162 ff
Pulsipher A G 121, 140
'Pure' democracy 1

Qualter T H 214–216
Quandt R E 73

Rae D W 1, 162, 164, 176, 177, 197
Rahman N A 73
Reapportionment revolution 9, 123, 125
Redistribution of Seats Act (1949) 8
Representation Commission (New Zealand) 9
Representation Commission (Canada) 10
Republican Party 7

Roberts G K 190
Robinson A 122
Robinson A D 6
Robson B T 149
Rokkan S 5, 7, 82
Ross J F S 179–180, 181
Rowley G 8, 89
Rydon J 57, 78, 85, 166

Sankoff D 212–213
Sauer C O 121
Schwartz M A 7
Schwartzberg J J 124
Scottish Nationalist Party (SNP) 83–84, 115–116, 173–174, 180, 182, 186, 193
Severo N C 226
Seymour C 122
Shepherd J W 143–144
Sickels R J 57–58, 122–123
Simeon R 7
Simms A 191
Single-transferable-vote system (STV) 164 176–188, 196
Skewness 66, 68–71
Sloman A 94, 99
Snedecor G W 153
Social Credit Party (Canada) 7, 92, 96, 107, 175
Social Credit Party (New Zealand) 6, 82, 102–103, 105, 116–119
Social Democratic Party (SDP) (Germany) 190–192
Socialist Party (France) 170–172
Soper C S 59, 166
South Africa [see also National Party (South Africa), Progressive Party (South Africa), United Party (South Africa)]
  basis of party support 7, 136, 137
  constituency proportion distribution 136–140, 230
  constituency size 38, 42, 45
  delimitation commission 137–140
  electoral bias 78
  electoral districting 10–11, 138–140
  electoral reform 3
  gerrymandering 135, 139–140
  malapportionment 58
  organisation of elections 4, 138–139, 164
  uncontested seats 90

South Shields 3
Spafford D 58, 93, 220–221
Steed M 8, 59, 64, 79, 173–174, 180–181, 192–193, 195, 197
Stokes D E 59, 60, 100, 129, 209
Stuart A 21, 26–28, 31, 46, 86, 129, 201, 206–207
Sunderland 142, 144, 149–151, 154

Taagepera R 39, 91, 209–212
Taylor A H 84
Taylor H 143–145
Thiel H 28, 198, 206
Tufte E R 11, 54–54, 63, 91, 129–130, 201–202, 204, 229
Tyler G 122

United Party (South Africa) 7, 11, 78, 133–140
United States [see also Democratic Party, Republican Party]
  basis of party support 6–7, 20
  constitution 2
  constituency size 38, 42, 44
  constituency proportion distribution 21, 46
  electoral districting 9–10, 55, 122–131
  electoral reform 3
  gerrymandering 122–125
  malapportionment 57–58
  organisation of elections 4
  seats-votes relationship 12
  voting swings 60, 63
Upton G 95
Uspensky J R 40, 41

Vickrey V 125
Vistre J du 171

Walmsley D 166
Ward N 10
Weaver J B 125–127
Wells D 122
Wells v Rockefeller (1969) 123
Williams P 172
'Women's Party' 5–6, 99
Wright v Rockefeller (1964) 124

Zelen M 226